JOSEPH IMHOF

Artist of the Pueblos

Joseph Imhof in his Taos home, 1945.

JOSEPH IMHOF

Artist of the Pueblos

A Biography by
Nancy Hopkins Reily
with Lucille Enix

SANTA FE

Sunstone books may be purchased for educational, business, or sales promotional use. For information please write: Special Markets Department, Sunstone Press, P.O. Box 2321, Santa Fe, New Mexico 87504-2321.

FIRST EDITION

10 9 8 7 6 5 4 3 2 1

Library of Congress Cataloging in Publication Data:

Reily, Nancy Hopkins, 1934-
    Joseph Imhof: Artist of the Pueblos: a biography/by Nancy Hopkins Reily with Lucille Enix.—
1st ed.
        p.   cm.
    Includes bibliographical references and index.
    ISBN 0-86534-259-8
    1. Imhof, Joseph, 1871-1955.   2. Artists—United States—Biography.   3. Pueblo Indians—
    Pictorial works. I. Enix, Lucille. II. Imhof, Joseph, 1871-1955. III. Title.
N6537. I45R45   1998
760'. 092—dc21
[B]   97-27712
                                                        CIP

Published by   SUNSTONE PRESS
                  Post Office Box 2321
                  Santa Fe, NM 87504-2321/USA
                  (505) 988-4418/orders only (800) 243-5644
                  FAX (505) 988-1025

Book design by Vicki Ahl

DEDICATION

*T*o my parents, Anna Pauline Richardson Hopkins Castleberry and Robert Howell (Hal) Hopkins, Sr., for my first adventures in New Mexico; and to my Aunt Helen Louise Richardson Morten and Uncle Winfield Morten for enriching those experiences.

CONTENTS

FOREWORD

My knowledge of Joseph Imhof's life and art began in 1944. As a girl of ten, I met Joe Imhof in Abiquiu, New Mexico while visiting my aunt and uncle, Helen and Winfield Morten, of Dallas, Texas.

Helen and Winfield Morten had met Joe earlier, in 1943, through mutual friends in Taos, New Mexico. At that time, Joe Imhof had told Winfield Morten of an old hacienda on acreage for sale near Abiquiu where the sunrise and sunset dissolve and replace the mesa colorations. Winfield Morten had been coming to New Mexico with his family since his child-hood, and his experiences while there caused him to dream of owning land in New Mexico. The Mortens purchased the old, ill-repaired hacienda near Abiquiu in the mid 1940s. Winfield did not hesitate to restore the old hacienda to splendor and to revive the worn-out land so that it produced far greater plant and animal yields. With his interest in protecting the environment, and wish to restore a historically significant building, Winfield, in his visions and dreams, lived as a man ahead of his time.

When he began restoration on the hacienda, Rancho de Abiquiu, my father, Robert Howell (Hal) Hopkins, Sr., coordinated the project. During construction, Mother brought their three children, Robert, Morten, and me to live in Santa Fe for the summer. It was during this time that I met Joseph Imhof. Winfield asked Joe, with his artistic vision, to assist with the hacienda refurbishing, and to bring Winfield's dream to life. The two visionaries, Winfield Morten and Joe Imhof, joined forces in Winfield's quest.

Without knowing it then, I began this biography when I met Joe Imhof. In our shared experiences, we became friends. From our first meeting, Joe took me on adventures to explore the Indians. We hunted arrowheads, witnessed dances, visited the sacred kivas, and I listened to his tales of the Indian Pueblo life. Joe Imhof taught me to see beyond the surface of objects, to feel the vitality of asymmetry, and to become sensitive to tonal values of gray in black and white. The values he taught me are those never seen at first glance.

As the years passed, I collected his memorabilia, and encountered his art in museums and galleries. Once I stood in Merrill's Gallery in Taos with my husband and experienced the disappointment of my husband's choice of a Nicolai Fechin lithograph over an Imhof lithograph. Perhaps that encounter solidified my determination to discover Imhof on my own.

Joe Imhof's jovial, gravelly voice, accompanied by his caring, gave me the patience to retain private memories until I actively began researching the Imhof legacy. By 1979, when I had accumulated enough biographical information on Imhof, I hired a secretary/typist to type my notes, a truly brave act for a woman who lived in a small town.

My few pages of notes prompted me to research further into Imhof's life and art. Because Winfield Morten had donated Imhof's "Corn Series" to the Maxwell Museum of Anthropology at the University of New Mexico, my first active research began at Maxwell. At Maxwell Museum, I hoped to find Imhof's personal letters and journals which would provide his relationships, concerns, prejudices, loyalties, commitments, responsibilities, values and personality. These findings would furnish the added dimension that would shów where Imhof had gathered his autonomy, the workings of his mind and spirit that allowed him to create.

Alas, I discovered that the Imhof archives at the Maxwell Museum are housed in two thin, manila folders. Within the folders, I found a list of artifacts, lithographs and paintings donated to the Museum, correspondence from Sallie, giving directions for the housing of Joe's archives, mention of a biographical sketch of Imhof written by Sallie, and the notation of Imhof's early photographic negatives housed at the Maxwell. Separately, an album showed photographic prints of Imhof's art donated to the Museum.

In one of Sallie's letters directing the archives, Sallie described Imhof as " . . . a gentle, dignified man who loathed the publicity and the limelight that other artists seemed to seek; he avoided publicity at all times, but I do understand that posterity through the collection should know something about the real Imhof."

The lack of personal documentation about Joseph Imhof's life comes partially from his dislike of documentation encounters, not his dislike of people or their ideas.

Yet, within this lack of "personal archives," lives the mind and spirit of Joseph Adam Andrew John Imhof. He desired that his art stand the test of time, instead of through biographical statements.

Further research at Harwood Foundation in Taos revealed Joe's personal note, in his handwriting, penciled to accompany a scant biographical form: "There let me live and die and not a stone tell where I lie."

Because Joe Imhof and Sallie preferred to remain invisible outside his small circle of friends and the world of Indians, my task of reconstructing Imhof's life and art has been difficult.

My research prompted my first hesitant telephone calls that eventually numbered a thousand. Courage took me to countless art galleries to hunt for Imhofs often ignored until my persistence brought forth Imhofs from the storage rooms. And it struck me as odd when these encounters brought remarks that Imhof had been overlooked.

Imagine my utter surprise, then the feeling that not only was I seeking Joe, but he was seeking me, when I opened the first archival file at Amon G. Carter Museum in Ft. Worth, and there, looking back at me, I saw a newspaper clipping that included a photograph, taken at the Grand Imperial Hotel opening in Silverton, Colorado in 1952, showing Joe Imhof and me. Not long after that, I felt such exuberance when Don, my husband, revealed his interest and support by buying our first Imhof. Then he traveled with me to New York City and helped me photograph, in a matter of three hours, over one hundred Imhofs housed at the National Museum of the American Indian. From there we journeyed to Santa Fe, Taos, La Junta, Colorado, and dozens of libraries and museums.

Finally, I received permission for a day of my choice to research at the Southwest Center for Research in Albuquerque. I came fully prepared with a briefcase so full that it refused to close and I had to carry it with both hands. Just as I reached the library door, I had an unnerving thought. I had left in the car now being driven away by Don all my identification and money needed for my research.

These journeys into Imhof's life of eighty-four years took me into events, societies, history and cultures through which I experienced the human condition. In exploring the root of Imhof's art, I discovered his aim of recording a culture in the process of being changed. Imhof's art tells more, though. It records how he escaped failure, thus value is gained by studying his art through his life experiences.

Over the years, I have catalogued Imhof's estimated body of over four hundred pieces of art that include oil paintings, lithographs, pencil and charcoal drawings, wood block prints, murals, watercolors, pastels, gouaches, wood carvings and sculptures. I assume that my research will never end, that I will always locate more art and biographical information. As the information continues to accumulate, I reluctantly publish this book.

An artist has as many biographies as individuals who knew the artist. Joe Imhof left an impression on each individual he knew. This biography is my impression of Joseph Imhof, aided and bound by all others who knew him personally or through his art.

Hundreds of individuals contributed to this work, all of whom I owe a debt of gratitude. A special thanks goes to those individuals at the Amon G. Carter Museum, University of New Mexico Maxwell Museum of Anthropology, National Museum of the American Indian - Smithsonian Institute, University of New Mexico Harwood Foundation, and to Mary Ann DiNapoli of Brooklyn, New York.

I thank Lucille Enix for her professionalism in transforming my fifteen years of research into readable form. The enthusiasm, friendship, and intuitive skills she brought to this project deserve my thank you. My gratitude can never equal her effort.

A very deserved extraordinary thank you to my family: Don Reily; Pauline Hopkins Castleberry; Jane and Mark Reily, Read, Thomas, John Mark and Anna; Donna Reily Davis, Carolyn and Julia for their understanding of my many hours devoted to this book.

ACKNOWLEDGMENTS

The individuals and institutions involved in nurturing a biography to life are many.

Words, ironically, become inadequate to properly express my appreciation to each contributor for the information and for each person's intangible contributions of time, encouragement, inspiration, promptness, interest, and cooperation. No one was too busy or bothered to contribute facts, correct errors, research and direct me to other sources. The priceless contribution of expectation encouraged me to assemble the information to reveal Imhof as a recorder, an artist and as an individual.

I gratefully acknowledge and thank these institutions and their personnel:

ARIZONA: Heard Museum, Phoenix, Glenn Taylor; Northern Arizona University, Flagstaff, Bruce Horn.

CALIFORNIA: Los Angeles County Art Museum, Anne Smith; San Diego Historical Society, Barbara Pope; San Diego Museum of Art, David L. Kencik; San Francisco Museum of Modern Art, Carol A. Wolf; California Historical Society, San Francisco, Jeffrey Barr; Butterfield and Butterfield Fine Art Auctioneers, San Francisco, Evalynna Ho.

COLORADO: Carnegie Library, Monte Vista, Dennis Wilson; Koshare Indian Museum, La Junta, Marvin Holbrook, Dena Salazar, Michael J. Menard, Del Orr, Joe Clay; Colorado Springs Fine Art Center, Judith L. Burdich; Denver Public Library, Eleanor M. Gehres, A. D. Mastrogiuseppe; San Juan County Historical Society, Silverton, Allen Nossaman; Anschutz Collection, Denver, Elizabeth Cunningham Miller.

ILLINOIS: Illinois State Historical Library, Springfield, George Heerman.

KANSAS: Wichita Art Museum, Lois F. Crane; Topeka and Shawnee County Public Library, Larry D. Peters.

LOUISIANA: Louisiana Auction Exchange, Baton Rouge, Sandra Causey.

MONTANA: Montana Historical Society, Helena, Brian Shovers; Tom Nygard, Bozeman.

NEBRASKA: Sheldon Memorial Art Gallery, University of Nebraska, Lincoln, Karen Merritt; Joslyn Art Museum, Omaha, Anne Dickerson.

NEW MEXICO: University of New Mexico, Harwood Foundation, Taos, David Witt, Betsy Wolf; Harwood Library, Taos, Tracy McCallum; History Library of Santa Fe, Orlando Romero; Museum of New Mexico, Santa Fe, Tom Livesay, David Turner, Phyllis Cohen, Steve Yates; University of New Mexico Maxwell Museum of Anthropology, Albuquerque, Marian Rodee, Natalie Pattison, George Duck; University of New Mexico Art Museum, Albuquerque, Alana Wolfe; Millicent Rogers Museum of Northern New Mexico, Taos, Karen S. Young, Vincente Martinez, Patrick Houlihan, Barbara Barrett; Kit Carson Memorial Foundation, La Morada de Don Fernando Taos, Taos, Victor Grant; Dar al Islam, Abiquiu, Walter Declerck; Western New Mexico University, Silver City, Nancy Davison; Albuquerque Museum, James Moore, Ellen J. Landis, Thomas Lark, Robert Dauner; Photo Archives, Palace of Governors, Santa Fe, Arthur L. Olivas, Richard Rudisill; University of New Mexico Center for Southwest Research, Albuquerque, Terry Gugliolotta; Santa Fe Public Library, Sallie Armstrong; Los Alamos Historical Museum, Theresa A. Strottman; Santa Fe Indian School, Olana McGratten; Taos District Court Clerk Martha Cordova; University of New Mexico, Albuquerque, Joseph Traugott; Van Vechten-Lineberry Taos Art Museum, Taos, Ed and Novella Lineberry.

Galleries in Taos: Governor Bent Gallery, Faye, Otto and Tom Noeding; Burke Armstrong Gallery, Burke Armstrong; Hensley Gallery Southwest, Michael Hensley; Philip Bareiss Gallery, Philip Bareiss, Susan Strong; Mission Gallery, Rena Rosequist.

Galleries in Santa Fe: Gerald Peters Gallery, Gayle Maxon-Edgerton; Woodrow Wilson Fine Art Gallery, Woodrow and Carole Wilson; Jamison Gallery, Zeb Conley, Jr.; Susan Tarman Antiques and Fine Art Gallery, Lisa M. Heitmann; Laurel Seth Gallery, Laurel Seth; Nedra Matteucci Gallery.

Galleries in Albuquerque: Brandywine Gallery, Louise Abrums;

Dartmouth Gallery, John Cacciatore; Peter Eller Gallery, Peter Eller.

NEW YORK: National Museum of the American Indian-Smithsonian Institute, Nancy Rosoff, Ruth S. Taylor, Molly Herron, Allison Jeffrey, Pamela Dewey, Ellen Jamieson, Shilice Clinkscales; *Life Magazine*, Paul Arbor; Rockwell Museum, Corning, Robyn E. Peterson; New York Historical Society, May N. Stone; Long Island Historical Society, Clara M. Lamers; Olana Gallery, Brewster, Bernard Rosenberg; J. N. Bartfield Galleries, New York City.

OKLAHOMA: Gilcrease Museum, Tulsa, Anne Morand; Philbrook Museum of Art, Tulsa, Thomas E. Young; Magee-Gerrer Museum of Art, Shawnee, Melissa Owens; Woolaroc Museum, Bartlesville, Linda Stone Laws; Melton Art Reference Library, Oklahoma City, Suzanne Silvester; Oklahoma City Art Museum, Jayne Hazelton.

TEXAS: Amon G. Carter Museum, Fort Worth, Paula Stewart, Carol Roark, Tom Southall, Jeannie Lively, Barbara McCandless, Mary Lampe, Helen Plummer, Melissa Thompson, Amy Kelly; Angelina College Library, Lufkin, Gloria Gilder, Earlon Williams; Dallas Public Library, Frances Bell; Archer M. Huntington Art Gallery, University of Texas at Austin, Meredith D. Sutton; Marion Koogler McNay Art Museum, San Antonio, Heather Hornbuckle; Panhandle-Plains Historical Museum, Canyon, Michael R. Grauer; Mildred R. and Fredrich M. Mayer Library, Dallas Museum of Art, Susan Shimp Torok; Museum of East Texas, Lufkin, J. P. McDonald; Fondren Library, Houston, Jet M. Prendeville; Kurth Memorial Library, Lufkin, Ryan Alworth; Butterfield and Butterfield Fine Art Auctioneers, Houston, Suzanne Staley.

UTAH: Southern Utah University, Braithwaite Center, Cedar City, Mandy Brooks; Utah Museum of Fine Arts, Salt Lake City, David M. Carroll; Springville Museum of Art, Provo, Vern Swanson; Brigham Young University, Museum of Art, Provo, Julia K. Lippert.

WYOMING: Buffalo Bill Historical Center, Cody, Peter Hassrick, Paul Fees; Teton County Historical Society, Jackson, Rita Verley; Wyoming State Museum, Cheyenne, Terry Kreuzer.

I gratefully acknowledge and thank these individuals:
ARIZONA: Mrs. Albert W. (Charlotte) Erkins, Sun City; Virginia Couse Leavitt, Tucson; Betty Lane, Green Valley.

CALIFORNIA: Walter A. Bailey, Robert and Linda Attiyeh, of Los

15

Angeles; Ray Dellenbaugh, Sunnyvale; Allen Willett, Carlsbad; Charlotte Dunn, Georgia Belaire, of San Diego; Mrs. James Bailey, Fair Oaks; Cornell Norby, Newport Beach; Harriet Ide Publicker, Beverly Hills.

COLORADO: Melvin Weimer, Colorado Springs; Kenneth Dellenbaugh, Mildred Wilson, of Creede; William F. Manke, Englewood; Charles Ewing, Antonito; Mr. and Mrs. Charles Howe, Boulder; Bud Hilker, Dorothy Harmsen, James Raughton, all of Denver; Mr. and Mrs. Leon Loughridge, Littleton.

FLORIDA: Veronica and Wilford Herron, Sarasota; David Ide, Ft. Lauderdale.

IDAHO: Robert Erkins, Bliss.

ILLINOIS: Donald L. Leone, Oak Brook.

KANSAS: Richard E. Firth, Leawood; Mrs. Robert Imhof, Colby; Ross McCausland, Wichita.

MINNESOTA: Charles Hynes, Minnetonka.

MISSOURI: Mrs. Freddine Parrett Heisey, Chilicothe.

NEW JERSEY: Wesley W. Ciampo, Ridgewood; R. H. Vander Clock, Blairtown.

NEVADA: Dr. and Mrs. Rodney Handsfield, Las Vegas.

NEW MEXICO: Doris Bailey Wakeland, Silver City; Kay Dicus, Susan Anneke Dicus Chittim, Walt Wiggins, Jackson Hensley, Joseph P. Hedrick Jr., Robert M. Copeland, Eleanor M. Crout, Suzan Campbell, Sandra D'Emilio all of Santa Fe.

In Taos, Jonathan Warmday, Charles A. Stewart, Ted Egri, Trudy Knox, Helen Kentnor, Gene and Phillips Kloss, Steve Eich, Marie Merrill, E. O. Floyd, Regina Cooke, Barbara Brenner, Mary and Gyrant Smith, Dorothy Brandenburg, Claire Brandenburg, Victoria Parrett, Martha Reed, Henry Sauerwein, Beatrice Vigil, Steven Villalobos, Melissa Eck, Jeff Gales.

Robert R. White, Mary Carroll Nelson, Garo Antreasian, Betty Sabo, all of Albuquerque; Ora Chase, El Prado; Diane Lund, Las Cruces; Peggy and Harold Samuels, Corrales; Helen Blumenschein, James Parsons, of Ranchos de Taos; Napoleon "Paul" Garcia, Sr., Abiquiu.

NEW YORK: Mary Ann DiNapoli, Brooklyn.

OKLAHOMA: Ralph L. Willets, Tulsa.

OREGON: Charlene and William G. Dady, Wilsonville; Robert L. Joki, Portland.

TEXAS: Mrs. Bruce (Carol Ann) Hale, Wichita Falls; Jane and E. Morten Hopkins, Joanne and Robert H. Hopkins, Jr., J. McDonald Williams, Roy Coffee, Jr., of Dallas; Mrs. Charles (Galen Burnett) Haynes, Midland.

In Lufkin, Tambra Correll, Kim Strong, Walter L. Borgfeld, Jr., Mark Hicks, Mary Read, Versia Sanders, Joyce Gray.

CHRONOLOGY: 1871-1966

1871: Joseph Imhof is born in Brooklyn, New York.

1876: Imhof receives a box of watercolors from his godfather.

1881: Imhof takes the ferry to Manhattan and the Ridley Mansion at 36 Beekman Street, an artists' studio located on the corner of Beekman and William. Imhof executes his first known still life.

1886: Imhof graduates from high school at age fifteen. His father refuses him an education unless Joe becomes a priest. Imhof spends his days at the Ridley Mansion, living in a pigeon loft, returning home to sleep at night. He begins his first job as an artist, hand lettering for Currier & Ives, Lithographers. Executes his first known painting, "Two Roses."

1888: Opens his bookstore in Brooklyn.

1890: Executes his second known painting, "Cupid Disappointed."

1891: Sells bookstore and uses the profit to buy passage on a ship to Europe to study painting. Meets W. F. ("Buffalo Bill") Cody on board ship, then spends time in Belgium sketching the Indians in Cody's "Wild West" show.

1892: Becomes a member of the St. Lucas Guild in Amsterdam. Travels and paints in Brussels, Munich, Italy, North Africa, Paris.

1893: Returns to New York, rents a studio in Flatbush, and begins to study the Iroquois Indians of New York and Canada. Meets Sarah Ann Elizabeth Russell, born in 1872 in Philadelphia.

1894: Imhof moves back to Ridley Mansion.

1895: Joe and Sallie become secretly engaged. Joe works freelance for Allen and Ginter, painting Indian Head Series for cards inserted in boxes of cigarettes.

1897: Joe and Sallie marry.

1898: Imhofs live in the Connelly Mansion, an estate along the Hudson River, then move to Staten Island. Magdalena Elizabeth Imhof is born to the Imhofs.

1899: Imhofs rent a studio apartment at 28 East 14th Street near Union Square, and later move to Englewood Cliffs, New Jersey where they rent a house. The Imhofs make a short trip to Canada to study the Indians before returning to New York to board a ship bound for Europe.

1900: The Imhofs travel in Holland and central Europe to allow Joe to paint in natural settings as well as to copy the great masters' paintings in museums.

1901: Imhofs return to the United States, living first in the Connelly Mansion, then a New Jersey home in Englewood Cliffs.

1902: The Imhofs travel to Ontario to allow Joe to paint the Indians, then return to New York before boarding a ship to Europe where Joe travels and paints.

1904: The Imhofs return to the United States, settling in Englewood Cliffs. Joe invents the tear tab mechanism for the cigarette package.

1905: Joseph Imhof meets Joseph Keppler, Jr. and they re-enforce each of the other's interest in Indians. Joe and Sallie begin attending Dr. Felix Adler's lectures, studying Adler's philosophical beliefs in the individual's responsibility to community and higher spiritual values. Imhof begins correspondence with the Albuquerque Indian School.

1907: Imhofs move to Albuquerque where Joe begins to travel among the Pueblos to learn their beliefs and customs and to photograph and sketch. Sallie enrolls as a student at the University of New Mexico.

1908: While dancing the Corn Dance with the Cochiti, who have made Imhof a member of one of their clans, Imhof envisions the Corn Series.

1910: Imhof builds his first home, constructing his studio in the manner of a kiva with its flooring below ground. Imhof welcomes Pueblo Indians who begin to spend time at Imhof's studio.

1912: The Imhofs return to New York where they move to their property in Montville, New Jersey they had purchased in 1905. Imhof builds another studio.

1914: Imhofs move back to New York City, near Greenwich Village. Imhof volunteers as scoutmaster for General McAlpin's Boy Scouts.

1918: Sallie enlists in the United States Navy where she is ranked Yeoman Third Class. Sallie is discharged from the U.S. Navy after being awarded a Victory Button and reaching Yeoman First Class.

1921: Imhof invents printing process using invisible color, sells a southern bread company on using it as a promotional insert in bread packages, then sets up press to run the invisible ink coloring books for children.

1922: The Imhofs buy a three-story brick home at 22 Willow Street in Columbia Heights, Brooklyn, where they then live.

1929: Joe and Sallie move to Taos where they build an adobe home, guest house, and studio next to property owned by the Taos Pueblo.

1930: Joe collapses from exhaustion, and the Imhofs move to La Jolla for six months to allow Joe to rest. Walter Bailey, a friend and artist, oversees their Taos property in their absence. The Imhofs return to Taos and Joe begins teaching in the Taos Field School of Art.

1931: The Imhofs meet and become friends with Gene Kloss, an artist, and Phillips Kloss, a poet and composer. Imhof exhibits at the Museum of New Mexico in Santa Fe during Fiesta. Imhof's art is exhibited at the Amarillo Art Association, Loan Exhibit of the Fine Arts Department of the Tri-State Fair.

1932: Emil Bisttram uses Imhof's lithography press. Imhof and Bisttram share their ideas and special interest in dynamic symmetry which both use to balance the content of their works of art.

1933: Elizabeth, the Imhof's thirty-five-year-old daughter, arrives in Taos to stay for a few months. She leaves for San Diego where she commits suicide. Gene and Phillips Kloss rent the Imhofs' guest house. Sallie begins working as secretary for Dr. T. P. Martin, Taos' physician.

1934: Imhof executes projects for WPA/FAP. Imhof exhibits at the Museum of New Mexico in Santa Fe during Fiesta.

1935: Imhof exhibits at the Museum of New Mexico in Santa Fe during Fiesta. Alexander Hogue uses Imhof's lithography press and expresses his interest in working with Imhof, a master lithographer.

1936: Imhof exhibits at the Museum of New Mexico in Santa Fe during Fiesta.

1937: Imhof exhibits at the Museum of New Mexico in Santa Fe during Fiesta.

1941: Imhof exhibits at the Museum of New Mexico in Santa Fe during Fiesta.

1943: Imhof meets Winfield and Helen Morten of Dallas. Imhof begins work on restoring and decorating Morten hacienda.

1945: Imhof exhibits at Western State College and receives a First Award for pastel and print.

1946: Imhof exhibits at the Museum of New Mexico at Santa Fe during Fiesta. Sallie Imhof receives the Selective Service Medal from President Harry S Truman for her volunteer work during World War II.

1947: Imhof exhibits in three different shows: the Museum of New Mexico's Print Makers exhibition, the Museum of New Mexico during Fiesta, and a second Print Makers exhibition at the same museum.

1948: Imhof exhibits at the Museum of New Mexico at Santa Fe during Fiesta. Imhof's work is shown at the Dallas Museum of Art in a traveling exhibition sponsored by the Museum of New Mexico.

1950: The Koshare Indian Museum in Colorado purchases their first Imhof.

1951: Imhof executes art works for Winfield Morten to use in his newly restored Grand Imperial Hotel in Silverton, Colorado. Imhof begins work on the work of art he regards as his legacy, the Corn Series.

1955: Imhof completes the Corn Series of sixty works, and dies two months later. A plane scatters his ashes over sacred Blue Lake where Taos Pueblo Indians' departed souls go to rest.

1961: Sallie Imhof donates the Corn Series and other art and objects to the University of New Mexico through the Helen and Winfield Morten Foundation.

1965: The University of New Mexico produces an exhibition of Imhof's Corn Series.

1966: Sallie Imhof dies and leaves the remaining Imhof art and Indian objects to the Harwood Foundation of the University of New Mexico and the National Museum of the American Indian, Heye Foundation. A plane scatters Sallie's ashes over sacred Taos Mountain.

CHAPTER 1

THE RECORDER

By 1946, Joseph Imhof had nearly depleted the income he had received for almost twenty-five years, money that had come from printing and publishing inventions he had patented in the 1920s. The inventions had served him well, freeing him to paint and create lithographs, and finally taking him to his spiritual home in Taos, New Mexico where the income from the inventions had financed his life's work. For the last sixteen years, he had painted and laboriously lithographed, with exacting accuracy, the Taos and other Pueblo Indians' daily lives and sacred ceremonies. However, the culminating work of his life, the rendering of a series of paintings that depicted the significance of corn to the Pueblo Indians, still lay ahead of him.

On this particular July day near the village of Abiquiu, he stood in the newly rebuilt Rancho de Abiquiu beside Winfield Morten who, though years younger, symbolized Imhof's idealized father, the man who would approve of his son's calling and who would financially assist Joe Imhof for the remainder of his life.

Joe reached with a feather-like grasp to place two blue and white Spanish Inquisition-era pottery vases from his extensive collection onto a two-foot-wide adobe windowsill at the Mortens' pueblo-style ranch house.

The Morten ranch window offered a panoramic view of the alfalfa fields, cottonwood trees that banked the Chama River, and the village of Abiquiu that nestled high on a bluff. Several centuries before, the bluff had served as a lookout for the land's first inhabitants.

Joe's loving arrangement of the Spanish vases must have reminded him of how and why he had collected antiques, paintings, books, lithographs, and valued artifacts since his adolescence. Numerous of these objects now brought him needed income, including the vases and other valuables he had sold to his friend, Winfield. In addition, the art objects allowed him to help Winfield visualize and sense beauty, which certainly fit into Joe's life goals of helping others see and experience the harmony in life by observing accurate details of a moment. Joe himself had begun to feel this kind of harmony in his later years after he had gradually undergone a kind of religious transcendence under the guidance of Dr. Felix Adler and his Society of Ethical Culture. Joe had since learned to balance his life with nature, something he had absorbed from observing the Native Americans' spiritual relationship to their surroundings. The harmony allowed him to appreciate beauty without an artist's interpretation. His discovery of this harmony that permeated his life laid the foundation for his own approach to painting the daily events in the lives of the Pueblo Indians, the nature that surrounded them, and the works he would create as a master lithographer.

The search for this kind of balance in his life had been with him since childhood when he had felt the wrath of his father's rejection. Joe had refused his father's direct order to enter a seminary and become the family's token priest. Joe's rebellion had caused his father to reject the son and withdraw support for any education the son might have wanted. Here had begun the rumblings of the discontented son searching for a sense of balance. As a boy of fifteen, Joe had left his parents' home in Brooklyn and moved into a pigeon loft. While his move only took him across the Brooklyn Bridge into Manhattan, he never again depended upon his parents for his livelihood. The loft gave him the autonomy he recognized that he needed. Here he began to learn the craft of lithography, and to search for the harmony he had never found during his formative years.

After he placed the Spanish vases in the spacious window of Winfield's home, the huge glass in the window reflected many of Joe's antiques that he had placed in the room. Had his search taken him in some symbolic way to his ancestral home, the one he'd always sought? Joe had been the one, in fact, who had told the Mortens about the Abiquiu land they subsequently purchased, and had helped them design their ranch home after a pueblo-style house, then assisted in its decoration and furnishings. At this moment, he could glimpse in the window's reflection the summation of his seventy-five years, and feel the dissatisfaction of what he'd left undone and must finish.

He had managed to surround himself with a family of his own creation: a father-figure who not only loved him, but understood Joe's pain, from having been abandoned by his own father. Indeed, Winfield Morten actively sought Joe's knowledge of the Indians' harmonious relationship between nature and man, and in return supported and praised Joe's paintings and lithographs. Winfield had even paid Joe to carve the home's full mantel of wood with a saying of Winfield's choosing: *La Casa de la Valle Feliz*, The House of the Happy Valley.

Toward the back of the room, Helen, Winfield's wife, had seated herself on a sofa situated near an archway above which Joe had painted a mural of Don Juan Oñate entering the valley at the confluence of the Rio Grande and Chama River in 1598. A Navajo rug draped parts of the sofa as if in celebration of the Navajo belief in man's imperfection made visible through the incorporation of one imperfection within a weaving. The Mortens and the Imhofs understood imperfection. Helen had always given Joe that unconditional love for which he yearned. Her presence comforted him, soothed the ache for his mother who had persuaded him, after he left home, to return and spend each night in his boyhood home.

Sallie Imhof, Joe's loving and handsome wife, stood opposite Helen, not far from another mural Joe had painted, this one of Helen and Winfield's family. The family looked out from above the archway that led into the trophy room. The words, "Enjoy Life While You Are Living, You Will Be A Long Time Dead," appeared in Joe's distinctive lettering above the mural's images. The saying could have capsuled Sallie's assigned role, to organize their lives in such a way that each could enjoy the fullness of the day.

Finally, I stood next to Joe. At the age of twelve, I reminded him of his only child, a daughter neither he nor Sallie ever mentioned. At the time, I could not have known that Joe thought many young women resembled his daughter. He seemed to think of her as the lively-minded girl who had traveled with him to Europe on his many journeys there to learn painting by studying the great masters of art, and who loved visiting art museums and watching him paint, not the thirty-five-year-old woman who had killed herself.

"Enjoy Life While You Are Living, You Will Be A Long Time Dead" mural by Imhof.

As Joe studied this reflected picture of his creation, he saw the massive, antique grand piano, its rectangular-shape standing to the side, begging to be played. Joe dared to turn back into the room and tell those he had gathered around him that at age seventy-five he had reached midlife, but did not yet feel old.

Unexpectedly, he turned to me. "Nancy," he said, "why don't you put the red tapestry on the back of the piano."

At my age, I felt unprepared to make any kind of grand gesture, much less a small statement in the company of my aunt and uncle. Dutifully, I placed the red tapestry, actually a somewhat off-true-red piece of woven cloth, onto the grand piano. The rectangular-shaped piano seemed to beg that I compose the tapestry into a straight line. I carefully folded the cloth to fit the length of the piano, placed it symmetrically on the back of the piano, then smoothed over all the wrinkles. I stepped back to admire my work and to make sure that the cloth hung evenly on all sides.

"Nancy," Joe said in his soft voice, graveled with age, "wrinkle it up and drape it off center."

As instructed, I gathered the tapestry, bunched it and threw it onto the back of the piano. Suddenly I saw how easily the folds created the tension and shading of colors. I caught the light in his eyes when he saw that his instruction had come as a revelation to me. He smiled in that way when two people share an understanding that belongs to them alone, one not comprehended by others.

"Nancy," he said, "let's go to the Corn Dance in Taos."

Without hesitation, we left the house and climbed into his car for the long drive to the Taos Pueblo that adjoined his home. He turned the car onto the two-lane dirt road that led from my uncle's ranch to a blacktop road. It had been some time since the county road grader had made its annual appearance to level the ridges left in the dirt road by the suspension systems of cars, the weather, and the extremes in temperatures that expanded and contracted the earth. Joe's car settled into a kind of rocking motion as he slowly drove over the ridges, taking us the two and a half miles to the blacktop road.

To our right, we could see the white cliffs of the palisades that had been carved from the earth by wind and rain erosion, and rose like sentries behind Rancho de Abiquiu. As the palisades snaked their dozens of miles to the north, their colorings would begin a slow transformation from the startling white near Uncle Winfield's ranch, into shades of pink, purple, mauve, tan, and yellows. By the time they reached Ghost Ranch, twelve miles to the north, the transformation would be complete.

At that time, Arthur Pack, a wealthy Easterner who practiced conservation and published *Nature* magazine, owned Ghost Ranch. Pack had bought the working ranch and rebuilt it into a dude ranch where the well-heeled could experience the howl of the coyote when the sun dipped behind the mountains, and awaken to the songs of birds. Georgia O'Keeffe had stayed at Ghost Ranch in 1934 before buying her own land at Abiquiu. She had climbed through the colored palisades at Ghost Ranch and returned to paint the palisades again and again.

O'Keeffe had first come to New Mexico in 1917, and returned on one of her trips with her good friend, Rebecca Salsbury Strand James. They had stayed with Mabel Dodge Luhan in Taos in 1929. Rebecca's then husband, Paul Strand, had been one of Alfred Stieglitz's colleagues. Rebecca, herself a painter and writer, was the daughter of Nate Salsbury, the business manager for William F. ("Buffalo Bill") Cody's "Wild West" show. In one of those strange twists of fate, Joe had had his first encounter with Native Americans

27

while Nate Salsbury served as William Cody's business manager for Cody's "Wild West" show. Their 1891 meeting would forever change Imhof's life, and give him his mission.

Later, when Georgia O'Keeffe moved to Abiquiu, Joseph Imhof would not always agree with O'Keeffe's artistic interpretations of her surroundings, or her avant-garde lifestyle. This judgment, however, had more to do with what Imhof perceived to be a too abstract representation of their shared environment, and not his personal regard for O'Keeffe. Imhof had judged the art produced by most of the other Taos artists as too commercial. Now, in 1946, Joe turned left onto the two-lane highway of asphalt that would take us the seventy miles to Taos. Had we turned right toward Ghost Ranch, the road would have taken us into Colorado because, at that time, a bridge had not yet been built across the Rio Grande Gorge that separated northwestern New Mexico from Taos.

Cedars, their branches rich with shades of green, and fields rich with corn and chilies marked the land on either side of the highway and, occasionally, gave way to an earth-colored adobe house tucked among the trees. The continual arroyos reminded us of the natural cycles of nature that sculpted the land through erosion. Twenty-five miles from the place where we had turned onto the blacktop, we arrived at Española, a town of about fourteen hundred people, populated with Hispanics, Pueblo Indians and Anglos, and the junction of the Rio Grande and Chama River. Here, the road forked. The main highway angled north in an almost direct line to Taos. The other road, the one to the right known as the High Road to Taos, curved up through the Kit Carson National Forest, in a more mountainous terrain. Along either road, the ancient land mixed with the growing contemporary ways of life.

Joe chose to follow the main road that paralleled the Rio Grande and took us through the settlement of Embudo, which had once served as an Indian pueblo. He laughed as his hand swept in an arc before us. This place, he said, reminded him of the years when he and Sallie had first moved to Taos. On their trips from Taos to Santa Fe, Joe had brought along sticks of dynamite to clear the dirt roads frequently blocked by rock slides. He had first learned to use the explosive when he had had to blast rocks and boulders that obstructed his routes when he had earlier searched for Pueblo Indians in 1907 through 1912. On their Albuquerque adventures, when the Imhofs had reached La Bajada, a trading point about nineteen miles south of

Santa Fe where other travelers gathered, they had encamped.

After five years in Albuquerque, Joe told me, he and Sallie had found that they could not earn enough income in this frontier setting, and returned to the East. Not until 1929 did they move permanently to Taos from New York, the same year O'Keeffe stayed at Ghost Ranch.

As the car moved along the meandering highway, the rolling crystal waters of the Rio Grande roared below on the left, cutting into the steep banks edged by piñon trees on one side and the highway on the other. The air smelled sweet and clean, as if to endow our minds with the clarity to understand each majestic view, which yielded to an even more magnificent view of soft white clouds against an ice blue sky framed by forest greens and anchored by the subtle earth tones Joe loved to paint. The setting formed the dynamic symmetry that fascinated Joe.

In the distance, Taos Mountain towered in the Sangre de Cristo mountain range that edged into Colorado. The mountain seemed to stand guard over the Taos Pueblo Indians who had saved their mountain from other men's intrusions; roads, buildings and noisy ways that brought disunity. The Taos Indians' mountain cradled one of their most sacred places, Blue Lake, from which they believed they had arisen and would return.

We drove through Taos, past the main plaza where all major and minor events transpired, and on to the edge of this small town of about eighteen hundred people that had become a magnet for artists and writers. At the northern edge of Taos, we passed Montecito Street that deadended into Highway 64, where the pink-walled "El Rancho de la Mariposa de Taos" resided. There, Duane Van Vechten, the niece of author Carl Van Vechten, had built her home in what had been an alfalfa field she had bought in 1927. If we had turned right at Montecito Street, we would have followed the pink wall to its end, then turned north on Seco Avenue, which would have taken us through the Imhofs' adobe front gate to their home that housed Joe's studio on two and a half acres that bordered the Taos Pueblo.

Instead, we drove past the front of the pink wall and just over two miles to the Taos Pueblo. We could hear the rhythmic beat of the distant drums as we neared. Joe parked the car close to the narrow entrance, the only way onto the grounds. We entered the low adobe wall that enclosed the dwellings of the Taos Indians. At one time, hundreds of years before, the wall had risen to a massive height, making the pueblo a fortress against

29

Imhof's studio sign at Taos home, ca. 1955.

raiding Plains Indians, such as the Comanches. Then, lookouts stood watch in each of the four towers located on the corners. The thick-walled five-story apartments had been there for hundreds of years when Captain Hernando de Alvarado of Coronado's expedition had come upon the Taos Pueblo four hundred years ago, in 1540.

Joe and I caught a glimpse of the costumed Indians dancing in the center of the pueblo's open spaced plaza. For now, though, Joe wanted to show me something else, the ruins of Father Zamora's fifteenth century mission church that had been destroyed by the American army during the rebellion of 1847. Only the adobe bell tower remained on these grounds, but a beam from the church, even more precious to Joe, had been given to him by the Taos Indians and then they had built it into Joe's home. We walked a few yards to the St. Jerome Mission, the one rebuilt after the rebellion, and peeked inside. Joe cautioned me that he did not find it inconsistent for the Indians to worship Christianity, while worshiping an aboriginal religion, and Native American religion because each religion had its own special message and offered its own tenets of faith.

From St. Jerome, we found our place among the crowd of spectators circling the dancers, men and women costumed in the tradition of the Corn Dance, a dance that asks for rain and is common to all Pueblo Indians. The Taos Indians regarded this particular July one-day Corn Dance one of many different kinds of Corn Dances asking-for-rain, and one of their less well-known *fiestas*. The Corn Dance offers a prayer in rhythm, movement and song to the Corn Mother, synonymous with the Earth Mother.

While each of the dozens of pueblos in New Mexico, Arizona, and Colorado creates its own traditions, art forms, and sacred rituals that are distinctive to each pueblo, all Pueblo Indians perform the Corn Dance. The influence of Catholicism makes its appearance in this dance because most pueblos select Saints' days to perform the dance common to all of them. Equally common is the *tablita*, a flat board of wood about ten inches in width and a foot high, worn upon the heads of the women dancers.

Though each pueblo may paint or shape the symbols variously, the tradition of *tablitas* predates the Spaniards' arrival. Upon the wooden tablet, the Indians have painted symbols to depict the content of their prayers. The blue paint on the board represents the sky, the uneven carving on top symbolizes clouds, and the sun appears in a touch of yellow.

The Taos Indians' dance, like all their Corn Dances, had begun at St. Jerome Catholic Mission that day. By the time we had arrived, the dancers, mostly women and a few men, had circled the pueblo's inner court in their slow shuffling dance. As the chorus sang songs especially for the moment, the dancers' movements symbolized the clouds, gently falling rain, the lightning, then the growing of corn.

Joe pointed upward and I saw Taos Indians standing quietly on top of the five-story apartments. As I squinted to see them, I saw them as Indians wrapped in blankets with the sun to their backs. In years to come, I observed that Joe read reverence into them. His thoughts revealed themselves in the simple lines, and the shades of black and white that he traced with crayon on lithography stones when he recreated these people with whom he identified.

In front of us, the women dancers wore cloth dresses that fastened on one shoulder and exposed the other. Underneath and below the dress hung another skirt, this one edged in lace. White buckskin leggings and soft buckskin boots covered their legs. A woven belt of reds, greens and blacks accented their costumes, as did the bouquets of wild flowers each woman held.

31

Colored ribbons flickered color in their black hair worn loose and free in a way that rain might fall.

When Joe moved my head slightly, the chorus came into view, old men wearing rainbow-colored blankets draped over their shoulders. The drummers, some standing, others sitting, beat their steady rhythm near the chorus.

Joe and I began to inch our way toward the kivas hidden below ground, revealing their locations with only a ladder poking above the earth. But, at the time, we could not see the ladders because the numerous visitors formed a human wall, cutting off our view. Pueblo Indians do allow outsiders to witness sacred dances, such as the Corn, Deer, Turtle, and Buffalo Dances. They never permit outsiders into their kivas where they perform their most sacred rituals. Except Joe. They had made Joe the exception.

In the year of 1907, when Joe and Sallie had first come to New Mexico, Joe had spent his time riding his horse into the semi-arid foothills to find the pueblos. As he slowly developed his relationship with the different Pueblo Indians, they found that he approached them with reverence, with respect, and as a friend. Of the nineteen settlements of Pueblo Indians living along the Rio Grande, it had been the Cochiti Pueblo Indians, who live about halfway between Albuquerque and Santa Fe, who had first allowed Joe into their kivas.

"He who comes as a friend," the Pueblos said, "is a friend." The Cochitis had sprinkled Joe with corn "to make him invisible," and thus enabled him to witness their secret ceremonies. Now Joe wanted to take me with him into the Taos kiva where he had spent hundreds of hours, sometimes dancing with the Indians, psychically absorbing their being, becoming as one with them as much as the human spirit allowed.

Finally, we broke through the crowd near the edge, and I could see behind one of the pueblo apartments the ladders, made of saplings, protruding from the ground. We soon stood ready to enter, and a Taos Indian sprinkled Joe with corn, making him invisible. The Indians regarded me as a part of Joe. When the corn rendered Joe invisible, I became invisible, too.

Years later, I learned from Sallie that Joe possessed a photographic memory. While he danced and meditated with the Pueblos, his mind was recording every detail that he would later sketch. At the time, I knew that the ceremonial dances had a purpose, a function beyond the ordinary, so I attempted to follow the cadences, thinking that the drums would somehow speak to me. I could not have known that as I stood in Joe's shadow, he had already begun to sketch in his mind the images before us.

He was the recorder, the artist who had found his harmony and balance through recreating, with exactness, the people who had taught him how to find his secret bliss.

Over the years that Joe lived in New Mexico, he sought to re-experience his bliss. In doing so, he created with exactness in his paintings and lithographs the daily activities, rituals and ceremonies of the Pueblo Indians. His search for himself produced one of the most complete, if not the most complete and accurate records of the Pueblo Indians.

The legacy he left in the body of his work could not have been fathomed by his parents, German immigrants who had established their lives in Brooklyn's German community. There they had found the economic, religious and political safety they had sought from the upheaval in Europe. They saw their legacy in their seven children, children who would complete the parents' dreams. The boy, Joe, though, had been different almost from the time of his birth.

CHAPTER 2

BEGINNING IN BROOKLYN

On Sunday, October 8, 1871, less than a mile from the Commandant's house in the Brooklyn Navy Yard on the East River, Magdalena Imhof gave birth to Joseph Adam Andrew John Imhof, her second son, and sixth of seven children.[1] John Joseph and Magdalena Imhof, the parents, would impose extraordinary expectations upon this son.

At the very hour of Joseph's birth at ten o'clock that night, halfway across the continent in Chicago, Mrs. O'Leary's cow kicked over the lantern that set off a conflagration that nearly destroyed the growing city.[2] The *Brooklyn Eagle* newspaper, on October 9, 1871, reported that half the block in Chicago was in flames before a single fire engine reached the scene. The *Brooklyn Free Press*, Brooklyn's only newspaper catering to the city's large German immigrant population, probably reported the same news about the fire in Chicago.

Within a few days, Currier and Ives, New York's leading lithographer, had printed the first black and white print of this historic news event. Because of the limitation of the day's printing presses, a colorist brought each lithograph to life by hand painting each print with the best watercolors.[3] Underneath the colored print, a craftsman had hand lettered, "The Great Fire at Chicago."

At the time of Joe's birth, John and Magdalena Imhof lived in a building they had rented just that year at 492 Atlantic Avenue.[4] Only a few months before, they had sold their two-story home at 408 Atlantic, where they had lived above the store where John plied his trade as a shoe and bootmaker.[5] In all the years John and Magdalena would live in the United States, from the time they had emigrated from Germany in 1853, they would live within a five block radius in Brooklyn, within walking distance of the East River.

John had been twenty-three, and Magdalena twenty-two, when they had arrived in Brooklyn.[6] By 1860, John's shoe and boot business had brought them a personal estate of over three thousand dollars.[7] In 1871, at Joe's birth, Magdalena had reached age forty-two, and the devout Catholic parents had a house full of children: Ann, age eleven, Mary at nine years, Frances at age six, George at four, and Kate only a year old.[8]

Brooklyn, like the Imhof family, had grown, too. In 1871, Brooklyn, Kings County, New York had a population of 419,921 and was the third largest city in the United States. Only New York and Philadelphia had larger populations. In fact, Brooklyn remained a separate city from its sister, New York City, across the river. Brooklyn, with its rich history of peoples who had occupied its land, managed to write its own charter in 1834, and accommodate itself to its current flood of transients, the Germans. Brooklyn had the largest seaport, horsecars that connected the neighborhoods and extended into Long Island's countryside, and ferries that took its citizens from Brooklyn across the East River to New York City. Brooklyn even had its own German-language newspaper, the *Brooklyn Free Press*. The city had its own highly regarded school system, fire and police departments, and boasted of being a major manufacturing center. People remarked that Brooklyn had a clean sense about it. Maybe that came from the salt air, the hills overlooking the East River, the openness of the neighborhoods, the tree-lined streets and the open country stretching along and across Long Island's land.[9]

The land had been long cared for by the Canarsee Indians, a branch of the Algonkian-speaking Indians who called themselves Leni Lenape, meaning "real men." This autonomous band of the Leni Lenape, the Canarsee, had lived on the land that became Brooklyn and had cultivated corn, squash, beans and other vegetables from the year 1000.[10]

The fertile flat lands of Long Island brought good corn yields and favored the cultivation of other crops in such abundance it forced the Indians to settle into villages to tend their agricultural enterprises. Corn became a main staple for the Indians, who also crushed the seeds and used them in sacred prayer offerings. The Canarsees lived within a complicated belief system that held that the elements of nature had been imbued with supernatural spirits. The Indians respected these spirits and developed ceremonies

35

around them. Trade developed among the villages and soon the Canarsee had worn paths connecting their villages. Europeans would continue using the paths and, in the nineteenth century, name them Kings Highway and Flatbush Avenue.[11]

In the seventeenth century, European explorers brought the arrival of the English in 1607 and the Dutch in 1624.[12] By the 1600s, the Leni Lenape had been renamed the Delaware Indians after Lord De la Warr.[13] More than once, had it not been for the Indians providing corn for the European colonists, the settlers would have died from starvation, particularly during the bitter winter of 1622 and 1623. That winter convinced the settlers of their need to learn the Indian ways of tilling and planting corn.[14]

During this time, the Dutch formed the New Netherland Colony, which included much of New Jersey, New York and Connecticut.[15] The Colony established its administrative and commercial center at New Amsterdam on Manhattan Island. However, the arrival of the Dutch brought conflict with the Indians over land ownership. This conflict finally erupted into a war between the Dutch and Indians from 1643 to 1645, and forced the Dutch to flee to New Amsterdam for protection. The Indians realized that they could no longer stave off the Europeans, and so made a peaceful settlement.[16] The Dutch then laid out a town on Long Island, with Brooklyn located in an Indian cornfield about a mile and a half from the ferry to Manhattan.[17]

Both the Dutch, with their seafaring and art history, and the Indians, with their religious beliefs and corn ceremonies, would impact Joseph Imhof's life with the visual remnants of their past cultures. It was as if the youthful Joseph Imhof would, in a curious way, use the Dutch and Indians as guideposts to absorb the past as he made his daily walks on Long Island.

In their beginning years, the Dutch prospered in their fur trade with the Indians, and developed agricultural communities on Long Island. By 1664, however, the English had conquered the New Netherland Colony and taken it from the Dutch. The next wave of immigrants had to wait nearly two hundred years for the political upheavals in Germany when agricultural failures and severe winters added to the German peasants' misery. Thousands fled their country between 1830 and 1860. Many, after their arrival in the United States, joined the westward movement toward California, but thousands of others settled into Eastern cities, primarily Brooklyn and Williamsburg.[18]

Few Brooklyn emigrants from Germany had wealth or university educations. Most had modest means or were among the poor, and their skills ranged from shoe and bootmaker, like John Imhof, to Catholic priests and engineers.[19] They brought their social customs of hard work, idealism, orderliness and industriousness. They formed social clubs, dance halls, and beer gardens.[20]

One German, Henry Roehr, who witnessed the German revolution in 1848, immigrated to Brooklyn and began the *Brooklyn Free Press* to inform the German immigrants of Brooklyn's activities and politics.[21] Another German, John Augustus Roebling, had studied in Bavaria the engineering of chain suspension bridges. Roebling's passion to design and build such bridges, however, was stifled in Bavarian Germany and he sailed for America where he would later engineer the design of the Brooklyn Bridge.[22]

By the time John and Magdalena disembarked at the Baltimore port of entry, Brooklyn had been incorporated as a city for nineteen years. John Imhof had been born in Kneibus, Baden-Württemberg, Germany and he and Magdalena were among the first Imhofs to arrive in America, where the original name, Imhoff, would become Imhof. The Imhoff heritage, though, dated back to Nürnberg, Bavaria as early as 1025 under Konrad the Second. By the late fifteenth century, Imhoffs continued to live in that area of Germany, as chapel and church records show, and where the St. Lorenz Church in Nürnberg remains the official church of the Imhoff family.[23] Its sanctuary displays wood and stone carvings by fifteenth century wood carvers and sculptors Veit Stoss and Michael Wolgemut.[24]

John and Magdalena Imhof, now of Brooklyn, thrived in their new world setting.[25] Others thrived as well and, with their prosperity, came a desire for greater comfort and closer connection to Manhattan. It was in this creative industrial-age environment that Joseph Imhof came to maturity.

* * *

For over fifty years, the people of Brooklyn had talked about building a bridge to connect Brooklyn, the country's third largest city, to Manhattan, the country's largest city. But the talk remained only talk until the 1860s. By then Brooklyn, as a major manufacturing center for glass, steel, chemicals,

37

hats, whiskey, beer and glue, had a population that had reached nearly half a million. Five different ferry lines, all operated by the Union Ferry Company, traveled from Manhattan and the mainland by different routes to Long Island. The ferry that directly linked Brooklyn to Manhattan, the Fulton Ferry, sometimes called the Brooklyn Ferry, streamed back and forth across the river, nonstop, night and day. Any person, whether banker, clerk, delivery boy, or butcher, doing business with either city, had to ride the ferry. Each day, thousands lined up and pushed or shoved their way aboard.[26]

In 1853, John Roebling and his fifteen-year-old son, Washington, happened to ride an ice-bound ferry, crossing the East River from Brooklyn to Manhattan. After the July Revolution of 1830 in Germany had caused Roebling to immigrate to America, he had tried farming, then engineering, before opening a wire factory in New Jersey. From there, he launched his successful career as a bridge builder. On that freezing ferry ride from Brooklyn to Manhattan, Roebling envisioned a suspension bridge over the East River, connecting New York's two major cities. A suspension bridge would give the height necessary for the clipper ships, with their tall masts, that plied the East River. Three years later, he made a sketch of his bridge and, in 1857, his plans appeared in the *New York Tribune*.[27]

New York's weather helped speed Roebling's plan. During the winter of 1866-67, the people of Brooklyn experienced one of the most severe winters on record. The commute to Manhattan by ferry became an even more burdensome and tiring trip.[28]

In 1867, John Roebling, as the engineer for the Brooklyn Bridge, met with his select group at the Brooklyn Gas Light Company on Fulton Street. John's oldest son, Washington, joined the group of men to study Roebling's drawings. The bridge would have immense towers and miles of wire cables. It fit right into the innovative engineering feats of the day. The French had almost completed the Suez Canal, and the Europeans had undertaken to build the longest tunnel through the Alps. In the United States, the Union Pacific Railroad continued to rapidly advance toward the West to become, in 1869, the first transcontinental railway. In 1869, the Atchison, Topeka and Santa Fe would lay its first seven miles of track to eventually join with the Southern Pacific to form the second transcontinental railway. In doing so, the railroads would usher in an era in New Mexico no one had envisioned, not even the locals.[29]

In New York, the Brooklyn bridge would turn Brooklyn into a boom town. Churches, stores, banks, factories, home builders would prosper. The cornfields that had fed the Indians would be turned into streets of gold. A shipbuilding company north of the Brooklyn Navy Yard would build the caissons for the bridge. The two caissons, 168-foot by 102-foot boxes, one for Brooklyn and one for New York City, would be towed down the river and then sunk into position for the towers. Their construction would become a daily spectator sport where people gathered every day. On May 8, 1871, with both caisson shells in place, construction began on the bridge that would become the gateway to Joseph Imhof's freedom.[30]

After Joe's birth that year, John and Magdalena continued their practice of walking the land with their children. Brooklyn provided the perfect setting, with its tree-lined streets, open fields, the salt air blowing in from the sea lanes, and sea gulls wheeling overhead.

Joe led the usual childhood of a towheaded boy.[31] His parents found him shy, yet outgoing to those with whom he felt comfortable. And he preferred to be called Joe. Three years after his birth, Magdalena gave birth to her last child, Elizabeth, born in 1874. That year the family moved to 493 Atlantic Avenue where they would remain until 1891.[32] By 1874, John Imhof had become a naturalized citizen of the United States.[33]

On August 25, 1876, the first man made a crossing on the cable that finally connected the Brooklyn and New York bridge towers.[34] Because the Imhof family lived only a few blocks from the Brooklyn tower, John and Magdalena probably gathered their children and joined the crowds to witness the excitement of the man crossing the East River by cable.

That year, Joe reached five years of age and another event would help shape his life just as powerfully as the coming of the Brooklyn Bridge. His godfather gave him a box of watercolors.[35]

The box contained the usual basic colors treasured by all beginners. Joe would dip his brush into a can of water, then touch a color with his brush, working the paint into the brush. When Joe touched the fully charged brush full of color to paper, he would move his brush from top to bottom, creating a graded wash. The spontaneous color electrified him and ignited his imagination.

The box of watercolors became his most precious possession. At night he would sleep with the box of watercolors under his pillow. Sometimes during the night, he would awaken and slip his hand under the pillow to touch the box and make sure the box of colors was still there.[36]

The desire to become an artist began for Joe at this early age. He kept a sketch pad and drawing pencil with him constantly. He learned to see details of the life around him when he joined his family for their daily walks through the neighborhood and into the countryside. He learned to use his drawing pencil so that it wouldn't leave unintended graphite marks on the paper, or engrave the paper. He drew with special care, and learned to use both sides of the paper. As Joe advanced in school, he continued his self-taught art training, and began to work with oils as well. By the time he had reached ten years of age, he had executed still lifes of such quality that one of his sisters would hang them in her home.[37]

American schools in the 1880s offered little in visual arts education. A student interested in being an artist learned by apprenticing with an established artist, by taking private art lessons, or by traveling to Europe for study at an art academy.[38] And even though people regarded the Brooklyn schools as far superior to those in Manhattan, public education had not advanced much beyond untrained teachers using the McGuffey Reader. Brooklyn school buildings that had been constructed in the 1840s needed repair, yet enrollment continued to soar.[39] High schools in the 1880s prepared students for the practicalities of living, instead of attending college.[40]

In 1881, Joe began to walk to the Fulton Ferry and watch the passengers.[41] As the Fulton Ferry from Manhattan docked, the passengers would come ashore after the loading gates of the ferryhouse would open. People from all walks of life would then fill the waiting room, which would empty immediately. An equally large crowd waited to load for the trip to Manhattan.

One day Joe embarked onto the Fulton Ferry, crossed the East River, and landed at Fulton Street in New York City. The trip must have commanded the full attention of the ten-year-old boy as he gazed at the ceaseless pageant stirring the waters of the river as seagulls called and wheeled above. Yachts, excursion steamers, ocean-going ships, clippers, schooners moved on the river at all times and told the boy of the many events taking place beyond his reach, but not his imagination.

Then Joe rushed off the ferry at Fulton Street in Manhattan, walked a few blocks west to William Street, then north to Beekman Street. At the corner of William and Beekman, at 36 Beekman Street, stood the Ridley Mansion. The Ridley family had moved further north, and their residence had been converted into studios for artists, such as painters, etchers, lithographers. Joe introduced himself to these artists, and began to make the trip from Brooklyn and Manhattan more frequently. He soon took his drawings, watercolors, and paintings with him to ask the advice of the Ridley Mansion artists.[42]

As Joe continued his self-taught art education with more frequent trips on the Fulton Ferry, the Brooklyn Bridge slowly neared completion. On May 24, 1883, the twelve-year-old boy and his family witnessed the most historic event to ever take place in Brooklyn: the opening of the Brooklyn Bridge. As the sun rose over the city, the flag was raised full-mast on the

Site of the Ridley Mansion at the corner of Beekman and William Streets, New York City, undated.

flagpole at the Commandant's house in the Brooklyn Navy Yard on the East River, less than a mile from the Imhofs' house. Simultaneously, flags rose throughout Brooklyn: from all official buildings, from the long-awaited bridge, from poles hanging from windows on houses. Others hung Chinese lanterns in their windows, and every building on Fulton Street flew streamers and banners, as did those who lived in the area that had come to be known as the Heights, the hills overlooking the East River.[43]

President Chester A. Arthur, and all the dignitaries, began their ceremonial march to Brooklyn on the bridge's elevated promenade. Others, who had been influential enough to receive a ticket admitting them onto the bridge, moved on roadways that ran on their side of the promenade. As the procession crossed the bridge, thousands cheered on either side of the East River with a roar that increased in volume with the marching bands. Below the bridge, on the river, ships had gathered to form an elongated flotilla, and had rigged their masts with colored flags that fluttered in the light breeze.[44]

When President Arthur arrived at the Brooklyn tower, guns boomed from the Brooklyn Navy Yard to the north, and cannons from either side of the bridge boomed their answer. The building of the Brooklyn bridge had taken thirty years from the time John Roebling had his vision in 1853.[45] Its gateway to Manhattan would enable the awe-struck twelve-year-old boy, Joseph Imhof, who was watching, to fulfill his own artistic vision. Joe's father was fifty-five and his mother fifty-four. The oldest child, Annie, was twenty-three, Mary twenty-one, Frances eighteen, George sixteen, Catherine was fourteen, and the baby, Elizabeth, was nine. Joe and Elizabeth remained the closest in their relationship.[46]

Three years later, in 1886, Joe graduated from high school.[47] His friends regarded him as being an inordinately serious fellow and unlike the average young man in Brooklyn.[48] By the time Joe graduated, he had long since used the Brooklyn Bridge to escape Brooklyn. More important, the bridge allowed him to escape his father's demands which would have condemned Joe to a life of failure.

CHAPTER 3

ON HIS OWN

Joe had always imagined himself attending college, and, naturally, assumed that his father would help him financially when the time came. The father had granted his oldest son, George, such an education. When Joe graduated from high school at age fifteen, in 1886, his father announced that instead of the anticipated college education, Joe would begin studies for the priesthood.[1]

The father's decision came as an astonishing revelation to Joe. Catholicism had played an exemplary role in their family life, and, certainly, other families had assigned children to the church.[2] But Joe found his father's desire to make Joe the token priest in the family more than he could fathom. Hadn't his father seen Joe's artistic talent? His drive to become an artist? His many excursions into Manhattan to consult with the artists living in the Ridley Mansion?

The father remained unmoved by Joe's arguments. If Joe refused to become a priest, his father said, then he would not pay for any education. Joe could either settle for the religious life, or nothing. Joe believed that the education was rightfully his, and insisted that he was going to become an artist of the first order. His father refused to speak of the matter.[3]

The denial of an education solidified Joe's determination to become an artist. Paradoxically, his family's religious devotion and the Catholic Church had taught Joe both self-discipline and determination. For Joe, his father's refusal became a turning point, and he decided he would not turn back from the vision he had all of his life from the time he'd received the box of watercolors; he took the responsibility for the direction of his life. In addition, he began to question his own religious beliefs, his own philosophical view of life. The father's decision had changed his son's life. The breach had been made. Joe would never look back.

At the age of fifteen, Joseph Imhof gathered his artist's supplies, walked the easy distance to the Brooklyn Bridge, crossed the bridge to Manhattan and walked the few blocks to join the artists at the Ridley Mansion. Only his mother's pleas, before he had left, managed to persuade him to return at night to sleep in the family home, and to eat breakfast with his beloved mother.[4]

The artists at Ridley gave Joe the kind of home he had sought, and introduced him to the kinds of employment available to apprentice artists. An elderly engraver, an emigrant from Switzerland, paid the five dollars a month rent for Joe's first studio, an amount the young man would repay after he received his first pay check. The garret on the top floor, a small space below the slanting roofline that Joe called his "pigeon coup," was all the space he needed.[5]

From the Ridley Mansion at Beekman and William Streets, Joe walked one block west to Nassau Street and into the Currier and Ives retail shop at 115 Nassau.[6] Here he contracted to draw the open-faced lettering for titles on Currier and Ives prints. He then received instruction on where to pick up his piece work in the lithographer's factory, a five-story building located one block north of the Ridley Mansion, at 33 Spruce. He learned he would letter directly on the stones used to make a print.[7]

Joe had already mastered the basic forms for all letters: using serifs, holding each letter on a horizontal line, drawing the uniform lengths of ascenders or descenders, achieving the right thickness for lines. Now he would learn to draw directly on the stone found at Solenhofen, near Pappenheim in Bavaria, regarded as the ideal lithography stone. No finer stone had been quarried. Its fine, compact grain permitted the stone to be split to achieve different thicknesses and sizes for printing. Before Joe ever saw the stone, it had been cut and sanded to flatten the surface. Then the lithography artist rubbed the stone smooth with a fine sand to give a rough enough surface to hold the greasy crayon used to draw upon the surface.[8]

Joe met other artists, lithographers and letterers who worked on the fourth floor of Currier and Ives. Because he worked on a piece-work basis, Joe would select his stone. Currier and Ives kept the stones within easy reach; the walls were lined with racks of stones on the upper three floors. Each stone was numbered on the end and ready for use. Stones containing art of the better-selling prints were kept for a while, and stones with less popular prints were ground by a man on the fourth floor who did nothing but grind and regrind stones. The third and fourth floors also housed the hand-operated presses.[9]

If the demand for a print resurfaced after the stone had been ground, a new stone was drawn, which accounts for some of the variation in prints seen today.[10] For example, Currier and Ives listed nineteen different prints of "The Great East River Suspension Bridge." Sizes available were large, small, and very small.[11]

The crayon Joe used to letter had been developed by Charles Currier, the founder's brother. Currier and Ives used exclusively the crayon made of beef suet, goose grease, white wax, castile soap, gum mastic, shellac, and gas black.[12] The crayon varied in size from the delicate diamond size used in letters, to the coarser grades of one and a half-inch thickness. Lithographers considered the Currier and Ives crayons superior to any others.[13]

Nathaniel Currier, the founder, as a boy of fifteen in 1828, had worked as an apprentice in lithography, a printing process developed only thirty-two years before, in 1796, by a Bavarian playwright, Alois Senefelder. In his search for an easy way to print his plays, Senefelder found that if he used an ink he had created, one made of soap, wax, and lamp black, that when he wrote on a porous stone, the stone absorbed water everywhere except where the ink had been applied.[14]

When Nathaniel Currier set up his own lithography business in America, in 1834, he realized that prints of major news events called attention to his prints. Six years later, his lithograph, "Awful Conflagration of the Steam Boat Lexington on Long Island Sound, on Monday Eve'g Jan. 13th, 1840, by which melancholy occurrence over 100 persons perished," appeared in the *New York Sun* only three days after the fire. The *Sun* heralded their reproduction as the world's first illustrated news "extra." Currier saw the endless possibilities of publishing pictorial reporting of newsworthy subjects.[15]

The first two Currier and Ives lithographs depicted fires. After that, the firm published thousands of prints on subjects as varied as fishing, hunting, animals, ships, steamboats, disasters, political cartoons, campaign banners, and portraits of notables. Currier and Ives became a national institution, a recorder of the American scene. Their lithographs pictured life in the city, the country, people at play, at work, on ships, in trains. Currier listed his firm as "Printmakers to the American People," and masses of people loved the prints, especially the colored prints that brought life to the depicted scene.[16]

During the fifty years that Currier and Ives remained at their peak, they produced an average of three prints a week.[17] Their catalogues listed seven thousand different prints.[18] Prices of prints varied according to size, scene and the prospective market. Small prints sold for six cents each at wholesale. Retail stores sold the prints for fifteen to twenty-five cents, and never more than three or four dollars. Sizes ranged from 2.8 inches-by-4.8 inches for the small prints, to eighteen-by-twenty-seven inches for the largest prints.[19]

By the time Joseph Imhof began his piece-work lettering, Joseph Keppler's *Puck*, the satirical weekly magazine which commented on the American scene, had been printing color illustrations, using chromolithography since 1876. Nathaniel Currier had retired and turned his business over to James Merritt Ives, a self-taught artist and native New Yorker whom Currier had hired as his head bookkeeper. Ives had proved his worth by giving birth to a trade name that continues to remain famous. While Ives remained active in the business, high speed, steam-operated presses had made the firm's hand-operated technology out-of-date, and Ives' print business had begun to decline. Still, the lithographer produced quality prints, and those prints sold by the thousands.[20]

Each day, Joe would pick up his stones at the Currier and Ives factory at 33 Spruce, return to his garret studio, and letter the small, medium and large stones with titles that added to a print's popularity and sales appeal. Over and over he lettered such key words as great, celebrated, grand, magnificent, champion, first, peerless, home, and American. After he had completed the work, he would take the proofs to the offices at 115 Nassau for approval. Once approved, he would carry the stones to the factory at 33 Spruce where printers transferred the work.[21]

Currier and Ives had long ago created an assembly process to produce their prints. As Harry T. Peters writes in *Currier and Ives, Printmakers to the American People*, "In the Currier and Ives shop the stock prints were colored by a staff of about twelve young women, all trained colorists and mostly of German descent. They worked at long tables from a model set up in the middle of the table, where it was visible to all. The models, many of which were colored by Louis Maurer and Fanny Palmer, were all first approved by one of the partners. Each colorist applied only one color and when she had finished, passed the print on to the next worker, and so on until it was fully colored. The print would then go to the woman in charge, known as the 'finisher,' who would touch it up where necessary. The colors used were imported from Austria and were the finest available, especially valued because they did not fade in the light.

"When large numbers of the rush stock prints were needed, extra help was called in. Then stencils would be cut for the various colors and the extras would wash in the colors. The prints could then be touched up by the regular girls. The larger folios were sent out in lots with models to regular colorists who worked outside the shop. Usually twelve prints from one of the large folio plates were sent out at a time. These outside colorists were often indigent young artists who earned a modest living at this kind of work while awaiting the recognition of their own work. Currier and Ives paid one cent apiece to colorists for the small prints and one dollar for coloring twelve of the large folios."[22]

Joe grasped at every piece of knowledge in his work. He learned to grain and clean the stone, use various crayons, to draw on the stone as well as on transfer paper, which the printer would run through the process to move the image to stone. While he found drawing on the transfer paper less inhibiting, he also learned that in the transfer process the prints lost their crisp tonal definition as compared to work drawn directly on the stone.

By his constant association with the prints, Joe discovered how to judge the quality of a lithograph. He observed that the margins around a print served as part of that print's aesthetic value. His most invaluable lessons though, came from his association with the printers who taught him to print. By the end of his year and a half with Currier and Ives, he neared becoming a master lithographer himself. His earnings rose with his mastery until he averaged about one hundred dollars a week, a handsome income for a sixteen-year-old in 1887.[23]

The increased income allowed Joe to move his studio in the Ridley Mansion from the garret to the main floor, where he added a reception room to his space. His more opulent surroundings cost him twenty-five dollars a month.[24] He continued, however, to return each night to his parents' home in Brooklyn where his father never gave up hope on Joe becoming a priest, and where he ate breakfast with his mother each morning.

Imhof demonstrates how to make a lithograph, 1954.

Joe's mastery of lithography brought him to the attention of Stecker Lithographers, a Currier and Ives' rival, though no other lithography firm equalled Currier and Ives' national reputation. Joe became art director for Stecker, a firm that purchased Currier and Ives used stones after a desired number of proofs had been made. Stecker reground the stones for their own use. In addition to the new position with Stecker, Joe's work brought him to the attention of other firms who hired him for freelance art work.[25]

By the late 1890s, the art of lithography began to disappear in this country, but the mastery of the process had been imprinted on Joe for his lifetime. Within forty years, he would bring the first lithography press to Taos. There he would use the skills he had mastered at Currier and Ives on his own Rutherford Machinery Company press that Currier and Ives used.[26] He would make his own prints of Pueblo Indians, teach lithography, and give other artists access to the press. In time, the art of lithography would see a revival in the United States in the form of the Tamarind Lithography Workshop established by June Wayne in Los Angeles during the 1960s, with Garo Antreasian the first master printer. The Workshop, which set standards and offered training programs, would continue its goals to serve as a training program for artists and produce American and other artists' finest works. The Tamarind Institute, in 1970, would become affiliated with the University of New Mexico College of Fine Arts in Albuquerque.[27]

For now, though, Joe painted for himself at night and on weekends. By the age of sixteen, he had executed an extraordinarily beautiful watercolor of two roses.[28] The nineteen-by-sixteen-inch watercolor depicts two pink, long-stemmed, fully opened roses lying on a background of a shaded and muted green. The viewer's eye goes immediately to the upper right rose whose white-edged petals appear to be rolling outward. Then the eye drifts to the left and the second rose of a slightly smaller size, and finally to the lower right signature, J. Imhof 87. The watercolor has been painted in the classic European style. Joe gave the watercolor to his closest friend, his sister Elizabeth, who took it with her when she married William Murphy. Elizabeth hung "Two Roses" (see page 161) in the living room of her Long Island home, and it remained with her until she died in 1960 at age eighty-seven.

Three years after Joe completed "Two Roses," he painted the watercolor, "Cupid Disappointed." Elizabeth also received "Cupid Disappointed" from Joe.[29] She bequeathed the painting to her son, Theodore T. Murphy, of Uniondale, New York, who worked as a meter reader for the Brooklyn Union Gas Company, which had emerged from the old Brooklyn Gas Light Company, the firm which had played such a pivotal role in the creation of the Brooklyn Bridge.[30] "Cupid Disappointed," an eighteen-by-thirteen-inch watercolor, depicts the back of a flesh-colored cupid, who appears much like a child-sized angel with white wings protruding from its nude shoulders. Cupid has raised its right arm to its forehead, as it stands at the back of center stage between a heavy drape on the right and a gold enscrolled screen on the left, and looks down into some unfathomable darkness. A discarded quiver with arrows lies on the floor in the right foreground. The torn half of a small paper note lies just beneath Cupid's feet, while the other half of the note has been torn into smaller pieces that lie to the right of the bow and quiver. Cupid's flesh tones contrast with the dark gray drapery that has been shaded to create folds. The painting speaks of loss and sadness (see page 162).

49

Elizabeth received "Cupid Disappointed," which Joe had signed in the lower left, J. J. Imhof 1890. Within a year, in 1891, Joe would board a ship heading for Europe and his first self-directed program to study the great masters. Upon his return to the United States, he would forever sign his paintings in one of several ways: J. A. Imhof, Joseph A. Imhof, Jos. A. Imhof, Imhof, or José Imhof. Never again would he identify his work as J. J., using his father's name in the initials, J. J., for Joseph John.[31]

Joe had already demonstrated his enterprising nature by his self-directed trips to Ridley Mansion as a ten year old, and his decision to leave home to pursue his art among those sympathetic to his interests. He continued to expand this enterprising asset when he added freelance work to his already industrious piece- work lettering for Currier and Ives. These pursuits introduced him to his financially successful position at Stecker Lithographers, and his other love: books.[32] Joe had always loved books, and now he began to collect them. On his way to the Ridley Mansion, or on his return to Brooklyn, he would stop in one or more of the numerous secondhand bookstores that lined Brooklyn's upper Fulton Street.[33]

He particularly searched for out-of-print books and first editions. Joe's mastery of lithography, his natural talent as a painter as seen in his youthful paintings, coupled with the continual critiques he sought from the artists in the Ridley Mansion, had helped him develop a critical eye for a well-printed book. His own self-directed reading program gave him knowledge about the value of books, for the ideas they contained and the quality of writing that conveyed those ideas.[34]

After about two years of collecting, Joe decided to open a bookstore that carried first editions, out-of-print books, and other books of exceptional value. In Brooklyn, he rented a store on Atlantic Avenue, near Court Street, not far from where his parents lived, and hired a young man to run the store. Every day, Joe arrived in the evening holding a load of books in his arms, and eased open the door to the already overcrowded bookstore.[35]

In a short time, the bookstore developed a reputation for the place to find valuable books. The store's selection of books proved so intriguing that a local newspaper wrote stories about unusual books found there. Soon, however, the numbers of books Joe brought to the store began to crowd the space where customers enjoyed browsing. Part of the store's attraction then became the crowd of customers who lined up outside the store, or stood in the doorway, unable to enter, to inquire if a certain book was available.[36]

The bookstore's success revealed various inborn talents Joe possessed, and must have given him the confidence in himself that his father refused to offer. Joe had an inherent ability to find and collect valuable works; he could translate his ideas into tangible enterprises that generated substantial income; he could live independently of his parents; and his work and his life had value, not just to himself, but to others who sought his creations.

This process of learning and producing income enabled Joe to envision his future. If he could not escape his surroundings, he would embrace them and make them his own. In what free time he did have, he began to make regular visits to the Metropolitan Museum of Art, which had been founded in 1870. By 1880, the Metropolitan was in its permanent home by Central Park at Fifth Avenue and Eighty-Second Street. The Protestants, who had helped found the Metropolitan, believed that art was an appropriate counterpoint to religion in ministering to the masses' needs. As the Metropolitan flourished, its collection of art would rank second to the major European museums that had had the advantage of centuries of royal collections. In 1891, the Metropolitan's Protestant trustees abandoned the Sabbath closing to remain open on Sundays. This allowed artists and everyday workers to visit on their weekly holidays.[37]

Joe continued his education at the Metropolitan where he became a regular, spending his time there studying the great masters to find solutions to his own drawing and painting problems. Rembrandt's "Portrait of a Man" revealed how the painter had abandoned the traditional Dutch smooth surface painting, and caked the surface using a heavily loaded brushstoke.[38] Joe would also find paintings by contemporary artists, among them Rosa Bonheur, the French painter. Bonheur's "The Horse Fair," donated to the Metropolitan in 1887, displays her knowledge of equine anatomy and motion by creating an uneven Baroque curving arc to create tension between man and the horse.[39] Bonheur, like Joe, would soon fall under the spell cast by Buffalo Bill and his "Wild West" show.[40]

Of equal interest to Joe at the Metropolitan was the 1890 gift, "Portrait of a Man" by Frans Hals. Joe saw demonstrated in this painting visible brushstrokes that, when viewed from a distance, fell into place.[41] Later Joe would copy Hals' "Baron Hasselaer" and "Mimi." These two copies later hung in the Taos living room of the Imhof home and were treated individu-

51

ally in Sallie's will.[42] By contrast, Joe admired Jan Vermeer's masterpiece, "Young Woman with a Jug." This Delft artist's painting at the Metropolitan showed Vermeer's use of minimum brushwork to avoid texture. The subtleness of this painting rewards the viewer with each discovery of detail, such as the objects, colors, reflection, light and shadow. The subject is a simple arrangement showing a woman in the corner of a room, yet it provides serenity. Vermeer attends to the negative space surrounding the subject by capturing the variety of ways light illuminates and reflects. The crystalline style of subtle horizontal and vertical light, with diagonal accents, does not take precedent over the flood of light creating a cool scheme more beautiful than reality.[43] Joe would make use of this light in his later portraits.

In addition, Joe had access to books that reproduced paintings by the great masters. In Jan Van Eyck's paintings, Joe observed how Van Eyck layered his oil pigments, of how he achieved light by using the thinnest of paint, then proceeded to achieve darkness by layering, creating thickness in the shadows. Van Eyck treated each color area separately and respected each color's boundaries.[44]

Peter Paul Rubens reversed the process by painting the lights thickly and opaquely, and the shadows thinly and translucently. Rubens' use of turpentine as a thinner helped him to achieve a variety of brushworks.[45] Joe saw that Eugène Delacroix never quite abandoned the cool studio light that emitted warm shadows. Delacroix used his paint at its thinnest to depict the turning of form in space, and used thickness to bring form nearest to the spectator.[46]

The new insights Joe gained from studying the great masters encouraged him to use new materials, to test different styles, and to think about statements he might make in his work. His visits increased his desire to live as an artist, and he increased his dedication and discipline.

Since Joe's father still believed he could control his son's destiny by refusing to acknowledge Joe's chosen interests and by withholding any financial help, Joe again turned to those who had guided his career. He closely questioned the artists at the Ridley Mansion. He also sought information in his treasured collection of books.

From these sources he determined the next step in his education, and his life. The decision would impact his direction as much as had his father's refusal to acknowledge Joe's interest.

CHAPTER 4

BUFFALO BILL AND THE SIOUX

Toward the end of the nineteenth century, art academies still provided most of the training for artists, particularly for Europeans. In the United States, the Pennsylvania Academy of Fine Arts had been founded in 1805 to educate artists. Other academies followed, but at a cost Joe could not afford.[1]

The Ridley Mansion artists tutored Joe in the alternatives available to artists at that time. So much had changed in the ways artists were trained, even in the last decade, from the origins of the earliest societies, known as lodges, which dominated during the medieval period. The lodges, a first step in establishing creative work as a fine art, were composed of groups of craftsmen working together on ecclesiastical buildings.[2]

During the eleventh and twelfth centuries, craftsmen and merchants of one particular occupation began leaving the lodges to form European guilds as a way of bettering themselves. In the early years of the guilds, the merchants dominated the guilds which took on economic and political overtones. Eventually, painters and sculptors broke from the lodges to join guilds. By the thirteenth and fourteenth centuries, craftsmen dominated the guilds. When at their height, guilds performed political actions, regulated trade, and provided professional education for the members as journeymen of a particular guild took on apprentices who later became assistants. During this process, guilds established art as a profession and craft, which allowed those without standing to train as artists.[3]

Still, the guilds had local control over artists and set standards of workmanship, length of apprenticeship and duties for an apprentice artist. Guilds also set the price of paintings. Guilds gained enough power and influence during the sixteenth century to house themselves in buildings designed for their purpose.[4]

Although the guilds provided economic stability, this system, too, gradually changed. Academies, which standardized an artist's training under a professor, replaced the guilds. The guild's master-apprentice manner of learning became the academy's professor-student relationship in which the student determined the length of his own training. The guilds, with their on-the-job training in the workshop, were replaced by the seventeenth century academy that had formulated a theoretical component to retain the Renaissance ideals of humanism with the study of design and drawing. Academies embraced the principles of perspective and anatomy.[5]

The academies taught that art should ennoble nature. However, since nature was not an ideal or perfect model itself, academies determined that artists should begin by studying the ancients, which were plaster casts of ancient Greek and Roman statues. In an academy, the student not only learned the grinding of color, how to clean brushes and prepare the surface for the painting, he learned painting techniques.[6]

The most famous academy, and the one other academies used for their role model, was the *Académie Royale de Peinture et de Sculpture*, founded in Paris in 1648 to overcome the restrictions guilds placed on court painters. Under the patronage of Louis XIV's minister, Jean-Baptiste Colbert, the *Académie Royal* had been modeled after the *Académia de S. Luca* founded in Rome in 1593.[7]

Academies flourished through the support of artists, who enjoyed an improved status. Artists could glorify their art and control the subject matter they painted, which they carefully ranked in order of importance. History and portraiture ranked highest, while still life, landscape and genre scenes ranked at the bottom.[8]

Upon the founding of the *Académie Royale*, other academies followed in Berlin, Antwerp, Amsterdam, Vienna, Florence, and the United States. The *Académie Julian* in Paris became one of the more popular among artists because it instilled in its students certain aesthetic criteria of composition, perspective, accuracy, anatomy, and a sense of value concerning the subject matter. Students mastered the use of light, shading, of how to create the folds of draperies; and, most importantly, academies raised art to the ranks of mathematics, astronomy, rhetoric and poetry.[9]

Unfortunately, the academies continued to train artists in a closed system that valued conformity and frowned upon originality. Academy professors believed that an artist's success was not based on ability, but on correctness of technique acquired through proper academic training. Academies respected the faithful transcription of nature, of classic values borrowed from the past.[10]

It was from this doctrinaire retrogression that the nineteenth century artist rebelled, leading to the eventual birth of Impressionism in the 1860s. The Impressionists, such as Edouard Manet, Claude Monet, Camille Pissarro and Edgar Degas, sought to create that which brought pleasure to artist and viewer alike, scenes of gardens and of ordinary families going about everyday life. In doing so, these Impressionists reproduced light, playing the sunlight and shadow on people and objects, giving them a natural, unposed appearance. With an object bathed in the natural light of the sun, the actual light on the object modified its color. The painter achieved the effect of vibrating brilliance by applying small individual spots of pure color instead of mixing paints on the palette.[11]

It was this very representation of vibrating color in brilliant light that Joe would see years later in New Mexico. He would see the color everywhere in New Mexico, in the sky, clouds, rocks, plants, so much so that he would never again take color for granted. This discovery would ignite his soul.

The academies in the Flemish countries of the Netherlands, Belgium and Luxembourg, by contrast to central European academies, offered artists freedom of expression without direct state patronage.[12] In the sixteenth century when the Reformation, and the Thirty Year War that followed, gave rise to Protestantism and saw the decline of Roman Catholicism in Northern Holland, artists reflected the changes. In the Flemish Low Countries (Belgium, Southern Netherlands, Luxembourg), Catholicism and the Roman baroque style still held sway with the presence of Peter Paul Rubens. In the northern provinces, Protestantism and the Dutch schools developed their own art subjects and styles consistent with their new religious, political, economic and social freedoms.[13]

Thus the Dutch School of Painting depicted the pictorial scenes of everyday life. Artists kept a good watch on their clients who were middle class burghers who wanted paintings to hang on their walls, showing their rise in

55

position. Religious iconography was replaced by a painter working, not for a patron, but for the market and to become a specialist in subjects that appealed to a market: landscapes, seascapes, cattle, horses, still lifes, and interior scenes. Independence from a patron gave the Dutch School freedom to succeed or fail. In doing so, the academies gradually evolved into exhibiting societies.[14]

By the age of nineteen, Joe had absorbed enough information about the various teaching methods used to train artists that he could make his decision concerning his next step. He decided to train in Europe. Several factors must have caused him to select Antwerp, Belgium as his home base. For one, the Red Star line steamed into Antwerp, a port considered one of the world's major shipping centers.[15] In addition, Antwerp served as an entry point for numerous artists on their way to Holland to paint a rapidly disappearing way of life in rural Holland, and the "out-dated methods employed by Dutch fishermen" that painters considered picturesque.[16]

Antwerp was a major artistic center as well. Its Antwerp School of Painting, founded in 1480 by Quentin Metsys who was involved with the Italian Renaissance but carried out the Flemish tradition of art, breathed life into the Southern Renaissance. In doing so, he abandoned the traditional Flemish composition for one set in a broad landscape full of atmosphere and sunlight. It was a straightforward, realistic approach. The Antwerp School of Painting continued into the seventeenth century, inspired by the rise of capitalism and humanism.[17]

Antwerp, where Joe disembarked, had such important buildings as the fourteenth century Cathedral of Our Lady, and the newly created Royal Museum of Fine Arts. In addition, this important industrial city had an impressive collection of Rubens and Van Dykes, paintings Joe had been particularly drawn to for their rich and warm tones in intimate settings. Clearly, his finances determined many of his choices, and Antwerp was a city where museums flourished. Their accessibility would have allowed him to teach himself by copying the great masters, an accepted way to learn art by the end of the nineteenth century.[18]

In 1891, Joe began to gather his finances to travel to Europe. That year he sold the bookstore for a substantial profit, and set his course for his self-directed European training. He never doubted his ability to earn the income to sustain his lifestyle, nor did he question that he did not manage his money wisely. He loved beautiful objects too well. As a safeguard, he left his mother in charge of his money and asked that she send him a monthly check to his address in Europe. He planned to live sparsely, not an unusual intention for an artist of his day, by renting a small room where he could cook his own meals.[19]

On April 1, 1891, at the age of twenty, Joe boarded the steamship SS *Noordland* of the Red Star Line. At 10:30 a.m., the ship pulled away from the New York harbor, and steamed toward Antwerp, Belgium.[20] On that same day, Joe's father bought a new home in Brooklyn at 227 Wyckoff Street, a few blocks from the former Atlantic Avenue address.[21]

By coincidence, and as timing would have it, William Frederick ("Buffalo Bill") Cody stood at the railing that same day on board the SS *Noordland* and watched the ship pull away from the New York harbor.[22] By 1891, as the Wild West slipped into history, only Cody remained to commemorate its glories.[23] Cody had not been without his troubles, however. Like Joe Imhof, he must have hoped that his biggest problems lay behind him.

Cody, who had had very little formal education, had turned a buffalo hunting job with the Kansas Pacific railroad construction crews into such a success that he had become known as Buffalo Bill. His showmanship exploits served him well when he organized a "Wild West" exhibition in 1883.[24] As his "Wild West" shows gained popularity, Nate Salsbury, as business manager, helped make them a financial success. The shows entertained throngs in the United States.[25] Even in Brooklyn, Cody became a latter-day genteel frontier hero, a kind of figure taken from one of James Fenimore Cooper's novels. And in Europe, Cody allowed the readers of American frontier adventure stories to see what frontier life was really like.[26]

On May 9, 1887, Cody had performed in London before Albert, Prince of Wales, later King Edward VII. Queen Victoria had enjoyed Cody's show so much that she had seen it twice.[27] Cody savored another triumph when Queen Wilhelmina of Belgium saw the performance in Brussels.[28] When Cody had come to Europe with his troupe of bronco riders and Sioux Indians for the Paris Exposition, in 1889, the French had become enthralled with his troupe's performances in Paris. The performances attracted large crowds and great sympathy for the Indians who, with other members of the troupe, had set up camp on the outskirts of Paris.[29]

Artists and writers felt particularly drawn to the troupe's magnificent performances. Among them was Rosa Bonheur, a French painter and sculptor known for her sympathetic and accurate depiction of animals. Rosa, by then a woman in her seventies, had set up her easel in the corrals of the Buffalo Bill camp and painted.[30] Eleanor Tufts wrote in her book, *Our Hidden Heritage*, "Rosa invited him [Cody] to By [France] to inspect her horses, and she seized the occasion to paint the Wild-West hero on horseback. He in turn sent her a gift of two spirited broncos."[31] Bonheur's most well-known painting may have been the life-size canvas of Buffalo Bill on his favorite white horse. Cody prized the work and shipped the painting to his wife, Luisa, perhaps to remind her of what he looked like during his long absences. Reproductions of the work appeared many times on playbills, posters and postcards.[32]

Of her experiences with the Indians, Bonheur wrote, "I was thus able to examine their tents at my ease. I was present at family scenes. I conversed as best I could with warriors and their wives and children. I made studies of the bisons, horses, and arms. I have a veritable passion, you know, for this unfortunate race and I deplore that it is disappearing before the White usurpers."[33]

Others took exception to Cody's treatment of the Indians. By 1890, reports had begun circulating in Europe that Cody mistreated his Indians, so he had gathered some of the Indians and headed to Washington to disprove the rumors.[34] A *New York Times*, March 7, 1891 article gives the best description of Cody's misadventure with his government.

"Col. Cody Gets His Indians

Mr. Morgan Finds He is Not a Bigger

Man Than Mr. Noble

"Washington, March 6 - Indian Commissioner Morgan has discovered once more that he is not a bigger man than the Secretary of the Interior. Somebody started the story last fall that the Indians who had been taken abroad by Col. William F. Cody to take part in the 'Wild West' had been badly treated and were surrounded by degrading influences.

"As soon as Col. Cody, better known as 'Buffalo Bill,' heard of this talk he rounded up his Indians, who were in Winter quarters at Strasburg, and brought them to Washington to give Commissioner Morgan an ocular demonstration of the falsity of the report. It was an expensive undertaking. When the Indians reached Washington, Col. Cody sought an interview with

Morgan. To his surprise, the Commissioner kept him waiting from day to day, and it was not until Buffalo Bill had secured the entire help of a prominent Cabinet officer that he was able to bring his troop before the Commissioner. Then the Indian troubles broke out in the West and at the solicitation of the authorities, Cody and his friendly Indians went to Pine Ridge and did good service for the government.

"But when the Colonel got ready to take his Indians back to Europe, he found a large-sized snag in his way. Commissioner Morgan flatly refused to permit a single red man to leave the reservation. He had been told that the Indians did not have proper surroundings abroad, and he considered it much better that they should remain on the reservation than be demoralized by foreign travel.

"No amount of evidence that Col. Cody could produce, including that of many leading Americans who had seen the show in Europe could affect Commissioner Morgan, or would he listen to the recommendations of Indian agents and Gen. Miles and Col. Forsythe that it would be the best way to prevent a renewal of troubles in the Spring to let Cody take a hundred of the Sioux out of the country. The Nebraska Senators and Representatives joined in trying to induce Morgan to issue the permits, but the only result was to call out an order from Morgan for the arrest of any agent of Cody who tried to take an Indian away from the reservation.

"It had cost Col. Cody a good many thousand dollars to bring his hundred Indians to the United States and take care of them here, and then to have them suddenly corralled by the Indian Commissioner after their return passage had been paid for was a little disheartening. Col. Cody has been here a week working hard to prevent the destruction of his show by Morgan's arbitrary act. The matter was finally laid before Secretary Noble, and today the secretary overruled the Commissioner and issued an order directing that Col. Cody be given liberty to take to Europe as many of the Sioux Indians as he wished. A fortnight hence, 100 of the redskins sailed with Buffalo Bill, and Commissioner Morgan, who boasted that he never attended a theatre or a circus in his life, will have to give them up to the demoralizing and degrading influences of foreign travel and contact with the civilization of the white man."[35]

Actually, the one hundred Sioux did not return to Europe on the same ship as Cody. They and their interpreter boarded the SS *Switzerland* of the Red Star Line two weeks later, on April 16, 1891.[36] Joseph Imhof would later meet Nate Salsbury and the Sioux, but for now he would learn of them through Buffalo Bill, his shipmate aboard the SS *Noordland*.

In another of those coincidences that seem to mark Joe's life, Nate Salsbury was the father of the artist, Rebecca Salsbury Strand James, who was a good friend of Georgia O'Keeffe.[37] Years later, Joe would meet up with O'Keeffe in Abiquiu, New Mexico and she would become a guest in his home at Taos. For now, Joe's life took a new turn with the presence of Nate Salsbury.

Cody may have been the impresario, but the credit for the business success of the "Wild West" show belongs to Salsbury. Salsbury had been born into a pioneer Vermont family in 1846, had lived in Illinois, gone on stage as a song and dance man in 1868, and in the 1870s had formed the successful Salsbury's Troubadours before joining up with Buffalo Bill.[38]

The winter that Cody had returned to Washington with the Sioux, Salsbury had stayed in Strasburg to manage the troupe's winter camp. Nellie Snyder Yost describes Salsbury's activities in her book, *Buffalo Bill, His Family, Friends, Fame, Failures and Fortunes.*

"Nate Salsbury, in France with the show, had not been idle that winter. Aware that the persistent tales of mistreatment of the Indians might make it impossible to secure Indians for the 1891 season, he had undertaken to gather an aggregation of the world's finest riders, for all the world seemed to love colorful displays of horsemanship."[39]

While Salsbury minded the show, Cody on board the S. S. *Noordland* took a special interest in Joseph Imhof, just as he had in Rosa Bonheur when he invited her into his camp outside of Paris. Cody always found artists and writers of special interest and often invited them to become a part of his entourage. Cody filled Joe with stories of the Indians, and of his troupe, all of which excited Joe's imagination.[40]

Joe's imagination may have played upon the passengers aboard ship as well. Certainly his wry sense of humor emerged in the notes he wrote on the SS *Noordland*'s printed cabin passenger list: "Mr. W. D. Bigelow, alias Doctor Koch; Miss Sophie Blum, Die Klenie; Mr. W. H. Cahill, Bill Nye; Mrs. Elizabeth D. Forst, Dock & I; Miss Minnie Frey, Bill Nyes No. 2; Mr. Rudolph Giger, Sultan; Mrs. Anne Giger, Sultana; Mr. Wm. J. Hauhart, Deadwood Dick; Mr. J. J. Imhof, McKinley; Mr. A. Kerckhoffs, Mrs. Bertha

Kerckhoffs, Budweiser, N.Y.; Mr. Levy Leon, Frenchy; Mr. N. Paulson, Capt.; Mr. S. Sorenson, Wandering Jew Ericson; Mr. E. Sonnenbrodt, Bismarck."[41]

In a letter dated June 2, 1994, Paul Fees, the Ernest J. Goppert Curator of the Buffalo Bill Museum in Cody, Wyoming, observed, " . . . the nicknames and notations [Imhof wrote on his passenger list] mean nothing to us. It could well be that they were names assigned in a skit. Bill Nye was a Wyoming humorist so it is possible that Cody's presence on board inspired the western nicknames. It seems just as likely to me that Imhof assigned the nicknames in jest or as a private joke. Note that the nicknames all have been assigned to people in the second cabin [where Joe stayed]."[42]

By the time the ship reached Antwerp, Cody had invited Joe to be his guest as long as Cody remained in Antwerp, readying his show for its London appearance. As Joe said, "Cody paid for my hotel room at the Hotel Antwerp for one week. Didn't know why, having landed with a pocket full of money."[43]

When the SS *Switzerland* arrived with Nate Salsbury and the one hundred Sioux, Joe spent the next several months talking with the Indians, studying their way of life, and sketching the first of his prized Native American portraits.[44] As Joe sketched, he practiced concentrating on his subject rather than the paper. At a comfortable pace, he began to trust his eyes, to find the lines, and the shading to establish the truth in his subject. The experience would mark the beginning in Joe's life-long mission to merge his life with the American Indians both spiritually and artistically. The Indians' way of life had opened paths for Joe he had not known before.

The extended time needed in Antwerp to ready the "Wild West" show had come about because Salsbury had made major changes during the time Cody had been in the States. In her book, Yost writes, "By the time Cody crossed the ocean again, with the new band of Indians, Salsbury had engaged twenty German soldiers, twenty British and twenty U. S. cavalrymen, twelve Cossacks, and six Argentine gauchos. These, with the twenty Mexican vaqueros, the twenty-five cowboys and six cowgirls of former years, and the thirty-seven mounted musicians, made an astonishing assemblage of splendid riders. When Cody arrived with his hundred Sioux warriors, the partners were able to present an exhibition of horsemanship that for speed, color, and action would soon be the talk of all Europe.

"The show now traveled from city to city in its own special railway

61

train, unloading at each stop with lightning speed, setting up the vast camp, putting on a morning street parade, giving afternoon and evening performances, then packing, loading, and moving on to the next stop. In Germany the show's speed and efficiency at loading, unloading, and feeding the hundreds of people and animals was of special interest to the army officers. Annie Oakley noted that 'at least forty officers of the Prussian guard [were always] standing all about with notebooks, [making] minute notes of how we pitched camp—the exact number of men needed, every man's position, how long it took, how we boarded the trains and packed the horses and broke camp, every rope and bundle and kit was inspected and mapped.' All this information would be translated into the rolling German field kitchens of World War I a quarter of a century later."[45]

Cody's "Wild West" show now had a subtitle, "Congress of Rough Riders of the World."[46] Cody's script constantly changed in an effort to outdo himself, but he always maintained two basic elements: the skills of the Indian and cowboy, such as bronco riding, and lassoing; and the dramatization of life in the West, such as Indian ceremonies, battles, and the Pony Express. It was truly an illusion of the highest form. But Cody reminded each audience that the exhibition came from the skill of the performer and the performance was not a result of a rehearsal.[47]

Like Joe Imhof and Rosa Bonheur, a whole generation of artists and writers fell under the spell of Buffalo Bill. Part of the understanding of how his "Wild West" show impacted artists can be found in the descriptions written by Cody himself and those who came to be transfixed. Cody described what happened when he and his troupe arrived in London.

"One of the first acts in the performance was to carry the flag to the front. This was done by a soldier. Walking around the arena, he offered the Stars and Stripes as an emblem of the friendship of America to all the world. On this occasion he carried the flag directly to the royal box, and dipped it three times before the Queen.

"Absolute silence fell over the great throng. Then the Queen of England rose and saluted the flag with a bow, her suite following her example. There was a wild cheer from everyone in the show, Indians included, and soon all the audience was on its feet, cheering and waving flags and handkerchiefs.

"This gave us a fine start and we never put on a better performance.

When it was all over, Her Majesty sent for me, and paid me many compliments as well as to my country and the West. I found her a most gracious and charming woman, with none of the haughtiness which I had supposed was inseparable from a person of such exalted rank. My subsequent experiences with royalty convinced me that there is more real democracy among the rulers of the countries of Europe than you will find among the petty officials of a village."[48]

By coincidence, John Young-Hunter, a young painter who had been born in Scotland in 1874, attended Buffalo Bill's London performance.[49] It would be twenty years before Young-Hunter would arrive in Taos and become Joseph Imhof's friend. Years later, Imhof and Young-Hunter would regale each other with memories of Buffalo Bill.[50] As fate would have it, the two men would also die within two months of each other in 1955.[51] For now, though, Young-Hunter arrived with his mother to witness the show that had taken Europe by storm.[52]

In his book, *Reviewing the Years,* Young-Hunter wrote of his reasons for coming to America for the first time in 1912.

"Furthermore an event of no small significance in my young life was the coming of Buffalo Bill to London. His 'Wild West' show, the first of its kind ever seen in England, was extremely popular, and it certainly was a thrilling experience for me. Had it been possible, I would have spent many hours behind the scenes, making friends, and gloating over all the details of the paraphernalia, including the typical cow-ponies, their trappings, the Indians and their 'tepees.'

"I happened to be in the audience the day that Queen Victoria and other members of the Royal family were present. This was an important occasion, and one not to be neglected by Buffalo Bill or his efficient manager, Nate Salsbury.

"The first part of the show was the introduction to the audience of the various participants, who entered the arena on horseback. 'God Save the Queen' and the 'Star Spangled Banner' were played by the cowboy band; the audience of several thousand, all standing, sang.

"The Indians then opened the performance. They were nearly all Sioux, representing several branches of that celebrated tribe, the Oglala, Wahpeton, Brule, Yankton, and Sisseton. At the far end of the arena I noticed some commotion, accompanied by typical falsetto yelping; then a group of about twenty feathered, painted, and gorgeously-apparelled Indians on ponies, dashed full speed around the large amphitheater, pulling up abruptly in front of the Royal Box, flourishing spears, bows, or guns, as a salute to Her Majesty. With renewed yelling, they backed toward the centre of the arena.

"Then came an announcement of a name on the megaphone, and a lone Indian appeared, 'The Chief.' Such dignity, such superb horsemanship, with the tail feathers of his war-bonnet floating behind him. He pulled up abruptly in front of the Queen, and then backed away.

"Again a loud announcement, and another band of Indians, Brule this time, repeated the performance, until each branch of Sioux warriors had made its characteristic obeisance before the improvised throne of the British Empire.

"As a moving spectacle, a colorful manifestation of dramatic effectiveness in the way of a salute, it is difficult to imagine anything more brilliant. The shouting of approval by the spectators was evidence of their appreciation.

"Next came the stagecoach, with a team of six horses driven by a venerable looking 'old-timer,' and accompanied by many cowboys and some Mexicans on typical western ponies. Following them rode Johnnie Baker, the expert rifle-shot, and the equally celebrated Annie Oakley and Lilian Smith.

"At the end of the procession, which now filled the arena, rode Nate Salsbury, who very rarely appeared, and last, Buffalo Bill himself.

"I cannot give a detailed account of what the program included, for my memory brings only a series of impressions: Buffalo Bill shooting glass or clay balls from a horse, with an Indian riding a short distance ahead and throwing them singly into the air; an old stagecoach attacked by Indians; bronc riding and roping of calves by cowboys and vaqueros. I seem to have been impressed by the expert rope spinning 'stunts' by a Mexican named Tony, and the picturesque, long-haired, bearded John Nelson, the driver of the Deadwood stagecoach. But the most vivid recollection is the rifle shooting of Annie Oakley, Lilian Smith, and Johnnie Baker—the 'Cowboy Kid.' Their marksmanship was an achievement which excited my boyish enthusiasm to the extent of attempted emulation.

"One other memory is the pony express rider, arriving with make-believe mail, a spirited and rearing horse being held for him as he approached at breakneck speed, and his remounting with fresh mail sacks thrown aboard behind him! This occupied but a few seconds, and he was on his way again. How many miles had he ridden, and how many more would he ride that day, before being relieved by another rider? Such were the thoughts of my excited imagination stimulated by this realistic episode.

"'Buffalo Bill's Wild West' show created a sensation in London. There was beauty as well as drama, expert accomplishment, and a colorful theatrical setting that produced the flavor of reality. Can anyone be surprised that I, a boy of twelve, was impressed?

"But to return to my decision to go to America. It was a spirit of adventure that made me restless in England. I wished to start life anew in an environment where tradition and influence did not exist, where a reputation of some sort had to be built without prejudice or past appreciation."[53]

Another artist who would later become Joseph Imhof's acquaintance in Taos, Dorothy Eugenie Brett, felt the same kind of impact from Buffalo Bill's show. Brett, who had been born in London in 1883, would visit Taos in 1924 with the English author, D. H. Lawrence, and his wife Frieda, and like the Taos area so much that she would remain and become a citizen of the United States. Brett said, "I fell in love with one of the Indians who rode wildly around the arena, naked, painted lemon yellow, wearing a great war bonnet with its feathers cascading down his horse's feet."[54]

As Buffalo Bill and his show reached their peak, President Theodore Roosevelt, who considered Cody his personal hero, imitated Buffalo Bill with "The Congress of Rough Riders of the World." Cody's show lasted thirty-plus years, until 1913, even though the West was becoming but a memory.[55] Already new forms of entertainment had emerged with the 1902 publication of Owen Wister's *The Virginian*, which combined frontier color, humor and adventure with a hero who was the popular image of a cowboy.[56] The first successful motion picture, released in 1903, "The Great Train Robbery," and written by Edwin S. Porter, marked the beginning of the art and industry of the motion picture.[57]

Joseph J. Arpad and Kenneth R. Lincoln state in their book, *Buffalo Bill's Wild West*, "Perhaps, Buffalo Bill is 'defunct,' as E. E. Cummings claims, but while he lived, he had the power, as Carl Sandburg tells us, to make the boy heart of America ache with the romance of the West."[58]

While the excitement of Buffalo Bill and his "Wild West" show reverberated through Europe, Joseph Imhof remained in Antwerp apprenticing himself to well-established artists to learn their techniques.[59] Joe learned the essence of line, to vary a line's width, to curve a line to strengthen and emphasize. As he refined his skills, he began to paint by first preparing a preliminary sketch. Joe would retain this painting technique all his life. He, like others trained in Europe at this time, would retain the skills and standards set by their first teachers. He moved on to Amsterdam where he continued to copy the old masters, worked as a lithographer and, in a short while, was honored by being elected to membership of the St. Lucas Guild, established in 1880 in Amsterdam.[60] In the St. Lucas Guild, "younger and less well-known artists did not so clearly risk being overshadowed by leading members of the Hague and Amsterdam schools of painting."[61]

St. Lucas Guild was located in Rembrandt Square which served as the heart of Amsterdam where people came for fairs and entertainment.[62] Among the Guild's esteemed members were such painters as Piet Mondrian who joined in 1894. This Dutch painter, born in 1872 in Holland, had begun, like Joe, as an academic painter. His landscapes, however, gradually began depicting the Dutch countryside with more original linear patterns, effects of light, and gradations of color. Finally, his paintings of trees, windmills, and sand dunes became so refined that he distilled the essence of objects into contours and primary colors with horizontal and vertical black lines.[63]

By contrast, Joe would not break with the roots of his academic training to the degree that Mondrian had succeeded in doing. Joe would eventually use color, as distilled by the light in New Mexico, to create a realistic style of painting using linear patterns and contours.

When Joe felt he had mastered all he could at this time from the Dutch masters, he set out traveling on his own. "In Europe the prominent Imhof name opened many doors for him. He traveled from Antwerp to Amsterdam, Brussels, Munich, Riviera, Italy, Cairo, Africa, and Paris often taking long walking trips to other small towns on the way." The Imhof name did open doors for Joe, but not in a literal sense at this time. All of his life he had heard stories of his family's European roots and this helped open his mind to his heritage and give him the necessary courage and security to travel on his own.[64]

Joe's future wife, Sallie, would remember the stories Joe later told of his travels. "Here was a strange story; while in Morocco he was painting a wine bark and the captain came along and was so pleased with the sketch that he invited Joe to sail with him on the next trip which he did. One of those violent storms so frequent in that part of the coast came up and they were shipwrecked and saved by the steamers that went out to save them; it was, and is, I expect, the law that a shipwrecked sailor is provided with transportation to his home; when Joe was asked for his home town he said Paris, which was his planned next stop, and so he had free transportation there."[65]

After spending time in Paris, he traveled to Munich where he studied artistic anatomy with Duke Carl Theodor, head of the Ducal line in Bavaria, and the father of Elizabeth who married Albert of Belgium.[66] The Duke was an oculist, the term then for ophthalmologist, whose hobby was anatomy. After receiving his medical degree at Munich University, he had set up eye clinics and hospitals in Tegernsee, Merau, and Munich in an effort to halt the spread of blindness rampaging through Bavaria. His daughter Elizabeth, who was a nurse, assisted him during eye surgery, which he performed daily at no charge. Those who could afford to pay left money in the hospitals' collection boxes and that money was contributed to charity as well. The Duke taught a large class in artistic anatomy in Munich.[67] Every time, even in later years, when the Imhofs went abroad for any length of time, Joe took a course in artistic anatomy, which accounted for his reputation among artists even up to his death, for his exceptional drawings of anatomy. Surgeons, particularly, admired his work that depicted the human figure.[68]

Joseph Imhof's emphasis on anatomy was in keeping with the Renaissance when man became the measure of all things, and artists approached the human figure by studying anatomy. Michelangelo, Leonardo da Vinci, and Albert Dürer were among those who studied anatomy to learn the structure of the body; the skeleton, movement of the joints and especially muscles, which held a primary interest for them. However, regardless of how much an artist studied the human figure, the art produced was the product of the artist's creativity. Originally, the study of anatomy had begun with pictorial books, but had progressed to an anatomical atlas for artists by the end of the seventeenth century. By the eighteenth century, France had become the center of artistic anatomical study. Joe planned to know anatomy so well that he could represent the body in such a way that it would appear fully dimensional, as if the viewer had walked around the subject.[69]

"Finally," Sallie recalled, "after three years, [actually, thirty months] Joe returned to Antwerp, where he spent his 21st birthday waiting for his check from New York, short of funds as usual. I believe he was about to cook beans for his birthday dinner when the postman arrived with the expected letter, and so he put the bean pot aside and went out to the Hotel San Antoine for his meal. That was the last of his stay in Europe, and he left Antwerp for New York on another Red Star steamer, in mid October [1893]."[70]

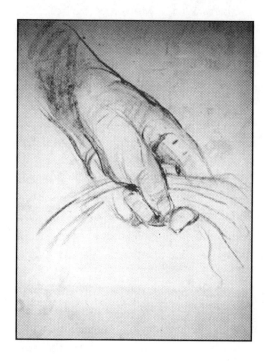

Imhof's sketch of a hand.

As usual, Joe had overspent his traveling money by buying objects. Because he could not afford to buy paintings by the great masters, he collected photographic reproductions made by photographers Anderson of Rome and Hanfstaengl of Munich.[71]

Photography, which had been in existence since the early 1500s, had had to wait for Louis Daguerre and his invention in the 1830s, the Daguerreotype, before others refined the photographic process of fixed images to make them acceptable.[72] In the 1850s, a small group of photographers began publishing photographs of the great paintings of Western art. For the first time, the public had access to its art heritage.[73]

In Europe, the English watercolorist, Isaac Atkinson (1813-1877), settled in Rome under the assumed name of James Anderson. He became a leading producer of lithographic reproductions of art until his interest in photography led him to photograph architecture, antique sculpture and paintings.[74] Anderson's son, Domenico (1854-1938), continued his father's work, and expanded the family business of photographic reproductions of paintings to over forty thousand plates.[75]

Anderson of Rome photograph of Jacopo Tintoretto's "Miracle of St. Mark," demonstrating dynamic symmetry and quality of reproduction, date unknown.

Franz Hanfstaengl (1804-1877) and Edgar Hanfstaengl (1842-1910) developed the same kind of photographic reproductions in Germany. Franz had astounded the photographic world in 1855 when he successfully retouched a negative.[76] Franz's and Edgar's joint ventures in art publishing in Munich established their photographs as near equals to paintings.

In later years, Joe would also collect "The Gallery of Masterpieces"

69

published by Doubleday, Page and Company. These reproductions in mezzotint included such great master painters as Frans Hals, Johannes Vermeer, and Albert Dürer.[77]

Sallie recalled, "The three years [thirty months] were most successful, and as he always had done, and did all his life, made it a point to read and converse and absorb information on interesting subjects. He had a wonderful memory and a photographic eye so that he could vividly recall so many things years after he had seen them. A face he never forgot, and with a very few lines could depict the face of the person in his story."[78]

During this period in Europe, while Joe traversed Europe, three of the six artists who would found the Taos Society of Artists in 1915—Ernest Blumenschein, Bert Phillips and Joseph H. Sharp—would study at the *Académie Julian* in Paris. In 1893, the year Joe returned to New York from his first excursion into Europe, Sharp traveled to Taos to sketch. Sharp's later meeting of Phillips and Blumenschein at the *Académie Julian* in 1895-96, would cause Phillips and Blumenschein to travel to Taos in 1898.[79]

The Taos experience would change all these artists, but for now, Joe's Taos days lay years ahead.

CHAPTER 5

A NEW FAMILY

When Joe disembarked from the steam-
ship that mid October in 1893, it would be with a sense of sadness over his
mother's death in his absence.[1] Still, his large, strong hands held packages
for his father and sister, Elizabeth. In addition, the shipping line unloaded
several crates accompanying him that held beautiful objects he had collected
for himself, the paintings he had copied as he studied the great masters,
European antiques, and a very fine guitar.[2] The collection, much like the
fine editions he had collected for his bookstore, would mark his life-long
obsession for collecting beautiful objects. His interest in history and fascination with Indian cultures would inspire him to collect Pueblo Indian artifacts in the same way.

The family greeted him with excitement in a house where he'd never
lived, 227 Wyckoff Street, and encouraged him to live with them.[3] Instead,
Joe rented a studio in the Flatbush section of Brooklyn, and continued his
previous habit of spending the night at his father's home before walking to
work in his own studio during the day.[4]

Joe's father still longed for his son to become a priest, but when he
saw how his son had dedicated his life to becoming an artist, he could not
push Joe openly. Joe, aware of his father's feelings, decided to continue
maintaining his artist's life separate and apart from his family's life.

At this time Joe began his study of the Iroquois Indians of New York
and Canada.[5] His approach to painting the Iroquois would forever set his
habit in painting. His curiosity rebelled at simply painting or sketching a
subject, because once he developed an interest in a subject, he had to know

71

everything about it. He recognized that if he knew fully the subject he intended to paint, he would paint it using his greatest talents. Thus, he would immerse himself in the subject's environment, its past and all that influenced its existence in an effort to become one with what he painted.

When Joe had left Brooklyn and home in 1891, he had considered himself a student, and now his self-directed education had solidified his identity and confidence. Besides, by now he had begun to sell his paintings. The works he found less than he thought himself capable, he discarded, a habit that he would follow for the remainder of his life.[6]

Though Joe spent most of his time in his own studio the year he returned from Europe, in 1893, he reestablished his friendships with the artists in the Ridley Mansion.[7] It was through new friendships that his life took another turn in the fall of 1893.[8] A group of people in Manhattan were in the process of producing Tom Taylor's English play, "The Ticket-of-Leave Man," whose central character, Detective Hawkshaw, takes the audience into English low life full of local color.[9] The playwright had a certain renown as the author of the play, "Our American Cousin" which President Lincoln had been watching when he was assassinated.[10] Within the Manhattan group, Sallie Russell, a handsome woman with hazel eyes, fair skin and dark brown hair, served as stage manager and treasurer.[11]

One evening after a rehearsal, one of the cast wished aloud that they had a good guitar for the play's heroine, a gypsy girl who wanders about London streets playing a guitar. Another cast member who played Hawkshaw, the detective, said, "I know a fellow who has just come back from Europe, and he has a fine guitar."[12]

Members of the theater group asked to meet this fellow, and Joe responded by personally taking his guitar to the group in their theater located in an old residence. When Joe entered the several storied former home, he seated himself in the parlor where he could see the broad stairs that curved into a broader landing at the foot of the staircase.[13]

Sallie, wearing a pale blue evening gown, descended the stairs in Joe's full view. As he watched the handsome woman of five feet, six inches float toward him, he remarked to himself, "That's the girl I want to marry."[14]

The woman Joe had chosen to marry was strikingly graceful in her carriage and ancestry. Sarah Ann Elizabeth Russell had been born on November 9, 1872 in Philadelphia, Pennsylvania into the ninth generation of a

72

family who had followed William Penn to the new world.[15] Two Russell brothers, who had been weavers in Edinburg, had come in 1683 with William Penn on his first visit. Penn, an English Quaker, had founded Pennsylvania as a refuge for the politically and religiously persecuted Quakers.[16]

Sallie's father, George Henry Russell, had been born on December 25, 1818 in Philadelphia. Sallie's mother, Elizabeth Barnes Stuart, had been born on November 11, 1830 in Philadelphia.[17] In 1880, Sallie, at age seven, lived at 909 Walnut Street with her sixty-three-year-old father, her fifty-year-old mother, one brother, Frank W., age twenty-four, a sixty-eight-year-old aunt, Sarah Ann Russell Branson, for whom Sallie had been named, and seven boarders.[18] When Sallie moved to Manhattan in 1893, she became the first of her family to leave Pennsylvania.[19]

Sallie's presence on the staircase left such an impression on Joe that he always carried that picture of her in his mind. During their fifty-eight years of marriage, he would insist that Sallie wear a pale blue dress even when her advanced age, and graying hair, made her feel less attractive in the pale color. Joe began his courtship according to the customs of the day, by meeting Sallie in a group of friends, usually at someone's home. Occasionally they attended a concert, the opera or the theater.[20]

As Sallie and Joe became better acquainted, he began to involve her with his research into Indian societies.[21] This is of special interest because as the Imhof marriage would evolve, it would take on the coloration and characteristics of the various Indian ways of life and philosophy the couple had researched and studied.

At that time, Manhattan had three libraries: the Lenox, the Astor, and the 42nd Street library. Eventually, the three would be consolidated into the library at 42nd Street, but in 1893 Sallie and Joe pursued their research in all three libraries.[22]

Since Joe had always lived on land once occupied by Indians, it was only natural that he focused on the Indians closest to his origins. In their research, Joe and Sallie discovered that the Canarsee, who had occupied Long Island, struggled to control their changing world when the Europeans arrived.[23] The exchange of trade goods was one way the Indians found they could control their lives. The trade goods, seen today as artifacts in museum cases and history books, are generally viewed for their functional use. This view misses an important aspect of the artifacts. The Indians believed these trade goods animate, and regarded them as being "alive." Indians placed such trade goods at the service of honor, and honored other people, and other-than-human spirits, by giving trade goods as gifts. Indians also honored people with spiritual power, whose aid they needed, by presenting them with trade goods.[24] In time, Joe would adopt this Indian belief to suit his own life.

In 1894, as Joe became more involved in his relationship with Sallie, he moved his studio back to the Ridley Mansion at 36 Beekman Street. Yet, he still spent each night at his father's home at 227 Wyckoff. In 1895, Joe and Sallie became engaged to be married and, because they valued their privacy, attempted to keep their upcoming marriage a secret.[25]

To help Joe increase his income beyond the paintings he sold, the artists among Joe's circle of friends encouraged, then introduced him to commercial art work. Throughout his life, Joe would always pursue his goal of creating original works of art, and then return to commercial art when he ran out of money.

In 1895, just before he married, he began doing substantial work for cigarette brands produced by Allen and Ginter of Richmond, Virginia.[26] Cigarette smoking had become the rage in the late 1800s. While most Americans thought the fashionable habit had come from the Turks, tobacco had actually originated in the Americas. Spanish explorers, who had first discovered the Aztecs smoking a kind of cigarette, had taken tobacco plants back to Europe. Tobacco cultivation and use had rapidly spread in the Iberian Peninsula and other Mediterranean areas, including Turkey.[27]

After the Crimean War of 1854-56, the Turks had introduced the cigarette to the British. Only in 1865 had cigarettes come to the United States when New Yorkers, sensitive to foreign influences, had quickly adopted this foreign fad from the British and taken up the smoking habit. At first, Americans preferred the hand-rolled cigarettes that produced the pungent aroma, but, in the early 1880s, New Yorkers began smoking their tobacco in cigarettes produced from a machine that rolled the cigarette. Competition, led by James Duke who had consolidated his competitors into the American Tobacco Company, known as the Tobacco Trust, now waged an aggressive advertising campaign of the brand names.[28]

To promote brands, cigarette companies blazed a trail in advertising by creating redeemable coupons or photographs of actresses which were enclosed in each package of cigarettes. Major Lewis Ginter earned the tag of "king of cigarette advertising." He stuffed cigarette packages with puzzles, maps, pictures of boats, flags, actors and actresses, all in numbered sets. When Ginter and Allen joined forces in 1875, and formed Allen and Ginter Company, they distributed booklets of famous buildings.[29]

In 1890, advertising under Duke's Tobacco Trust took the form of prizes and redeemable coupons that accompanied each box of the particular brand advertised. Smokers and nonsmokers began collecting coupons and photographs in a craze that swept the country for over a decade.[30]

Among the most prized coupons were the series of Indian heads that Joe lithographed for Allen and Ginter cigarette brands in 1896. The Imhof Indian Head Series of Chippewa, Pawnee, Apache, Blackfeet Sioux, Delaware and others appeared in their authentic dress, as only Imhof would have it. *Life Magazine*, in a January 2, 1950 issue, published an article on early advertising and featured six of the Imhof Indian Head Series that, even today, remain collectors' items.[31]

MAN AND CHIEF,
PAWNEE

RUSHING BEAR,
°PAWNEE

Imhof's cigarette cards as featured in *Life*, 1950.

RED 'BIRD,
CHIPPEWAY.

'GREAT BEAR,
DELAWARE.

GERONIMO,
APACHE.

RED THUNDER,
BLACKFEET SIOUX.

Imhof's cigarette cards as featured in *Life*, 1950.

As another part of his commercial art work, Joe served as director of the art department for H. A. Thomas and Wylie Company, a publisher that produced theatrical papers. Joe said of himself, "I was a big guy, tip your hat to me. [I] made one hundred dollars a week."[32]

"Lillian Russell, The Nineties," (media unknown, 100 X 50 in.).
Pictured left to right: unidentified, unidentified, John Derek, James Cagney, 1952.

It is believed that during this time he created the portrait, "Lillian Russell," which he later secured for Winfield Morten's hotel in Silverton, Colorado. The 90-by-42-inch unframed work, apparently executed in chalk, currently hangs in the Grand Imperial Hotel, Silverton, Colorado. The formally posed Lillian Russell appears larger than life under glass, surrounded as she is in the wood and gold 100-by-50-inch frame. A carved wood ribbon at the top of the frame reads "Lillian Russell, The Gay Nineties."[33]

Her creator obviously intended for her to look down on her subjects. She has a rather sly, bemused seductive look in her white and pink strapless gown that reveals her ample breasts. Her right arm hugs her waist as her fingers touch her right shoulder, as if to say, "Look at me. I know your secret desires." The large hat she wears tends to emphasize her feminine assets, as does a fan-like piece of fluff she holds in her left hand. The tilt of her head to the right, and the slight turn of her body convey a coy statement, calling attention to her seductive quality. She appears believable, yet remains a part of the myth that belongs to the long since vanished West.

Joe's interest in recording personalities of the West, such as Lillian Russell, and authentic Indian lore, which Buffalo Bill and his Indians had originally stimulated in Imhof, actually came at the end of the Western movement. Artists living along the Eastern shores had begun to move West as early as 1820 when the explorer artists, such as Samuel Seymour, an important engraver, accompanied Major Stephen Harrison Long's expedition to the Rocky Mountains. Seymour's duty was to sketch the landscapes and the Indians. Seymour made the first field drawing of a Plains Indian dance group and, in 1820, sketched the headwaters of the Platte River.[34]

George Catlin's mother, who had been captured by the Indians, influenced his early life. In 1824, when Catlin saw the Indian in his regalia, he decided to rescue from oblivion the Indian and his customs by painting over six hundred Indian portraits. Catlin's accurate ethnographic work, in which he showed great sensitivity to the Indian life and customs, forms much of our present-day knowledge of Indian life.[35]

Karl Bodmer, who had studied the paintings of Catlin and Seymour, rendered many of the same scenes as accurately as Catlin, but did so in an academically trained manner that displayed his skills in polished renderings. Bodmer had been born in Switzerland, and had accompanied the Prussian Prince Maximilian on an exploratory expedition to the American West in 1832.[36]

By the late 1830s, the railroad artists, such as John Mix Stanley and Gustavus Sohon, arrived in the West. Stanley had first come to the West as the artist to the Stephen Watts Kearny military expedition. Later, Stanley became the official artist for the northern railway survey, resulting in sketches for a huge panorama. Sohon, as an army man, had been assigned to surveying parties of the Rocky Mountain passes. His pictorial series of the West are "the most authoritative pictorial series in pre-reservation days."[37]

After the Civil War between the States, from 1861 to 1865, artists came to the West as correspondents. The Rocky Mountain school of artists brought Albert Bierstadt to the West in 1858. His panoramic landscapes became quite popular, only to be later rejected because they did not look the same as current painters. Still later, his work would be appreciated for its melodramatic, heroic view of the Rocky Mountains.[38]

Samuel Colman arrived in the West in 1870, a short time after the transcontinental railroad had been completed. His series of paintings of western subjects allowed the American public to become more aware of the natural wonders of the West.[39]

Thomas Moran, in 1871, accompanied a surveying expedition to the Grand Canyon of the Yellowstone to paint the grandeur. He later returned to paint the Grand Canyon of the Colorado and other magnificent scenery. He placed no value on literal interpretations, because he preferred to convey his emotional response to nature.[40]

Simultaneously, pioneer artists, such as George Ottinger in Utah in 1861, painted Western genre, and Theodore Gentilz painted Texas genre in 1870.[41] Pioneer photographer and painter, William Henry Jackson, made the first photographs of Yellowstone Park in 1871.[42]

The myth makers, Frederic Remington, an illustrator, and Charles Russell, came to the West in the 1880s.[43] The Oklahoma land rush on September 16, 1893, when fifty thousand people claimed land in a six and a half million acre area, acted as another powerful lure to the Westward movement.[44]

Writers, such as James Fenimore Cooper, with his tales of the frontier packaged in moral messages, added to the interest in the West.[45] Adolph Bandelier, who had had little formal training as an anthropologist, found solace in studying the Indian cultures of the Southwest after a forced business career. In 1890, he published his fictionalized Pueblo ethnography, *The Delight*

79

Makers.[46] Charles F. Lummis, a late nineteenth century California-based writer and photographer of Indian and Hispanic cultures who had lived for five years in the Indian pueblo of Isleta, made most of the photographs to illustrate the book. Lummis did not always accurately portray a particular Indian mode of dress, place the correct basket or blanket with the Indian who used them, but his work looked right. He combined a slice of life with posed, staged activities.[47]

Many years later, when Joe Imhof joined others in assessing Bandelier's scholarly work, he would remark about *The Delight Makers*, "As for the dance description, much better descriptions and more accurate ones have been made by later anthropologists."[48] At the time of publication, however, the book sharpened Joe's interest and served to bring the West closer to the Eastern seaboard.

The Romantic artists who settled in Taos began arriving in 1898 with Ernest Blumenschein and Bert Phillips who established the Taos art colony.[49] Cowboy artists, who adopted the West, included Olaf Wieghorst and Burt Proctor, who specialized in painting horses.[50]

A later group who discovered the West were the modernists, such as Robert Henri of Santa Fe, in 1916, and a student of the *Académie Julian* of Paris. Henri did not want to record the Indians' passing, but to express what he had found in the Indian.[51] Edward Hopper came to Santa Fe in 1925, and applied the same technique he had used in the East to record the West.[52] Georgia O'Keeffe first visited Taos in 1929, and returned permanently to Abiquiu, New Mexico in 1946 to paint the Western scene in simplified, austere, pristine canvases.[53]

In 1896, Joe Imhof, too, helped attract Easterners to the West with his lithographs that depicted authentically dressed Indian heads. For Joe, personally, the sale of the Indian head prints to Allen and Ginter, and his other commercial art work enabled him to marry.[54]

Sallie and Joe had announced their marriage only a few weeks before the ceremony on February 3, 1897 in New York. The family wished them well. The couple rented a flat on 81st Street and Fifth Avenue in the heart of the museum district. In their on-going need for privacy, the couple allowed the family to think the newlyweds had departed on their honeymoon to Washington, D. C. In reality, they had chosen to remain in their flat, located one block from the Metropolitan Museum of Art, and to visit museums where they could meet the museum staffs and continue Joe's research on Indians.[55]

The museums were important to Joe, not only for what he saw, but how he felt while in the presence of art. Museums gave him the means to evaluate other artists, to judge other works which, in time, would equip him to judge his own works. In addition, he found museums as a storehouse of history, a place where he could learn about the condition of man. Joe's curiosity of man demanded that he attend museums. Sallie and Joe frequently discussed with the museum staff the place of an artist's participation in museum life. They eventually concluded that while the museum and artist remain interdependent, they must also maintain a distance as a way to preserve a balance.[56]

Joe's father, John Imhof, continued to live at the 227 Wyckoff residence in Brooklyn until he sold it on October 4, 1905.[57] The next year he would sell the 493 Atlantic Avenue house on July 18, 1906.[58]

Soon after their marriage, Sallie became Joe's secretary, collaborator, and business manager. Joe could pursue his commercial art, inventions, and paintings while Sallie served as his secretary and manager of their businesses and homes. They would work as a unit. Sallie commented, "Business and serious art don't mix."[59]

In the late summer of 1898, the artist, Howard Moore, who was the nephew of Sir Humphrey Moore, invited Joe and Sallie to live on an enormous estate in upper Manhattan. The Imhofs would live in a part of the estate's mansion that had been converted into an apartment. Howard Moore, his family, and Sir Humphrey Moore's widow, the Countess of Hildebrandt, a Hungarian, would live in the remainder of the mansion.[60]

The estate had been bought and the mansion built by Richard B. Connelly, who served as treasurer of the notorious Tweed Ring of Tammany Hall. For his misdeeds, Connelly had been sentenced to prison where he died. His property was confiscated and sold by New York City to Anheuser Busch. For insurance reasons, the Moore family now lived on the estate.[61]

The property resided on the land where Spuyten Duyvil, "Spouting Devil," divided Manhattan from the New York shore, and the site of many historic battles during the Revolutionary War. One Hundred and Eighty-First Street bounded the property on the south. Lafayette Boulevard (now Riverside Drive) served as the boundary line on the west which also ran parallel to the Hudson River. On the north, the property ended at the estate of several hundred acres owned by James Gordon Bennett, owner of the *New York Herald*, later the *Herald Tribune*. To the east of the estate, a wide gravel road led to the estates to the north. Hundreds of trees and shrubs transformed the estate into a forested area.[62]

As was Joe's habit, he developed an interest in James Gordon Bennett who had died in 1872. Bennett had founded the *Herald* as a four-page penny paper with a stated purpose that read, "We shall support no party—be the agent of no faction or coterie, and care nothing for any election, or any candidate from president down to constable."[63] But another facet of Bennett's life made the greatest impression on Joe when he learned that Bennett had been educated for the Roman Catholic priesthood in Scotland. By chance Bennett had read Benjamin Franklin's autobiography, and that encounter with Franklin's life caused Bennett to abandon his plans for the priesthood and resolve to immigrate to America. Joe learned that Bennett's shaky start in the newspaper business had led to an enormously successful life.[64]

The Connelly mansion equally intrigued the Imhofs. Connelly, who had descended from an Irish peasant family, had built the mansion to resemble an Irish mansion. Full length mirrors covered the walls of a large ballroom lighted by candles held into candlesticks bracketed to the mirrored walls. One mirrored wall harbored a secret spring lock that, when released, swung the mirrors back to a secret room that contained a catholic altar. Here a priest could hide and live as might have been done during past days in Ireland.[65]

The mansion had numerous balconies that looked out over the Hudson River. Wisteria from a tree that grew among other trees a short distance from the wall covered the wall of balconies. Joe painted the wisteria in 1898 and the painting would recall many fond memories for them in the years to come.[66] When Joe and Sallie moved permanently to Taos in 1929, they took a farewell trip up the Hudson River to catch one last glimpse of the Connelly mansion that had given them so many pleasures. They found instead a long line of ten-story apartment buildings and no evidence of trees or shrubs.[67]

After their time in the Connelly mansion, the Imhofs returned to their flat, but decided they did not enjoy city life. They then moved to Staten Island to the old town of Huguenot. They found a house said to have been built in the days when the Huguenots inhabited the small town.[68] In the year they lived in Huguenot, Sallie gave birth to their only child, a girl they named after the two women whom Joe loved most in his family, his mother, Magdalena, and sister, Elizabeth. They would call her Elizabeth, the name carried by Sallie and her own mother. Magdalena Elizabeth Imhof was born on November 19, 1898.[69]

That same year, the Spanish-American War began. As a result of the war, the United States expanded its navy and showed its power in the Caribbean and the Pacific.[70] When Sallie and Joe returned to live again in Manhattan, they discovered several changes. Tents had been set up in Union Square, and American flags flew from numerous poles, where the military recruited for the war effort. Sallie, especially, admired the naval recruiting she observed in the Square. American patriotism flowered.[71]

The Imhofs rented a studio apartment at 28 East 14th Street, just south of Union Square, in the midst of renovated studios, that ran as far as Fifth Avenue, for painters, engravers and lithographers.[72] Just down the street from the Imhof's studio apartment, George E. Miller Lithographers maintained workrooms for artists to produce their work. Miller Lithographers had become an institution and would remain at this address for some time.[73]

Historically, an artist and a printer collaborated in producing an artist's lithograph. In Europe, such lithography workshops were the norm, but were limited in the United States. Consequently, many American artists traveled to Europe to produce their lithographic works. Even the finest lithographic workshops in the United States did not compare to the European lithographers of the day.[74]

Joe's lithography experience was so skilled by now that he did not require a printer. He needed only an assistant to work on opposite sides of the press to help him position the paper, dampen it, and engage the press in the printing process. By acting as his own printer, Joe could incorporate his lithography skills into his art, avoid any friction that he might have with a printer, and refine his own printing and lithography styles. This also allowed him to make his mistakes privately, rather than being distracted by the presence of a printer.

The year on 14th Street proved fruitful for Joe who was painting. He also created the first of his many inventions. Sometime during this period, Joe invented pictorial devices for two lithography companies in New York.

On November 19, 1901, the U.S. Patent Office granted Joseph A. Imhof, Assignor to H.A. Thomas & Wylie Lithographing Company, a patent for a pictorial device which was a cutout of papers joined to form a structure that appeared three dimensional. The paper structure, when stood on its edge and viewed from the front, appeared to be a cage enclosed by walls and bars. Upon the back section could be printed, or stamped, pictures of wild animals, or a room interior with furniture. The cutout had been joined on four sides in such a way that an open space existed between the front and back sections. The purchaser was only required to cut away the wild animals or furniture and stand the pieces in the interior.[75]

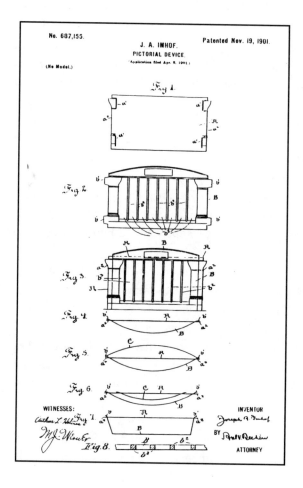

Pictorial Device
invented by Imhof,
November, 1901.

As an Assignor for American Lithographic Company, Joe received the patent on April 29, 1902 for a cutout of tabs on a curved surface. Previously, such tabs had been used on heavy paper to prevent the cutout from falling over. Imhof's pictorial device used lighter paper, and the use of tabs on a curved surface prevented the device from falling over.[76]

"We were living the carefree life of that era," Sallie remembered. Once or twice a month, they invited a large group of young male artists, who lived along 14th Street, to a stag party in a kind of gathering of men where they could talk of their work and general trends in art. Sallie would take the baby, Elizabeth, and leave the men at the studio while she traveled to Brooklyn to stay.[77]

"As I look back at that time," Sallie recalled, "I can remember some names and faces of those who rose to recognition in the arts; alas, I seem to have long outlived them all."[78] Joe still produced all of his own lithography, and preferred to act as his own printer. It took infinite patience and the ability to accept responsibility for failure, efforts Joe found worthwhile to work without a printer.

That summer Sallie and Joe rented a summer house in Englewood Cliffs, New Jersey, just opposite Spuyten Duyvil on the northern end of Manhattan Island and near a large German settlement just south along the Palisades. For years they kept the house made of stone, set among a Dutch settlement of Hudson River shad fishermen and their families, as a retreat from their active city life. Their neighbors all had good, old Dutch names, and eventually accepted the Imhof family from across the bay. The house fronted a sandy beach where they could swim in the clear Hudson waters. Oil-burning ships had not come as yet into existence to pollute the rivers.[79]

To reach the Englewood Cliffs house, the Imhofs took the train run by the New York Central Railroad from New York City. The train, which pulled a freight car and a passenger car, made two trips daily along the Hudson River. It made stops after 125th Street and as far down as 28th Street. To reach his 14th Street studio, Joe had to cross the Hudson to New York, Sallie recalled. "We had a Negro workman married to one of the Dutch women and he managed the boat which Joe took most every morning." Tides from Spuyten Duyvil were often so strong that the boat drifted several miles north or south, according to the tide run, before reaching shore and the train station.[80]

Sallie made regular trips into New York, too. In September of 1899, Admiral George Dewey returned to the United States a hero, and Sallie joined the great crowd welcoming his return.[81] That same month, Sallie and Joe made a short trip to Iroquois Indian country near Ontario, Canada.[82] The Iroquois Confederacy, composed of the Mohawk, Oneida, Onondaga, Cayuga, Seneca, and Tuscaroras, held a particular interest for Joe. The Confederacy had occupied a continuous territory that extended from the Hudson River to Lake Erie, across Lake Ontario, and south of Huron country in the headwaters that flowed into central New York. Less than one hundred years before, they had formed a huge trade network and were regarded as the most powerful political grouping of Indians north of Mexico.[83]

As Joe sketched the Iroquois, he learned from them. The Iroquois society believed that a person's status depended not on the goods he possessed, but rather on what he or she gave to others. It endangered the tribe to be in possession of goods when others were in need. It appeared to Iroquois that it was much safer to be generous. Members attained status by redistribution of their goods. In doing so, the status did not carry an increased authority.[84]

Joe found the Iroquois a far different experience from his European heritage in which people achieved respect by authority and the ability to command others. It was the Iroquois who eventually became the diplomats between the French and the English, and who thus held the balance of power.[85]

Joe was aware that the Iroquois laws of confederacy had not been written, but were transmitted orally from one generation to the next by members who had learned the laws. For many generations, the Iroquois preserved their confederacy by using a collection of wampum belts and strings. Each string recalled a law. The Iroquois believed that all important statements should be accompanied by a gift, a wampum.[86]

In all probability, Joe combined this Iroquois belief with the Canarsees' trade goods practice to formulate his own habit of gift giving. He never wanted a friend to leave his home without first receiving a gift from himself. This became a habit that Joe followed all his life.[87]

The knowledge Joe gained through his exchange with the Iroquois may have been the seeds of his developing philosophy toward life. Certainly his preference for giving away his paintings, instead of selling them, fit this philosophy. Joe did not keep detailed records of the works he created, either. While this trait would anguish art historians in the years ahead, his generosity to friends and strangers would always astonish the recipients.

When Joe and Sallie returned from this excursion to sketch the Iroquois, they began to consider a journey into Europe. The Spanish-American War had ended and Spain had turned its interests inward. Europe felt safe again.[88]

CHAPTER 6

THE BIRTH OF STYLE AND SUBJECT

By 1899, the Imhofs had been married for two years, and their year-old daughter, Elizabeth, was being molded to fit into their close family unit centered around Joe and Sallie striving to create their own lives. In the winter of that year, they boarded a steamship for Holland to enable Joe to pursue two years of painting and lithography in Europe.[1]

During this two-year European tour, two important events would occur: Joe would evolve a more free-flowing painting style and develop the confidence to paint subjects that interested him, rather than imitate the great masters and follow the painting styles taught in the academies. And, at some level, Elizabeth would realize her assigned role as an extension of her parents, possibly a kind of appendage that would lead to a weak sense of her own self and her later self destruction.

On a mild winter day, so characteristic in Holland, the Imhof family disembarked from the ship and settled in Amsterdam. Joseph Imhof, apparently like other American painters in the Netherlands, recognized the transitory nature of Holland's pre-machine-age state and saw himself as the recorder, the preserver of the old and picturesque way of life passing away. Other artists in Holland clearly saw their mission to record the European peasant with his vanishing traditional way of life and trades. These artists saw the urgency in recording other life forms, which included the American Indian, they perceived as disappearing. It may have been here in Holland that Imhof conceived his idea for his later mission to record the Pueblos, a people whose way of life he saw as disappearing.[3]

Imhof (left) in New York before his first trip with Sallie to Europe, 1900. Sarah Russell Imhof in New York before her first trip with Imhof to Europe, 1900.

As was their custom by now, the Imhofs walked the land, taking in the seventeenth and eighteenth century red brick multi-story homes that bordered the narrow streets and wandering canals. They frequented the Rijksmuseum, with its castle-like towers, and an exterior embellished with sculptures and tile work. The museum, surrounded by a park, had opened in 1885, and provided the Imhofs with ample examples of Rembrandt, Vermeer, Frans Hals, Goya, van Dyck and Rubens.[4]

As winter passed into early spring, cup-shaped tulips began showing themselves in the countryside to the west of Amsterdam, and the Imhof family, having acclimated themselves to their new surroundings, decided to move on.[5] From Amsterdam, they traveled some eighteen miles east and south to Laren by Hilversum where the landscape displayed a series of thatched-roofed cottages along a few roads surrounded by wastelands whose only growth produced heather and stunted pines.[6]

Laren, which had become an artist's colony of the first dimension, attracted artists from throughout Europe and the United States. "Joseph Israëls, the father of the Hague School, is thought to have discovered Laren in the early 1870s . . . [and] he apparently spread the word among his

89

colleagues about this unknown village full of dark interiors and peasant subjects."[7]

The Imhofs, like many artists attracted to the area, stayed at the Hotel Hamsdorff enjoying the hospitality of widow Hamsdorff. And Joe, who had years before established the need for a private studio, rented a small, dark room in the home of one of the local farmers. Here he painted portraits and Dutch interiors, and the dunes. He gave especial attention to detail and smooth surfaces.[8]

On other days, the Imhof family walked the several miles to the dunes bursting with color from the wild flowers. At times, they stayed long into the day to allow Joe to use the light, with all its gradations, in his paintings. When darkness seemed to come upon them suddenly about eight in the evening, they would make the long walk back to Hotel Hamsdorff, their appetites ravenous. After a hearty meal, Joe and Sallie oftentimes talked into the nights with fellow artists.[9]

The dunes outside Laren attracted others, in addition to artists drawn to the area. Nineteen-year-old Queen Wilhelmina I, her mother, Emma, and her entourage came to the dunes to hunt. Although the queen did not herself hunt, she remained with the hunting party, and the hunting activities afforded Joe opportunities to paint the hunt and horses. It was here that the Imhof family first met Queen Wilhelmina I.[10]

The young queen lived only about thirty miles east of Laren, in Apeldoorn, in a fifteenth century castle, known as the hunting lodge, Castle Het Loo, surrounded by a forest in central Holland. The castle's foundation had been laid by Princess Mary Stuart of England in 1685, and the gardens' box hedges had been clipped in decorative patterns as lovely as those in Versailles.[11]

Sometime during this period, the Imhofs packed and moved on to central Europe, as evidenced in two landscapes. The first, an untitled lithograph, would become representative of Imhof's landscapes in which he gave minor attention to people. In a rural, European village, a large stucco house sits slightly to the left in the 8½-by-15½-inch format, and dominates the scene, while a smaller stucco house on the right gives the landscape balance. The lines of the larger house appear to be drawn free hand to indicate the structures were hand finished. The rear light source highlights a man, woman and dog walking along a dirt road in front of the larger house, while three other figures remain half-hidden in a doorway and to the left side of the house. On the far right, a man carries water buckets on poles balanced on his shoulders. A pig can be seen in the background, as can a few birds and clouds that dot the sky.[12]

First known lithograph by Imhof of Europe, (17 X 19½ in.), ca. 1900.

In a painting titled, "Outside Munich, 1900," a more free-flowing style emerges in the kind of landscapes that would follow until the end of Imhof's life. In the painting, an elongated tree trunk explodes from the left bottom corner to dominate the vertical format. The branches vibrate with movement and the vivid greens in the leaves. In the foreground, colors flow, then ebb, and swirl about the grounds, and lead the eye to a remote light colored farmstead in the distant background. The lighted sky empowers the tree's vitality. Yet, no people appear to enliven the scene (see page 164). Landscapes devoid of human inhabitants began to take root at this time and would forever remain typical of Imhof.[13]

Just after the spring tulips bloomed in 1901, and the summer crops began to thrive, the Imhof family boarded a steamship for the United States.[14] By now Elizabeth had turned three, and her curious relationship with her parents, which continued to unfold, could, many years later, be discerned when Sallie wrote Joe's biography. Sallie referred to Elizabeth by using different designations for her: our daughter, his girl, our baby. Never once did Sallie use her daughter's name, Elizabeth.

At the end of their oceanic voyage, the Imhofs headed for the Connelly mansion to visit their friends, the young artist, Howard Moore, and his family in the Upper Manhattan mansion.[15] Sir Humphrey Moore's widow, Louise, the Hungarian Countess of Hildebrandt, still lived there and entertained them with her eccentric ways. Sallie described themselves as having become fast friends with the Countess. From here, the Imhofs returned in the spring of 1901 to their home in the New Jersey Palisades for a winter stay before undertaking a summertime journey in 1902 to Ontario to enable Joe to spend time with the Huron Indians, and to sketch and paint their portraits. Substantial research on various East Coast Indians remained for Sallie before the family could travel through Iroquois territory, and on into Huron country in Canada.[16]

Although Joe Imhof sought to live in close proximity to the Hurons, the Imhofs would have to pass through ancient Iroquois territory in upstate New York, and cross into Canada before reaching the Huron reservation. This same journey had been made by numerous explorers, as Sallie's extensive study of the Iroquois and their relationship with the Huron showed.

It was Giovanni da Verrazano who first discovered New York Bay and the Hudson River, in 1524, which became the European gateway to Iroquois and Huron territories.[17] These and other Indians had long before developed sophisticated alliances to advance warfare, had cultivated vast acreages of orchards and agricultural field crops, and constructed villages filled with housing tracts.[18] But it remained for Henry Hudson, in 1609, to penetrate Indian territory in Upstate New York in his boat, the *Half Moon*. The Dutch East India Company had employed the Englishman to find a new water route to the Far East.[19] After an unsuccessful attempt to sail around northern Europe, he had sailed into New York harbor and on up the "river of the mountains" to a site near Albany. Hudson's reports aroused the interest of the Dutch traders.[20]

In one report that year, Hudson wrote, "I saw there a house well constructed of oak bark . . . a great quantity of maize or Indian corn and beans of last year's growth, and there lay near the house for the purpose of drying enough to load three ships, besides what was growing in the fields."[21] Hudson found the Indians friendly and the fur trade prosperous. What he could not have known was that the Iroquois had formed a league with five tribes—Mohawk, Oneida, Onondaga, Cayuga, and Seneca—into a Confederacy of Five Nations in about 1570. The league controlled the waterways, the fur trade, and had unified themselves to wage skilled warfare.[22]

The various Algonkian tribes, who lived in the lower New York valley and Long Island, relied less on war-making skills and, instead, lived in more autonomous bands whose religions tied them closely to nature. They lived in harmony with their neighbors and shared the land and power among themselves.[23]

In 1621, the ruling council of the Netherlands granted a charter to the Dutch West India Company which gave it a monopoly in trade for twenty-four years along the shores of the Americas. Five years later, the appointed governor purchased Manhattan from the Algonkian-speaking Delaware Indians, and this settlement became known as New Amsterdam. The village grew to one thousand by 1650 and then to fifteen hundred in 1664.[24]

Europeans also replaced the Canarsee through land purchases and war, and began to import African slaves. The Canarsee, who found their lives transformed by conflict, disease, and a new technology that disregarded the spirit of nature, fled into Pennsylvania, Ohio, Indiana, and finally to Texas and Oklahoma.[25]

The Confederacy of Iroquois, unlike the Canarsee, did not flee.[26] Since 1300, when the Iroquois had invaded upstate New York, they had lived on their vast tracts of land cultivated into hundreds of acres of corn, beans, cucumbers, muskmelons, watermelons, pumpkins, and squash. Their villages extended for miles into valleys cleared of forests.[27]

They constructed their longhouses of elm saplings bent and secured at the top to form a tall frame with a curved roof, then covered the longhouse sides with elm bark. Inside the houses that extended a length greater than a football field, they built firepits at either end of the central corridor. Compartments along the corridor housed each family and, within the compartment curtained by a mat, bunks on the walls served as storage spaces and seats for family members. In the central corridor, assorted paraphernalia for daily living hung on pegs, while dried plant foods they had smoked above the firepit hung from the rafters.[28]

These Indians had developed a matriarchal society in which mothers and daughters lived in the longhouses. The eldest and most able-bodied woman assumed the leadership in each clan segment. She directed and coordinated the clan's domestic and economic needs, yet she chose two men to lead the clan, a civil chief and a war captain. Out of respect for those who protected and gathered food for the clan, senior women saw that the men always ate first.[29]

After marriage, a man joined his wife in the longhouse belonging to the wife. However, since the man still belonged primarily to his clan of women rather than his wife's, the marriages tended to end shortly. In addition, the men served as hunters and traders and stayed away for months at a time. Usually the brothers of wives assumed the role of father in raising a couple's children because the brothers belonged to the same clan as the wives.[30]

While the Hurons belonged to the Iroquoian linguistic family, and shared similar characteristics with the Iroquoian matriarchal family, longhouse communal villages, and agricultural methods, the Hurons remained bitter enemies with the Iroquois. They competed for the same fur trade and agricultural lands. Though the Hurons, too, had established a Confederacy, which included the Bear, Cord, Rock and Deer people, they lived in smaller groups.[31]

In 1534, when the French explorer, Jacques Cartier, had first discovered the Gulf of St. Lawrence, he found the Huron living in their settled agricultural villages near the St. Lawrence River. By 1603, when Samuel de Champlain arrived, the Iroquois had driven part of the Hurons from the St. Lawrence River and into Ontario.[32]

The animosity between the Hurons and Iroquois expanded when Hurons received the French as friends, but the French, under Champlain, made the fatal mistake of firing upon a small detachment of Iroquois. From that moment on, the Iroquois became bitter enemies of the French and took up the cause of the English. When the French realized their error, they began a campaign to break the power of the Iroquois Confederacy. For the next one hundred years they waged war against the Iroquois by destroying vast acres of crops and villages.[33]

The Iroquois fought back by orchestrating a campaign of terror against the French and their allies, the Hurons. Iroquois war bands destroyed dozens of Huron towns, killing, torturing, and capturing Hurons to replenish Iroquois lost in war.

The fragment of remaining Hurons drifted west and north, settling in Michigan, Wisconsin, Ohio, Ontario, and Quebec. By the time Joe Imhof began his journey to study and paint them, a short one hundred years in the future, only about a thousand would remain, and several hundred lived on a reservation near Middleport, Ontario.[34] The Iroquois, of course, had suffered the same fate as their hated Huron. A much larger population of Iroquois survived, but they, too, lived on reservations in upstate New York and on two reservations in Ontario, near Grand River and Muncytown.[35]

When summer arrived in 1902, the Imhofs, having steeped themselves in the histories of the Indians who had settled the northeast coast, set off for Ontario. In the midst of Huron country, the Imhofs arrived at Caledonia, an old town in Ontario about two miles southeast of Middleport, that Sallie regarded as still primitive. Here they settled in Ontario, some fifty miles west of Niagara Falls on the Grand River. Just as they had done in Holland, they stayed in the town's only hotel, described by Sallie as small, comfortable but not elegant, for a week to acclimate themselves to the surrounding area. Each day they traveled into the countryside for Joe to meet, then sketch Indians whom he visited.[36] The sketch was preparatory work for a permanent, larger scale work, and served as Joe's way of writing. In his sketches, he did not attempt to produce a replica of a future painting, which would cover the entire surface of a canvas.

After Joe felt a sense of familiarity with these Indians he sketched, the family boarded a train to travel the two or so miles to Middleport where a chain ferry provided the only entry into the Indian settlement. They rented a room in a small hotel in Middleport for the duration of Joe's summer working tour. Each day, as they boarded the chain ferry, four-year-old Elizabeth's attention riveted on the elderly woman who owned and operated the chain ferry.[37] Elizabeth's interest became so centered on the highly individual woman who wore a sunbonnet and smoked a very smelly pipe that Sallie made a note of it in her journal. It is possible Elizabeth was attempting to identify with the woman's clearly defined self, as compared to her own weak-centered being. She might have wondered how she could become her own true person.

As the days piled one upon the next, the Indians seemed to grow fond of Joe, who had become a familiar figure in their midst.[38] By now, Joe had trained himself to sketch the human figure by utilizing the knowledge he had learned in the anatomy classes while in Munich. His hand quickly captured an Indian's physical being on paper, while the conversations he encouraged as he sketched helped draw out the essence of his subject. His skills gradually developed in combining a subject's anatomy with their essence of being.

Sallie and Elizabeth, as Joe's appendages, found acceptance among the Hurons. In time, they became friends with Chief Jimmie Jamison, and witnessed the visit of the Prince of Wales, who happened to be touring the United States and Canada. In the Huron-style flag ceremony, a tall flagpole lay upon the ground before the Prince of Wales and Chief Jamison. When the Prince presented Chief Jimmie Jamison with a huge English flag, Chief Jamison clapped his hands and numerous men came running to tie the flag to the pole and raise it while the company sang an Indian song.[39]

Though the working tour had expanded Joe's knowledge of Indian life, and the pervasive influence of corn on Indian religion, myth and survival, he felt disillusioned, then disappointed in the condition of the Indians and the hovels in which they lived. Still, his skills as an artist had expanded as well, and his work continued to take on his individuality.[40]

Perhaps to distract themselves from the Indians' condition, Joe and Sallie began to excavate sunken graves on the white man's side of the river. As always, direct observation of the diverse features of man gave him a better understanding of the complex process involved in the cultural development. When Joe found nothing in the sunken graves to interpret the special characteristics of the natives, and when he felt he had accomplished what he had sought in the Hurons, the Imhofs decided to return to New York to prepare for another extensive European working tour.[41]

When they left Ontario, one Indian, Gus Yellow, walked the fifteen miles to their hotel in Middleport to say goodbye. As a token of his esteem for Joe, Gus Yellow had brought an enormous turtle rattle whose handle consisted of the turtle's outstretched neck. The rattle sealed their friendship, and engendered years of correspondence between the Imhofs and Gus Yellow and Jimmie Jamison. Yet the Imhofs, who had talked of returning to other tribal villages, never visited the Huron villages again.[42] Too many other interests held an allure for them. At the moment, the Fall seemed to beckon them to Europe, as if Joe might find direction in a continent where the people had given him the freedom to claim himself.

On Saturday, November 29, 1902, the Imhof family boarded the twin-screw steamer Holland-American line, *Potsdam*, bound for Antwerp, Belgium.[43] Once in Antwerp, Joe guided his family to the old hotel, *Fleur de Or*, where he had lived as a student the first time he had arrived in Europe. The three generations of women who managed the hotel welcomed his return and his new family. To Joe, it felt as if he'd come home again.[44]

The hotel served as their central homing place as Joe proudly guided Sallie and Elizabeth to the source of the bells emanating from the nearby Cathedral of Our Lady whose spires had been carved to resemble lace.[45] They walked to the city's center to admire the sixteenth and seventeenth century Guild Houses, and then to the building, now a museum, the Plantin Moretus, that intrigued Joe the most. The sixteenth century printing establishment, created in 1549 by the French painter and bookbinder, Christophe Plantin, still contained all of its original elegance of fine typography and engraving.[46]

The Imhofs then toured the zoo in preparation for Joe to paint in one of the small rooms, built especially for painters, behind the cages of animals. In the days to come, Joe would spend hours in one of the rooms, painting scenes of wild animals.[47]

From Antwerp, the family moved on to Brussels for a few days before departing for Amsterdam. They planned to remain in Amsterdam until the weather cleared and allowed them several months in Laren for Joe to paint and renew his friendships. They made the most of their time, as always, while in Amsterdam by living in a pension on Spiegel Gracht located near the Rijksmuseum. During that period in Amsterdam, strict pension rules stipulated that boarders must furnish their own beds. The pension provided everything else essential, so the Imhofs purchased the first of several pieces of furniture they would acquire during this trip.[48]

Each day, Joe took Elizabeth with him to the Rijksmuseum where she "began her appreciation of art" by his side. There they spent long hours, with Joe copying more great masters while teaching Elizabeth how to recognize the great painters. She not only came to recognize each painter's work, but with a child's receptive ear for different sounds, she gradually began speaking French,

Flemish, and became fluent in Dutch, a language Joe spoke as well.[49]

Sallie would recall, long after Joe's and Elizabeth's deaths, that Joe had always felt disappointed that "his girl" had never wanted to become a painter. Sallie believed that their daughter held the same interests as Sallie: chemistry and biology, and had wanted to become a surgeon just as had Sallie, though Sallie had never made any attempt to pursue such a career.[50] But Elizabeth, by now, as a constant companion to Sallie and Joe, had accommodated herself so completely to her parents that it's possible that the aspirations of her real self remained cloaked even from herself. Neither parent left any record of friends Elizabeth might have had, nor of any associations beyond her parents. Sallie spoke of their daughter as having similar characteristics as Joe in his goal setting, but what else could Sallie have imagined if Elizabeth had had no other associations?[51]

When Spring arrived, and the weather cleared that year in 1903, the Imhofs packed their sparse furniture and goods and headed the eighteen miles southeast to Laren. They rented the Sunday part of a large, and old, farm house where Joe established his studio. However, he spent most of his time with Clifford Snyder, a painter who had grown up in Wisconsin, but had become an expatriate living in Europe.[52] The thirty-nine-year-old Snyder had earned his degree in dentistry at the University of Michigan before setting up his dental practice in St. Paul, Minnesota. After a year, he established a practice in Berlin and became the dentist for the royal family. When he became financially independent, he practiced dentistry part time and used his free time to paint. Eventually, he opened a studio in Paris, which became his permanent art headquarters.[53]

Joe accompanied Snyder into the countryside to paint the actual lives of Dutch peasants living in the outlying areas, and Dutch interior scenes. At the same time, Joe and Snyder relished discussions with painters who had come from other parts of the world to capture on canvas these same Dutch experiences. The two men enjoyed each other immensely and would remain friends until Snyder's death in 1928 in Paris.[54]

Within a few months, the Imhofs packed again, and this time traveled to a geographic area new to them: Veere, a village situated on the north side of a peninsula some one hundred miles south of Amsterdam on Holland's west coast. The Imhofs had the adventure of hiring a canal boat to transport them and their goods to Veere.[55]

Some five hundred years before, Veere had been a thriving port owned by a powerful Scottish family with marriage ties to Scotland's royal family. The port became important to shipments of Scottish wool. In the early twentieth century, Veere had become the home to deep sea fishermen and shipbuilders, as well as an attraction for artists who sought to soak in the centuries-old village. Its authentic houses and warehouses, built in the sixteenth century to service the wool trade, remained, as did the Dutch House built during the time of Mary Queen of Scots. Veere became Joe's most loved destiny in Holland. Sallie would recall toward the end of her life that their time in Veere had been the happiest of their lives.[56]

The Imhofs' rented sixteenth century house resided on the same street as the Scotch House, a mansion built by a Scottish wool merchant who had constructed his warehouse and office adjacent to his home. The town hall near the Imhofs still housed much of the records, paintings and manuscripts created during earlier eras. The remains of Veere's great cathedral, which had been built by travelers coming to take the cure from water found in Veere's sacred wells, had been partially restored from one of Napoleon's campaigns when the general had converted the cathedral into a six-story hospital for his wounded.[57]

Gradually, the Imhofs began buying sixteenth century furniture for their narrow, three-story house. Joe's already acquired knowledge of antiques helped them carefully chose each piece, and the family accommodated themselves to becoming one with the village.[58] Though Veere's sacred well still existed, the villagers no longer used it. Instead, they drew water from a village cistern kept replenished by the daily rains guided into the cistern from water drained from roofs. The Imhofs drew from the same cistern, but boiled their water for cooking and drinking.[59]

Joe spent his evenings discussing art with the many artists who had taken up residence in the village. However, he preferred to focus his conversations on the great masters. He refused to talk about modern art or his own work, because he said he thought his art was his own business. Nor would he discuss art with the young, for whom he had a particular fondness, and, instead, felt a responsibility to train them to see the beauties and possibilities in life. In Veere, as he would in every country, he engaged young people in conversations about life and all the facets of beauty he saw as a part of life because, Sallie said, he especially loved the young.[60]

Most mornings, weather permitting, Joe would join the fishermen who had anchored their boats along the wharf next to a boardwalk. Here they knelt in prayer before eating their morning meal on the dock, and setting out to sea. Joe often joined them in their meal and, because he spoke their language with fluency, became acquainted with not only them, but almost every male in the village. Many times Joe boarded someone's boat and set out to sea for the day. For Joe, whose life-long hobby had been boats and shipping, this must have seemed a dream come true. He painted their ships, the same ships used by their forefathers. Though he sold a few of these works, he gave away most of the paintings to friends who admired his work. Sallie always approved of his giving away his possessions because it made him so happy.[61]

In the evenings, he would join the townsmen in their meeting room located in the village lighthouse built on the dunes. Here they smoked cigars and talked of the day's events. On Sundays, the small boys, even the five year olds, were permitted to smoke a small cigar as they sat on the church stoop. Joe was amused at their antics and spoke to them in their language.[62]

When Queen Wilhelmina I and her mother, Emma, arrived for a visit, the Imhofs joined them for a reception at a friend's home where they renewed their acquaintance from previous visits.[63] It's possible the Queen, who had seen Buffalo Bill and his "Wild West" show as an eleven year old, and Joe exchanged stories of their experiences with Buffalo Bill.[64]

On December 6, 1903, the Imhofs took Elizabeth to the village children's celebration of Saint Nicholas where they received toys, then the family celebrated Christmas Day at the church with the village elders. The Imhofs had been in Holland for almost a year that Christmas Day, so began making plans to move on. They wanted to spend time in Nürnberg, Germany where the Imhof line had begun.[65]

In early 1904, they packed their furniture and other household goods and shipped them to New York for storage. They talked of building a Dutch house on land once settled by the English along what is now the New Jersey coastline stretching from Leonia to Fairview, but the dream never materialized and, in time, they sold the sixteenth century furniture they had collected in Veere.[66] They later built a summer camp on property purchased in 1905 in the Township of Montville, just southwest of Towaco, New Jersey.

Elizabeth had reached the age of six in 1904, and Joe would turn thirty-three and Sallie, thirty-two. Before leaving Holland, the Imhofs returned to Amsterdam for a short visit, then traveled north the short distance to the town of Edam. Then they returned to Antwerp and Brussels before heading toward their next destination: Frankfurt am Main. To reach Frankfurt am Main in southern Germany, they took a long and circuitous route by first stopping in Cologne, an ancient city ringed by streets that followed medieval walls. Among many sights that impressed them, they especially remembered the Cologne Cathedral of mostly vertical lines, with its dominating twin spires, and located in the city's heart.[67]

It was early Spring now, and the Rhine River flowing through Cologne had been swollen by the winter melts in the Swiss Alps. The Imhofs climbed aboard one of the boats plying the Rhine and charted a course down river for St. Goar, passing Bonn and Koblenz along the way.[68] At St. Goar, the river narrowed dramatically, its waters funneling into a treacherous maelstrom of rapid currents and eddies. It was at St. Goar, with its river gorge of rushing torrents, that the legend of Lorelei originated. On the 430-foot cliffs above the river, the bewitching water nymph sat combing her golden hair as she sang her strangely beautiful siren songs, luring boatmen to their destruction.[69]

St. Goar, itself a beautiful town, with its towering ruin of the thirteenth century Castle Rheinfels, handwoven linens sunning on lawns that fronted their creators' homes, and lilacs in bloom, charmed the Imhofs. Since the boat tied up in St. Goar for the night, the Imhofs stayed in Hotel Karl Horberich and vowed to return at another time for a long visitation.[70]

The next morning, their boat pushed off for Frankfurt am Main, which would serve as their launching point for Munich where they planned to stay for a period of time. From Frankfurt am Main, they boarded a train for Munich, a city renowned for its museums, theater, cathedrals, and music. It also acted as a magnet for artists from throughout the world.[71]

In Munich, they decided, they'd stay at the San Franciscan Hotel, the same hotel where they had stayed in 1900. Much to their surprise, the hotel's porter recognized them when they got off the train. He gathered up their luggage as if he knew they intended to take up residence in the San Franciscan.[72]

As summer approached, they decided to look for a large apartment Joe could use for a studio, one near the heart of the city. They found what they had been looking for on Roudolph Strasse, in the home of an Austrian physician's widow. The location placed them in the heart of Munich, away from American colonies, and near foreign students, artists and professional men, all of whom Joe preferred to Americans because he did not wish to live by American customs. Within a short time, they had a standing table reserved in St. Peters courtyard where, every afternoon after five, they met their friends for conversations and refreshments. The well-known Imhof name also entitled them to a reserved table on a balcony overlooking Munich's main parade route.[73]

Joe disciplined himself to work every morning in his studio from eight until ten o'clock. He made it known to the artists and models, who collected about the steps of the art museum, that he served breakfast to his wife and the model in his studio. From that moment on, he never had a problem finding a model to pose for his morning's work.[74]

Later in the day, as he made his rounds about Munich, he carried a bag of candies, and sometimes pennies, which he handed to children of the poorer families, for whom he felt a particular compassion. His pennies would, in time, grow to nickels which he carried in his pockets to disperse. It became a habit that he would continue until the end of his life.[75]

In Munich, as in Amsterdam, the Imhofs shopped the weekly out-of-door sales held at fairs, usually located on the edge of the city, where people sold wares of all kinds, from rusty nails to valuable antiques. Some of the most beautiful objects they bought came by acquainting themselves with the sellers who would invite them to look at the "good pieces" in their homes.[76] They also spent time in the Bavarian National Museum founded in 1855. By 1904, the Bavarian National had collected so many pieces of art that it had had to move its location several times.[77] Here Joe studied various periods of German and northern Italian art closely related to the Bavarian culture.

With summer upon them, the Imhofs packed again. This time they headed for Nürnberg to trace the Imhof line that reached as far back as 1025.[78] And, they wanted to spend more time studying the life and paintings of Albert Dürer, a famous sixteenth century artist who had painted many portraits of Hans Imhoff, Dürer's banker and, more importantly, his patron.[79] Joe Imhof had descended from the Hans Imhoff line.[80]

During the fifteenth and sixteenth centuries, Nürnberg was considered to be a medieval splendor, and the center of the German Renaissance that brought together the Italian Renaissance and German Gothic traditions. Here the guilds flourished with the presence of such great artists as Albert Dürer, Veit Stoss, and Michael Wolgemut.[81]

In the heart of Nürnberg reposed the magnificent St. Lorenz Church, started in 1220 and completed in 1475, now replete with twin towers that flanked the entrance, a stained glass rosette, and a sanctuary filled with wood and stone carvings by Veit Stoss and Adam Kraft. Albert Dürer's teacher, Michael Wolgemut, had created the painted wood panels where the choir chairs began. In the church, with its soaring vaulted ceiling, carved pillars spoke of the redemption as did the mass of wood carvings in the entrance that extended the theme, beginning with Adam and Eve and continuing to the Last Judgment.[82]

Among other discoveries, Joe and Sallie found the Imhoff chapel on Imhoff Strasse with a parish house connected to it. Inside the parish they saw a drawing of Valentine Imhoff, a lexicographer, depicted asleep at the foot of a tree which grew from his body. The Imhoff lineage, dating from the fifteenth century in Nürnberg and extending into the nineteenth century had been recorded on the branches of the tree.[83]

Joe Imhof, who had longed for his father to serve as his patron, felt particularly drawn to his distant relative, Hans Imhoff, who had been Dürer's patron. It was Dürer himself, however, with whom Joe sought to identify. For in the mirror image of Dürer, Joe saw himself, as if he had embodied Dürer's spirit.

When Joe and Sallie entered the Albert Dürer house a few blocks north of the St. Lorenz church across the Pegnitz River, they found it typical of the half-timbered houses of the fifteenth century. Dürer had bought this house near the medieval walls in 1509, at the height of his fame, and had painted many of his masterpieces here. Dürer, the Imhofs knew, had been regarded as the first genius of the German Renaissance.[84]

Dürer, like Joe, had been an engraver and designer as well. In some ways, their shared traits seemed uncanny. Dürer had been born in Nürnberg in 1471, exactly four hundred years earlier than Joe's birth in 1871. Dürer had apprenticed at the age of fifteen to the leading Nürnberg painter and book illustrator, Michael Wolgemut.[85] Joe had apprenticed himself at age fifteen to the artists living in the Ridley Mansion.

Dürer, however, had family connections. Albert Dürer's father had been a goldsmith, while his godfather had been Anthony Koberger, one of Germany's foremost printers and publishers. Wolgemut, Dürer's teacher, had been a lifelong friend of the patrician and humanist, Willibald Pirckheimer, whose daughter married Hans Imhoff. Koberger, Wolgemut and Pirckheimer contributed to Dürer's genius, teaching him the rudiments of drawing, the devotion to craft and meticulous detail, the painter's and woodcarver's expertise and, above all, the value of books and learning directed toward the new humanism in Italy.[86]

Joe Imhof taught himself the value of books by reading voraciously and by collecting books, many of them out-of-print collectors' editions. And he had apprenticed himself to the leading lithographer in the United States, Currier and Ives.

After completing his apprenticeship in 1490, Dürer traveled through the Netherlands and Germany before finally setting up his workshop in Nürnberg.[87] Exactly four hundred years later, Joe Imhof traveled through the Netherlands and Germany before settling himself in Manhattan as a painter and lithographer.

Dürer's work, while traditional in subject matter, was revolutionary in subtlety of technique.[88] Joe Imhof, whose work eventually focused on the Pueblo Indians, was traditional in his subject matter at the time, but his technique, in rendering historically accurate a people and their way of life that would gradually vanish, proved to be as revolutionary. At the time Joe painted the Pueblo Indians, artists tended to romanticize the Indian, to present him in false images which have plagued the Indians and poisoned the relationship between whites and Indians. Joe, in his accuracy, gave added importance to the differences in the white and Indian relationship.

In so many ways, Dürer's and Imhof's personality traits seem similar. In 1507, Dürer had been in Venice, and away from his work for seventeen months, long enough that his patrons had become eager to acquire more of his work. One, Jakob Heller, a Frankfurt merchant, commissioned Dürer for an altarpiece depicting *The Assumption of the Virgin*. Max Steck, in his book, *Dürer and His World*, wrote that Dürer grumbled about the fee while, at the same time, he stressed his goodwill. "Dürer was almost invariably engaged in disputes," Steck wrote. "He was not avaricious; on the contrary, he sometimes verged on extravagance. He was quick to give things away, squandered money thoughtlessly on trifles which caught his fancy . . . yet he never entirely lost his . . . fear of not being able to make ends meet . . . . Finally, after receiving an arrogant and unsympathetic response from the Frankfurt business man, he [Dürer] lost patience and declared the contract void, instructing his banker, Imhoff, to return the deposit . . . . At this Heller backed down . . . ."[89]

In another instance, Steck wrote that after Dürer had been in Antwerp for a period of time, the city council offered him an annual retainer and a "well-constructed house," if he would remain. Dürer longed to return to Nürnberg, and so when "Dürer's thoughts turned to departure, [he] dispatched a succession of bales to Imhoff in Nürnberg, some of them filled with the most bizarre assortment of articles—buffalo-horns, fish-fins, coral, Indian feathers, caps, porcelain vases, twelve pairs of gloves, bolts of silk, large nuts—all things which he had purchased or been given."[90] All the kinds of objects that Joe Imhof collected four hundred years later. Steck's description of Dürer's extravagance in giving things away, while squandering money on trifles, could have been a fitting description of Joe Imhof.

Dürer painted his banker and patron, Hans Imhoff, many times. One portrait hangs in the Gardner Collection of the Boston Museum.[91] Another, painted in 1521, hangs in the Prado in Madrid, a museum that has a particular interest in Albert Dürer since the artist was a favorite of Emperor Maximilian I.[92]

Eventually, Joe Imhof acquired a photograph of Dürer's portrait of Hans Imhoff. Joe hung the prized photograph in the studio of their Taos home. He also acquired two copies of lead transparencies. One is of Dürer's coat of arms that Dürer designed himself in 1523. Another depicts a branch of the Bavarian Royal family. Sallie Imhof attached an importance to the lead transparencies and willed these to the University of New Mexico College of Fine Arts.[93]

Before returning to Munich, the Imhof family sought out Berchtesgaden, a village deep inside the fold of the Bavarian Alps and, as the crow flies, about sixty-five miles from Munich.[94] Sallie and Joe saw Berchtesgaden as the noblest town in the Bavarian Alps, not only for the salt mining that provided the basis for its wealth, but for its most famous resident, the fifteenth century wood carver and painter, Veit Stoss. They would later study his wood carvings that graced churches throughout Europe.[95]

105

From here, the Imhofs traveled to Salzburg to enjoy the Music Festival, then made a brief excursion into Italy, simply as tourists. Joe sketched as they traveled, but existence of these sketches or drawings remain unknown since Joe gave them away to friends or people who admired them.[96]

With money once again running low, and Elizabeth now school age, the Imhofs returned to their Munich studio to pack. The steamer returned them back up the Rhine River to Cologne where they again stayed at the Dom Hotel, which stood in the shadow of the Cologne Cathedral. Much to their delight, they received a room with a bath, only to discover that their bathtub had no fixtures, or water. A maid remedied the problem by filling the tub, then emptying it of water after they had all bathed.[97]

The next day, October 8, 1904, Joe celebrated his thirty-third birthday by walking his family to the Cologne Cathedral in a pouring rain. After one last look at the relics of the Magi and the crown jewels, the Imhofs took the train to Antwerp where they remained for a few days before boarding a ship home.[98] The time had come for Joe to search out profitable commercial art work to pay for their next excursion into Europe.

CHAPTER 7

JOINING PHILOSOPHY WITH ART

When the Imhofs returned in 1904, they found New York vibrating with competition; competition for readers of every form of printed matter, for followers of new faiths, new ideas, new products, and for the control of trusts by fabulously wealthy men who monopolized the banking, oil, steel, copper, sugar, tobacco, and shipping industries. The industrial age had shifted into high gear and Joe intended to profit from his own inventive ideas.

The income from his previous commercial art work had taken him and his family to Europe twice and to Canada, had provided for a home in Englewood Cliffs on the New Jersey shore, a community next to the more fashionable Palisades where financially successful Germans lived, and an art studio on 14th Street in Manhattan.[1] By 1904, he still could not clearly define the future direction of his life, but he did know that he had not yet finished with Europe.

His previous work for Allen and Ginter had provided the money to marry Sallie, so now he called on people in the cigarette industry again.[2] Much had changed during the two and a half years he had spent in Europe. Although the United States Congress had passed the Sherman Anti-Trust Act during 1890, Congress extended its scope in 1904 in an attempt to prevent trusts from monopolizing industries.[3] A study made in 1904 listed 318 industrial trusts that had capitalized at seven billion dollars and represented the merging of 5,300 individual plants. The seven big trusts in banking, steel, oil, copper, sugar, tobacco, and shipping were capitalized at two and a half billion. Census figures showed that one-eighth of American businesses employed more than three-fourths of the wage earners and produced four-fifths of the manufactured products. In anticipation of the new Anti-Trust law, the Tobacco Trust had incorporated into the American Tobacco Company. Still, health concerns and competition plagued the company.[4]

When the Imhofs had left the country, a wave of anticigarette legislation across the country had caused fourteen states to prohibit the sale of cigarettes entirely, and all but Texas prohibited sales to minors. The campaign against cigarettes had arisen out of health concerns, then spread to warnings that linked cigarettes with the decline of morals and all manner of physical ails, from baldness to a weak mind. However, the spread of cigarette use continued unabated, and then picked up with incredible speed.[5]

Despite the fact that the American Tobacco Company now owned all the significant cigarette brands, competitors still waged bitter price wars, wars that James Duke, who had put together the Tobacco Trust and served as president, had originated to drive all other tobacco companies out of business.[6] Though American Tobacco controlled eighty-five percent of the American cigarette market, profits had been cut in almost half by the tobacco wars.[7] Profits, then, had to be increased by other methods. Americans now accepted machine-rolled cigarettes, which had helped cut labor costs.[8] In 1902, American Tobacco directors managed to get taxes cut to fifty-four cents per thousand on small cigarettes with a wholesale value of two dollars or less per thousand, and to a dollar and eight cents per thousand on more expensive cigarettes.[9]

Packaging innovations offered one of the few remaining developments in cigarette sales that could increase profits.[10] In 1904, cigarettes were usually "priced in even nickels, and a number of price classes of cigarettes developed according to the possible combination of five-cent multiples and packs of ten and twenty." Reductions in retail prices, say five cents a box or increases from ten to fifteen cigarettes per box, could eliminate the profit entirely.[11]

Attractive, easily used packaging, though, could attract more smokers. When Joe Imhof called on American Tobacco, he came away with an assignment as an idea man.[12] American Tobacco first wanted to develop a tear tab to open a cigarette package. At the time, cigarette manufacturers used tin foil as a package wrapper. Not until 1907 did manufacturers use paper-backed foil as a cigarette wrapper inside packages.[13] Cellophane packaging had not yet arrived, so Joe's assignment concentrated on the package itself. He returned to his 14th Street studio and used his knowledge of the mechanics of printing to make sketches of a tear tab mechanism to open the cigarette package. American Tobacco, which had no interest in completed drawings, wanted Joe's ideas in the form of sketches for such a mechanism. These sketches for such a device were then patented.[14]

As Joe worked in his studio sketching ideas for American Tobacco, Sallie opened their house in the New Jersey Englewood Cliffs and both again began their daily boat rides across the Hudson before boarding the train into Manhattan; Joe commuted in the mornings and Sallie most afternoons to continue research in the Lenox Library on the Northeastern Indians.[15]

On one such commute, Joe met Joseph (Udo) Keppler, Jr. who would not only introduce Joe to the commercial art work in the newspaper publishing business, but become the Imhofs life-long friend.[16] The similarity between the men was striking. Joseph Udo Keppler, Jr., like Joseph Imhof, was the son of a German immigrant. Udo Keppler, Jr. had been born into a St. Louis German immigrant community six months after Joe Imhof had been born in a similar community in Brooklyn. Both men had developed a passion for North American Indians when each discovered he lived on land once occupied by the Algonkian.[17] Both had trained as artists, and received much of their training in Europe.

Now, in 1904, Joe Imhof would board the train near where he crossed the Hudson at Spuyten Duyvil, and Joseph Udo Keppler, Jr. would board a short distance later, in Inwood, an enclave of New York's wealthy.[18] Udo Keppler, Jr. worked as the chief cartoonist for *Puck*, a magazine of political satire that contained cartoons, poetry and prose, and had been founded by Udo Keppler , Jr.'s father in 1876.[19]

The senior Keppler had grown up in Vienna where he had satisfied his artistic talents decorating cakes and sweet confections created by his father, who owned a bakery. The father had left Vienna however, for a better life in United States, and had taken two of his sons with him. Udo Keppler, Jr.'s father had remained in Vienna with his mother, received his academic training as an artist, and began drawing cartoons and illustrations for a new humor magazine.[20]

Coincidentally, Joseph Keppler heard from his father who had departed twenty years before. The father's two sons had died and now he wanted his third son, Joseph, to join him. After a tearful reunion in 1867, the small family left for St. Louis, Missouri, a common destination for German immigrants. The unstable political situation in Germany had sent thousands to America, and swelled St. Louis by fifty thousand Germans, making the city the fourth largest after New York, Brooklyn, and Philadelphia.[21]

Joseph Keppler enrolled in medical school, but soon abandoned medicine, and became involved in St. Louis German theater. He also tried selling his caricatures to St. Louis English-and German-language publications. In the growing number of friends he made were other German immigrants, and among them were Joseph Pulitzer, a star reporter on the St. Louis German newspaper, and Udo Brachvogel, a librarian, who later would write for *Puck* and for whom Joseph Keppler would name his first son.[22]

At age thirty, Joseph Keppler was still intrigued with comic satire. His German friends who had enjoyed such publications in Europe encouraged him to start such a publication since none existed in the country. In 1868, roughly one out of twenty publications in America was published in German. On March 18, 1871, the first issue of *Puck* appeared in German. No subject was too mundane or monumental for Keppler's cartoons that depicted his opinions that ranged from overheard conversations in bookstores to world events.[23]

A few weeks into publication, Joseph Keppler caricatured the German Press in St. Louis and drew his friend, Joseph Pulitzer, who had just bought into the *Westliche Post*. The next month, in August, *Puck* suffered the same fate as all previous satirical publications: death by undercapitalization.[24]

Joseph Keppler, however, determined to continue. He had remarried after deaths of his first wife and sons, and now his second wife, Pauline, had given birth to their first son, Udo, on April 4, 1872. Joseph Keppler sent his work to the publisher of *Illustrated Newspaper*, one of the leading news magazines in New York. When the work was published, Joseph Keppler determined to move to New York City, the country's publishing center. Four years later, in 1876, a new *Puck* appeared on New York newsstands, this time with adequate financing from a partner and friend, Adolph Schwarzmann.[25]

German-Americans took to *Puck* from the start even while the nation suffered in the midst of a depression. New York City had three times the German population of St. Louis, and Joseph Keppler's caricatures brought to life the German-American bankers and businessmen parading around the New Jersey Palisades wearing their yellow vests and sky-blue coats. The ten-page weekly carried more color than the St. Louis edition had carried. European cartoon magazines splashed their caricatures with color, while color remained absent in most American publications. *Puck* changed that even though the lithographic printing process using color was still in a crude state.[26]

The color added appeal, and within a few months the magazine's success caused the owners to began an English-language edition. At the same time, the magazine's demands left almost no time for Joseph Keppler to spend with his family, which had grown to five children, plus his St. Louis in-laws and mother from Vienna who had moved into the household in 1879. That same year, the seven-year-old Udo, a quiet, shy boy, discovered the old Algonkian Indian settlement nearby, and began a life-long love affair with the Indian culture.[27]

In 1883, the acclaim and financial rewards *Puck* brought sparked an interest in Joseph Pulitzer, who had just purchased the failing *New York World*. *Puck* dazzled Pulitzer and he wanted part of its glory. He offered to buy Joseph Keppler's magazine. Joseph Keppler refused. When freelance cartoonist Walt McDougall offered Pulitzer a cartoon that Joseph Keppler had already rejected, Pulitzer saw it as a chance to take on Joseph Keppler. He published the cartoon on page one of the *World* and hired McDougall as the newspaper's first editorial cartoonist. Pulitzer's action transformed the art made famous by Joseph Keppler into another feature in American newspapers.[28]

While Joseph Keppler and Pulitzer remained friends, and continued to meet over an occasional meal, Joseph Keppler never celebrated Pulitzer's publishing feats by granting him another caricature. Though they both embraced the common man, they went about it differently. Joseph Keppler, a proud American, celebrated his German heritage and remained in that social circle. Pulitzer sought the powerful and embraced the leading money men, many of whom the *World* criticized in print. Joseph Keppler detested this kind of duplicity.[29]

Puck's success now allowed Keppler to hire a number of cartoonists and editors, which gave him more time with his family. In 1889, Joseph Keppler took his family to Europe, and, while there, Udo Keppler spent part of his time painting. At the end of the trip in August, Joseph Keppler left Udo, now seventeen, in Munich to begin training under Wilhelm Dietz at the Academy of Arts. Udo Keppler excelled in his studies, but became so

111

homesick that he wrote his father and requested to return home. Joseph Keppler, who felt badly that he had never been close to his son, assured Udo that he would always have a place at *Puck*.[30]

Udo Keppler returned home where he joined the staff as a cartoonist. However, within six months, he returned to Germany, this time to Heilbronn, to finish his studies. When he returned permanently to New York City, he took his place at *Puck*, where Joseph Keppler began grooming him to eventually run the magazine. Udo Keppler took his place sooner than anyone could have imagined. Joseph Keppler died of a heart attack in 1894. His death made page one news across the country. Shortly after his father's death, Udo legally changed his name to Joseph Keppler, Jr. and, in 1901, became chief cartoonist.[31]

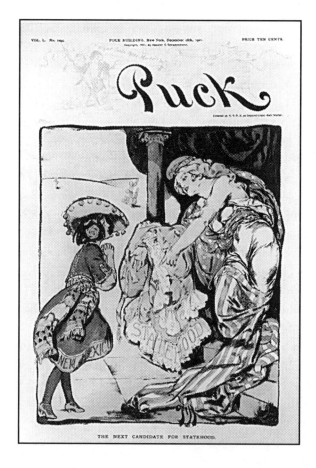

Chromolithograph cover for *Puck* magazine, December 18, 1901.

Puck's remaining days were numbered, however. Technological changes in printing presses, the use of photographers whose pictures could be instantly printed, new inks and papers all made the chromolithographic process which had produced the beautiful and striking color in *Puck* too costly.[32]

When thirty-three-year-old Joe Imhof met thirty-two-year-old Joseph Keppler, Jr. in 1904, *Puck* still commanded national attention, but its importance had already begun to wane. The ferocious newspaper wars which had started in the 1870s now continued full tilt with a completely different group of men.[33]

In 1870, Charles Dana and his *New York Sun* had changed the course of newspapering from the older penny press to the new journalism. Dana's readers consisted mostly of the average New Yorker, workers and small merchants. Dana prized writers who could make a story come alive, who could recognize "the poetry in life." Above all else, a story had to be interesting. It was one of Dana's editors who told a young reporter, "When a dog bites a man, that is not news; but when a man bites a dog, *that* is news." One of the *Sun*'s editorial writers answered the still famous inquiry of a young girl named Virginia, "Is There a Santa Claus?"[34]

The new journalism helped spread the message that Charles Darwin's emphasis upon the struggle of individual existence, which saw the rise of "individualism," had a negative impact on the common man. Social and political scientists pointed out that unrestricted exercise of individual power by some brought misery and poverty to others. The outcome, they said, was not national strength, but national weakness.[35]

Newspapers used their editorial pages to now champion the common man. They became aggressive in pursuing news, which newspaper owners had determined to be the primary obligation of the press; crusaded actively in the interests of the community; and appealed to mass audiences through the use of better graphics, headlines, well-written human interest stories, and use of illustrations.[36]

When Joseph Pulitzer's *World* came along in 1883, Pulitzer wrote a "ten-point program on the editorial page: tax luxuries; tax inheritances; tax large income; tax monopolies; tax the privileged corporations; a tariff for revenue; reform the civil service; punish corrupt office-holders; punish vote-buying; punish employers who coerce their employees in elections." Pulitzer declared he believed in the aristocracy of brains and honor, the aristocracy of labor, and the aristocracy of virtue.[37]

113

When James Gordon Bennett, Jr. took control of the *New York Herald*, he led his reporters into becoming the most skilled in gathering and transmitting the fastest communications. It was the *Herald's's* reporter, Henry M. Stanley, who spent two years searching in Africa for the missing missionary and, when he found him, inquired, "Dr. Livingstone, I presume?"[38] Bennett had already seen the value of a Sunday edition, which his paper had long published. Pulitzer, though, first showed the potential of the Sunday edition as an entertainment medium. He began to feature material for women, children, and for sports enthusiasts. Pulitzer's Sunday editor began to exaggerate and popularize factual information, and directed writers to interpret advances made by American scientists. One of his staff described their approach:

"Suppose it's Halley's comet. Well, first you have a half-page of decoration showing the comet, with historical pictures of previous appearances thrown in. If you can work a pretty girl into the decoration, so much the better. If not, get some good nightmare idea like the inhabitants of Mars watching it pass. Then you want a quarter of a page of big-type heads— snappy. Then four inches of story, written right off the bat. Then a picture of Professor Halley down here and another of Professor Lowell up there, and a two-column boxed freak containing a scientific opinion, which nobody will understand, just to give it class."[39]

In 1893, Pulitzer installed the first color presses, which enhanced the illustrations in the *World's* regular comic section, the first such comics carried in a newspaper. The most successful of these artists was Richard F. Outcault, whose "Hogan's Alley" depicted life in the tenements. The central character was a toothless, grinning kid in a ballooning dress. The *World's* presses ran a daub of yellow color on the kid's dress, and he became known as "the Yellow Kid."[40]

When William Randolph Hearst arrived in New York with his *New York Journal*, the *World* had a Sunday circulation of 600,000. Hearst immediately began hiring Pulitzer's most successful editors, and one of them took the artist, Outcault, and the "Yellow Kid" with him to the *Journal*. Pulitzer selected another talented editor who brought in another artist, George B. Luks who later became a well-known artist, to continue the "Yellow Kid," and the contest was on. Both newspapers heavily promoted the Kid on posters and in other features. From this came the phrase, "yellow journalism" as newspapers escalated their war to grab readers. In all, fifteen daily English-language newspapers battled for readers in 1900. While newspapers thundered their concerns for the common man, their reporters produced shrieking, gaudy journalism filled with sex, violence, and sin.[41]

From the sensationalism of the news, the crusades begun in the name of the common man, arose the muckrakers. By the 1900s, the flood of immigrants had doubled from the past twenty years, and four out of five of New York's residents were either foreign-born or children of foreign-born parents. At the same time, the percentage of children attending school had risen to seventy-two percent, and the illiteracy rate had dropped to ten percent. The time was right for the rise of books that exposed the excesses in society.[42]

Upton Sinclair wrote *The Jungle* in 1906, and laid bare the unsanitary practices of Chicago meat packing houses; Frank Norris wrote *The Octopus* in 1901 to reveal the struggle of California farmers against the power of the Southern Pacific Railroad; then came his book, *The Pit*, that protested Chicago wheat speculators. More exposés followed.[43]

In this environment, Joe Imhof found himself wanting to become a part of the publishing innovations creating so much excitement. Joe already shared the income for the pictorial device he had invented and patented in 1902. However, he had created the device while employed by American Lithographic Company and, as a result, received no credit for his work. J. V. Sloane of American Lithographic did syndicate the device to newspapers and, in a silent agreement with Joe, paid Joe a royalty.[44]

In the meantime, Joseph Pulitzer's *World* had withdrawn from the sensationalism of news when Pulitzer recognized that yellow journalism would eventually destroy itself, which left the *World* as the premier newspaper in New York City. In 1904, Pulitzer's son, Joseph Pulitzer, Jr. now managed the *World* after Pulitzer's health forced him to retire.[45]

In all probability, it was Joseph (Udo) Keppler, Jr., whose father had remained friends with Joseph Pulitzer, who introduced Joseph Imhof to Joseph Pulitzer, Jr. All three were sons of German immigrants, and each son had worked on the cutting edge of publishing. While not one of the three continued to immerse himself in the German community as had his father, each still maintained his ties to his German heritage.

Imhof's contact with Pulitzer's *New York World* produced work for the

115

World's Sunday supplement. Joe created a children's page which contained the educational cutout he had invented in a project that Joe loved, but one that the *World* held all rights to circulate. Sallie would later comment that Joe constantly mourned this Sunday supplement for which the *World* held all rights. Joe's sense of loss probably meant that he had hoped to receive a royalty from the work which would have brought in a constant source of income during the lifetime of the children's page. Instead, he apparently received a one-time payment for the work as a "work for hire."[46]

His disappointment did not interfere with the Imhofs' friendship with Joseph (Udo) Keppler, Jr. Sallie began to ride the train with the two men each morning so that each could give her ideas on what information they wanted her to research on Northeastern Indians. At the end of each day, the three would meet again and, as they rode the train, Sallie would review her findings. Their friendship blossomed and would last until Udo Keppler, Jr.'s death in La Jolla, California in 1956.[47]

For now, the next decade would bring the death of Joseph (Udo) Keppler's wife; his remarriage to a woman who shared his interest in Indians; his decline of President Theodore Roosevelt's offer to serve as Commissioner of Indian Affairs; his sale of *Puck* in 1913, which Hearst would purchase to use as a Sunday comic magazine section as well as a comic magazine sold separately. Hearst then discontinued *Puck* in 1918. Keppler retired to Woodland, New York to live near an Indian tribe that had accepted him as a member but, in 1946 when his health declined, he moved to La Jolla where he would again play an important part in the Imhofs' lives until he died.

As Joe and Sallie attended their usual concerts and theaters and made their walks around and through historical places in New York City in 1905, the year they first met Joseph (Udo) Keppler, they began to discuss Joe's still unsettled direction in life.[48] They also invested in property. On February 21, 1905, Joseph Imhof purchased six and a quarter acres of land in Montville, New Jersey, almost thirty miles west of the Palisades. The deed stated: "The use of the water from the spring situated on the westerly side of the said lot . . . . Together with all and singular the houses, buildings, trees, ways, waters, profits and privileges and advantages . . . ."[49]

Perhaps the Imhofs purchased the property as a safe haven, a place where they could settle once Joe could determine his direction. The spiritual lives of American Indians spoke to Joe in ways he could not yet articulate,

and Europe continued to call to him. He had long since divested himself of
any beliefs he might have had in Catholicism. In time, the Imhofs' discussions led to a growing interest in attending one of Felix Adler's lectures held
each Sunday at Carnegie Hall.[50]

Felix Adler and the Society of Ethical Culture, which he had founded
in 1876, had become famous before the turn of the century. By the time Joe
and Sallie began attending his lectures, Adler's followers regularly filled
Carnegie Hall. Adler proved a natural fit for Joseph Imhof. Adler, too, had a
German immigrant background and, like Joe, had rejected his father's dictate to become, in Felix's case, the family rabbi. Felix Adler, too, had searched
for his individual calling and had found it while attending the Universities
of Berlin and Heidelberg. Not only that, but Adler's search for "The New
Ideal" had a marked emphasis on humanism, just as Albert Dürer's education three centuries earlier had had an emphasis on the new humanism in
Italy.[51]

At the age of five, Felix Adler had accompanied his family from Alzey,
Germany, a town not far from Worms in Rhine-Hesse, to New York. Felix's
father, Dr. Samuel Adler, who had accepted the offer to become the rabbi of
Temple Emanu-El in New York City, had a highly regarded reputation for his
Judaic learning, and his work in the Reform movement of German Judaism.
Rabbi Adler sent his two sons, Isaac and Felix, to the Columbia Grammar
School where they received an excellent education primarily in Latin,
Greek, English, and mathematics. Felix remembered the mental disci-
pline as "severe."[52]

Dr. Adler devoted himself to his sons' religious education, which in-
cluded instruction in Hebrew, in Bible, Jewish history, and in elements of
Judaic learning. Felix, much like Joseph Imhof, felt more drawn to his mother,
Henrietta, who brought emotional warmth and caring to her children's needs,
while believing with her husband in the principles of piety and active faith.
To allow Dr. Adler time for his scholarly pursuits, Mrs. Adler made regular
visitations to neighbors and on errands of helpfulness to homes of the poor.
Felix, who enjoyed the companionship of his mother, accompanied her on
these excursions of charity where he witnessed the meaning of poverty. Dr.
Adler's passionate attachment to the antislavery cause, and his open weeping
after Lincoln's assassination made a deep impression on Felix, one that
lasted the remainder of his life.[53]

Felix followed his brother, Isaac, into Columbia College in 1866, but felt a dissatisfaction with his education. On July 6, 1870, Felix Adler arrived in Paris on the eve of the Franco-Prussian War, which broke out on July 19. In 1871, Felix witnessed the crowning moment of German glory in Berlin, of the ushering in of the modern German Empire. Bismarck and his policies would forever mark a crucial question for Felix: right versus might in the exercise of power and its validity in terms of the human condition.[54]

Felix's studies at the University of Berlin led him toward understanding the psychic patterns and thought of different peoples—Semitic, Aryan, Chinese, and others—which, in turn, introduced him to the ethical systems and religions of mankind. This approach allowed him to make comparisons and place his Judaic studies in a larger context. He wrote his father and requested permission to study this subject area further in Leipzig. Dr. Adler wrote that he did not object to Felix spending the summer in Leipzig, but he must return to Berlin and limit himself to the study of Talmud, which was the future of his career.[55]

Felix did not go to Leipzig, but he did pursue his philosophical interests. He began to study Kant, with its varying forms of neo-Kantianism, which were in vogue in German philosophy at that time. Immanuel Kant, who had lived 1724-1804, was a German philosopher who continues to be regarded as one of the greatest figures in the history of metaphysics. Kant showed that "the great problems of metaphysics—the existence of God, freedom, and immortality—are insoluble by scientific thought." Kant's ethics center on his imperative, or absolute moral law, "Act as if the maxim from which you act were to become through your will a universal law."[56]

In 1873, Felix Adler transferred to the University of Heidelberg and became a candidate for a Ph.D. in Semitics. When he returned to New York, he introduced his ideas, as successor to his father as rabbi, in a sermon before the Temple Emanu-El congregation. His thinking did not inspire the trustees. Even though Felix's father, Dr. Adler, was distressed, knowing that his son was no longer a candidate, Dr. Adler continued to support Felix's idealism.[57]

Felix Adler, who now held his doctorate in Semitics, was, in many respect, a creature of the times in his rejection of individualism, and in his championing causes and behaviors for the common good, for the common man. Felix favored what he called "organized democracy," in which the essential organs of a society—family, occupation, state, school, and religion—each would have their own rights and responsibilities over which no sovereignty, such as the state or leaders of an elite class, would have total authority.[58]

Felix believed that the "New Ideal" of the Ethical Culture should forward "a universal task" by attending to the "great practical problems of the age," by spreading "truthfulness among the people" and "education for moral welfare." The Ethical Culture began its deeds with two projects that would change forever a city/state's responsibility for its citizens.[59] These same projects, and the philosophy that lay behind them, would also forever change Sallie Imhof. In the coming years, and throughout her life, Sallie would follow Felix Adler's teachings in the work she sought in her effort to discover the substance and center within herself, her own identity.

In 1877, the Ethical Culture Society sent nurses to visit the homebound sick in poor districts. The nurses reported their visits to doctors, who provided free services, and who either instructed the nurses on the next courses of action or visited the homebound themselves.[60] This visiting nurse service continues to serve as an important adjunct to city/county public health services.

The Society's second project launched a free kindergarten in which each child living in poverty was given regular medical examinations and adequate nutrition. In addition, the child was engaged in arts and crafts, taken outdoors to play in parks, and products and persons in the city were brought into the classroom.[61] In time, Felix Adler's project became the model for every elementary school in the country.

By the time the Imhofs began attending Dr. Adler's lectures, Adler's projects had become a part of the Imhofs' surrounding society, and Dr. Adler was a highly regarded Professor of Social and Political Ethics at Columbia University, teaching alongside his colleagues John Dewey and William P. Montague.[62]

The Imhofs listened to Dr. Adler's reconstruction of religious thought, what Adler called "the spiritual ideal," ideas that Joe eagerly sought to comprehend because Adler served to reinforced what Joe verged on believing. Dr. Adler's concepts and maxims nudged Joe in the direction that he intuitively had wanted to take. Adler "maintained that 'a social conception of Godhead,' that is, a vision of the spiritual universe as an infinite life of

119

interaction between uniquely diverse members, should replace the traditional monotheist idea of God as a single individual Being." He said that two fundamental parts of religious services should be rejected in his Sunday meetings: the repetition of scattered Bible verses for young people, which he maintained the young could not comprehend at that time in their lives; and he proposed the Society exclude prayer and every form of ritual.[63]

In Adler's "organized democracy," he proposed that five or six families live "cooperatively" in adjacent homes with certain quarters and facilities shared in common, such as the kitchen, laundry, garden, kindergarten, and an "art room." The idea was to bring groups of children together without separating them from their mothers who would also be "kindergartners." It would save duplicated housework and, finally, afford the group to undertake to rear one or more "neglected" children.[64]

Joe and Sallie Imhof must have recognized that Adler's idea, in more ways than not, described the living arrangements the Iroquois and Hurons had created in their longhouses. During the time that the Imhofs attended Dr. Adler's lectures, Joe began a correspondence with the superintendent of the Albuquerque Indian School, which had opened in 1881 as a Presbyterian boarding and industrial school.[65] In 1886, the Bureau of Indian Affairs had taken over the operation of the boarding school with an enrollment of about three hundred students who studied and lived in a few board shacks located on forty-four acres. The school concentrated on teaching Indian boys a trade since, as a later Superintendent, Reuben Perry, said, "An Indian father visiting the school was more impressed with a table or chair his boy had made than with the fact that the boy also had learned to read, speak and write English."[66]

In his correspondence, Imhof was reaching out for answers for himself, though he must have known that the answers did not lie in a school setting that was alien to the Native American culture. Still, the school would serve to open a door for him and to introduce him to the Pueblo people. Sallie's research had plumbed certain basic beliefs held by Native Americans, beliefs she and Joe learned that held that humans are connected to all beings on earth, both animate and inanimate.

Adler, however, saw women as having certain limitations, that they should build up their "natural vocation to motherhood." He said, "Let there be equality of opportunity for higher education of women in colleges, professional, and post-graduate schools." Yet, Adler did not believe that women should use their higher education to follow diverse careers, but should use the education to become "more complete partners of their husbands, more intelligent mothers of their children." And he opposed women's suffrage.[67] Joe Imhof would not have agreed to Adler's stand on women's suffrage, but Joe shared Adler's belief, as did men of his time, on the role of women as Joe demonstrated in his own marriage.

When Adler touched on the "Spiritual Ideal," he accepted the supremacy of Mind. Mind, he said, "is a world-building power having 'reality-producing functions' that transcend sense experience and order it in universally binding" ways. Adler's view of moral freedom implied a more explicit mutual regard for the moral freedom of others. "Elicit the best in others and thereby in yourself," he admonished his listeners. "We grow and develop in proportion as we help others to grow and develop," he said, and Joe Imhof applied the maxims to his own behavior.[68]

While Dr. Adler disliked being described as having "mystical" qualities, he admitted that features of mysticism were present and vital in his relation to the unique individuality of each member in the infinite "spiritual manifold . . . . My ideal of the divine life," he said, "is that of . . . a spiritual society infinite and composed of infinite members, infinitely diverse, each necessary to the whole and the whole necessary to each. It is this ideal of the perfect life in which I seize the symbol of the utter reality in things."[69]

Most of the ideas that Dr. Adler expressed, he framed in abstract thought. The psychoanalyst, Dr. Arno Gruen, would write years later, "One of the factors that gives rise to and perpetuates splitting of the self, as well as violence in our life, is abstraction. It is in part the overvaluation of intelligence which has made us glorify abstract thought—at the expense of passion, enthusiasm, and openness . . . . Ideas based solely on the logic of their own interrelationships, now lay claim to a kind of 'higher reality' that can be far removed from the actual circumstances these ideas were originally intended to mirror."[70]

Abstraction, Dr. Gruen maintained, "is admirably suited for filtering out feelings . . . . Abstraction promotes depersonalization, the splitting off of embarrassing or painful feelings . . . . The oppression of women and the psychic impoverishment of men are prime examples . . . . Men see themselves and women in terms of abstractions in keeping with a philosophy that proclaims the necessity for strength, domination, and power rather than with the true reality of the other person." The abstraction of "woman" comes to a man's "aid, for she, in her supposed inferiority or at least lower station, is assigned the task of building up and stabilizing his self-image by recognizing his 'strength' and 'higher station.'" The path to power, Dr. Gruen cautions, "leads to a self that mirrors the ideology of domination." And power, domination and control over others provide one way to inflate one's self-esteem.[71]

By 1906, Dr. Adler possessed enough power as a religious leader, with his legion of followers, that he could speak openly about his belief that it was quite possible, and even likely, that there existed non-human beings capable of an intercommunicating that furthered mutual maturing. Again, the Imhofs must have recognized the way in which Adler's belief paralleled that of Native Americans. Adler believed that within each person lay the "crystal fountain" of rightness, and this unique rightness held an eternal component of the "spiritual universe."[72] It was another way of belonging to eternity. These ideas resonated in Joe and Sallie Imhof.

Sallie came to believe that Joe's attendance at Dr. Adler's lectures touched Joe's soul and developed to maturity the character in Joe that made him the lovable man he developed into being; that Adler awakened Joe's realization of duty to others to help them see the beauty of life from its finer aspects; and that money and the strife to obtain it were not the secret of happiness and success. Joe's success in arousing in so many young people the appreciation of beauty in the world was evidenced in the years after Joseph Imhof's death when Sallie continued to receive letters from men and women who told of their gratitude for the advice and assistance Imhof had offered that helped make them successful.[73]

The question, however, that Dr. Adler asked himself still plagued Joe. "What has [my] life meant, and in view of that what does the whole world mean?"[74]

Joe sensed that he could find the answer among the Pueblo Indians who believed that all elements of the earth are humans' peers, whether mountains, streams, trees, rocks, insects, birds, or other animals that can teach us about living. But one must listen in profound silence to hear what nature has to say.

Native Americans know, the Imhofs had already learned, that humans must walk in balance with nature, and balance means that if you give of yourself, you must take back energy and nourishment. Inner balance means that courage must be tempered with wisdom; tenacity with flexibility.

Black Elk, a Lakota medicine man, said, "Everything an Indian does is in a circle, and that is because [nature] always works in circles, and everything tries to be round . . . . The sky is round . . . the earth is round like a ball and so are all the stars. Even the seasons form a great circle in their changing . . . ." The life cycle of a human completes itself in a circle as it becomes a part of the greater universe.[75]

When the Hopi adopted Albert Einstein, he observed that when people see themselves as separate from nature and the universe, they live in a kind of delusional prison, restricted by personal desires and to having affection for only those closest to them. "To free ourselves from this prison," he said, we must widen "our circle of compassion to embrace all living creatures and nature . . . . Nobody is able to achieve this completely, but the striving for this achievement is in itself a part of the liberation and a foundation for inner security."[76]

Native Americans continually ask, like Dr. Adler, "Why am I here? What is my purpose?"[77] Joe Imhof, who had found success in his inventions, his efforts as a portrait painter, continued to ask this universal question and to feel the magnetic pull of the spirituality found in the Native American beliefs and way of life. His restlessness caused him to close his 14th Street studio and house in Englewood Cliffs to again board a steamer for Antwerp with Sallie and Elizabeth.[78]

In April of 1907, the Imhofs met up with Albert Vogel, a German-born American, and his wife in Antwerp. For the first time, the Imhofs transformed themselves into happy tourists traveling with the Vogels through Belgium for a month, and then the Rhineland where they visited many ruined castles. After several months, they worked their way across Germany to Munich where Joe set up another studio from which he journeyed to sketch peasant life.[79]

In Munich, the Imhofs discovered their friend, Clifford Snyder, and, after several months in Munich, Snyder accompanied them to Holland and then to Delft and Edam for more sketching and sightseeing. During this trip to Amsterdam, or perhaps an earlier one, Imhof learned to use casein. Finally, the group returned to Munich where Sallie sensed an intensified restlessness in Joe.[80] Elizabeth, who had reached age nine, had grown more inward, more silent on this trip, yet Sallie, as always, focused her attention on her husband's needs.

While in Europe, Joe continued corresponding with the Albuquerque Indian School superintendent. One day in the early Fall, as Joe and Sallie sat in Joe's Munich studio, Joe abruptly said, "You know, I am getting tired of European culture. Let's go out to New Mexico and see the Indians out there."[81]

Within a few days, Sallie had packed the contents of their studio, and had shipped them to Antwerp where the Imhofs soon followed to board a steamer back to New York. In late October, they spent time saying goodbye to their families and friends, settling business, and making arrangements to leave for Albuquerque, and another way of life and thought.[82]

CHAPTER 8

ALBUQUERQUE BOUND

In 1907 when the Imhofs boarded the train in New York for the Territory of New Mexico, it is doubtful they had any realistic understanding of their destination that lay 2,000 miles to the west. They decided to take, as Sallie said, "a leisurely trip" the last part of October.[1] The timing couldn't have been worse. Unknowingly, they had left just in time for the on-set of the heartland's winter.

They planned to stop first in Washington, D.C. to show Elizabeth, now almost nine years old, the nation's capital. They, of course, hadn't seen the capital either, but Elizabeth always gave them reasons to make decisions that proved satisfactory to themselves. They had all toured the capitals of many European countries, but never their own country. In addition, Elizabeth had attended various schools in Europe and, at intervals, schools in New York and New Jersey.[2]

Because the Imhofs were more experienced in European travel, they possibly thought that train travel across the heartland into the New Mexico Territory would be much like what they'd experienced in Europe; close proximity to villages, well-established cities that could provide them with amenities that would add comfort to travel; frequent stops for personal investigations of their surroundings; and smooth running trains.

Train tracks had been laid across continental United States only thirty-eight years before. Passenger trains had been in use even less time. By the time the Imhofs began their journey across country, at least most passenger cars had been enclosed and the passengers' seats had been cushioned with horsehair underneath the straw-woven seat covers.

In the first week aboard their train, even Sallie confessed to the discomfort they experienced.[3] This marked a major concession on her part since she tended to use euphemisms to gloss over their hardships. When they ran out of money, for example, she usually said they needed to place Elizabeth in school at another location, or that Joe had other business that he needed to take into consideration.

By the time they reached Kansas City, they had decided to get off the train. Sallie recorded that they wanted to get acquainted with midwesterners.[4] More likely, they needed to rest and recover from the train trip. It's equally possible that Joe needed to earn more income working as a printer, something he did regularly when they lived and traveled in Europe, though the Imhofs rarely mentioned this kind of employment.

During the several days the Imhofs stayed in Kansas City, Sallie expressed surprise at the vast differences between the people in Kansas City and those who lived on the Eastern seaboard.[5] What awaited them in Albuquerque, however, would trigger cultural shock when they discovered what seemed more like a foreign country within their own land. It was a country where Anglos made up the minority and the Imhofs would need to adjust to the Spanish and Pueblo cultures.

It is unknown what Joe Imhof learned from his correspondence with the Albuquerque Indian School superintendent. It is certain, however, that Imhof's correspondence provided a catalyst for his seeking the Pueblo people. The Pueblo Indians' need for education probably dominated their letters. Prior to the coming of Anglos, Spanish conquistadors had assigned all education of the Indian and Spanish populations to the Franciscans who tended each mission. After the Spanish withdrew, formal education virtually disappeared, leaving only a few Pueblo Indians who could read and write. In 1858, it was The Reverend Gorman who had started a Baptist missionary at Laguna Pueblo west of Albuquerque near Acoma who first suggested to Agents a central school for the Pueblos. In 1864, United States Indian Agents had recommended that Indian Commissioners build schools and hire teachers for each Pueblo, but the government did nothing.[6]

In about 1880, an Indian Agent solicited Pueblo leaders to send their children to the Carlisle Indian Training School in Carlisle, Pennsylvania. The Zuni Pueblo near Gallup, New Mexico sent two boys and two girls, Laguna sent two boys and a girl, and San Felipe, north of Albuquerque, sent three boys, a small contribution from nineteen pueblos with a population of over 10,000. The next year, the Presbyterian church opened its boarding and industrial school at Albuquerque for the Pueblos. Within six months, Albuquerque bought 65.82 acres of land and donated it to the United States for the Albuquerque Indian School complex. The school was relocated on the land near Albuquerque where Indians could be trained in animal husbandry and agriculture. In addition, day schools began to open in several pueblos.[7]

Even with the dedicated work of a few Indian Agents, droughts, primitive agricultural methods, poor health, and especially smallpox and diphtheria epidemics compounded by worthless vaccines sent by the government, devastated the Pueblos. Within a four year period, from 1890 to 1894, in the Acoma Pueblo, alone, death claimed seventy-eight people.[8]

In 1899, when Indian Agents recommended that the government employ farmers and matrons who would teach better farming and health practices in the pueblos, health and agricultural production began to improve. At the same time, conflicts broke out between Pueblo traditionalists and the newly educated children. The Acoma governor and officials took to whipping people who put on "citizens clothes and cut their hair." An Indian Agent recommended that the governor be removed, saying, "A part of the people of Acoma are disposed to get rid of their old customs and habits, but if they are to be treated as these parties have been it will be bad on all the people; the better class will be discouraged."[9]

The rigid policies of both the United States government and the Indian traditionalists exacerbated the conflict. Agents observed that returning students who had trained as tailors, printers, painters or in other occupations that people had no use for in pueblos, became subject to ridicule by older members of the pueblo. In other instances, the equipment needed for a student's newly learned trade could prove too costly to purchase. Then a number of Pueblo students at the Indian Training School at Carlisle, Pennsylvania refused to return to their pueblos. Even Pueblo elders who visited the Carlisle school could not deny that children who had been listless and dull when they had left their pueblo had blossomed into healthy, alert students whose sharp minds became evident in their enthusiasm for learning.[10]

Joe Imhof's urgency in reaching Albuquerque could have been fueled by the observation that Pueblo traditions and customs had been in a state of flux since the invasion of the conquistadors. Now, at the beginning of the

127

Imhof painting at Acoma Pueblo, 1907-1912.

twentieth century, with the United States government programs and legislation dedicated to assimilating and destroying Indian cultures, these cultures would soon change and possibility become lost forever. The Pueblos were the last Native Americans who not only lived within their own traditional communities, but still governed their own people. The United States government had not yet managed to herd them onto reservations, though it had allowed most of their land to be confiscated by Anglos.

Later in November, when the Imhofs reboarded the train in Kansas City, the Atchison, Topeka and Santa Fe tracks would generally follow the original Santa Fe Trail still in use only a short forty years before. Don Juan de Oñate had founded the village of Santa Fe in 1598, and it had grown to become the center of economic trade for the vast territory north of Chihuahua, Mexico. The long trail south from Santa Fe into Chihuahua had developed into a trade route with the Indians and farming along the Rio Grande. Soon, stories of wealth brought Americans searching for commercial relations with Mexico, all of which the Spanish rejected.[11]

By 1821, however, a regular trade route developed between Independence, Missouri, Kansas City's neighboring town, and Santa Fe. Pack Mules, then heavy wagons drawn by oxen and loaded with glass, cotton cloth, tools and hardware began cutting deep ruts across the vast Kansas plains. The 775-mile journey through the sparsely marked and tediously flat plains moved the traders into Indian territory and the almost impassable Rocky Mountains spilling down from southern Colorado. Santa Fe and Albuquerque lay between the fork created by the Rockies as they plunged into northern New Mexico. The western range of the fork formed the San Juan Mountains which then joined the Jémez Mountains. Within the body of the Jémez rushed the Chama River, a major tributary of the Rio Grande. While the Chama watered and shaped the Jémez, the Rio Grande cut through the entire mountain fork, separating the western range from the eastern that formed the Sangre de Cristo Mountains that became part of the Sandia Mountains near Albuquerque. It took the traders seventy days to reach Santa Fe. The return journey of American traders, loaded with furs, gold, wool, silver and Indian crafts, took only thirty-eight days. The high tariffs and fees charged by Mexican officials still left room for a twenty to forty percent profit for traders. When the United States seized Santa Fe in 1846, and the Mexican War concluded, business rapidly expanded.[12]

The railroads continued laying tracks across the continent when the Union Pacific, building westward from Nebraska, and the Central Pacific, building eastward from California, met in Utah in 1869 to form the first transcontinental railway. That same year, the Atchison, Topeka and Santa Fe

129

Railroad Company completed its first seven miles of track in Topeka, Kansas. The train, traveling fifteen miles per hour, made the seven mile trip in thirty minutes. Santa Fe Railroad intended to extend their tracks to San Francisco and the Pacific, to Galveston and the Gulf of Mexico, to Mexico City and to Santa Fe, New Mexico to capture that legendary trade. In 1878, the first train entered New Mexico. Three years later, in 1881, the Atchison, Topeka and Santa Fe connected with the Southern Pacific in the southwestern corner of New Mexico, at Deming, to form the second transcontinental railroad. Soon the Atchison, Topeka and Santa Fe Railroad overtook the Old Spanish Trail stagecoach as the fastest, least dangerous and most economical way to travel to the West.[13]

The Santa Fe Railway may have improved travel, at twenty miles an hour, but travelers still faced severe hardships as they moved across the flat Kansas plains devoid of towns and other humanity other than buffalo hunters, cowboys, bandits, Indians, miners, and traders. Railway travelers faced days of being exposed to the heat and/or cold, and uneatable food at stops where the train took on water and fuel.[14]

Almost no hotels existed, and the few that had been thrown up along the tracks consisted of shacks with a few cots. Passengers usually found food served by bartenders or saloonkeepers who had no motivation to serve home-cooked meals in the middle of nowhere and without access to food supplies. Those brave enough to order food found rancid and greasy meat, days old coffee, biscuits made without leavening and so old that people called them "sinkers," and canned beans.[15]

If a passenger did order a meal, he usually had twenty minutes in which to order and eat, because the trains stopped only for short periods of time. Many accused the food servers and railroad crews of deliberately planning this scheme to profit from uneaten meals later served to the next innocent traveler. It became a necessity for passengers to carry a shoebox of foods: fried chicken, cheese, bread, fruit, and other edibles that suited different tastes, all of which left passenger cars filled with the constant food odors that did not blend well inside a closed railroad car.[16]

Frederick Henry Harvey knew all about bad food forced upon railroad passengers. He traveled constantly on the Chicago, Burlington, Quincy Railroad, working as a freight agent for that railroad. In his constant travel on Burlington, here was a man who knew the effects of bad food and poor housing on his own precarious health. He also saw an opportunity.[17]

In 1875, he joined with a partner to open two cafes on the Kansas Pacific Railroad, one in Kansas and one in Colorado, while still working full time for Burlington. To further add to his income, Harvey sold advertising for a Kansas newspaper. The standards Harvey demanded for the restaurants helped make them financial successes, but he had to guide them from a distance. His partner disagreed over Harvey's demands for standards, and the two men dissolved their business within a year.[18]

Harvey's extra work in the restaurant business and advertising solicitation provided him enough financial savings to develop his idea of a system of restaurants linked by the railroad. He took his idea to his employer, Burlington Railroad. That railroad's officials were not impressed, nor did they believe that the food business warranted their financial investment. They told Harvey to take his idea to the Atchison, Topeka and Santa Fe Railway, where they "would try anything."[19]

In 1876, the president of Santa Fe Railway not only liked Harvey's idea, but made a handshake agreement to give Harvey a small depot restaurant in Topeka and transport all his needed supplies free of charge. If Harvey made any profit, he could keep it. Harvey hired a friend as manager and the two set about scrubbing floors, cleaning silver, ordering new linen tablecloths, and creating a new menu. Within weeks, train passengers, local businessmen, families, and railroad crews stood in line for the privilege of dining in the new environment. Harvey ordered even fresher food and better recipes. Customers jammed the place.[20]

Two years later, Santa Fe Railway made a more formal agreement for Harvey to manage the depot restaurant in Florence, Kansas. This contract ran for five years, and this time Santa Fe agreed to stop its main passenger trains for two meals per day at the Florence dining room. Santa Fe also agreed that if the railroad added dining cars, the company would take over the Harvey House and pay Harvey an agreed upon price.[21]

Santa Fe renewed and expanded Harvey's contract until 1889 when the railroad management agreed to give Harvey the exclusive right to manage and operate the restaurants, lunchstands and hotel facilities which the Harvey company then owned, leased or would lease in the future on the Santa Fe lines west of the Missouri River. Santa Fe would furnish the coal, ice, and water, and provide free transportation for all Harvey supplies and employees.

Fred Harvey would receive all profits. Harvey restaurants, lunchrooms and hotels expanded west, to Newton, Hutchinson, Dodge City, Kansas; in La Junta and Trinidad, Colorado; and then in Albuquerque; and in small towns in Arizona before reaching California.[22]

The first Harvey restaurants existed under the same roof as the Santa Fe depots and offices. In the more remote areas of New Mexico and Arizona, Harvey used boxcars to house his restaurants. Regardless of the structure, the inside of each Harvey House looked the same: scrubbed floors and facilities, fresh linen and polished silver on each table. Customers found gourmet foods on the menu: fresh fish shipped on ice from the Great Lakes; sea turtles and sea celery from the Gulf of Mexico; cantaloupes from California; beef from Texas, and pork from Kansas; fresh dairy products from Harvey's own dairies in Texas, New Mexico, Arizona and Colorado; various cheeses from northern states; and a multitude of fresh fruits and vegetables.[23]

The Harvey Girls joined Fred Harvey in 1883 after the waiters in Raton, New Mexico got into a brawl one night and cut each other up so badly they couldn't work. Fred Harvey fired all of them, the manager included. According to an article by the writer Erna Fergusson, who would later become a personal friend of the Imhofs, Harvey's new manager suggested that Harvey hire women since they were less likely "to get likkered up and go on tears . . . . Those waitresses were the first respectable women the cowboys had ever seen—that is, outside of their own wives and mothers. Those roughnecks learned manners."[24]

Fred Harvey set up a system for hiring women in the same way he had set standards for his restaurants and hotels. He wanted well-educated women, those with a high school diploma and in more remote areas, at least completion of the eighth grade. Harvey Girls had to speak clearly, use good manners, present a neat appearance, undergo rigorous training, obey all employee rules, and sign contracts of at least a year's length. Thousands applied through advertisements placed in newspapers and magazines.[25]

All Harvey Girls dressed in black shoes, stockings and dresses. A starched white apron and white collar completed the look, while a white bow set off a woman's hair that had been piled on her head. The women lived in chaperoned dormitories, received good wages and railroad passes. Most became fond of the Harvey management that treated their employees fairly, though many found the regular inspections by superintendents daunting.[26]

Santa Fe Railway and Harvey located their restaurants, lunchroom and hotels every hundred miles. In order to keep the trains on schedule, yet allow passengers to enjoy a meal with pleasure, conductors dispensed menus and took orders in advance before telegraphing the information ahead. When passengers arrived, foods had been cooked to order, which allowed the Harvey Girls to work quickly and efficiently.[27]

Still, the West harbored the outlaws, cowboys, railroad crews and miners, men who spent vast hours in the open territory without rules. When they entered a Harvey establishment, however, Fred Harvey expected them to obey the rules and behave like gentlemen. Lamy, New Mexico, the railroad stop where the Imhofs expected to continue their travel by train to Albuquerque, remained the roughest town served by Harvey. Not long before the Imhofs arrived, a gang of gamblers and confidence men had taken over Lamy, robbed the Harvey employees of their money, and ordered meals for which they refused to pay. Then they had ordered the manager to leave town when he refused to give them more food. Instead, he wired Las Vegas, New Mexico, the Santa Fe stop some forty miles northeast of Lamy, for instruction.[28]

Fred Harvey and the cashier from the Harvey Hotel in Las Vegas arrived. The next morning, a dozen toughs barged into the Harvey House, ordered food, ate, and demanded to see the manager. Fred Harvey asked them why they wanted to see the manager. They said they planned to hang him. Harvey replied that he hoped they wouldn't since he needed the manager to run the restaurant. However, the men could hang another man as soon as they paid for their meals. Harvey pointed to the cashier from Las Vegas, a great bull of a man. The cashier glowered as the men threw money on the table and left. Such stories gave rise to the saying that Harvey, his managers, and the Harvey Girls "civilized the West."[29]

The West also took its toll on Fred Harvey who had suffered from yellow fever and typhoid much of his life, and now experienced the agony of recurring colon cancer his last sixteen years. He died in 1901, during the midst of an expansion program with Santa Fe that had seen its passenger loads increase greatly through the imaginative efforts of the Harvey organization. However, Harvey had foreseen his death, and had trained his sons Ford and Byron, and his son-in-law to take over the management and expansion program.[30]

133

To entice even more tourists to travel on the Santa Fe, the Harvey organization commissioned Charles Whittlesey to design a modern railroad complex for Albuquerque, and Mary E. J. Colter, an architect and interior designer, to design buildings and select their furnishings. Colter, an authority on southwestern art and archaeology, used her knowledge to develop structures that combined the traditional Spanish and Indian styles. Colter created a "mission" Spanish and Indian style that made use of porches, adobe, heavy wooden beams, subtly colored tiles, and earth tones of red, brown, blue and orange.[31]

Colter's first large commission from the Harvey organization came with the assignment to design the interior of the Alvarado Hotel and Indian Museum built beside the hotel. The buildings quickly took shape, and the Alvarado Hotel opened in 1902 at Albuquerque. Albuquerque, like many railroad towns, had divided itself into two sections when the railroad came. The original town, founded in 1706, was known to locals as Old Town. New Town came into being when the Santa Fe built its tracks on land one and a half miles east of the original plaza because the company feared flooding from the Rio Grande that flowed nearby. Townspeople watched in dismay as old and new businesses moved to the tent and shanty town forming around Santa Fe's depot and tracks.[32]

In 1901 when Fred Harvey died, Albuquerque consisted of perhaps a hundred wooden shacks and houses built on the sandy soil that held almost no vegetation. The Alvarado Hotel would help change that. When the Alvarado opened, its massive adobe structure imposed itself beside Santa Fe's tracks, and included eighty-nine rooms, a restaurant, and a museum which sold Indian artifacts and crafts. Now New Town had more than tents, a few shacks, a large saloon and red light district close to the railroad station.[33] Though Albuquerque could boast of a first class hotel, civilization would be slow to arrive.

The Santa Fe Railway and the Harvey organization, however, were working on that, too. In 1895, the Santa Fe management hit upon the idea of buying the rights to Thomas Moran's great painting, "Grand Canyon." Moran sold the rights, and Santa Fe had superb lithographic reprints made, which they had framed in handsome gilt frames, then sent to hundreds. The lithograph proved so popular that Santa Fe sent thousands more to schools, offices, hotels, and into homes, any place that might attract passengers.[34]

In another stroke of brilliance, Santa Fe Railway discovered its own advertising genius working as a passenger clerk, William Haskell Simpson. By 1900, he began sending artists into Grand Canyon for two-to-four week excursions to capture the Canyon's grandeur, and these works of art found their way into books, magazines, newspapers, and onto calendars. Simpson then expanded his idea to center on paintings by talented artists who captured the "Santa Fe Southwest," works that portrayed Indians, landscapes, and other Southwest subjects in a kind of romantic realism.[35]

Rather than attempt to continue buying rights to a painting, and thus forever struggle with infringing on an artist's rights, Simpson proposed that Santa Fe Railway buy the paintings outright. In 1903, Simpson purchased Bertha Menzler Dressler's painting, "San Francisco Peaks," the first work that would start a collection of over six hundred paintings. In 1907, alone, he purchased 108 paintings. The romance of the West began to come alive in the minds of Americans as these works of art began appearing on posters, calendars, and in advertising in all print media.[36]

As Santa Fe Railway arranged to send artists into the Southwest to paint the country's magnificent scenery and native peoples, these artists' excursions caught the imaginations of other artists. Simpson acquired most of his paintings from artists who lived in Santa Fe and Taos, and this attracted more artists to New Mexico. Artists whose works Simpson acquired included, in addition to Thomas Moran, Oscar E. Berninghaus, Gunnar M. Widforss, William R. Leigh (known as the "Sagebrush Rembrandt"), Elliott Daingerfield, Walter Ufer, W. P. Henderson, E. Martin Hennings, Gerald Cassidy, Louis Akin, Frank Paul Sauerwein, Bert Geer Phillips, and E. Irving Couse. Through mass distribution of these artists' works, a popularity developed to not only see the Grand Canyon, but to experience the entire Southwest depicted.[37]

In 1907, Santa Fe's advertising director bought three Bert Geer Phillips portraits of Taos Indians to launch the famous Santa Fe Railway calendar which would find its way into 300,000 homes, schools and offices.[38] Joseph Imhof must have been affected by this burgeoning interest in a part of the country that he already felt drawn into.

In fact, the Imhofs could not avoid seeing the art that Santa Fe Railway used to decorate the interiors of its passenger trains and Harvey establishments. It's even possible that the Imhofs became fascinated with one of the Santa Fe menus designed by E. I. Couse, or probably by Oscar Berninghaus, artists they would later know when living in Taos.[39] Joe and Sallie must have anticipated, even perhaps been eager, to see Indians greet them at Las Vegas and then Lamy, New Mexico where they could leave the train to purchase Indian artifacts before reboarding for Albuquerque. By 1907, Santa Fe had blanketed the country with photographs of Indians in New Mexico and Arizona selling their pottery, silver jewelry, and woven blankets to tourists as they stepped off Santa Fe trains.[40]

Santa Fe Railway brochures boasted of outstanding examples of Indian, Spanish, and Mexican antiques and crafts. One Harvey ad read: "See patient Navajo squaws weaving blankets, their men engaged in fashioning showy bracelets, rings, and trinkets . . . . Undisturbed by the eager tourist, the stoic works on as unconcernedly as though in his reservation home." What had started out in Albuquerque as an Indian Museum, built on the flank of the Alvarado Hotel, that took pride in offering only authentic Native American and Spanish art and antiques, evolved into a crafts shop that promoted the mass production of Indian crafts.[41]

By 1907, the Santa Fe and the Harvey Company had begun a dramatic shift away from Indian traditional arts, and toward fulfilling the mass tastes of the Easterners. The mass production of crafts provided financial assistance to the Indian artisans, and a new awareness of native crafts to tourists.[42] All of this awaited the Imhofs, still only vaguely aware of what awaited them as they made their train journey across Kansas.

Not far out of Kansas City, snow began to fall and, within the day, the Imhofs found themselves caught in a howling November snowstorm. Before nightfall, as the train began to slow as it made its way through snowdrifts, they realized that a blizzard raged around them. Powerful winds drove the snow through the windows of the unheated train, and the wet snow further chilled the passengers who now huddled to protect themselves. Those who sought to stop the snow drifting upon them had to tip a porter to secure pillows to stuff against the cracks in the windows.[43]

As children wept from fright and misery, their parents distracted them with the only treat available: a cup of water taken from a tank and drunk from a community cup dangling alongside the tank. Only the fortunate few who had made previous trips knew to bring their own drinking cups. The Imhofs resisted the community cup. What was to have been a few days' journey turned into a nightmare of cold, hunger, and concern about arriving anywhere. Since the train had no dining car, the conductor roamed from seat to seat, asking passengers if they desired a reservation to dine at the Harvey restaurant at the next stop in western Kansas.[44]

The train moved on, slowly pushing its way through the drifts until it arrived in Las Vegas, New Mexico two days later than scheduled, over fifty miles east of Santa Fe, and a good one hundred miles from Albuquerque. Snowdrifts prevented the train from moving any farther. The famed Montezuma Hotel in Las Vegas had long since burned to the ground, but the Harvey organization had built, this time, a more elegant hotel, the eight-year-old Castañeda. This hotel hosted the annual reunion of Teddy Roosevelt's Rough Riders, and had become the favorite among Harvey employees because the people who lived in the small community accepted and welcomed them.[45]

The Castañeda, with its two-story, U-shaped building that had porches extending around its outside walls, faced the great open plains of northeastern New Mexico. The view offered little to the Imhofs, who looked out across a vast snowfield that ended in infinity. The Santa Fe Railway offered the Imhofs one of the hotel's thirty rooms, and welcomed them into its large dining room, and a lunchroom for the few days it would take to clear the tracks.[46]

"We had not expected the tropics," Sallie complained, "but [we] had not realized we would experience such cold weather."[47] At the least, Santa Fe had laid wide tracks to Albuquerque to accommodate its flanged steel wheels, instead of building the kind of narrow gauge tracks that ran from Lamy to Santa Fe. Those passengers had to ride open-sided trains that made their way through mountains by using switchbacks, and, in the dizzying ride, managed to nauseate the passengers. Sallie had still to learn of that ride she would later take.

Within two days, the tracks had been cleared, and the Imhofs reboarded the train for Albuquerque. The reststop had helped them acclimate themselves to their new environment so that now they found the last leg of their journey interesting rather than foreboding. Periodically, the train stopped in what seemed to be the middle of nowhere to pick up hunters bringing their deer horn trophies on board. The Imhofs, always eager to investigate their surroundings, fell into conversations with this new breed of

137

people who were only too willing to regale the uninitiated New Yorkers with tales of adventure. Soon the Imhofs succumbed to the charm of New Mexico ranchers and accepted their western hospitality to visit their ranches. The Imhofs were delighted at invitations to stay as long as they liked. The ranchers, in turn, were charmed by the lively Elizabeth, a small blonde girl of nine years.[48]

The last one hundred miles of train travel to Albuquerque served them well. They made their first friendships among well-known ranchers who would remain their friends in the years to come. For now, though, the Imhofs wanted to hurry on to their destination, possibly to relieve the anxiety that had been building about this Territory where they hoped to live.[49]

The Alvarado Hotel came as a disappointment. Sallie saw it as a small hotel facing the railroad tracks at the end of Central Avenue. Regardless, the people of New Mexico saw the Alvarado as an elegant, first class hotel. People bragged of the Alvarado's sun parlors, its barbershop, club, and reading room in addition to its dining room that served gourmet meals. All the rooms had electricity and thermostatically regulated steam heat. In the spring, summer, and fall, the Alvarado's landscaped surroundings displayed lawns of green grass, walks, shrubbery, and the ever-warm sun parlors.[50] It was the one place where people all over the New Mexico Territory could go for relief from the harsh elements of nature. That, too, would introduce a problem for Sallie.

When the Imhofs stepped into their room, on the second floor at the Alvarado, they hurried to the window for an elevated view of their new town. Instead, long icicles clinging to the window obstructed their view.[51]

CHAPTER 9

LIFE IN ALBUQUERQUE

*F*oreign. Albuquerque was all so foreign, like nothing the Imhofs had seen before. As days piled one upon the other, the foreignness of it did not diminish. Rather, it became more evident. Foreign languages they'd never heard before were spoken by round-faced men with reddish tints to their skins. Their costumes of handwoven cloth were filled with bright colors taken from the rainbow. Other men had more elongated faces, more hair, and still the Imhofs could not understand the language.

For the moment, the blanket of snow seemed to have silenced the land, making the landscape, even the 10,000-foot mountain the Imhofs could see to the east, softer than they might have imagined. Perhaps the snow spoke of their new environment, of living on a more simplified plane, one that would give them relief from their more hectic life in New York.

In the following weeks, as the days warmed, Sallie quickly discovered that the Alvarado Hotel, built in the middle of Albuquerque's New Town, was not the place to keep their young daughter. Cowboys, mountainmen, hunters, and men working on railroad crews sought relief in the Alvarado's cantina where "nobody cared if a man took a drink or if he didn't . . . a handful of men were building the town . . . men [who] could visualize a city behind the frame shanties . . . vast population and a city life . . . the real pioneer spirit, doing the best you can with what you have."[1]

"Doing the best you can with what you have," aptly described the Imhofs' new adventure. They found themselves in a place like no other they had encountered or understood. For the first time, Sallie bumped up against the kind of vulgar, crude behavior she had never before witnessed. She had

139

no idea what awaited her, nor how she would cope. She simply knew she had accommodated herself to other unlikely environments. To her, it was becoming increasingly evident that she viewed and experienced life quite differently from her husband. She realized that she had no choice but to stay in the Alvarado since no better hotels existed in the area. Only time would enable her to meet enough locals to help her evaluate their situation.[2]

Here and there where the snow melted, tufts of native grass began to appear anchored in sand as far as the eye could see to the west, to the south, to the north. The excitement of discovery inspired Joe to inquire about walking the land. He'd already ventured out several times to study the Sandia Mountains that rose with breath-taking suddenness just to the side of the Alvarado Hotel's long verandas. He knew the mountains had to be a good ten miles east from where he stood, but they seemed closer.

This constant watching of the Sandia's northern end gradually began to mesmerize him. He saw that their rugged peaks appeared to glow toward evening, taking on the hues of gold, then pink and mauve. Even the shadows that fell into the crags of the Sandia's sides glowed with reds and shades of mauve. Yet, the sky remained cloudless, an icy deep blue to match the stillness in the air. Was it the air that made him see so clearly? In time, this

"North End of Sandia Mountains, Albuquerque," (oil, 21¼ X 32 in.), ca. 1907.

view of the Sandia Mountains would appear as one of the first paintings he would execute in New Mexico, a twenty-one-by-thirty-two-inch oil titled, "North End of Sandia Mountains, Albuquerque."[3]

Albuquerque's high, dry climate, the Imhofs soon discovered through others they met, attracted people with health problems who sought the healing environment. This high elevation, Joe began to realize, made the air less dense and the dryness created an atmosphere free of distorting particles. The air was clear, almost transparent. The unfiltered light provided him a clarity he had not experienced before and this made him want to see more, to feel the land and understand the people. He pulled on a pair of hiking boots and struck out to the west of the Alvarado Hotel. The Alvarado itself faced west and into the railroad tracks which ran north to south and appeared to act as a dividing line between the new town of wood shacks and tents growing to the east, and the original town to the west. The local residents had built the original town of Albuquerque, Old Town, around the traditional Spanish plaza flanked by the churches, government buildings, and houses. Those of long residence took pride in its bustling population of over six thousand souls.

As he walked, trying to keep his balance to the edge of the road and away from the deep muddied ruts made by wagon wheels, he wondered about these people. He had noticed that the hotel and Indian Museum attached to the hotel employed many people from the surrounding area. He'd seen a supply store and a general store near the hotel, but these hired only a few. At the same time, he felt the confidence of having put aside his earnings from his printing and lithography inventions, his newspaper and advertising creations that now allowed him this time in New Mexico. Still, he wondered how these people survived outside of those who lived off the hotel and general stores.

Most people walked, he noticed, or rode horses. He saw a few families riding in buggies and wagons pulled by horses. He realized that he had had limited experience with horses, including those he had painted in Holland, and in Cody's "Wild West" show. The idea of owning a horse stuck in his imagination.

By the time he reached Old Town, he had not seen one paved road. Now he saw a length of boards nailed together into a walk elevated above the mud and sand. He climbed the steps to the boardwalk that fronted the few stores built around the central plaza. The idea of living on a frontier had its fullest impact: isolation—an isolation that gave him a singular sensation of oneness with himself. As he stepped into the different stores selling feed, clothing, various dried and canned foods, gear for horses and wagons, farm implements, he sensed how he, Sallie and Elizabeth would live.

He introduced himself and discovered these people found him a novelty with his Brooklyn accent and work as an artist, but they accepted him, too, with his openness and his outgoing friendly manner. He inquired about a place to live, and most told him about various boarding houses, places where newcomers lived until they could secure a house. On his walk to Old Town, he had noted that most houses were made of wood, and looked to be three or four rooms, small compared to the stone house where he and Sallie had lived in New Jersey. The idea of living in a boarding house did not trouble him, however, since this would give him time to become acquainted with the pueblos and to determine the length of time he might stay in Albuquerque.

He could see clearly, standing in the plaza, that Albuquerque lay on a sandy plain, almost on a desert floor. Yet, the Rio Grande flowed just out of his sight at the western edge of town. Still, the few hundred wood-framed houses scattered near Old Town did not obstruct the distant mountain ranges shimmering in the distance to the west. They almost looked like a bank of storm clouds, laying the way they did, close to the ground. At dusk, he had seen them turn illusionary, their changing colors of mauve, then purple playing tricks on his eyes. If he had read his maps correctly, and this was a big if because no one had accurately mapped the New Mexico Territory, he would find the Acoma Pueblo some fifty miles further to the west, just before the mountain range.[4]

He looked south and again saw the illusionary cloud bank of purple shapes in the distance resting on either side of the Rio Grande in the flat valley. The Isleta Pueblo would be closer, about forty miles closer. One of the clerks in the Indian Museum had said the Isleta Pueblo lay about twelve miles south. Yes, he and Sallie would visit Isleta first. He headed toward a barn to inquire about buying a horse, maybe a buggy, too. He knew he would need to find a place for his family to live before he purchased a horse and buggy, but he could at least inquire. Perhaps he could rent a horse and saddle.

By now, he had begun to understand many dimensions of New Mexico Territory, things he and Sallie could never have known unless they had experienced them firsthand. He had not expected to see so many Spanish and so few Anglos. When he had inquired at the Alvarado Hotel's Indian Museum, he had been told that the three separate cultures—Spanish, Indian, and Anglos—lived side-by-side in the Territory, but lived separately. The Spaniards, who had failed in assimilating the Indians into the Spanish way of life after nearly four hundred years of killing and deprivation of these original inhabitants, had stayed, even in their failure, to form the majority. Anglos now comprised the new minority. When Joe thought about this, it coincided with what Sallie had found during her research just before they had left New York.

Had it not been for the ancient Aztecs who had spoken to the Spanish conquerors of the Aztec ancestors who lived in the legendary seven cities to the north, the invaders might not have been so persistent. When the Spanish invaders heard the stories of these cities, their dreams of easy riches transformed legendary Indian cities into the fabled seven cities of gold. When, in 1532, the news reached New Spain that Francisco Pizarro had discovered rich deposits of gold in Peru, the information served to confirm New Spain's conquistadors' quest for the legendary El Dorado.[5]

Cabeza de Vaca's and Estévan's, his Moorish slave, arrival in 1536 at Mexico City with tales of their six-year journey from Florida further excited the Spanish. Cabeza de Vaca told of crossing swamps and inlets in their own hand-made boats, of hiding from Indians in forests, and coming across the Rio Grande before turning south into Mexico. At this juncture, he said, they had discovered Indians to the north living in multistoried houses and wearing handwoven clothes of cotton adorned with jewelry of coral and turquoise. These tales seemed to confirm the Spaniards' belief that cities of gold awaited in the north for their taking.[6]

The Spanish organized an expedition to the north, using Estévan as guide and Franciscan friar Marcos de Niza as leader. After months of travel, Estévan did discover several Zuni villages scattered over a fifteen mile area, but, instead of streets paved with gold, they found mud houses, some multistoried, made by a people living in them. Within a short time, the Zuni killed Estévan, and his companions fled back to Fray Marcos' main expedition. Marcos retraced his steps to Mexico City and told stories of their

143

wondrous discoveries: cities of "emeralds and other jewels—vessels of gold and silver—whereof there is greater and more abundance than in Peru."[7]

Perhaps Marcos, too, had experienced the transforming magic of the evening light that might have played tricks on his vision, turning the distant desert into cities of gold. Marcos referred to his discovery as *Cibola*, which the imaginative Spanish then termed the Seven Cities of Cibola, and later, the Kingdom of Cibola. King Charles V, grandson of Isabella and Ferdinand and ruler of Europe from Holland to the boot of Italy, placed the thirty-year-old Vasquez de Coronado as head of the expedition to conquer Cibola. He also implored Coronado to treat the Indians well, since he'd received reports of their mistreatment.[8]

In 1540, Coronado set off with a massive expedition of 336 Europeans, four friars, eight hundred Indians, ten European and Indian women, and over one thousand horses, plus hundreds of sheep, goats, and cattle. It was Coronado who introduced the first horses to the Southwestern region that would cradle the first European civilization in the interior of the United States. In full armor and decorated, steel helmets, Coronado and his men finally came upon the Zuni villages near Gallup, New Mexico. The Zuni resisted, hurling stones at the Spanish whose superior weapons helped them force the Zuni to surrender.[9]

Much to his amazement, Coronado discovered a dusty village where the Zuni barely scraped out a living from the high desert soil. He sent Fray Marcos back to Mexico City in disgrace. Coronado then set up his base in the Zuni Pueblo, and sent out smaller expeditionary forces: Pedro de Tovar and Fray Juan de Padilla went north to the Kingdom of Tusayan, which happened to be where the Hopi lived; Garcia López Cárdenas marched toward a large canyon, which happened to be the Grand Canyon; and Hernando de Alvarado set off for reported villages along the Rio Grande and Pecos River located in New Mexico.[10]

Alvarado traveled into the Rio Grande Valley, and then turned north until he came to the Taos Pueblo. He sent word to Coronado that an area he called Tigeux had impressed him most. Coronado and his forces arrived first near the Isleta Pueblo, then turned north, following the Rio Grande to Tigeux near Bernalillo, before exploring Taos and then east of an area around the Santo Domingo Pueblo where they discovered the turquoise deposits that the Indians had mined for hundreds of years.[11]

That winter in 1541, a Plains Indian living in the Pecos Pueblo told Coronado of a village to the east where the people made gold jewelry. Coronado gathered his forces and followed the Indian, but when a severe winter halted the group, he ordered his forces to take over an Indian Pueblo where he confiscated their food supplies. The Indians rebelled and Coronado had hundreds of Indians burned at the stake after he destroyed a village. In the Spring, with the Indian guide, he and his men moved east, looking for gold. They crossed the Texas and Oklahoma panhandles and got as far as Salina, Kansas before they discovered they had been tricked by the Indian. They executed him and returned to Tigeux.[12]

In 1542, Coronado, who had been injured when his horse had fallen, led his forces back to Mexico City with news that they had found no gold. It would be forty years before the Spanish invaded again, this time looking for silver. In 1581, Fray Augustine Rodríguez and Captain Francisco Chamuscado set out through Chihuahua, Mexico for Tigeux. They established the El Camino Real which, in time, would become the trading route followed by North Americans as they traveled the Santa Fe Trail to New Mexico then turned south into Mexico. Had Chamuscado's expedition continued north-west some two hundred miles into the San Juan Mountains, they might have discovered the fabulous silver veins near present-day Silverton, Colorado. Instead, Chamuscado passed through the desolate land, *Jornada del Muerto*, where over three hundred years later the first atomic bomb would be dropped.[13]

Chamuscado's expedition found no gold or silver, but believed a trade route could be established with the Indians who made exceptionally fine cotton goods. Three friars remained, just as had three remained from Coronado's group. A year later, Antonio de Espejo and Fray Bernaldino Beltrán led another expedition and discovered that the Indians had killed all of the friars. Espejo's name remains in history records because it was he who coined the name Nuevo Mexico, New Mexico.[14]

Not until 1598 did the Spanish return. Many changes had taken place by this time: Spain was in decline, and the Spanish in New Spain (Mexico) had begun to intermarry with the Indians. The expedition's leader, Juan de Oñate, had married a descendant of both Cortez and Montezuma, the Aztec chief. This time Oñate brought four hundred men of whom one hundred and thirty of the men brought their wives and families, and seven thousand cattle. Oñate followed the Camino Real to the valley bordered on the east by the Sangre de Cristo Mountains, so named the Blood of Christ because the red and mauve colors toward evening transformed the mountains into a red glow that reminded the Spaniards of Christ's blood.[15]

Oñate took over an Indian village east of the Rio Grande and renamed it San Juan de los Caballeros, before taking the settlement to the west side of the Rio Grande. This pueblo he named San Gabriel del Yunque. Immediately, Oñate had a chapel built. When the settlers could not find enough Indians to perform the farm labor, they had to resort to farming the land themselves. The experience further frustrated the new settlers to the hard life, because the soil did not easily give its fruit to anyone. Oñate decided his group needed room to expand, and sent his nephew to take food from the Acoma Pueblo.[16]

The Acoma Pueblos did not take kindly to this act of theft. They killed the nephew and several other Spaniards. Oñate retaliated, killing over six hundred Acoma before capturing the remaining villagers and hauling them off to Santo Domingo where he cut off one foot of all males over twenty-one and carted away sixty girls to convents in Spain. The killings and destruction continued in other pueblos, creating a reservoir of hatred for the Spanish.[17]

In addition, Oñate did not command respect even as a leader among the Spanish, so he began exploring into other areas west, including California. Most of the Spanish settlers deserted before the viceroy of Mexico recalled Oñate and sent Pedro de Peralta with orders to establish a provincial capital of the kingdom of New Mexico that was defensible and had good grazing for cattle. Peralta's expedition moved near an abandoned pueblo in northern New Mexico where he laid out the town of Santa Fe in 1610. There it has continued as the capital city, making it the oldest capital in the United States. Peralta also built the Palace of the Governors as official residence for himself and subsequent rulers.[18]

Then he began building mission churches. By 1625, over fifty such missions dotted the Rio Grande valley where Franciscans set about claiming Indian souls. In 1680, eighty missions had been built. While attempting to re-educate the Indians to Christianity, the Franciscans added to the Indians' knowledge of building multistoried houses of mud, instructing them how to use sun-dried bricks called adobe. The Franciscans, using Indian labor, had trees cut into forty-foot beams to brace the adobe walls that rose thirty-five feet in height and were five to eight feet thick. The mission churches' twin towers now rose high above the Indians' dwellings.[19]

While Spanish-imposed laws allowed the settlers to use Indian labor a certain number of hours for building, farming, and weaving garments, the settlers and Franciscans became greedy, and eventually turned the Indians into slaves. During the 1630s, Indians in the Jémez and Taos Pueblos rebelled against this forced labor and killed their Spanish priests. Again, the Franciscans and Governor revenged their losses, this time more savagely. Then in 1675, the Franciscans resorted to hanging and imprisoning the Pueblo Indian religious leaders, or shamans, the Spanish accused of practicing witchcraft. Systematically, the priests burned and destroyed all the kivas.[20]

As a result, seventy Pueblo warriors stormed the Palace of Governors and demanded the release of the jailed shamans. Otherwise, the Indians said, they would refuse to help fight the marauding Apaches who now used Spanish horses to raid the missions. One of those released, Popé, fled to Taos where he helped organize the 16,000 to 30,000 Pueblo Indians against the nearly 2,400 Spanish. In 1680, the Indians attacked, killing at least four hundred Spanish, and twenty-one of the thirty-two priests. Survivors took refuge in the Palace of Governors where they managed to kill over three hundred Indians, but, still, the Spanish had to surrender. Over one thousand Spanish retreated to Mexico. By then, the more than ninety Indians villages that Oñate had counted in 1598, had shrunk to half that number.[21]

The Pueblo Indians then reconstructed the Palace of Governors to suit their needs before destroying any evidence that the Spanish had ever existed on Pueblo land. Only the Isleta Mission Church and the Acoma Mission Church survived the rampage.[22]

But the Spanish were not discouraged. Twelve years later, in 1692, Captain General Diego de Vargas Zapata Lujan Ponce de León y Contreras led an expedition back up the Rio Grande to New Mexico, this time arriving peacefully at the Hopi mesas. He returned to Mexico, triumphant. The next year he led a resettlement group of soldiers, families, more priests, a few Indians, and animals to Santa Fe. They camped outside the Palace of Governors and, when winter arrived and their food supply dwindled, they asked the Indians to allow them into the Palace and to share their food. The Indians, who observed that the Spanish had little changed, refused. A ferocious battle ensured and the Spaniards killed nearly one hundred Indians while taking another four hundred as slaves.[23]

In the coming three years, some of the most terrible battles in Pueblo history erupted in the San Ildefonso, Jémez and Acoma Pueblos. Many Rio Grande Pueblo people fled to live with the Navajo and Hopi. In 1695, fifteen hundred more settlers arrived in Santa Fe. Vargas founded two more towns, or villas: Santa Cruz de Cañada, and Villa de Albuquerque, in 1706, named for the Viceroy of New Spain.[24]

With more established villages, the Apache raids increased. Their marauding attacks finally gave the Spanish and Pueblo Indians a common enemy. Together, they fought the Apache, then the Comanche, and finally the Ute. In 1739-40, French explorers began arriving at the Taos summer fair, an unorthodox event in which both friendly and hostile Indians traded with the Spanish. Within ten years, however, the Spanish closed the fair to French, fearing their encroachment.[25]

In 1779, the Spanish made Juan Bautista de Anza governor of New Mexico. Anza had already helped settle California, and founded the city of San Francisco. In New Mexico, he managed to finally subdue the Comanche, the Apache, and the Hopi who had suffered even more from drought and an epidemic of smallpox brought by the Spanish.[26]

By 1805, Lieutenant Pike, on an expedition, had found the Rockies. He built a stockade in the San Luis Valley where the Spanish found him and took one member of his expedition back to Santa Fe for questioning. However, trappers based in America had already discovered Santa Fe and trade had already begun. Then the people of New Spain revolted against their Spanish oppressors in a war that lasted from 1810-1815. When the Mexican revolution finally ended, Spain granted Mexico independence in 1821. The Mexican government, in turn, granted the Pueblo Indians full citizenship.[27]

Gradually, the Spanish began withdrawing their Franciscan priests from New Mexico since the costs of maintaining the missions had become too great. In addition, the priests, after all these years, still had not been able to convert the Pueblo Indians to Christianity. Then more turmoil ensued when the new government in Mexico decided to install a Mexican governor instead of allowing a New Mexican Hispanic to assume the position. For once, the Indians joined with the Spanish New Mexicans in a revolt that drove the appointed governor from the Palace. They captured him in the Santo Domingo Pueblo, and killed him.[28]

148

Immediately, the General Assembly of New Mexico elected an Indian living in the Taos Pueblo as governor just before the Mexican government could send troops to put down the rebellion. When troops did arrive, the New Mexicans drove out the troops at about the same time Texans pushed the Mexicans from the Republic of Texas. In 1845, the United States annexed the Republic of Texas. The next year, President James Polk declared war on Mexico when the Mexican government refused to negotiate a transfer of lands east of the Rio Grande claimed by Texas. General Kearny led his troops into New Mexico and retook the territory.[29]

At General Kearny's direction, Fort Marcy arose just north of Santa Fe's plaza to become the first American fort in the Southwest. Before General Kearny departed for California, he chose Charles Bent of Taos as governor. In several months, however, the Spanish in New Mexico began to fear losing their lands and they, in turn, conspired with the Pueblo Indians to oust the Americans.[30]

The rebels struck at Taos first where they murdered Governor Bent. American troops stormed the mission church at Taos Pueblo where the last of the rebels held forth. Cannons blew holes through the mission church walls, demolished the church, and killed two hundred Pueblo Indians.[31] The Taos Pueblos never rebuilt the mission church, nor did they clear away the ruins. Instead, they kept the partially demolished structure to remind them of their sovereignty. In time, they would honor one man, Joseph Imhof, with a charred beam from the ruins.

In 1848, the next year, Mexico transferred the New Mexico Territory to the United States which, in turn, paid Texas for its claims to the land.[32]

With continued Apache, Comanche, Navajo, and Kiowa Indian raids, the United States built more forts to protect its settlers and travelers. The realization that the last conqueror, the Americans, had used tax and other laws to strip the native New Mexicans of Spanish descent of the thirty-five million acres originally owned by them must have struck Joe as a paradox as he felt the land beneath him. He could not fathom how much the Pueblo Indians must have lost.[33]

Was it any wonder that the superintendent of the Indian School had described the Pueblo Indian children as dull and listless? The superintendent had written of this demeanor as if it reflected a natural state. It was a wonder that the Pueblos even existed after nearly four hundred years of

149

killing and re-education by the Spanish and Americans. Joseph Imhof again felt the urgency of a mission that he knew belonged to him: the accurate rendering of the Pueblo people and the beliefs that had sustained their survival for thousands of years.

When Joe returned to the Alvarado Hotel, he described to Sallie what he had found, the information he had learned about where they might live, and his urgency to begin work. In his absence and in the previous weeks, she had been making inquiries, too. She agreed that they should move to a rooming house soon, that she knew where they could secure a letter of reference and introduction.[34]

By the time the snow had cleared in the next few weeks, the Imhofs had their letter of reference and an introduction to a widow who owned a large house at Second and Gold Streets, about a half mile west of the Alvarado Hotel.[35] In reality, there were no houses at Second and Gold, only buildings that rented rooms. Sallie recorded that they "rented two apartments, shall we call them, and those were our quarters for some time."[36] The so-called apartments amounted to two rooms in a boarding house, and the time they lived in those two rooms would amount to possibly two years. For now, though, Sallie had something else nearby she wanted to explore: The University of New Mexico.

The Imhofs, of course, had heard of the University before they had arrived. They hadn't imagined that it would become Sallie's refuge from isolation and cultural shock in this harsh land, and the source of her friendships. It had, after all, only been in existence for fifteen years before the Imhofs had arrived.[37]

Like all other creations shaken into life upon this land, the University had had a difficult birth in a Territory so poverty stricken that it did not even have a high school. The United States Congress, in 1854, had granted the Territory of New Mexico 46,080 acres to establish a university in the Territory. However, the grant was not available until New Mexico became a state, and no one knew when that might transpire.[38]

What few schools existed in the Territory were in deplorable condition and, since laws did not permit towns to levy taxes for educational purposes, most people depended upon private or church-related schools. Congress had granted a certain amount of money to each state and Territory for agricultural experiment work. In the Territory of New Mexico, various districts and counties began to compete for these funds.[39]

After the territorial legislature accepted these funds, legislators began to debate over where they would locate an institution to use the money. There were some who did not want to establish any institution of higher learning, because the Territory had so few financial resources. Others wanted a singular university located in Albuquerque. A consensus finally concluded that Albuquerque "could not hope to obtain a school that would include the University, Agricultural College, and School of Mines, and that it would be best to accept the University."[40]

In an act of courage and faith, the territorial legislature passed a bill, in 1889, that provided for the location of the University at Albuquerque, the School of Mines at Socorro, the Agricultural College at Las Cruces, and the Insane Asylum at Las Vegas.[41] In 1892 the University of New Mexico opened the doors to its first building and 108 students.[42]

The University made its home on a mesa about two miles east of the village of Albuquerque, all due to the legislative bill that stipulated "that the school should be located not more than two miles north of Railroad Avenue on high and dry ground." Land was then donated for the University's specific location.[43]

When Joe, Sallie, and the ten-year-old Elizabeth walked the three-quarters mile from their boarding house to the University campus, they found an incongruous campus located in a scattering of trees that had been planted in the sand: one wood shack used as a gymnasium, a pueblo, and two square, red-brick multistoried buildings that looked like they belonged in the age of Queen Victoria. The just-completed brick and sandstone science building, "Hadley Climatological Laboratory," shone against surrounding desert sands. Hadley Hall, as it was called, had come to life through donations from students, the legislature, and the widow of the late Walter Hadley whose father had been the University's vice president under the University's first president.[44]

Only the one building, a boys' dormitory built in the style of a pueblo, looked as if it belonged to its surroundings. It was one of the first pueblo-style buildings the Imhofs had seen and, when they inquired among their new acquaintances about its origin, they learned of Dr. George Tight, the current and third president of the University.[45]

George Tight had received his doctorial degree in geology from the University of Chicago in 1901, the same year he became president of the University of New Mexico at a salary of two thousand dollars per year. Dr.

Tight, who had already taught geology at Denison University for fourteen years, had been born in Ohio.[46]

As a geologist, Dr. Tight knew how to look at the land. In one of his first actions, he sent students into the mountains to bring back trees, and began a tree-planting program that brought in trees from all over New Mexico. From his native Ohio, he brought back squirrels to help propagate the trees. He found water and improved a deep well on the campus where he started an experimental irrigation project. By late 1908, a total of five thousand trees and plants had been set out, a well dug to irrigate, and a windmill built to power the irrigation project.[47]

In the pueblo, he saw not only the artistry of what the Pueblo people had created, but he found an ecologically sound building. As he traveled on University business throughout the Territory, he began a study of pueblo buildings. He photographed the pueblos and mounted the photographs in his office for further study "until his room looked like a sort of picture gallery."[48]

He measured and graphed every detail: windows, walls, ladders, building materials. Then he put the faculty and students to work with him, constructing University buildings using the pueblo design. Faculty members, including John D. Clark, a newly appointed chemistry professor, and Dr. Tight, acted as architects, carpenters, plumbers, painters. "Dormitory walls were left 'entirely bare of decoration, paper.'" The University's yearly student magazine, *Mirage*, in 1907 noted that the Indians designs were taken from art at a time when the Pueblo Indians had reached the height of their civilization. The dormitory chandelier was shaped like an Indian swastika with electric lights suspended from each corner. The fireplace andirons were "gigantic swastika pins." And students decorated their own rooms, using "Indian blankets on the floor, Indian pictures on the walls, curtains decorated with Indian symbols." The University's English teacher, Ethel Hickey, christened the men's and women's dormitories Kwataka and Hokona, names taken from Indian legends.[49]

The addition of the pueblo style women's dormitory had come into being by September 1908, as had other pueblo style buildings: the president's home, the Tri-Alpha fraternity, the large administration building, and the central heating plant. The arbor-theater, which would become an important part of Sallie's life, had been started and the campus boasted of an outdoor gymnasium of bars, rings, and swings, plus two good tennis courts.[50]

152

In a stroke of advanced technology, Dr. Tight designed a solar heating system for the dormitories, using a tank and heater on the roof of each building. The heating system saved the University water, time, and expense. The pueblo designs and solar system also cost Dr. Tight his position.[51]

Bitter hostility arose over Dr. Tight's new ideas for the University campus. A common opinion complaint: "If you are going to be consistent, the president and faculty should wear Indian blankets around their shoulders and feathered coverings on their heads." As one faculty member pointed out, " . . . the people did not seem to think it odd to go back several thousand years to copy Greek architecture, but they could not tolerate what belonged to their own land."[52]

Dr. Tight was dismissed in 1910. That same year, Hadley Hall burned and the University's new president decided that he would use more economy in any future building. However, others had already seen Dr. Tight's vision, and the Santa Fe Railway began using the pueblo design for all of their hotels and restaurants. Dr. Tight's artistic vision for the University's architectural design would not be realized until 1927 when the Board of Regents formally adopted the pueblo style for the University's building program. In time, the design would be recognized as the Southwestern contribution to the American culture.[53]

The Imhofs' excursion onto the campus in 1908 would bind them in a relationship with the University that would last decades beyond their lives. For Sallie, the University offered her an opportunity to extend her education and make new friends. For the time, she decided she could walk the distance to class since Albuquerque's lone form of transportation, a horse car, only traveled from the New Town railroad station to the jail on West Central Avenue in Old Town.[54]

After making inquiries at the University, Sallie enrolled in "Chemistry of Foods and Nutrition," taught by Professor Clark, who had also arrived in 1907. The class became the first of many that Sallie would take at will. By the time classes started, Charles Weber of the University had given Sallie a fox terrier, the first of many dogs the Imhofs would own. Years later, Sallie recalled that the fox terrier loved to attend Dr. Clark's chemistry classes. "She would sit there quietly all day," Sallie said, "and trot home again at night."[55]

Within two years, Sallie would enroll in classes taught by Miss Josephine S. Parsons who had been hired as "Secretary of the Faculty at a salary of

153

$100.00 a year."[56] Her skills would soon take her to becoming Principal of the Commercial Department.[57] The English, spelling, grammar, composition, and stenography Sallie would learn under Miss Parsons would help her manage Joe's work, and prepare her for later secretarial positions in New York and Taos.

The 156 students enrolled at the University of New Mexico that year in 1908 with Sallie may have received a superior education. The University had already produced a Rhodes Scholar in 1905, and would produce another in 1908. Karl G. Karsten, a 1911 Rhodes Scholar, would become one of the Imhofs' best friends.[58]

While Sallie attended classes at the University, Joe, who had already established himself as a portrait painter on the East Coast, began to paint as he waited for the roads, that would take him to the Isleta Pueblo, to become passable.[59] In one of his first portraits painted in Albuquerque, and one of the few he dated, he depicted an elderly man, his eyes shifted to the left, either in deep thought or concern with some event to his left.[60] Imhof painted the oil in the style of the seventeenth century Dutch painter, Rembrandt, when his self-portraits conveyed "Everyman's painful journey through the world."[61] Like Rembrandt, Imhof made use of the psychology of light cast on the facial expression to communicate the care-worn face. Imhof's subject wears the clothes and facial hair typical of men who traveled and lived during this country's frontier period at the turn of the century. The man's dark coat probably represents the best he has to wear. His full, bushy mustache has been carefully trimmed, and tufts of hair puffed on each side of his head add to the impression that he has aged beyond his years. It is the kind of aged, and concerned look that Joseph Imhof himself would develop during his years in New Mexico (see page 163).

Perhaps the painting hinted of a revelation to the Imhofs, that they had been touched as never before by a land of great hardship and poverty. Hardships had come in such unexpected ways. Even New Mexico's dry climate added to an individual's aged look.

As the road dried in the Spring of 1908, the dirt hardened into ruts that began to fill with sand that shifted and spun with the winds that picked up velocity in March. For two months, the wind storms would alter life in the plains surrounding Albuquerque. Joseph Imhof would need to learn to protect himself when he made his way into the countryside.

CHAPTER 10

DISCOVERING THE PUEBLOS

In the Spring of 1908, Joe bought the first of three horses he would own while living in Albuquerque. In time, he would buy three conveyances: a buggy, surrey and wagon. The wagon he would outfit with a covering that would protect him and his family from the harsh rays from the sun, and from the sudden and powerful thunderstorms that continually formed in the summer when heat, moisture and electricity collided. The horse-drawn vehicles would take him and his family across distances, such as the trip he now planned to take to the Isleta Pueblo.[1]

He bought a saddle, too, in case something should happen to the conveyance. He could saddle his horse and ride for help, or he could park his rig and ride his beautifully gaited saddle horse into terrain made difficult by the landscape. He learned to rig the wagon with hoops, then use tarpaulin to cover the hoops, making it into a covered wagon where he could live in the wilderness for weeks.[2]

That Spring, Joe packed the buggy with his sketchbooks, paint supplies, and camera before he set off with Sallie and Elizabeth for Isleta.[3] The pueblo lay twelve miles to the south, a leisurely day's journey. As they followed the trail south, the intricate patterns of the land began to weave themselves into his life. Cottonwood and willow trees grew densely along the banks of the Rio Grande, and the river exposed the rich volcanic ash hidden beneath the sand. This was the river, he knew, that had given birth to the golden age of the great Pueblo civilization.

As they drew near Isleta, he saw in the flat bottom land of the Rio Grande an entire village rising from the earth. The countryside, indeed, the

155

whole territory, seemed made up of earth villages that he could not have imagined unless he had seen them with his own eyes. It was awesome.

Imhof by his white covered wagon near a Rio Grande pueblo, 1907-1912.

When they entered the pueblo, Indians appeared everywhere, their clothing splashed with the colors he had seen when he had first arrived in Albuquerque. As was the custom of the time, Joe pulled the buggy up to the Isleta's general store where he would introduce himself and make his inquiries. Here he met Pablo Abeita who had, since 1905, operated his family's store at Isleta.[4] Abeita, no doubt, wore the typical Isleta fashion. His ever-present red undershirt sleeves and neck could be seen peeking from under a lacy-front white shirt. His Pueblo-style belt was a handwoven red sash with fringes carefully placed on the right side. When outdoors, he always wore a tall, white Stetson hat with no crease, and a straight brim.[5]

In another of those strange coincidences that marked Joe's life, he would discover that Pablo Abeita had been born in the same year as himself, in 1871.[6]

For now, though, he fell into conversation in his easy-going and friendly manner, with the kind of openness that caused others to trust him. As he introduced himself and his family, he must have been aware that he had met an extraordinary man in Pablo Abeita.

In 1889, at the age of nineteen, Pablo Abeita had been appointed by the governor of his tribe to serve on the All Indian Pueblo Council. It was a position he still held when Joe met him. Abeita's exceptional abilities had years before been evident to the local Catholic priest who enrolled Abeita in a Jesuit school at Old Albuquerque. From there, Abeita transferred to St. Michael's College in Santa Fe. His ten years of formal education became a rare scholarly achievement in the Territory. When he completed his education, he returned to Isleta Pueblo.[7]

However, before joining his family's business, he worked as a typesetter at the Albuquerque newspaper, and as a resident farmer, the equivalent of an extension agent, for Pueblo Indians. In 1913, Abeita would be appointed a judge, then, in 1922, elected Secretary of the All Indian Pueblo Council, "which fought the Indian Service in favor of self-government within the pueblos." In his capacity with the Pueblo Council, he would travel to Washington, D.C. and counsel nine Presidents of the United States, four of them before having met the Imhofs.[8] In the years ahead, he would also visit the Imhofs in New York, and name one of his five sons, Andrew, after one of Joe's middle names.[9]

Pablo Abeita was respected by all the Pueblo Indians. Some said he might have become governor of the state of New Mexico if he had so chosen. He spoke English, Spanish, and his own language, Tiwa, fluently. His wry sense of humor must have appealed to Joe, as did his use of "quaint sarcasm rather than malicious barbs" when criticizing an opponent.[10]

In time, as the relationship between Joseph Imhof and Pablo Abeita evolved over their lifetimes, Pablo would be among the first of the Pueblo people who would teach Joe about the ancients as told through the Pueblo people's collected memories, and their song and dance ritual ceremonies. It's possible that Imhof did not know that "these people had no written history; theirs was an oral system of maintaining the records of ages." The Pueblo people passed the history of their people from one generation to the next through reverent narration expressed through ritual dance and mime.[11]

They believe their ancestors, Aboriginal people, roamed throughout the Southwest, gathering seeds, plants and hunting, as far back as ten thousand years before Christ. Joe S. Sando, the godson of Pablo Abeita's son, José Simon, points to research that suggests that some native North Americans originated in the Tehuacan Valley of Mexico. In a period of about 5,000 B.C., these people began consuming chilies and avocados. Two thousand years later, they had domesticated a grain, corn, that had originated in the Americas.[12]

Sando indicates that the Pueblo Indians probably brought fragments of the Mesoamerican civilizations with them to the Southwest, and that this can be seen in the similarities between the Pueblos and the Olmec, Toltec and Mayan civilizations. By the time the Pueblo Indians brought domesticated corn to the Southwest, corn could be found being used by most Indian civilizations in the southern hemisphere. Columbus and his brother, Diego, found corn growing in Cuba, Central America, Peru, Bolivia, and Mexico; in each country, they observed how the Indians attended every aspect of corn by sacred ceremonies.[13]

The story of corn, Joseph Imhof would learn throughout his years in New Mexico, is the story of the Indians; that the Indian is corn. The Pueblo Indians' traditional story of their relationship with corn begins with their emergence from the underworld. Although there are three different language families among the Pueblos, they all define themselves by a similar emerging story. They believe they struggled to ascend through four different worlds: the world of fire, that split from the sun to create earth, and has the color of red that opens to the east; the world of breath, since it is an act of prayer to breathe, that has the color of blue that opens to the south; the world of water, born from underground lakes and rivers, and has the color of yellow that opens to the west.[14]

These stories tell of the destruction of the earth several times. Those people who kept their pureness and connection to the spirit were saved. In the last destruction, they went underground and lived with the ant people until the earth was ready to be repopulated. At that time, the people ascended into the fourth world that has the color of white, the color of light that opens to the north.[15]

The people then came from their sacred place of origin, Shibapu (spelled Shipap and Sipapu by different Pueblos), in the north, and emerged by way of a lake. The Great Spirit who accompanied the emerging people gave them corn, and that is how they lived. In the mornings they prayed, scattering corn pollen as a gift to the Great Spirit. At the naming of a baby, they gave the child a first meal of corn. From then on the child became a part of corn. Pueblo Indians vowed to always keep the trust of the corn, the only grain that depends on the hand and care of man. Of all the grains, only corn cannot sow itself.[16]

Pablo Abeita continued the ancient ritual of scattering corn pollen to the winds in his prayer every morning, and he possibly described this prayer ritual to Joe. Sometimes Abeita prayed at night to the creator and to the stars.[17]

The traditional story tells of how the Great Spirit guided the ancient ones through many arduous tasks and, for ages, led them from place to place upon the continent. Many of them settled in the Four Corners area where they developed their civilization over hundreds of years. To prevent the people from being annihilated, the Great Spirit caused them to move in different directions, which is how they developed different dialects.[18]

According to their oral history passed down by many generations, the Tanoans arrived first in the Southwest and settled around the Cortez, Colorado area, and moved into Mesa Verde. The Keresans arrived sometime later and occupied Chaco Canyon. They brought with them the Bear Cult and Corn Dance.[19]

The Pueblo Indians, having arrived in these different groups, have three different language groups and, among the language groups, dialects. Tiwa, spoken by Pablo Abeita and the people of Isleta Pueblo, belongs to the Tanoan language which has three dialects: Tiwa, Tewa, and Towa spoken by eleven different pueblos. Joseph Imhof, with his faculty for speaking languages, probably learned the Tanoan language to enable him to speak freely with the Isleta and Taos people. In time, he might have spoken the Keresan language of the Acoma, Cochiti, Santo Domingo, and four other pueblos. Only the Zuni, he would discover, spoke the Zuni language.[20]

Somewhere between 2,000 and 1,000 B.C., the Pueblo Indians began to plant small ears of corn and, over a period of some one thousand years, the growing of corn began to change their lives. Between 500 and 300 B.C., they established permanent villages, planting corn, squash, beans, chilies, and other vegetables. They dug pits to store their corn and keep it safe from rodents and spoilage.[21]

They used this same idea of the pit to construct their homes. They would excavate a shallow pit and build walls with upright poles, then fill in the spaces with mud before plastering the walls with more mud. For the roof, they used timber, brush and twigs plastered with mud. The sunken floor protected them from the heat and cold.[22] Joseph Imhof would use this same design to build his own studio to protect his work from the sand driven by the winds.

One of the last migratory groups to come down from Western Canada were the Athapaskan hunters. Their arrival in about A.D. 1500 would cause the Zuni Pueblo Indians to call them "Apache," which means enemy. Over time, the Spanish would name them "Apache de Nabaju." Eventually, they would split apart and become known as two separate people, the Navajo and the Apache.[23]

From the Pueblo Indians, the Navajo learned sandpainting, weaving and lodge building.[24] The Pueblo people were multilingual long before the Spanish arrived, speaking the Keresan language and the Tanoan dialects, as well as Zuni and Hopi. Many could converse freely in the Navajo, Kiowa, Apache, and Comanche languages.[25]

During the twelfth century, a severe drought ensued that lasted over many years. The ancient ones told of Mother Earth splitting apart. The Pueblo people then moved from the four corners area to the land around the Rio Grande and its tributaries. This began the coming of their Golden Age, and is where the Spaniards found them in the 1500s. When Coronado first came across a Pueblo Indian village, he named it Isleta, meaning little island. In 1581, when the Fray Augustine Rodríguez expedition arrived at Isleta, the Spaniards began building a mission, San Antonio de la Isleta, which they completed in 1629. While the Isleta Pueblos did not take part in the rebellion against the Spaniards in 1680, the Spaniards stormed the village anyway. The few remaining Indians fled to live with the Hopi and did not return until 1716 or 1718.[26]

By the time the Imhofs arrived at Isleta, the mission church had long since been rebuilt and now distinguished itself with a single bell tower. At first, Joe found it puzzling that the Isleta Pueblos worshipped so faithfully at the St. Augustine church while, at the same time, following Pueblo ancient beliefs set forward by their religious official, cacique, the Indian selected to guide them spiritually.

"Two Roses," (watercolor, 19 X 16 in.), 1887.

"Cupid Disappointed," (watercolor reprint, 18 X 13 in.), 1890.

Untitled portrait, (oil on canvas, 40 X 33 in.), 1908.

"Outside Munich, 1900," (oil on canvas board, 11 X 8 in.).

164

"Taos Lilacs," (oil on canvas, 36 X 30 in.).

"Chamisa," (oil, 29 X 38 in.).

"Cottonwood Tree,"
(oil on board,
22 X 18 in.).

166

Untitled Tree, (oil on
board, 24 X 20 in.).

"Rainbow,"
(oil, 3 X 3 ft.).

167

"Navajo Canyon,"
(watercolor, 22½ X
26½ in.).

"Santuario de
Chimayo," (oil on
board, 32 X 27½ in.).

"Indian Pueblo," (oil, 14 X 18 in.).

"South Taos Pueblo," (oil on canvas board, 16 X 20 in.).

"Rebuilding the Mission at Rancho de Taos," (oil, 3 X 5 ft.).

"Buffalo Dance-Taos," (watercolor with gouache, 23¼ X 18¾ in.).

"Taos Drummer,"
(oil and casein,
24 X 19 in.).

"Native American Potters," (oil on canvas, 30 X 36 in.).

172

"The Camofleurs," (oil on canvas on board, 30⅝ X 46¾ in.).

Untitled, (watercolor,
28 X 20 in.).

"Pedro Mirabel," (watercolor,
18 X 13 in.).

174

Untitled Indian Man, (media
not known, 2½ X 1½ ft.).

"Bonnet Mender,"
(oil on canvas,
30 X 22¾ in.).

"Lucinda Castellano," (watercolor, 22 X 29 in.).

"In the Kiva," (oil on canvas, 34½ x 44 in.).

176

"Governor's Cane," (oil
on canvas, 36 X 30 in.).

"Santana Sandoval," (oil on board, 24 X 25 in.).

177

"The Governor of the
Pueblo," (watercolor,
30 X 23 in.).

"The Singers of the Plains,"
(oil on canvas/board,
29 X 22 in.).

"The Governor of Taos," (oil, 5 X 3 ft.).

"Winnowing Corn," (oil, 4 X 2½ ft.).

"Cleaning the Ditch," (oil, 4 X 3 ft.).

"Braiding Corn, Acoma," (oil, 4 X 3½ ft.).

"Husking Colored Corn," (oil, 3 X 4 ft.).

"Grinding Corn, Acoma," (oil, 3½ X 4½ ft.).

"Making Wafer Bread," (oil, 2½ X 3½ ft.).

"Baking Cornbread," (oil, 3½ X 3 ft.).

"Burial Ceremony, Taos Pueblo," (oil, 3 X 2½ ft.).

"Koshares at Kiva," (oil, 4 X 3 ft.).

"Ceremonial Smokers," (oil, 3½ X 5 ft.).

"Procession, Pueblo of Picuris," (oil, 4 X 5 ft.).

"Winter People Resting, Pueblo of Santo Domingo," (oil, 4 X 5 ft.).

"Apache Visitors to Corn Dance," (oil, 2½ X 3 ft.).

"Votive Offering During Corn Dance, Santo Domingo," (oil, 3 X 4 ft.).

"Prayer After Dance, San Felipe," (oil, 2½ X 3 ft.).

"Corn Dance," (oil, 8 X 12 ft.).

According to the ancient ones, when they arrived into the last world, the world of light, the Spirit warned them to respect and obey the laws of nature, and the orders of their leaders whom the people selected among themselves: the chief, the war captains and the cacique.[27] The war captains in each pueblo would lead the people to their destinations, while the cacique was "responsible for observing the movements of sun, stars and moon; and for the days of planting and harvesting; and for the spiritual ceremonies of benefit to crop and tribe."[28]

Under this government, the Pueblo Indians made religion a part of their daily lives. They and their selected officials set the rules that all the people agreed to follow. In their daily prayers for rain, and their need to know the best times for planting, cultivation and harvesting of crops, they developed rituals of songs and dance as a way to show reverence to nature and to preserve the history of their people. They also became keen observers of nature and astronomy. They knew the world was round, as shown in their pottery and baskets designs, while the church in Europe declared that the world was flat.[29]

Yet, centuries later, Joe observed, the Pueblo Indians began many of their rituals and ceremonies on Catholic holy days. At other times, Pueblo Indians asked the local Catholic priest to bless their dances and songs that celebrated corn, rain, the sun and sky. This, despite the fact that the Spanish priests had tried to destroy the Pueblo Indians' spiritual beliefs.

The priests had, unwittingly, only succeeded in driving the Pueblos to practice their spiritual beliefs secretly. Four hundreds years ago, the Pueblo Indians pretended during the day to follow religious practices dictated by the local priest, while during the night at great distances from their pueblo, they secretly performed Pueblo dances and rituals.[30]

Over several years, Joe came to understand that the Pueblo songs and dances recorded not just the stories of the ancients, but the continual un-folding of the Pueblo Indians' lives. This included the coming of the Span-iards and the Americans. Spiritually, the Pueblos knew, "All paths lead to the same summit."[31] Joe would come to understand the naturalness with which the Pueblos incorporated Catholic rituals into Pueblo religious practices.

Daily living practices held Joe entranced as well. At Isleta, he saw for the first time women carrying their water supply in jugs, or ollas, balanced on their heads. The tall, thin-walled jug, with its narrow opening at the rim, prevented the water from splashing out or evaporating. This first encounter with ollas inspired him to began an extensive collection.[32]

Joe Imhof's initial encounter at Isleta would cause him to return many times in the next four years. On occasion, Sallie would accompany him, and, eventually, Isleta became one of Sallie's favorite pueblos. However, most of the time, Joe would come by himself to sketch, photograph, and live with families who invited him into their homes. It was there in the Isleta Pueblo that Joe met Maria Chewiwie, who would become one of his models for many years. When the Imhofs moved to Taos after a seventeen-year absence from New Mexico, Maria Chewiwie would visit them when she came to see her cousin, a Martinez, in Taos.[33]

These journeys into the landscape brought Joe a familiarity with nature that came not just from spending great portions of time under the open sky, but from his effort to see nature and the land as the Pueblos experienced it every day. This helped him understand how the Indian reaffirmed his kinship to the land by telling of it in their songs and stories. The telling of it gave them ownership which they fought to protect.

Within the year in 1908, Joe decided to make the longer journey of fifty miles to the Acoma Pueblo.[34] At first, he went to Acoma with Sallie. Once there, they camped at the base of Acoma where they lived while exploring the pueblo. On these longer journeys into the land, he began to carry dynamite to clear a road through the boulders for his covered wagon. Debris thrown from the Jémez Mountains to the north, and the extinct volcanos to the west that dotted the land, presented formidable obstacles to any traveler.[35]

The Jémez Mountains embraced one of the world's largest extinct volcanic craters, the *Valle Grande Caldera*, measuring over sixteen miles in diameter. The volcano's explosive forces forged much of the New Mexico country west of the Rio Grande. Ash from its eruptions accumulated in depths of hundreds of feet and spread as far as Oklahoma and Kansas. In time, the rock hardened into a honeycombed form called "tuff." Out of the rock, wind erosion chiseled caves where some of the first Anasazi settled. Much of the scarred volcanic rock Joe traveled upon in his journeys to Acoma had long been covered with soil that had given birth to wildflowers and grass.[36]

"There were no barbed wire fences," Sallie reported, "and Joe would cut across wherever he thought from the incomplete maps to be obtained that his direction was right. He often said he began many of the roads leading into pueblos. He was blessed with keen powers of observation . . . .

"I spent many hours wondering if he and the horse were all right, especially for water, for Joe had little thought for his own comfort, but after making a trip to a marked water hole he would find water that the horse refused to drink, or no water at all and the next hole twenty miles away. Then he would track back to the railroad where there were tanks of water for the engines. There were often objections to watering a horse, although a man was never refused, but Joe in his quiet way and his friendliness caused the water man to relent and the horse had his drink. Animals and children were objects of his affection, and it hurt him so very much to see any of them abused."[37]

It was during this period that Sallie came to realize that Joe was not just a wanderer, but a dreamer.[38] Joe, however, saw life through the eyes and instincts of an artist. On his first journey to Acoma, after he crossed the Rio Grande, and drove his covered wagon west from Albuquerque, the surrounding sage, piñon, and juniper awakened his senses. The terrain gradually rose in the gentle rolling hills until Joe found himself atop a plateau looking west.

As the horse picked its way across, then down the plateau slope through low-lying scrub brush, dwarf cedars, sage and prairie grass, the terrain began to flatten into a valley. From this vantage point, Joe could see the San Jose de la Laguna Mission, built in 1706, in the Laguna Pueblo to the north. But the most stunning sight arose to the west: the Enchanted Mesa, a four hundred-foot monolith of pinks and yellows shimmering in the distance. The sheer immensity of this giant that rose from the valley must have quickened his breath.

The word Acoma, itself, meant "a place that always was," in the sense of home or eternal resting place.[39] Joe had heard the legend handed down by the ancient Acomas who had once dwelled there long before the birth of Christ. When the Acoma had first arrived at their "place that always was," they had lived atop the Enchanted Mesa. One day, so the legend went, as the people tended their crops in the valley, a sudden rainstorm had burst upon the mesa and washed away access to the top. After the storm calmed, the Acomas discovered a young girl and her grandmother had been left stranded on top. Rather than starve to death, they had leaped from the mesa's cliff walls.[40]

195

In the distance, just beyond Enchanted Mesa, Joe saw a slightly smaller mesa, the one he sought that held a citadel, Acoma, on a sandstone cliff that rose 357 feet above the surrounding valley. It would be the most ancient city he had ever visited. Tribal legends also told of Acoma having been inhabited since before the birth of Christ, though archaeologists can only document habitation since A.D. 1200.[41]

In land surrounding Acoma's fortress height, lay fields of cultivated corn, beans, melons, squash, wheat, alfalfa, peach trees, onions. He saw large groups of animals as well: cattle, goats, chickens, turkeys, burros, horses, hogs and sheep. He looked for the way to ascend to the top.[42]

He followed a footpath to a narrow slit in the sandstone where he found well-worn steps and handholds cut to human scale. With slow, laborious steps, he made his way to the top.[43] When he stepped onto the flattened top, what he saw made him think he stood in the middle of a painting. Men who wore white pantaloons to the knees, and leggings of wool above leather moccasins, covered themselves with colorful wool blankets. When they moved toward him, he realized that some of them wore leather leggings. These were the people, the Pueblos Indians, who had taught the Navajo weaving.

After he introduced himself and Sallie, and discussed his interest in learning from them, the Acoma agreed to allow Joseph and Sallie to live at the base of their mesa, and spend days and even nights with them in their pueblos. In future excursions to Acoma, Joe would come to live with the Acoma as a way to know them.

In their welcome to him, they took him through their pueblo, a seventy-acre sky city that looked out over their fields and animal pens below. From this height, he could see the extinct volcanos that peaked upon the land, and the lava beds that stretched to the west. High above the valley floor, he could see other outcroppings of wind-eroded sandcliffs, and the rolling peaks of Mount Taylor to the north.

The pueblo itself had been well tended. Streets of hardened earth separated the rows of adobe homes, two and three stories in height. Ladders made from stout trees leaned against the adobe walls and led to entrances that faced south. The few windows on the south sides had been fitted with thin pieces of mica, a mineral chiseled from the earth. The solid adobe walls faced north to protect the people from fierce north winds during the winter.

The original pueblo had been destroyed, of course, by the first Europeans to see Acoma. Captain Hernando de Alvarado and his traveling companion, Fray Juan Padilla, described Acoma as the "strongest ever seen, because the city was built on a high rock. The ascent was so difficult that we repented climbing to the top. The houses are three and four stories high. The people [are] of the same type as those in the province of Cibola [Zuni], and they have abundant supplies of maize, beans, and turkeys like those of New Spain."[44]

As in other pueblos, the Spaniards had built a mission. What made San Estevan del Rey Mission perhaps more remarkable than other pueblo missions were the forty beams supporting the sixty-foot ceiling. They had been hand carried by twenty to thirty Acoma Indians in the 1600s from the sacred Mount Taylor some thirty miles to the north. The priest had instructed the men that for sacred reasons the beams were not to touch the earth in their journey from Mount Taylor. The four beams that did touch the earth were placed upright at the altar just beyond the earthen floor of the church.[45]

The courtesy shown Joseph Imhof had a long history among the Acoma, actually all the Pueblo Indians. A member of Alvarado's expedition wrote, "The natives . . . came down to meet us peacefully, although they might have spared themselves the trouble and remained on their rock, for we would not have been able to disturb them in the least."[46] This kind of peacefulness, and a basic pacifism, Joe came to believe in the years he lived and associated with the Pueblo, ruled all aspect of the Pueblo Indians' lives.

Still, Joe realized that these were a defeated people, and four centuries of defeat had taken their toll. The most recent invasion had come in the form of the railroad, which now brought traders on a regular schedule to buy the exceptional pottery and woven cloth made by the Acoma. At the insistence of Anglos, Acoma elders had already sent children to schools in Albuquerque. In a few years, Acoma men would join the railroad for work, and that would create more problems for these people. The Acoma, as well as other Pueblos who had lived in peace and in a cooperative society for centuries before the arrival of the Spaniards, would continue to follow their ancient beliefs in peace and cooperation.[47]

While the Acoma spoke English, Imhof wanted to learn their language, Keresan, to enable himself to understand the content of their songs during ritual dances. His affinity for these people came in part, too, from a

197

belief he shared with them. The Acoma believed that a tribal member should perform public service without pay as a way of making the world a better place.[48] This making the world a better place was an ethical responsibility all must share voluntarily. Joe had learned and accepted this from the teachings of Dr. Felix Adler. In addition, Joe held that he must never use his paintings as commercial tools, but to use his gifts as an artist for the betterment of man. In a curious way, the Acoma confirmed to Joe that he had acted correctly in giving his paintings and sketches to friends and acquaintances.

Joseph Imhof made dozens of sketches and took even more photographs of the Acoma. Through them, he saw that the individual became absorbed into a collective identity during ceremonial dances, that "the needs of individuals in Pueblo culture are secondary to the goals of the group; in turn, the group is guided by traditions intended to maintain harmony with nature through ceremony." The times spent at Acoma were the beginnings of Joe's later paintings that captured Pueblo life by "uniting figure with figure and figure with earth in rhythmic patterns of shape, color, and line," in an effort to suggest the spiritual wholeness of Pueblo Indian life.[49]

These people acquainted Joe with Pueblo clans, an entirely new idea to him that would become important in his future relationship with the Cochiti Pueblo Indians. The Acoma's emergence story told of two sisters, Nautsiti and Iatiku, who were the first two people to emerge from Shipapu. "All the people and other living things came to life with these two girls— everything at Acoma awakened to the sun and to the world and the sisters received husbands and multiplied. Then Nautsiti disappeared to the east but Iatiku remained and gave each girl child a clan name when she was born."[50]

The first clan mothers were named in order, the oldest in loving memory of Nautsiti, who called herself of the Sun Clan. Clan bloodlines descended from the mother, and the Pueblo Indian family structure, Joe would come to know, would evolve around the common female ancestor.[51] This clan structure would affect his privileges in the years ahead when the Cochiti Pueblo Indians made him a member of the Turquoise Clan at Cochiti Pueblo.

The Pueblo Indians had already made accommodations for incorporating others outside their clan long before the Spaniards arrived. The head of a family could invite someone outside the clan into the moiety, a kind of societal structure for ceremonial and social purposes. The invitation was associated with marriage and friendship. With the constant pressure of out-siders making their presence felt after the Spaniards arrived, the moiety be-came a more constant part of Pueblo societies.[52]

The most recent arrival of Anglos had come with the railroad, when the tracks came through Laguna Pueblo around 1880. The tracks brought American engineers and surveyors. Three of these Anglos married Laguna women. The marriages influenced another development in Pueblo societies: the "progressives" who approved outside marriages and education outside the pueblo, and the "conservative" factions who believed members of their pueblo should adhere to traditional Pueblo life and teachings.[53] Joe would experience these effects, too, at Cochiti Pueblo.

It was at Acoma, in all probability, that Joe felt the full impact of this ancient land occupied by descendants of "the Ancients." He must have real-ized that he had entered a period of self-education, that he would apprentice himself to these people, just as he had apprenticed himself to the master painters of previous centuries in Europe.

As he listened, observed, and sketched, he saw that religion was a way of life, that every event did have meaning. Anglos had told him that Pueblo songs sung during different ceremonies and dances were mostly nonsensical sounds that added to the rhythmic beat of the drums. Now he found that all of the ceremonies and rituals were religious and carefully memorized prayerful requests for an orderly life, rain, good crops, plentiful game, pleasant days, protection from violence. Even the dances were a form of prayer.

In the coming months, Joe lived with the Acoma and Isleta Pueblo Indians, learning their languages, customs, sacred beliefs, and always sketch-ing and photographing. In the animal dances, the Pueblos asked the Great One for permission to appear in the animal form before the animal was killed because the animals had an inner spirit as well.[54] He watched the Rainbow and Butterfly Dances and, of course, the greatest of rituals, the Corn Dance.

Douglas fir branches, the symbol of everlasting life, adorned the bod-ies of dancers in all of these dances. The Pueblos, he found, informed the Great One, as they danced, that they did not intend to mutilate the tree that they had climbed upward into the fourth world, but held the Douglas fir tree sacred and used its branches in honor of him. After a dance, the Pueblos would take the branches and float them on the river, or burn them in their fireplaces to produce the fresh odor of the fir tree.[55]

In the Corn and Harvest Dances, women wore *tablitas*, a wood carved elevated headdress that formed a kind of altar. In these dances, the women always wore a black or white one-piece dress belted with a woven cloth, white cotton leggings, colored scarves over one shoulder, and silver jewelry inlaid with turquoise and shells.[56] When they danced, the dirt stirred under their feet and rose around them. The swirl of dust seemed to give a mystical quality to these people as they came row upon row toward each other, caught in the oneness of their prayer. For now, Joe was satisfied to watch, to sketch and record. He would learn the sacred meanings of each movement in the years ahead. For now, he wanted only to feel their ritual, their religion.

The Corn Dance, as always, touched Joe in a more personal way, perhaps because corn had given life to these people. Corn was life. Long before the Spaniards had come, the people at Acoma were growing many varieties of corn: sweet, dent, flint, flour, and popcorn. From these they made hominy, succotash, cornbread, cornmeal mush, and they especially liked tortillas and tamales. But corn was much more than food for the body.[57]

Indians had taken a grass plant and, through a process not yet understood, converted "it into the most versatile and adaptive of all cereals, a plant so efficient in turning raw resources into food and other useful materials that it dominated ancient American agriculture for thousands of years and had since gone on to extend its influence all over the world . . . . The Indian further found time to develop around it a great culture of art, science, literature, and religion . . . . The story of Old America is the story of corn and the Indian."[58]

Corn permeated every facet of life. Corn silks, after having been soaked in water and drunk, served as a medicine for various ailments. Husks were used to make tamales, to smoke, for wrapping, and as stuffing for cushions or mattresses. Cobs could be used for fuel, as a scrub brush, stoppers for jugs or pottery bottles, and for medicinal purposes. Stalks were used as building materials in walls, fences, toys, religious figures, funereal objects carved of stone or made of clay as a more lasting source of food in the next life.[59]

The metates, stones used for grinding corn, were passed on from one generation to the next as heirlooms in a gesture to retain the loved women who used them. Some Pueblos women placed several metates side by side to grind corn coarse, medium and fine. As the women worked, they developed a rhythm to music of the flute, which gave rise to grinding songs sung by the women.[60]

Over the years that Joe visited the Acoma Pueblo, he would purchase, or receive as gifts, these women's creations: a seed jar, small ollas, a wide-mouth bowl, polychrome ollas.[61] At the end of his life, he would return these and other Indian-created objects to the Indians. He had enjoyed their beauty and they had enriched much of his life. Now he wanted them returned to their rightful owners. In returning the objects, he acknowledged not only the intellectual and spiritual expressions of the Indians, but the importance of the Native Americans' continuity and survival.

As always, Sallie took care of Joe's business, and this business of returning Pueblo artifacts. She had found pleasure in the distant excursions to pueblos, but she had also found her home with new-found friends at the University of New Mexico. She would bring Joe into this part of her life, just as she shared his. The exchange would enrich the University's theater productions, bring the craft and art of lithography to the campus, and introduce the Cochiti and Santo Domingo Pueblos to the University.

CHAPTER 11

A HOME AT LAST

By late 1908 and early 1909, Sallie had developed a circle of friends at the University of New Mexico and begun to think of herself as having a place in Albuquerque. She was thirty-seven years old and, from the lengthy description she recorded of a home they bought, she must have longed for a place of her own. She clearly wanted Joe to become more a part of her life and circle of friends. Joe, while accommodating, had become obsessed with the Pueblo Indians' relationship to the universe. He had learned more from the Santo Domingo and Cochiti Pueblos he met selling their pottery at the museum attached to the Alvarado Hotel.

Sallie recorded that, in 1909, they bought land and built a studio.[1] However, Imhof did not appear on the Albuquerque, County of Bernalillo deed records until May 4, 1910 and then it was for a one-third interest in two strips of land, one containing 8.24 acres, and the other containing 10.3 acres. The land lay between Carlisle and Princeton, south of the present Interstate 40 and north of Indian School Road, all of which is part of the present-day Netherwood Park. Joe sold this land on May 20, however, sixteen days after he bought it, to Ada Netherwood.[2] The sale spoke more about their financial situation, because the transaction appears to indicate that Joe was speculating in real estate. However, he left no records of any profit or loss.

In 1910, according to the Albuquerque City Directory for 1910-11 and 1912, Joe and Sallie Imhof lived on the east side of Yale Avenue, and south of East Central, where Joe built his studio. Because they did not buy the Yale Avenue property until June 1912, shortly before they moved to New Jersey, it's possible they leased, then improved the property with an option to buy.[3] For now, though, the Imhofs made a short trip to New York, probably to take care of their finances.[4]

The Imhofs' University Heights property, which they rented or leased, lay some five lots south of the University of New Mexico, on Yale Avenue on a piece of land that ran between Silver Street and the old Railroad Avenue, now renamed Central Avenue.[5] The property had a three-room house, a cellar, and a chicken house where Sallie judged someone had been unsuccessful in raising chickens. After they made arrangements to move onto the property, they built several rooms onto the house. Sallie recorded that except for the home of Mrs. Werner, the postmistress, who lived far to the southeast, "there was not a house for fifteen miles all the way to Tijeras Canyon, and the wild flowers and beautiful cactus were all the way to the canyon."[6]

Imof's home on Yale Street south of Central Avenue, Albuquerque, 1912.

"The extension of Railroad Avenue east of High Street," Kenneth C. Balcomb recalled in *A Boy's Albuquerque*, "became a wavering sandy lane as far as the University; from there a wagon road wound uncertainly till it entered

203

Tijeras Canyon, which in Spanish means scissors, so called because it branches at its upper end into two canyons—Tijeras and Cedro. On its way to the canyon it passed an adobe and rock structure that had the reputation of harboring ladies of questionable reputation, but displayed the innocent sign, 'Tea and Cakes.'"[7]

When Joe built his studio, it was the first of its kind built in Albuquerque, and one that would cause a great deal of comment. The large building incorporated design that Joe had learned from the Pueblos. Like the ancient ones, he dug more than one floor below ground level. In the first ten feet, he used poured adobe, then placed bricks above the adobe.[8]

The outside entrance to the first floor was three steps down from ground level. The lowered entrance prevented the dust storms from interfering with Joe's work. The studio itself had one large room, a separate smaller studio for his small work, a library where he kept his valued book collection, and several other rooms. On the southeast corner of the studio, he built a room with an outside opening for visiting Indians. He placed benches around all of the walls for those who wanted to sleep there. For the fireplace, he kept a good supply of piñon outside the door.[9]

He then built a stable below ground so that it would not interfere with their view of the Sandia Mountains, and attached to it an open shelter that housed the buggies, and riding gear. Already, the friends Joe had made in his travels to the pueblos would bring visitors. Soon, Santo Domingo Indians, who had hitched rides on the freight trains and sold their pottery in front of the Alvarado Hotel, would begin to arrive at the Imhofs during the evening.[10]

"We never knew how many would come across the field to our house for breakfast," Sallie recalled. "They politely waited until they saw smoke coming from the chimney. They were well-behaved and so thankful for our friendship."[11]

When they finished the studio at the end of June in 1909, they raised a pole, and Sallie set off to buy a flag to fly on July Fourth. "I searched from store to store, and there was none to be had," she recorded. "Mr. and Mrs. Strong from Philadelphia had just opened a book and stationery store on Second Street, and she, like me, was horrified. She said then that as long as they had a store there would be American flags for sale, and during our lasting friendship up to their deaths there was always a good selection."[12]

Sallie's pride in her country would soon be fulfilled in a more direct expression.

July 1, 1909 brought the Imhofs another good friend, Edward Dundas McQueen Gray, the new president of the University of New Mexico. Gray had been born at Croftonhill, Lanarkshire, Scotland, the son of Dundas McQueen, the ambassador to Louis Phillipe, and the great grandson of the twelfth Baron Gray. President Gray had received his higher education at the University of Heidelberg and the University of London where he took honors in Arts.[13]

Before settling in New Mexico in 1893 at Loving, a small town near Carlsbad, he had traveled and lived for many years in Europe, Egypt, North and South America. He belonged to many societies and clubs and had written several books, novels, and a drama, the "Red Harvest."[14] President Gray's interest in the arts excited Sallie, especially since she had a special affinity for the theater.

That year brought Joe the greatest honor he had received. The Cochiti, in a simple gesture, sprinkled him with corn to make him invisible.[15] They now thought of him as the "invisible man" and made him a member of the Turquoise kiva where he would learn the secrets of their society.[16] Before becoming a member of the Cochiti Turquoise kiva, in all probability, Joe first spent time at the Santo Domingo Pueblo located south of the Cochiti Pueblo where the Galisteo River connects with the Rio Grande. The many Santo Domingo Indians who had visited Joe's studio had welcomed his friendship. And, Joe had long realized that when an Indian extended his friendship, he gave all without reserve.[17] Besides, the Santo Domingo Pueblo lay just over thirty miles north on the east side of the Rio Grande, which was the same side of the river where Joe and Sallie lived.

The road to Santo Domingo Pueblo was probably as well traveled as any during this time simply because the Indians themselves had formed a trail that connected the Isleta, Santo Domingo and Cochiti Pueblos long before the Spaniards arrived. The Santo Domingo had built their pueblo in a place that the Spaniards would later designate as the Camino Real, and the railroad would follow. Beyond Santo Domingo, by twelve miles, lay the trading point of La Bajada, which marked a geographic, economic and political dividing line.[18]

La Bajada, which means the slope, had taken its name from the mesa that at this point dropped seven hundred feet. Shepherds had once sheltered their sheep at night along this mesa. In time, travelers would carve the Santa Fe Trail and the Chihuahua Trail up and down the steep mesa between Santa Fe and Albuquerque. To ease the sudden climb and drop in land, travelers had carved out switchback trails. La Bajada then became a dividing line in New Mexico; anything north of La Bajada was considered northern New Mexico; anything below the mesa drop off, southern New Mexico.[19]

Joe's first visit north would take him to the Santo Domingo Pueblo, a less arduous journey than if he traveled to the Cochiti Pueblo which was some six miles north across the Rio Grande near the volcanic tent rocks. Only the infrequent floods from the river plagued the Santo Domingo whose pueblo, in 1909, had been in its present location since 1700. In previous years, attacks from the Spaniards and floods had forced them to relocate and reconstruct their pueblo many times.[20]

The Santo Domingo Indians held several special interests for Joe. They had originated the Corn Dance and all Pueblo Indians regarded them as not only performing the most impressive Corn Dance in existence, but they were the most conservative, the most bound by tradition to their spiritual beliefs. They did not welcome outsiders, especially white men, but they made an exception for Joseph Imhof.[21]

Joe rode his gaited horse to the edge of the pueblo that squatted on the sandy plain near the curve of the Rio Grande. Patches of cottonwood trees provided some relief to the eye from land that held little vegetation and stretched into the distant northern mountains. He tied the horse and made his way to the edge of the pueblo. He had arrived to observe the beginning of the Spring Corn Dance.

A long, earth-pounded lane opened into the pueblo and, as he watched, four rows of men dressed in their brightest color shirts and full-legged pants, carrying a sprig of evergreen in each hand, came toward the center of the pueblo. Beside them walked a man beating a drum whose powerful throb reverberated into the wind. With him walked the flag carrier.[22]

"Behind them in two files slouched the dancers—perhaps a hundred and fifty men, women, and children." As they moved " . . . forward against the wind, colors screamed against the dun grey walls, a life emerged into the monotone of sand and sky . . . . It was a great ceremonial dance by which the corn must be lifted into life; corn for all. So everyone participated.

"The men, naked to the waist, were painted a golden copper. Their freshly washed hair fell to their wide shoulders and held entwined a few blue and green parrot feathers. Each wore a white Hopi ceremonial kirtle embroidered in red and green, and tied with a red and black wool sash, the long fringe dangling from right knee to ankle. At the back swaying between their legs, hung the ever-present fox skin. On their legs tinkled straps of little bells, sea shells, and hollow deer hoof rattles. Their ankle-high, fawn-colored moccasins were trimmed with a band of black and white skunk fur. They carried in the right hand a gourd rattle, in the left a sprig of evergreen.

"The women, alternating with the men, shuffled along bare footed in the eddying dust. Their squat heavy figures were covered by loose, black wool *mantas* beautifully embroidered around the hem in red, leaving one bare shoulder free, and belted around the waist with a green and scarlet Hopi sash. Their waist long hair, like that of the men, rippled free in the wind. Each carried on her head a turquoise-blue *tablita* held by a string passing under her chin—a thin wooden tiara perhaps a foot high, shaped like a doorway, painted with cloud symbols and tipped with tufts of eagle down. They wore heavy silver bracelets and rings, silver squash-blossom necklaces, and strings of turquoise and coral, and carried in each hand a sprig of evergreen.

"The two files stopped, facing each other, the children on one end. Between them the flag carrier dipped his long pole over their heads, the drummer began to beat the great drum . . . that throbbed hoarsely. The gaze of the fifty old men turned inward, became fixed. They began to chant—a powerful soughing like the wind among the pines . . . . The sprigs of evergreen lifted and fell. Then came a tinkle of bells, the clatter of deer hoofs, a rattle of gourds . . . . In two long rows, the stable, stolid women alternating with the leaping men. Then in four shorter rows as the women stepped back to face the turning men. And now in a great, slow-moving circle breaking up into two circles, each woman a shadow at the heels of her man . . . .

"The insistent, down-pressing stamp that sinks down deep into the earth, as the throb of the drum sinks deep into the unconscious. And the insistent rising chant that lifts, lifts up into the shaking spruce twigs, up to the rain feathers on the pole to the clouds in the sky. The two dual life-forces that flow downward and upward in man. But here now arrested, rigidly controlled and rhythmically freed as the psychic in-breathings and out-breathings of meditative prayer made visible in patterned motion. A prayer whose mesmeric beat closed the mind to sight and sound, to wind and dust. Beating through the flesh of the earth and the earth of the flesh, through the growing corn and the people who would envelop the ripened corn again for the strength and power to perpetuate both . . . ."[23]

The dance kept up all day, with the Santo Domingo emerging from a kiva at one end of the pueblo, and then others emerging from a kiva at the other end. What Joe witnessed gave true meaning to prayer, a communal prayer that lifted the energies from the earth and the people and connected it to the sun and clouds and rain.

Joe had been given permission to photograph, and in his mind he recorded not just what he saw, but the impact of the energies upon his own being. At the end of the day, he often spent all night sketching what he had witnessed and experienced.[24]

Imhof's photograph of Santo Domingo Corn Dance, August 4, 1907-1912.

The artist, John Marin, was so intrigued by the Corn Dance that he had witnessed at Santo Domingo Pueblo that he wrote Alfred Stieglitz, "Certain passages in the dance itself are so beautiful that to produce something having seen it—becomes well nigh worthless—it's like grafting on to perfection—it's like rewriting Bach."[25]

Joseph Imhof knew this as well. Many years into the future, in 1951, Joe would paint this Santo Domingo Corn Dance. For now, his idea for painting the Corn Series waited to be born. It would soon find birth, however, when the Cochiti drew Imhof into joining their dance. Imhof's painting of the Santo Domingo Corn Dance, a 27-by-37-inch gouache and pastel, does capture what he saw in the motion of dance as the flag carrier, his red blousey shirt and white pants above leather leggings, dips the flag borne by Aztec priests. From the long, smooth pole hangs the narrow hand-woven white banner, the kirtle, with the ceremonial fox skin dangling from the end. A bunch of colored parrot and hummingbird feathers—the crest of the war god Huitzilopochtle—tip the end of the pole. The drummer, with his great belly drum, beats a rhythm behind the flag bearer. Rows of men dressed in white, sprigs of evergreen some tucked into their woven waist bands, and some held high with one hand, bend their knees to the beat. Across an opening, rows of men, naked to the waist and their bodies painted copper, bend to the beat. Behind them shuffle the women, their feet touching the earth and their blue *tablita* altars stepping toward the sky (see jacket cover).

A *Koshare*, his body naked except for a loin cloth, dances his white-painted body splotched with black strips toward a row of dancers. The ever-present corn husks spring from his head where they have been tied. A rainbow arises above the dancers, as if acknowledging the prayers released through the communal energies.[26]

In 1909, however, Joe had painted nothing, or, if he did paint, he produced few canvases even though he had photographed and sketched Pueblo Indians in many separate pueblos for two years.[27] He had so much yet to understand before he could paint with the confidence of knowing that he had captured the authentic Pueblo Indian.

When the Cochiti honored him with membership and made him invisible by sprinkling him with corn, they gave him permission to record their ceremonies both in photographs and the sketches he returned to his studio to make.[28] To reach Cochiti Pueblo, Joe followed the Rio Grande valley north to Santo Domingo in his covered wagon. From Santo Domingo he continued to follow the river north. The permeable soil held little vegetation in this desert-like terrain but as he neared Cochiti, the soil colors began to vary from grays, to browns, and then reds. The color variations revealed the secret of whence they had come, having been washed from the Jémez Mountains that loomed immediately to the north, and from mesas that sloped into the river valley.[29]

Fields of corn grew on both sides of the Rio Grande, and Joe saw a bridge across the river that would lead him into Cochiti. As the wagon and horses rattled across the bridge, he noticed the caissons, eight and ten feet in diameter, bracing the bridge. Baskets of branches filled with rocks enclosed each caisson, to prevent beavers from eating the timbers. The sight might have reminded him of his youth in Brooklyn, of crossing the Brooklyn Bridge to study art. In 1882, one year before the opening of New York's Brooklyn Bridge, and when Joe rode ferry boats across the Hudson to Manhattan, the only means of crossing the Rio Grande at Cochiti Pueblo was to board one of the ferry boats owned and operated by the Cochiti themselves.[30]

Cochiti Pueblo rested on an elevated plain, about a half mile west and twenty-five feet above the river. Occasional cottonwood trees grew in the village that looked out over a broad plain. Only 237 Cochiti lived in the pueblo now, even though they had occupied this place for at least seven hundred years, except for the sixteen-year interruption of the Pueblo Revolt in the late 1600s. Joe had seen numerous corrals at the edge of the pueblo where he had staked his horses.[31]

A number of Hispanics also lived in the pueblo, and they owned and operated the only two stores in the pueblo. It was here at Cochiti that Joe probably first saw a Penitente's *Morada*, or chapel. The Penitentes, a facet of the Catholic church, whipped themselves in a ritual reminiscent of the earlier Spanish invaders. The Penitentes would play a larger role in Joe's life in the future, but for now, he discovered the flagellants' belief in superstition was connected to the belief that their efforts would bring clouds, and then rain.[32]

The pueblo had a plaza with two-story adobe homes on either side. Almost every family had an oven on the roof or in the yard. The windows had been made of selenite mosaics and a white clay had been used to caulk the segments of selenite. When the Cochiti wanted to prepare "the gypsum plates for their windows, they boil them in hot water so as to further the cleavage." The church was old and dilapidated, and the cross had fallen to the ground where it lay in ruins.[33]

From his Cochiti friends, Joe learned that the people had split into two factions. The Conservatives, who believed in the "supernatural powers of the cacique, in the supernatural knowledge and powers of the medicine men and in the authority of war captains," and the Progressives, who obeyed only the governors, the *fiscales* and the Council of *Principals*. Thus, the pueblo had two kivas, the eastern kiva that belonged to the Turquoise people, or moiety, those outside a clan who had been invited to join, and the western kiva that belonged to the Pumpkin people. They called their kivas shipap, reflecting the tribal place of emergence on the earth. The Turquoise and Pumpkin kivas were oriented toward the plaza, and members entered the eight-foot hole in the top of the kiva by a ladder. A staircase of ten steps led to the ladder hole.[34]

The Turquoise kiva ladder had a decorative cap at the top; the Pumpkin did not. The Turquoise had various rainbow and lightning designs and Ku-sha-li figures painted on the plastered and whitewashed wall. The gypsum for the whitewash had been gathered by war captains near the old La Bajada and baked in an outdoor oven for twenty-four hours or more, then ground into a fine powder. The Pumpkin kiva looked perfectly plain inside. No bench or seat could be found along the wall.[35]

Inside both, a hearth graced the south side below the roof opening. A firebox of a foot long and three feet high had been built at the back, directly under the hatchway. Anyone climbing the ladder had to pass directly over the fire. Two large posts supported the roof; attached to the posts were simple broad shelves on which to place candles. These walls were plain except for wooden pegs on which to hang scalps and to support the long pole on which the scalps were carried.[36]

"Kivas are like churches; there shouldn't be any fights or bad feelings in them," Cochiti believed. In their emergence story, the Cochiti described ascending to earth by climbing a tree similar to a Douglas fir tree from Shipap after a great flood. At first, they lived at White House, far to the north, with all the other people of the earth. Joe would later learn that the Cañari of Ecuador told of a similar emergence story.[37]

The Cochiti farmed extensively, growing fields of corn, beans, pump-kins, watermelons, and they raised horses, burrows, pigs, sheep, chickens, turkeys. They hunted continually as well, living on deer, wildcat, bear, bad-ger, rabbits, squirrels, turkeys, ducks, quail, and dove. They used the fur of the fox, wildcat, bear, skunk, and other animals for warmth and for ceremo-nial use. From eagles, hawks and hummingbirds they extracted feathers. The Douglas fir, their most important ceremonial plant, could be found growing at the foot of the Jémez Mountains.[38]

Their drums, however, set them apart from all other Pueblo Indians who regarded the Cochiti as the greatest of drum-makers. The best drums were made of mountain cottonwood, or aspen, with heads made of cow or horsehide. Because Cochiti drums had two voices, one head was made from the flank hide, and the other of the thicker hide from the back of the animal. The thickness of the hide created the two voices. A small hole was drilled, one of either side under the tie thongs, to allow air to escape when a drum was beaten. While most men made the drums, only a few became renown for their remarkable drums. Women usually painted the heads and sides. No two were alike. If a drum was ever repainted, it was painted in its original design. Each drum could always be recognized by its design.[39]

When Joe first attended Cochiti ceremonial dances, he simply ob-served, becoming a student of the people. On dance days, the drums were brought to the kivas where the drummers, while alone, warmed them by the fire to obtain the proper voice. The drummer then fed cornmeal to the drums as a form of blessing and request for power.[40] With the encourage-ment of the Cochiti, Joe eventually joined them in the Corn Dance.

At around noon on the day Joe first danced among the Cochiti, both men and women dancers emerged from one kiva and two men, side by side, with two women behind them, walked to the center of the plaza. The men had stripped to the waist and wore the white Hopi kilt worn also by the Santo Domingo. They had tied evergreen to their arms, and wore parrot feathers in their hair, while wearing skunk fur around the heels of their moccasins. In one hand they held a rattle, in the other a sprig of evergreen. A turtleshell tied behind one knee rattled with each step.[41]

The women wore the traditional black dress, leaving one shoulder bare, their long hair freshly washed and streaming down their backs. They wore no shoes and held a sprig of evergreen in each hand. Their blue *tablitas*, tied on their heads with a string under their chins, appeared as altars stair-stepped into the sky.[42]

Suddenly the great belly drum began to throb, and the dancers' feet pounded the earth as they slowly moved in an intricate pattern, their arms pumping the sprigs of evergreen in the air. Their banner carrier waved the pole over the dancers, and then they disappeared into their kiva before dancers emerged from the second kiva. Sometimes both groups joined in the plaza, their flag carriers waving their banners over them, as they wound among each other, singing, their feet pounding the earth to the voice of the drum.

Sometimes the drum stopped, and it seemed as if the earth had hesitated to breathe. Then the voice spoke again, this time in a higher tone and at a faster pace that joined the dancers in a different kind of prayer. All day the people seemed to become one in the sea of evergreen, moving to the voice of the drum, their singular voice carried into the wind, their spiritual reverence one with each other and all of nature around them.[43]

After the dance, singers tossed a few grains of cornmeal on the drum and inhaled from the drum, rubbing meal on their throats, as a way of assuring the continuance of their own voices and well-being. Drummers then returned the drums to the proper kiva where the drums were again fed. The cacique came to each kiva and thanked the drums for their help in the day's activities. He, too, drew out their breath.[44]

Over the next three years, Joe returned again and again to study and learn, to photograph and sketch. Sometimes he brought Sallie when he wanted her to experience ceremonial dances. On these occasions, they would arrive the night before the dance so that they could observe the preparations, and then they would sleep in their covered wagon. At other times, Joe lived with the Cochiti in their homes, sometimes for weeks.[45]

Through this apprenticeship period, the Cochiti taught him that supernatural powers were of supreme importance to their culture; that at specific times, certain individuals were deemed worthy of being invested with such powers. These persons had met the Cochiti ideals of "industry, kindness, helpfulness, and interest in, but not intense curiosity concerning others' affairs, an awareness of communal responsibility, providence, honest and sincere respect for traditional items and beliefs that are Cochiti."[46]

The individual who became so empowered received no privileges, no material gain or other benefits. They used their supernatural powers in an official way, and for the benefit of all. For this they received respect.[47]

The message of the dance, no matter which dance, carried similar teachings. "The unity and rhythm of nature; the correlative interdependence of nature and man; natural law as the basis for human law; the pervading power of prayer, ritual, art, and concentration on the 'good'; the folly of quarrelsomeness, pride, and non-cooperation; freedom through education and self-discipline."[48] Order and rhythm were the nature of things. Man must study them and bring his life and his society into harmony with them. Only then could man be free. The Cochiti teachings reinforced beliefs Joseph Imhof already held, beliefs he had come to know and bind to his soul. These were the beliefs that Dr. Adler had referred to as the "spiritual ideal, a vision of the spiritual universe as an infinite life of interaction between uniquely diverse members [that] should replace the traditional monotheist idea of God as a single individual Being."[49]

When Joe felt himself ready, he prepared himself for prayerful thanksgiving, and joined his kiva of moiety, the Turquoise people, in dance. The drums spoke to him in a voice he had before now never consciously understood. As the drum throbbed, it was as if his mind had finally allowed him to acknowledge his own origin in the universe. His feet pounded the earth to life, and at last he felt the heartbeat from which he had arisen.

His voice joined others as it floated and sighed in the wind, becoming part of the space around him. Imhof transcended into the rhythm of the universe. In a vision, he saw the story of corn as the same story of his life: planting, watering, nurturing through the tilling of the soil; he saw the ceremonies as reverence for all elements of nature, and the various rites that legitimatized his being. He became one with all. His ideas of his life coalesced with the Indians' relationship to corn, to all of life. He ascended and became one with the community in the swelling universe of energies. The beat of the corn became his beat of life. At that moment, he knew he would return. He had found his home among the Pueblos. He would tell their story, his story, the only way he could speak, by painting the story of corn.

When the dance ended that evening, he knew he had experienced more than the raising of the corn. He had given birth to the direction of his life. His own life had been transformed, ignited by the voice of the drum as his feet pounded the earth in unison with the community. He finally dwelled in harmony.

From the Cochiti Pueblo, Joe ventured into the trading point, La Bajada, where other travelers gathered in the small village. His dynamite became necessary to clear a path through boulders as his team of horses dragged the covered wagon along the switchback trail. Sometimes he had to place the boulders under the wheels of his wagon to prevent it from rolling unchecked downhill.[50]

Other times Joe camped at the foot of the surrounding Jémez Mountains, and spent time among the strange rock formations in Peralta Canyon just beyond Cochiti Pueblo. There hundreds of spiral shaped rocks jutted from the earth. During the evening, the volcanic ash, that had been belched from the Jémez Mountains a million years ago and then shaped by wind and rain, showed him a symphony of colors as the setting sun layered the gray creatures shades of orange and pink. Sometimes they looked like giant guardians of the earth, perhaps even spirits arising from the earth. Other times they appeared as ghost tents from the people's ancient past.[51]

Joe's experiences fired Sallie's own imagination. She loved for him to regale her friends with stories from his travels in Europe, his excursions into the landscape, of his life among the Isleta, Acoma, Santo Domingo, and Cochiti Indians. Joe thrived on the attention as well. One day in July, Mrs. Louis Ilfeld, a dear friend of Sallie's, invited Sallie and Joe to a tea. "In those days," Sallie recalled, "a TEA was a tea; there were no cocktails served."[52]

At the tea, Joe elaborated on his trips to the Santo Domingo Pueblo, and suggested to the guests that they use the few automobiles in Albuquerque to take those interested to Santo Domingo Pueblo to witness the Corn Dance. They could drive up the evening before, camp overnight so that they could be present when the dances started in the morning.[53]

"Quite a few met us there [at Santo Domingo Pueblo], and were interested," Sallie recorded. Among those interested was Erna Fergusson, then a student at the University, and Miss Ethel Hickey, sister of the Judge in Albuquerque.[54]

When Erna Fergusson graduated from the University of New Mexico in 1912, she received another degree from Columbia University before working as a reporter for the Albuquerque *Herald*. Fergusson's desire to travel more in New Mexico, coupled with her experiences traveling with Sallie and Joe to Santo Domingo, prompted her to pioneer, with Ethel Hickey, their own business, the Koshare Tours, in 1912. The Koshare Tours took tourists to primitive sites in New Mexico. The couriers knew the history of the area and made it interesting for the tourists when they attended the Pueblo dances and had a difficult time understanding that the dances were religious ceremonies.[55]

The Harvey organization liked her idea so much that they bought her business and put her in charge of their new tour business, Indian Detours. Just as Fred Harvey had done, she trained young women on the ethics and skills of leading tourists into primitive sites to view Indian ceremonials, and taught them the history of the Pueblos. In 1926, Indian Detours carried tourists into the unknown, to Taos, the cliff dwellings, to San Ildefonso Pueblo, Carlsbad Caverns, the Painted Desert, all guided by well-educated young women.[56]

Erna Fergusson later pursued her writing and reporting, authoring books on the Southwestern Indians, and traveling throughout South America and Germany to gather articles for the many publications that assigned her work.

Sallie and Joe met another accomplished student, Karl Karsten, who would play an important part in their lives. Karl had attended the University of Illinois in 1907 and 1908 before attending the University of Chicago for another two years. In 1909, he enrolled at the University of New Mexico where he met the Imhofs and spent many hours conversing with Joe. Karsten played on the football team, joined the debating team, and served as president of the Dramatic Club in 1910 and 1911.[57]

In 1911, President Gray helped launch the first dramatic production on May 30 at the University of New Mexico. The comedy, "Rose O'Plymouth Town," was set in the Massachusetts' colony, and featured historical figures such as Miles Standish, John Alden and Priscilla. Sallie, of course, worked on the production, and brought Joe into her world. He painted the sets, making them of paper, and installed indirect lighting at the Elks' Crystal Theater.[58]

During this period, President Gray had begun recruiting exchange professors for the Spring and Summer classes. The first year, he recruited two professors, a Frenchman and a German, who became acquainted with the Imhofs. " . . . They were much puzzled and bewildered men who visited us," Sallie said, "and tried to have Joe explain some of our manners and customs. It was laughable to see their bewilderment at the easy way we seemed

216

to educate the young, and after the formalities of the foreign universities it was easy to understand." Sallie credited President Gray with bringing students the rudiments of social manners and graces not known in the South-west.[59]

President Gray also appointed Ms. Josephine Parsons, Sallie's stenography instructor, faculty secretary, and, in 1910, made her Principal of the Commercial Department. Sometime during this period, Joe volunteered to originate and teach classes in lithography. However, he received no income for this project. Still, Sallie was in her element, and the University had an enrollment of 163.[60] "Our studio was a happy place where our friends and the students of the University would come, and we would have a happy time together," Sallie recalled. "I myself was studying at the University of New Mexico, and all knew they were welcome.[61]

"Then we had a friend at the Shortle Sanitorium and he had a sister in New York who was a teacher in a school our daughter had attended."[62] Albuquerque had several sanitoriums, but in 1910 Dr. Abraham G. Shortle opened the first privately owned facility, the Albuquerque Sanitorium, on East Gold at Sycamore Street.[63] "That was another project of ours," Sallie said, "to have the patient and his friends at the Sanitorium come up for little tea parties and for Thanksgiving, Xmas, and all the other holidays, and we later learned how much it did for their morale."[64]

These were also the days when practical jokes offered a diversion from the sameness in this harsh Territory. Boys invited the preacher up the hill to judge a debate that didn't materialize. Sports included wearing " . . . wide ties 'like gigantic butterflies,' blue spotted socks, fobs without watches, and jerseys of every shade of red . . . ."[65] Joe, with his whimsical sense of humor, was in his element. He kept a collection of hats he had gathered from around the world and entertained guests by greeting them at the door wearing one of his unusual creations. When guests left, however, Joe never failed to give each a gift.[66]

Karl Karsten became a Rhodes Scholar in 1911 and sailed for England that fall. Sallie recorded, "A group of students from the University, of which I was one, waved him onward towards England." After Joe's death in 1955, Karl Karsten wrote to Sallie. She had not seen him for fifty-one years. It was "a lovely letter of appreciation for what Joe and I had done for his formative years . . . . I confess it was an unexpected tribute to Joe."[67]

217

By 1912, the Imhofs had lived in Albuquerque for five years, and still Joe could not find a means of earning a living. However, they decided to buy the property where they lived and Joe had built his studio. On June 18, 1912, for $1,250.00, Joe bought lots 6, 7, 8 of Block One of University Heights of a plat filed in July 1906. Each of the lots, located on the east side of Yale Avenue between East Central and Silver, measured 50-by-142 feet.[68]

Three months later, on September 10, 1912, Joe borrowed five hundred dollars from the First Savings Bank and Trust Company in Albuquerque, using the Yale Avenue property for collateral. The note, at eight percent interest, was due two years after the date it had been secured.[69] On August 20, 1913, Joe repaid the note seven days after they sold the property for nine hundred dollars, on August 13, 1913. With that sale, Joe took a three hundred dollar loss.[70]

Sallie recorded that in 1912, "after these years of being with the Indians," they decided to return to their New Jersey home, and later New York, because they had become concerned about their daughter's education. Elizabeth had turned fourteen. Yet, Sallie recorded that they had "pending a trip to Spain to study the Spanish influence here." It is more likely that the Imhofs had finally run out of money. When they left Albuquerque that year, they first took the train to Santa Fe to visit their friends for several days at the Staab home, now La Posada Hotel. Traveling with them was the fox terrier that Sallie had become so attached to, and who lived with them for another sixteen years before it died in New Jersey.[71]

After several days in Santa Fe, the Imhofs and their dog took the narrow gauge train from Santa Fe over the switchbacks to Lamy. "It was a rough trip," Sallie said. "We sat on benches along the side and rode around a succession of curves and many were train sick."[72]

At Lamy, they boarded the Santa Fe train for Chicago where they planned to visit their "dear friend," Ina Law Robertson, who had founded, in 1898, the first Eleanor Club for business women. Ina Law Robertson, like so many of the Imhof friends, worked her entire adult life helping other people. She had come from Oregon to do post-graduate work at the University of Chicago. What she saw happening to working women, however, caused her to found the Eleanor Clubs.[73]

In the early part of the twentieth century, people attached a social stigma to all single working women in America. Women who worked were socially inferior and morally suspect. Men did not admire the independent woman. That admiration was reserved for males. The attitude could explain, in part, why Sallie waited until her early forties to seek employment.

The Eleanor Clubs would eventually accommodate more than six hundred girls in and near Chicago, to provide "homes where working girls earning a low wage could live in safe, comfortable and pleasant housing, yet free from charity. Her great aim was to prove that a club for working girls could be maintained on an absolutely self-supporting basis. Her experiment proved a unique success . . . ."[74]

From Chicago, the Imhofs rode the train to Buffalo for a short stay, before arriving in Montville, New Jersey where Joe began immediate construction on another large studio. Sallie was forty years old and almost giddy to be back in New Jersey. "It was amusing," she recorded, "to be greeted with joy [back] to civilization after those years of roughing it in the Southwest."[75]

The year the Imhofs left New Mexico, it became the forty-seventh state with a population of 327,000. Already, Joe was making plans to return. Among the people of New Mexico and the Pueblo Indians, he had discovered his own personal sense of place, his destiny and purpose in life. First, he would need to earn the money to sustain his family in New Mexico.

CHAPTER 12

NEW YORK AND FINANCIAL SECURITY

The coming seventeen years in New York City would bring not only financial security for the Imhofs, but become a turning point for each of them. Immediately upon their return, changes invaded their lives from every direction. The arrival of modern art created by European artists when the Armory Show opened in 1913 irrevocably changed the world of art in which Joe lived. The collapse of the older academic system, which had been in its heyday before 1870 and had already begun to crumble with the emergence of Impressionism in the early 1870s, became evident during the Armory Show. Artists began to argue among themselves over the value of academies.

Though Joe did not envision himself belonging to a particular school of art, other artists described his work as realism, and it, too, came under attack, but the arguments stimulated and excited Imhof's imagination. He intensified his search for the ideal and service to the greater good through art, all the while experimenting with ideas current among artists.

Europeans further engaged the United States in the global community by dragging the United States onto European shores to make the world safe for democracy. Prior to 1914, the United States Congress thought of the heavily armed peoples of certain European countries as blunderers when they began shooting at each other. America had not thought of itself as a world power up until this time since it had been building its own nation. Besides, the Atlantic Ocean separated Americans from strife-worn Europe. In 1914, Americans began to realize that Germany's militarism threatened the beliefs of all western civilization, and thus the stage was set for the United

States to throw off its isolationism and defend its beliefs in democracy.

At the same time, World War I provided Sallie the perfect opportunity to create a life for herself while her husband disappeared into his studio to invent a process that would sustain them financially for most of their lives.

Immediately upon arrival in New York City, the Imhofs settled onto their property in Montville, New Jersey, some thirty miles northwest of Manhattan.[1] They had purchased the six and a quarter acres in 1905, two years before leaving for Albuquerque. Since the property contained a house, several buildings, and its own water supply provided by a natural spring, the Imhofs set about making it livable.[2] Joe immediately began building a large studio for his work.[3]

Prior to living in Albuquerque, Joseph Imhof had been a well-established portrait artist, as well as a highly regarded lithographer and printer. The quality of his portraiture work can be seen in the one known portrait that he painted while living in Albuquerque, New Mexico. It is possible that upon his return, he immediately reestablished himself in portraiture. That he immediately returned to the printing and publishing industry can be found in the patents he filed in 1913 and 1914 with the assignor to Kaufmann & Strauss Company of New York, New York.

The patent that he filed on November 17, 1913 involved the invention of a new kind of Display-Stand that provided a means for positioning a carton to a Display-Stand, then locking the carton to the Display-Stand once it had been set up. The drawing in the patent application showed a hand holding a carton that projected from the Display-Stand. The completed Display-Stand provided an attractive advertising medium for a commercial product.[4]

A second Display-Stand invention, filed on December 23, 1914, depicted a hand extending from the Display-Stand that could support a heavier commercial product. The product contained in the Display-Stand showed a bottle filled with a product, and supported by bendable wings that slanted behind the Display-Stand. The Patent Office granted both patents.[5]

Shortly after Joe submitted the application for the second patent, he had moved his family from Montville into an apartment at 294 West 11th Street, near his studio in a historical part of Greenwich Village known as Abington Square.[6] The original Greenwich Village in which they lived existed within a triangular-shaped area bounded on the north by 14th Street, on the south by Spring Street, and west from Broadway. Within the triangular area lived writers and artists regarded as the center of America's literary and artistic Renaissance. The area around what is now Avenue of the Americas consisted of a maze of streets that wound around old burgher dwellings of the early eighteenth and nineteenth centuries. The narrow, crooked streets still contained homes with lawns and gardens. Nearby, on the southern side of Washington Park known as "genius row," lived the best-known artists— Reginald Marsh, Morris Kantor, Edward Laning, and Raphael and Moses Soyer. These artists eventually emerged as the group around Kenneth Hayes Miller and became known as the Fourteenth Street School, one of the more important groups that thrust realism into prominence again after it came under assault by the adherents of modern art with the opening of the Armory Show in 1913.[7]

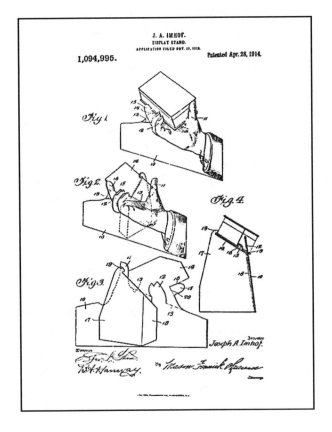

Imhof's invention
of a Display-Stand,
November 17, 1913.

Up until this critical year, 1913, the same year Joe had located his studio and his family within the ten-block radius where he had worked and kept a studio since 1898, American art had been dominated by the academies, whether located in the United States or in Europe, but particularly in France, where technical proficiency was paramount. Artists who painted outside the domain of the academies, including Joseph Imhof and others unknown or unconventional, rarely had access to public exhibitions, since the academies dominated the major art markets and publicity channels.[8]

The technically proficient artist—those trained in academies—fit well into the social structure and expectations of the late nineteenth century and first decade of the twentieth century. The country at this time had entered the machine age where science triumphed, and "the practical application of such physical research resulted in an amazing array of inventions . . . ."[9]

Simultaneously, more and more Americans saw the rising acceptance of power and wealth as an end unto itself while thousands of children continued to live on the streets where their poverty-stricken parents had abandoned them.

At this time a new group of artists, who became known as realists, were keenly aware of the social problems that festered in the streets. Most had worked as illustrators for newspapers and magazines before devoting themselves to painting.[10] It had been Robert Henri of Philadelphia who had led this new group of realists who changed the way artists and Americans approached art. In another of the strange coincidences that marked the Imhofs' lives, in 1891 Robert Henri lived at 806 Walnut Street in Philadelphia, less than a block from where Sallie had been born at 902 Walnut Street in 1872.[11]

The power of Henri's influence filtered through him as a teacher and crusader. "Aside from (Alfred) Stieglitz, there [was] no more important personality in twentieth-century American art" than Robert Henri. In the late nineteenth century, Henri had returned from Europe to teach, and became associated with a small group of artists, among them John Sloan, William Glackens, George Luks and Everett Shinn, who gathered in Henri's studio to discuss and argue art, literature, ideas, and occasionally play in amateur theatricals.[12]

Within the decade, they laid the foundation for what the academicians labeled, with derision, the "Ash Can School" of American art. Henri believed, like Joe Imhof, in the ethical ideal and in the innate goodness of man. "Whereas Henri believed in art as the expression of life, as part of life, and life as the province of art, Stieglitz saw artistic creation as an end in itself," as seen in the life and work of those artists, who included the painter Georgia O'Keeffe and photographer Paul Strand, whom Stieglitz championed.[13]

" . . . The Ash Can School stood for 'truth' as against 'beauty,' for 'life' as against 'art,' for the 'real' as against the 'artificial.'" They loved life in all its crudeness, its ugliness, and fought against the isolation and effeteness that they found in academic art. They had great sympathy for the poor, the underdog, and the lower classes. In their paintings of pictures that did not look like pictures, they captured their surroundings: street life in New York, the overcrowding, the workers, poverty, bawdy nightlife. Their work, of course, outraged the academicians.[14]

The Armory Show grew out of the academicians' rejection of new approaches to art and the desire by artists to exhibit freely. In 1907, when the National Academy of Design exhibition jury rejected two of Luks's paintings, Henri, who was serving on the jury, became so incensed that he withdrew two of his three accepted paintings, and instigated the action that led to the Armory Show.[15]

When Gertrude Vanderbilt Whitney opened the Whitney Studio Gallery the next year, the realists found support for their work and exhibited as a group. As a group, they began to gain an importance they had not had as individual artists. It was this group, led by Henri and the artist Arthur B. Davies, who brought the Armory Show into being in 1913.[16]

These young, independent artists formed the Association of American Painters and Sculptors with the purpose of mounting a large exhibition of American art. When Arthur Davies became president, he conceived the idea of including radical European art "to shatter the narrow provincialism of American taste." To this end, he helped secure an exhibition of modern art at the *Sonderbund* in Cologne. Added to this selection of modern art, which included such painters as Picasso, Braque, Matisse, Marquet, Van Gogh and Gauguin, were a selection of contemporary American artists, including John Sloan, John Marin, and Maurice Prendergast. For the first time, lithographs and etchings received status in America as works of art when a large number of important European prints appeared in the Show. In all, the Show contained 1600 works.[17]

City at the Sixty-Ninth Regiment Armory, and ran less than a month, from February 17 to March 15, 1913. Immediately, the Armory Show became page one news. Reporters, critics, and academicians expressed shock at the Show's content. One hundred thousand people came to ridicule, laugh, and express astonishment at the "fakers" who had created the works. Yet the Armory Show changed forever the way Americans came to view art. Investors began to buy the Impressionists and galleries started to open shows that not only exhibited modern art, but welcomed not only the Ash Can School and Fourteenth Street realists, but the very artists and photographers whom Alfred Stieglitz had championed.[18]

Although modern art had been imported to this country, it had been brought by American artists, and Americans, after overcoming their initial shock to such a radical departure from their understanding of art, embraced the modernists. The modernists seemed to speak to the social unrest evident before and during World War I, and the realization by Americans that the world had not been saved for democracy. At the center of these new ideas and discussions on economic/social reform sat Mabel Dodge in her salon at 23 Fifth Avenue in New York. Her evening gatherings brought together poets, writers, artists and advocates of the Armory Show, suffragists, psychoanalysts, trade unionists, people like Lincoln Steffens, Emma Goldman, John Reed, Walter Lippmann, and just plain people.[19] Joseph Imhof, in all probability, had an awareness of Mabel Dodge and the ideas flowing out of her salon, but Mabel Dodge and Joseph Imhof would wait until the Taos years to become friends and neighbors.

In the years following the Amory Show, younger artists, for the first time, felt an acceptance. Modern art denied the dogmas of the academies and allowed artists to create using concepts of color, design, and form. The academicians, of course, disapproved. However, Henri's group of realists faced a dilemma of their own. While they accepted modern art, most were unable to change their own artistic outlook because of their social beliefs about life. They simply could not reject the belief that art represented an expression of life, nor could they separate their identification with people, and their sense of social responsibility as expressed in their art. Most had a problem accepting the modernists' preoccupation with abstract forms.[20] Imhof's portraiture and scenic paintings, numerous inventions, commercial and newspaper work placed him squarely in the middle of the realists.

225

"The great majority of the realists both in literature and in art had their start and developed their styles as newspapermen . . . . The cultures which produced Matisse and Picasso, Proust and Joyce, were far different from that which produced [Theodore] Dreiser and [John] Sloan."[21] The degree to which Joseph Imhof shared the realists' views would become evident in his Taos years in his relationship with the Taos Society of Artists and neighboring Georgia O'Keeffe.

Academicians fought the modernists' idea that in art the individual, drawing upon intuitive expression, reigned supreme. In the confusion, many artists sought a more modern approach to the art academy, turning to science in an effort to establish an orderly system of universal laws under which artists could work. This would not only democratize art, but expose the charlatan masquerading as an artist, as compared to the true artist. Science, through the discovery and use of universal laws, had raised the standard of living and ushered in the industrial era. Many artists believed that such universal laws could be found for the creation of art.[22]

Shortly after 1900, Jay Hambidge developed the principles of dynamic symmetry, but his theory received minimal attention until after the Armory Show. Other theories that came into existence included the inhalation theory whose founders postulated that the thorax served as the center of emotional life. These proponents argued that all Greek figures were depicted inhaling, rather than exhaling. Another group of artists believed that there existed a theoretical relationship between color and sound whereby a color palette, and subsequent painting, could be arrived at by the mathematical use of color in the same manner that mathematics determined musical scales. Of all the so-called scientific theories, only dynamic symmetry survived.[23]

Jay Hambidge wrote that he "was impelled to take up the study of symmetry because he could not entirely agree with the modern tendency to regard design as purely instinctive."[24] Hambidge, like Imhof, had run away from home at age fifteen. He had worked as a surveyor's helper in Iowa, then moved on to Kansas City where he became a reporter before joining the *New York Herald* as a reporter. While in New York, he studied painting under William Merritt Chase's school, the New York School of Art. On an assignment from *Century* magazine in 1900 to draw Greek ruins, he developed his theory that the Egyptians and Greeks had used a mathematical formula to create balance and proportion, rather than used their instinct for design.[25]

Hambidge believed he had recovered, through the study of natural shapes such as those found in leaves and shells, and in the shapes of Egyptian and Greek art, the principles of proportion. "There is no essential difference," he wrote, "between the plan of a Greek vase and the plan of a Greek temple or theater . . . . The curves found in Greek pottery are identical with the curves of mouldings found in Greek temples."[26]

Artists Henri, Bellows and Knoll used Hambidge's mathematical compositions to proportion the content of their paintings.[27] The curator of Greek art at the Boston Museum of Fine Arts wrote a book on Hambidge's application to Greek vases, and the Metropolitan Museum of Art's curator of classical art defended Hambidge against attacks.[28] Hambidge's teaching positions at Harvard and Yale tended to add credibility to his theory.[29] Joseph Imhof and fellow artists argued dynamic symmetry and other so-called scientific theories on art late into the nights.

Like other young self-taught artists, Emil Bisttram, an illustrator and designer who began his career designing catalogue covers, fell in among advocates of dynamic symmetry. Within a short time, he developed the largest commercial art studio in New York City, which became the model for subsequent successful advertising agencies. Bisttram and his partner eventually closed their studio, and he began studying under some of the leading painters such as Leon Knoll, and at the National Academy and Chase's New York School of Art. Jay Hambidge, teaching dynamic symmetry, was among his instructors.[30]

Almost an entire generation of American painters had attended Chase's New York School of Art. There, Henri had taught such painters as George Bellows, Guy Pène du Bois, and Edward Hopper.[31] During the early 1930s, these same artists, in addition to Emil Bisttram, Joseph Imhof and Georgia O'Keeffe would arrive in Taos. However, this loose gathering of the Ash Can artists who had helped form the backbone of the Armory Show would not generate the same excitement in New Mexico. Only Bisttram and Imhof would become friends and teaching colleagues of dynamic symmetry. Mabel Dodge would also appear on the scene to provide another salon for those who simmered with ideas, and to befriend Bisttram and Imhof.

Imhof and Bisttram shared several beliefs, professionally and personally. Although Bisttram created abstract as well as traditional paintings, he and Imhof saw dynamic symmetry as a useful tool in which the artist drew

227

lines across the picture plane to aid in achieving a balance in the precise weight, mass and volume of the painting's content.[32] The harmony they sought in their paintings reflected the kind of spiritual harmony they sought in their personal lives.

Both men had a strongly developed social conscience, yet, unlike the Ash Can School of artists, neither so strongly identified with the surrounding poverty and social inequities of people around them that they painted their lives. Imhof strongly identified with the Indian. In the Indian, Imhof had found dignity and a centuries-old belief system that prevailed despite the government programs and legislation that attempted to destroy it. Like the Indian, Imhof had confronted rejection and prevailed. He had held to his own belief system and pursued his artistic interests, even strengthened these despite their lack of popularity. He had never belonged to any school of art, and apparently knew that he would always create as an outsider. While Stieglitz insisted upon the nobility of art, Imhof believed that the Indian, as a people, embodied the nobility of the human race. It was to this end that he devoted his art.

He was not, however, blind to his surroundings in New York City. From 1913 until 1918, the end of World War I, Joe volunteered his time and used his art to instruct boys, many of whom lived on the streets, about life beyond the streets.[33] Hundreds of children, most from poverty-stricken immigrant families, still lived on the streets. From 1853 until 1929, two hundred thousand boys and girls were picked up from New York streets and placed on trains headed West where people picked them out of line-ups to either adopt or employ.

It had been two artists, Ernest Thompson Seton and Daniel Carter Beard, who had originally addressed the changing youth population that had evolved by 1900. It was a world where urbanization robbed the youth of a place to roam freely, ride a horse, manage domestic animals. Such a loss caused the youth to become virtually physically weak and less resourceful.[34]

Seton and Beard were well aware that the upper classes had vast privileges, while four-fifths of the population bordered on poverty as the middle class erupted from the Industrial Revolution. Seton began a Woodcraft Indians organization in 1902 while Beard, in 1905, began a group he called Sons of Daniel Boone.[35]

Simultaneously, in England, Robert S.S. Baden-Powell was designing a similar youth group with military organization which would become the foundation for the Boy Scouts of America, though it would not become official in the United States until February 8, 1910. Soon, other groups came to the scouting field to recruit young boys. William Randolph Hearst of Hearst newspapers organized his American Boy Scouts aimed at training young soldiers.[36] This organization would later become known as the United States Boy Scouts headed by General E. A. McAlpin.

Joe became a Scout Master of 260 neighborhood boys for United States Boy Scouts, the military organization whose president, General McAlpin, believed that military discipline was the only way to control the millions of boys in the country.[37] After the Boy Scouts of America formed in the United States, General McAlpin expressed his desire for a friendly rivalry between the two organizations. McAlpin had graduated from Phillips Academy too late to serve in the Civil War, and had joined New York's Seventy-First Regiment in 1874 where he had risen in the ranks until 1895 when New York's governor had appointed him Adjutant General. He commanded New York's national guard to suppress disorder in Brooklyn when the street car riot erupted, and headed the United States Boy Scouts until his death in 1917. Officers from Governor's Island in Upper New York Bay near Brooklyn trained the boys in military and naval drills on a regular basis.[38]

On Thursday nights, Joe gave illustrated lectures to the United States Boy Scouts in the auditorium of Houston High School located at the edge of Greenwich Village. Sometimes he illustrated his lectures with his own drawings, and soon the auditorium began to fill with boys, many of whom brought their fathers. Each week the boys made their requests for subjects to be discussed the following week. Most requested western subjects.[39]

Sallie recalled, "The boys were brothers of Hudson Dusters, tough boys with guns. Yes, they had guns but were afraid of butterflies." As scout-master, Joe took them into the countryside where they camped out as he taught them to love nature, the night, and to watch the fire. Nearly forty years later, in 1954, Sallie would remark, "Imhof, lover of fellow man; he loved children, spent many years in New York City with General McAlpin and . . . gave to worthy causes, and let [me] Sallie give to worthy causes."[40]

When the United States entered World War I in 1917, many of the boys who had reached the appropriate age and had been well drilled, joined the military as corporals and sergeants. Before World War I broke out in July of 1914, though, New York prepared to celebrate the tercentenary of the establishment of chartered commerce, and the Imhofs welcomed their Indian friends who had been invited to help publicize the event.[41] Rodman Wanamaker, son of Wanamaker's Department Store founder, and President Grover Cleveland took command with an exhibit at Grand Central Palace on Lexington Avenue. On November 8, 1914, the *New York Times* reported, "A wrinkled Indian Chief with a big medal on his breast which proclaimed him to be White Man Runs Him stepped out of a tepee arranged on the ground floor of the Grand Central Palace at 7:30 o'clock last night and raised his right arm, pointing the first two fingers upward. At the same time a wireless instrument at his left began to sputter and lights flashed on in a replica of the Woolworth Building, which stood beside the tepee.

"The Indian's sign was a message of peace to all the world, and the wireless instrument caught it up, flashed it out in code to a receiving station across the long floor space and to a sending station on the roof, which wafted it out to space in general . . . . The ceremonial function was the way those in charge of the New York Commercial Tercentenary Exposition, which will remain open at the Grand Central Palace until Nov. 21, chose to usher in the first evening. The exposition was arranged so that New York business could show goods of the day's markets in a historical setting commemorating the town's 300th trade birthday.

"Most all of the space on the ground floor of the Grand Central Palace was taken up with commercial exhibits, but the walls and the general setting were arranged purely for sentimental, historical, and scenic value. The pictures brought back from the Western Indian country by Rodman Wanamaker Expedition formed the background for an arcaded entrance to the model of the Woolworth Building, and an Indian village pitched down beside it."[42]

Dr. Joseph K. Dixon, leader of the three Wanamaker Expeditions, was there to help erect the tent of Chief White Man Runs Him whom Dixon had brought back from the Crow Indian country in Montana. When Dixon asked White Man Runs Him to help erect the tepee, he refused, saying, "Heap no savvy . . . catch 'em squaw. Squaw fix 'em."[43]

Such high jinx seemed to have followed the Wanamaker Expeditions. Wanamaker had long had an interest in calling attention to the fate of the American Indian. In 1909, he had proposed that a National Memorial to the

Indian be erected in the New York harbor. In 1911, President Taft, after an act by Congress, authorized the Memorial. But two more years passed before Taft, his Cabinet members, and thirty-two Indian chiefs gathered to sign a Declaration of Allegiance to the United States.[44]

The Memorial never got built, but Wanamaker financed three expeditions led by Dixon: one filmed the movie "Hiawatha" in the Valley of the Little Big Horn; another filmed The Last Great Indian Council, a gathering of chiefs representing every major Indian community; and, finally, Dixon took the American flag, as a symbol of citizenship, to every Indian community, whereupon the Dixon group recreated the New York ceremony.[45]

In 1912, John Young-Hunter, by now a professional photographer, had recently arrived in United States. His interest in Indians led him in 1913 to the Crow Agency in Montana to record the event. In his book, *Reviewing the Years*, Young-Hunter wrote, "My arrival at the Crow Agency was coincident with a special occasion; a group of photographers from Philadelphia [Wanamaker Expo.] has just left for Lame Deer, the agency of the Northern Cheyenne Indians, a few miles distant, the object of their visiting the Crow Agency being to record Indian types for a forthcoming publication.

"The Indians, I discovered, were not too well pleased with the result of the inconvenience to which they had been put, having come many miles in anticipation of a feast; whereas, I was told, they were presented only with a flag, an emblem which they complained they already possessed!"[46]

Of the New York celebration, Sallie Imhof remembered, "Indians from all over the U.S.A. were entertained. Our Pablo Abeyta (sic) was one, and another was White Man Runs Him, a Ute from Utah who was said to be the only Custer scout that escaped the massacre because Custer had sent him on some mission."[47] Although the *New York Times* identified White Man Runs Him as a chief from Wyoming, and Sallie labeled him a Ute from Utah, White Man Runs Him was a Crow from Montana who served as Custer's Chief of Scouts.[48]

"So for many days," Sallie remembered, "these two men went out of our house and the studio, and at the Palace the scouts [the group Sallie always referred to as General McAlpin's Boy Scouts] met with them and were so happy to be greeted in Indian style.

"There were funny incidents all the time. White Man was warned about dropping lighted cigarettes. One day while walking along with Joe and Pablo

231

he threw his cigarette out into Lexington Avenue, remembered, and dashed out amid the traffic to step on it and had to be rescued by Pablo. Again at Pennsylvania Station the three had been seeing some Indians off to Washington. At that time the ceiling decoration of the main room was the sky and the constellations, and with the great knowledge the Indians have of astronomy White Man stopped and gave a demonstration and as he was in full costume the commuters began to collect until the guards had to ask them to leave as the trains were being run late."[49]

While in New York, Pablo Abeita discussed the completed history of Isleta Pueblo that he had written. He remarked to Joe and Sallie that he would not bequeath the completed text to his people until after his death. Later, in the 1930s, after Joe and Sallie moved to Taos, Pablo again mentioned his completed Isleta history text. In the years after Pablo's death, Sallie would wonder if the manuscript were known by Pablo's people.[50]

The Imhofs' concern for recording the Indian people took various forms, one of which included the creation of life casts with a composition invented by Joe and one of his partners and great friends, the artist/sculptor Sigurd Neandross, a Norwegian born in the same year as Imhof, 1871. They had been experimenting with the process for several years before Pablo Abeita and White Man Runs Him arrived for the Tercentenary; so, during that time, Imhof and Neandross made casts of both men.[51]

"The process consisted," Sallie said, "in covering the entire head," the hair included, and shoulders with the composition invented by Imhof and Neandross. Tubes were inserted into the subjects' nostrils as a means for breathing, and communication was accomplished by the use of a pad of paper and pencil.[52] The life cast, or life mask, created a portrait made from touch and allowed subjects to see themselves in three dimension, a rarity since individuals usually see themselves in reflected mirrors. The mask had the capacity to give subjects new insights into themselves.

During these years, Imhof and Neandross made many life casts of explorers. One such explorer, Theodore Roosevelt, had an appointment to have his life cast made at his Oyster Bay home with the artists when, on the morning of the appointment in January 1919, Roosevelt died.[53] Joe gave the life cast of White Man Runs Him to a California museum. In May 1961, Sallie gave the life cast of Pablo Abeita to Maxwell Museum of Anthropology of the University of New Mexico, Albuquerque in memory of Joe.[54]

Imhof's life cast in
studio, ca. 1912.

The California museum had replicas made, "Joe said not very successfully and they sent him one which he gave to his friend Thomas Gilcrease" in
Tulsa, Oklahoma.[55] In 1961, Sallie wrote to Dr. W. W. Hill of the University
of New Mexico about the value of Pablo Abeita's cast. "I was surprised that
the 'bust' of Pablo Abeyta (sic) was not valued at a higher rate than $200.00.
Pablo was such a prominent Indian in Washington and among the Pueblos—
the official interpreter for all the Pueblos on their trips to Washington as he
spoke all the different tongues. When he died the publication "Indians at
Work" published a long obituary; he was a dear friend of ours and visited us
in New York where the <u>Life Cast</u> was made by Joe in 1916 [actually 1914] so it
is not just a bit of sculpture but a perfect showing of the man as he actually
was. This is not a criticism, but I thought you would like to know something
of the history which I gave to Dr. Hibben, but I fear he had forgotten to tell
it to you."[56]

Imhof's photograph of Theodore Roosevelt, ca. 1919.

Through the years in which the Imhofs lived in Greenwich Village, they had many Indian visitors, "especially from Canada, and Joe continued to paint and talk to them, but all the time his interest in the Southwest increased. Much time was spent in libraries, and he had others searching the libraries for more information, and the traders would come bringing him artifacts of the Pueblos and with his determination with the fixed idea that we were coming out to stay [in New Mexico and] he worked to that end."[57]

By 1915, Joe had reached age forty-two, Sallie forty-one, and Elizabeth graduated from high school that year at age sixteen.[58] The Imhofs' social life continued to be full and unabated. They renewed their attendance at Dr. Felix Adler's Ethical Culture lectures, this time becoming personally acquainted with Dr. Adler. "We became members of that cult," Sallie said.

"Every Sunday Dr. Adler filled Carnegie Hall for his talks. In many ways Joe's outlook was changed, and he became more serious and dedicated to his profession and the great desire to convince youth of its great opportunities." Sallie observed, "In many ways he did succeed and was happy to live his life to see some results in his desires. To this day [1963] I receive letters from happy people who thank Joe for showing the way."[59]

In 1916, George G. Heye, an independently wealthy New York banker, founded the Museum of the American Indian and located it at 155th Street at Broadway, near Washington Heights. Just after the turn of the century, Heye had become obsessed with collecting artifacts of Native culture. His purchases filled boxcars which he sent back to New York. Not until 1922 did the museum open to the public, and then its focus went beyond the simple display of objects.[60]

The Heye Museum devoted itself to the exhibition, study and preservation of the culture of the Native American of all the Americas. The curators hoped to develop a better understanding of the Indian through archaeology and study of the origin, early migration, and ancient civilizations of the Indian. By ethnology, the museum staff sought to study the living people, their customs and history. The Imhofs became devoted to the Heye Museum where they conducted some of their research, and later donated artifacts.

The year after the Heye Museum opened, when the United States entered World War I in 1917, the Imhofs watched with a measure of pride and regret as a Marine recruiting ship, the *Leviathan*, anchored in the New York harbor and many of the boys from Joe's Scout troop enlisted. Both of the Imhofs were overage for military duty, though that did not deter Sallie from enlisting in the United States Naval Reserve Force at the Third Naval District, 61 Chambers Street, in New York City. She listed her birth date as November 9, 1879, shaving seven years from her actual birth in 1872. In all probability, Sallie became one of the first women to serve in the United States Navy known as National Yeoman (F).[61]

On August 28, 1918, she received her rank as Yeoman Third Class (F) NRF. The following month, on September 3, 1918, the Navy called Sallie to active duty and transferred her to the Fleet Supply Base, South Brooklyn, where she was attached to the Admiral's staff as secretary. Within two months, World War I ended, though Sallie continued in the Navy for another two years, and commanded several hundred women.[62]

On January 20, 1920, she was awarded a Victory button, and on November 19, 1920, the Navy discharged her at Brooklyn as a Yeoman First Class (F).[63] A photograph made of Sallie during her Naval service shows a handsome, trim woman with pure joy written in her smile. It was the kind of joy that stayed in her conscious memory for the remainder of her days and thereafter, for she never parted with her uniform, even into her afterlife.

During the time Sallie served in the Navy, Joe had been experimenting with aniline color dyes, synthetic dyes prepared from coal tar, and the first such dye from a source other than that taken from plants and minerals.[64] The first aniline dye had been discovered by an English chemist, Sir William Henry Perkin, in 1853; he had the process patented in 1856.

At the time Joe began his experiments with aniline color, Sallie reported, "It was a time of trouble for me; long days and nights spent in the studio, and he would come home with his blond hair stained with color and his clothes also."[65]

Sallie in her Navy uniform, 1917-1920.

On May 23, 1921, Joseph Imhof filed an application with the United States Patent Office, the Assignor to Invisible Color Print Corporation of New York, for a Method of Producing Color-Prints. Imhof's application described a printing process whose main feature had an apparently uniform color but latent and substantially invisible color released and made visible upon application of a solvent, such as water.[66]

Joseph Imhof, who had invented a printing process using invisible color, had two partners, John Charters and a man named Pearson, with whom he formed the name of their corporation by using the first letter of each last name: Imhof, Charters, Pearson; Invisible Color Print.[67] The Patent Office granted Imhof's first patent on July 12, 1921. He filed subsequent patent applications that used only water to reveal hidden images using a four-color process, an improved printing process, the use of varnish, and a way of superimposing one color upon another. The Patent Office granted three other patents on March 6, 1923, September 2, 1924, and March 10, 1925.[68]

When the first experiments succeeded during 1920, Joe came into the house one day and announced to Sallie, "This is it! This patent will be the means of our retiring from everything commercial, and I can paint."[69]

Immediately Imhof and his partners went into business. They leased a large loft on White Street where they installed three printing presses, and Joe supervised the quality of the materials printed: sets of twelve pictures of educational subjects. One side carried the invisible picture, and other side contained a story about the picture's content. The partners sold the sets of pictures to large southern bread companies which used them to promote bread product sales. Children collected the sets and received gifts for the sets.[70]

Income from their business had finally provided financial security for the Imhofs. Joe now operated three studios, one for his experiments and inventions, another for his painting and lithography, and the third for printing the invisible color sets. In May 1922, they sold the property in Montville, New Jersey and began making short trips of a few months into Canada to continue their study of the Indians, and for Joe to paint. That year they spent several months in Newfoundland where Joe studied and painted the native fishermen. "He did some wonderful seascapes of stormy seas," Sallie related.[71]

The next year, in 1923, the Imhofs purchased a three-story century-old brick home at 22 Willow Street in Brooklyn Heights, the site of the original Dutch settlement and only a few blocks from where Roebling lived at 110

Columbia Heights as he oversaw the building of the Brooklyn Bridge.[72] Brooklyn, whose geography consisted primarily of flat land, had so few high points that the people designated names for them. It must have been with great pride that Joseph Imhof returned and bought a distinguished home in the area of his origin.

Brooklyn Heights resides on "a bluff above the East River cut off from the rest of the borough by Brooklyn's Fulton Street. It is thus isolated on its high eminence with a breathtaking view of the tip of lower Manhattan."[73] In 1923, the houses on Willow Street consisted of "row houses, extending row block after block, on tree-lined streets, interrupted only by an occasional school or church or apartment house."[74] The Imhofs' house measured twenty-two feet wide and forty-five feet deep with large porches on the back overlooking gardens.[75] The house, now in the designated Brooklyn Heights Historic District, is described as a fine Greek Revival house.[76]

Joe, while never a sportsman, found archery, target shooting, soccer and baseball of interest.[77] The early Brooklyn baseball teams used players only from Brooklyn and managed to win the pennant in 1916 before sliding into the basement.[78] Joe became an avid and loyal fan of the Brooklyn Dodgers who boasted of some of the most loyal fans in baseball.[79] In 1922, pitcher Clarence Arthur Vance joined the team and hurled them into competition again.[80]

Although the Imhofs never succeeded in their travel plans to Spain to explore the Spanish influence on the Pueblo Indians, in 1925 they managed to travel the eastern coast of South America. There they stayed in Rio de Janeiro and Buenos Aires, and other cities. While they had wanted to visit Peru, their time constraints did not allow them to reach their goal.[81]

After they returned, Sallie began working as executive secretary for the American Legion, which had been formed after World War I, and incorporated by an act of Congress in 1919. The Legion dedicated itself to veterans, community, and national interests related to rehabilitation, child welfare, national security, and patriotism. Sallie's work with the American Legion in New York began her life-long devotion to the organization.[82]

In addition to her work with the American Legion, Sallie began making authentically dressed Indian dolls. Most of the dolls measured ten-by-four inches and included Matachine Dancers who danced during the time of early Spanish settlers in the pueblos; San Juan Deer Dancer; Santo Domingo

Corn Dancer; Malinche-Virgin Dancer, a ten to eleven-year-old girl; Hopi Dancer/Basket; and Hopi Eagle Dancer.[83]

"I wish to convey," she wrote of this time, "that our life was the usual life of a family of three, socially and professionally. I was prominent in New York City Legion affairs, and we were both interested in Greenwich House under the direction of the beloved Mary Kingsbury Sankowich, who married a Russian Professor from Columbia College. It was a wonderfully run foundation, and the teachers of about everything the young of that neighborhood demanded were there. Joe had a class in drawing, another in pottery making, and every so often he would get a group around him and tell them of other towns and countries. Sometimes Mayor Jimmie Walker would come around and visit. He was a lovable boy who never really grew up, and everyone liked him in his earlier years."[84]

Walker's later years lost their luster when charges of corruption marred his administration. However, subsequent investigations showed that Walker had been more careless than corrupt.

During these same years, Sallie would recall to a Taos friend, Walter A. Bailey who would live in the Imhofs' Taos guest house, "In the 1920s we were rich beyond all means."[85] Even though Sallie served as Joe's manager, the Imhofs engaged the professional services of Joseph Henry Ide, who headed the certified public accounting firm of Joseph Henry Ide & Company of New York City. "When the Imhofs left New York, . . Imhof turned over every penny to have Joseph Ide invest the money and send him an allowance, allotment."[86]

The Imhofs and Ides had already enjoyed a long-term relationship before the Imhofs left New York, as can be seen in the Ide's daughter, Harriet, who knew the Imhofs as Uncle Joe and Aunt Sarah. This close relationship in their professional and personal friendship would continue long into the future. Later, in Taos, when the Ides visited the Imhofs, not only did the Taos Indians permit the Ides into a kiva, but the Indians came to the Imhofs' house and baked bread for them in an Indian oven. On another occasion, in 1937, the Ides met D. H. Lawrence and his wife Frieda, Georgia O'Keeffe and other artists in the Imhof home. Over the years, Joseph Imhof sent the Ides many gifts, including jewelry, carved totem poles, etchings, and paintings. Harriet corresponded with the Imhofs, writing numerous thank you letters. But all this lay in the future.[87]

When the Great Depression shattered so many lives, the economic catastrophe left no scars in the Imhofs' lives. Their pain, particularly for Sallie, was felt in leaving their environment. For Sallie, this meant the American Legion that she had come to love. "And now the time grew near to forget all the frivolity and the culture of the New York scene," she wrote. "There was a certain reluctance and sadness in cutting off old ties, and the task of trying to make our friends understand that we were not making a great sacrifice in giving up our normal life and going to that wild Southwest."[88]

Sallie's regrets can be understood by reading the memoirs she wrote of the American Legion testimonial given to her that took place in 1930 before the Imhofs left New York for Taos. "The following testimonial was given me at the large farewell party at the Hotel Pennsylvania where several thousand were present. It is the document in hand lettered in Roman character beautyful [sic] illuminated and is of beautyful [sic] workmanship. The signature is by the Legion Chairman of New York county and adjutant of the county. It is done on Vellum and cover cushioned leather.

"The letter from the National Commander was written from London England. He was elected to his office in Paris, France at the convention celebrating the 10 anniversary of the Legion, a dear and trusted friend for years before and after World War I."[89]

On May 21, 1930, the National Commander of the American Legion wrote Sallie: "I am sorry that you are leaving New York permanently. Many a disabled man in that City is going to miss you. When Judgment Day rolls round and you have an opportunity to look at the Judgment Book, I am sure that you will find your name leading all the rest, for it will certainly be recorded there that you are one who loved your fellow-man. The unselfish service which over this long period of years, you have freely given can never be sufficiently rewarded upon this earth. But I want here and now to testify as to that of which I have personal knowledge. There has never been another like you."[90]

Sallie had reached age fifty-seven when Joseph Imhof, age fifty-eight, closed his three studios. Elizabeth was now thirty-one and apparently still living at home. "With all the arrangements and the packing of the contents of three studios and our large house and all the rest of it, Joe was very tired."[91]

The unknown that loomed in Taos, their next destination, must have taken its toll on all of them. For Joe, there was no turning back.

CHAPTER 13

HOME IN TAOS

At the age of fifty-eight, Joseph Imhof embarked upon a new career in Taos. In that summer of 1929, when he and Sallie came to buy land and cut timbers for their adobe home, which would include Joe's studio with an attached room for his lithography press and a guest house, Sallie must have reflected on their previous life in Albuquerque, then steeled herself for what she knew lay in store for her.[1]

Don Fernando de Taos, as it had been known before 1884, was only an isolated village of dirt roads, its name having been given to distinguish it from Ranchos de Taos, another village a few miles south. Although ancient peoples had been living in the area since 3,000 B.C., Don Fernando de Taos officially sprang into existence somewhere between 1777 and 1800 when a number of Spaniards, who had been living in the Taos Pueblo, had settled together a short distance from the pueblo.[2]

In the late 1920s, Taos was also home to about twenty-five artists who had established, shortly after the Imhofs had moved from Albuquerque to New York, a kind of celebrity about themselves and their art. Sallie knew Joe shrank from this kind of public seeking of adulation, but that he would soon lose himself in his art and the Indians living in the surrounding pueblos.[3] She, in turn, would summon her courage and make a life for herself. Since neither Sallie nor Joe left any record of whether Elizabeth joined them in Taos, it is possible that Elizabeth might have been attempting to cut herself adrift from her parents. At age thirty-one she still had not separated from them. Too, the prospect of living in such an isolated area, no matter how beautiful, must not have held much appeal to a young woman in the prime of her life.

For an artist, though, the area around Taos offered the very essence of life: pristine light, diverse cultures and a land so vast with space, geological features, and rich, varied vegetation that it expanded the mind and spirit. In fact, artists had been drawn to the primitive soul of the area for several hundred years. The Dutch painter, Jan Mostaert, had been so taken with the northern New Mexico area after reading a report of Coronado's expedition of 1540-42 that in 1545 he had painted an imagined landscape.[5]

An engraving, "Don Fernando de Taos," by W. W. H. Davis and dated 1857, depicted an adobe village tucked in the foothills of the Sangre de Cristo mountain range.[6] Alex Compera, a pioneer Colorado landscape artist who had studied in Paris in the 1870s, had arrived in Taos in 1879 and become perhaps one of the first to paint the village.[7] Henry Rankin Poore, an artist trained in Philadelphia and Europe, visited Taos several times in the 1870s, 1880s and 1890s. One of his paintings completed in the 1880s, "Pack Train Leaving Pueblo of Taos, New Mexico," illustrated an 1890 census document he participated in gathering from sixteen pueblos.[8]

Poore's art became one of the most widely circulated illustrations of Taos.[9] However, it was Joseph Henry Sharp of Ohio who gave birth to Taos' future art colony. After he received training at Cincinnati's Art Academy, Sharp traveled to Europe in 1881 and, like Joseph Imhof, furthered his art studies in Antwerp. In 1883, at the age of twenty-four, he made his first sketching trip to Santa Fe and points west. He was particularly impressed with the fact that Indians in the Southwest and West still lived in a natural state.[10]

Sharp returned to Europe for further study and painting, then returned to New Mexico in 1893 and spent the summer painting and sketching in Taos. One of his illustrations from this trip appeared in *Harper's Weekly* where it received wide circulation. Sharp returned to Europe for study at the *Académie Julian* where he met two young Americans, Ernest Blumenschein and Bert Phillips. The eagerness and enthusiasm with which Sharp described his experiences in New Mexico ignited Blumenschein's and Phillips's imaginations.[11]

Blumenschein, who had also grown up in Ohio and studied at the Cincinnati Art Academy, actively sought a means to reach the West. When he received an illustration assignment from *McClure's Magazine* in 1897-1898, Phillips joined him on a sketching trip into the mountains of Colorado. In the late summer of 1898, they bought a wagon and team of horses and set off for Mexico and, after many mishaps, found themselves stranded with a broken wagon wheel in Northern New Mexico's San Luis Valley.[12]

Perhaps Blumenschein's view of what he experienced as he rode one of their horses twenty miles into Taos while Phillips waited best describes the magic that drew artists to Taos. "I was receiving under rather painful circumstances the first great, unforgettable inspiration of my life. My destiny was being decided as I squirmed and cursed while urging the bronco through those many miles of waves of sagebrush. Sharp had not painted for me the mountains or plains or clouds. No artist had ever recorded the New Mexico I was now seeing. The color, the reflective character of the landscape, the drama of the vast spaces, the superb beauty and severity of the hills, stirred me deeply. I realized I was getting my own impressions from nature, seeing it for the first time with my own eyes, uninfluenced by the art of any man."[13]

Joseph Imhof would see this awesome and natural beauty in 1907. To this he would add the power of New Mexico's ancient people who had complex origins, religions, and moral values which they preserved in an oral history never divulged to outsiders, because that would offend their religious privacy. These were the elements of life Imhof sought to reexperience and record; why he had worked so diligently for seventeen years in New York to secure the financial means to return and live out his remaining days.

The Taos area in 1898 clearly impacted Bert Phillips, now thirty, in the same way it had affected Blumenschein and would affect Imhof. Phillips stayed, and eventually married the sister of Dr. T. P. Martin.[14] Dr. Martin had arrived in 1889, after having studied at College of Physicians & Surgeons, Baltimore, to become Taos's first physician. Blumenschein returned to France where he and Sharp continued their enthusiastic conversations about Taos. Coincidentally in 1899, Oscar Berninghaus of St. Louis, an artist traveling through Colorado as guest of the Denver and Rio Grande Railroad, heard of Taos and took a side trip to the area which so impressed him that he decided to return every summer.[15]

E. Irving Couse, who had been trained at the Art Institute of Chicago and was studying in Paris at the time Sharp and Blumenschein spoke so glowingly of Taos, became caught in the imaginative idea of painting an unspoiled land and its people. In 1902, Couse arrived in Taos for the summer. Taos and its people continued to draw him back every summer until 1927 when he made Taos his permanent home.[16]

By 1905, Blumenschein had married Mary Shepard Greene, a prize-winning artist in Paris, and persuaded her to return with him in the summers to Taos.[17] Two years later, in 1907, Joseph, Sallie, and Elizabeth Imhof had arrived in New Mexico, but their destination had been Albuquerque to give Joe a home base from where he could travel to sketch, photograph and come to know Pueblo Indians in the New Mexico Territory.

The Blumenscheins first settled in New York where Ernest worked as an illustrator for book publishers of such authors as Willa Cather, Jack London and Booth Tarkington, and the major magazines of the day: *Harper's*, *Century*, *Scribner's*. He also taught at the Art Students League.[18] Here he met W. Herbert Dunton of Maine who had studied at the Cowles Art School before going off to Montana to join a "cow out-fit" which eventually took him to New Mexico. When Dunton returned to New York where he, too, worked as an illustrator for magazines, he enrolled in Blumenschein's class. Blumenschein recommended that Dunton spend the summer painting in Taos. Upon his arrival, Dunton knew Taos held what he wanted as an artist. The following summers he returned to paint until 1912 when he moved permanently to Taos. Blumenschein, his wife, Mary Greene, and their daughter, Helen, would finally settle in Taos in 1919.[19]

Four of these six artists—Sharp, Blumenschein, Phillips, and Couse—had studied in Europe, and at the *Académie Julian* in Paris. All had discussed the possibility of forming an art colony in their own country, a colony similar to the ones in France where artists gathered to paint in a natural setting.

America had nothing comparable to the fine art academies and museums found in Europe, which was why most American painters studied in the European environment. When these artists returned to their own country, many suffered cultural shock when they again found themselves in a country that nurtured and celebrated commercial enterprise while denigrating artistic endeavors. Numerous of these artists sought to establish a kind of school of art that was uniquely American. In the late 1890s, American art colonies, such as those formed at Laguna and Carmel, California and Provincetown and Gloucester, Massachusetts, used Barbizon, France as their model.[20]

Barbizon, which had been founded in the 1830s, was the most famous of the French art colonies, and served as the model for all of the French colonies that followed: Giverny, Pont-Aven, Concarneau, and Etaples. These colonies offered a kind of summer retreat from the pressures of urban living, an opportunity to paint in a natural setting, and the enjoyment of the relaxed camaraderie of fellow artists. The settings and companionships nurtured the painters.[21]

This kind of environment was what the painters who settled in Taos had in mind. " . . . if (our) your, I mean, scheme goes through," Phillips wrote to Blumenschein from Taos, "we can come together better prepared for a mutual aid to each other . . . . We'll be . . . like the group of Barbizon painters and writers . . . ."[22]

Six years later, in 1906, Joseph Henry Sharp, who had divided his time between Taos and the Crow Agency in Montana, wrote to the Director of the Cincinnati Art Museum, " . . . you see, we are at our first love and stomping ground. Bert Phillips is here year round. Couse has just bought a little place, fitted up a studio and is at work, and likely for many summers. Young Berninghaus of St. Louis has just left and Curtis and Sauerwein and others are coming, so there may be a Taos colony a la Barbizon yet!"[23]

During the late 1800s and early 1900s, the subject matter of Taos and other American painters who lived in art colony type settings located in the United States began to speak of a powerful sense of place and of a unique people, while European artists turned more to style. The Taos and Santa Fe artists created their own subjects that fit well into this emerging depiction of America.

In July of 1915, these six Taos artists met in the home of Dr. T. P. Martin, Taos' local physician who had a well-established reputation in the dusty community, to form the Taos Society of Artists. The newly formed Society existed, they determined, to educate others about their work through the use of traveling exhibitions, since Taos had no galleries; to promote and stimulate expressions of art; and to develop a high standard of art among members. The doorway to membership came through sponsorship by two members, having lived or worked in Taos for three years intermittently, and having exhibited in some capacity. All new members had to receive a unanimous vote and pay one dollar annual dues.[24]

Within three years of the Society's formation, members' canvases were being shown in New York galleries, and in their own traveling exhibitions in major American cities. Active, Associate, and Honorary memberships never exceeded eighteen artists at any one time. In 1927, when the group disbanded, only twenty-one artists had been selected into the elite group's twelve-year existence. But the Society had achieved its goal.[25] Now travelers and tourists stopped in Taos to view and purchase art. Some of these travelers would, in time, become friends and clients of the Imhofs.

By the time Joe and Sallie arrived in 1929, the artists who had originally established homes in Taos had bought the existing buildings and converted them into homes and studios. Phillips had bought a house and remodeled it into a home and studio; E. Irving Couse had bought an abandoned convent and turned it into a studio/home; J. H. Sharp had reworked a chapel into a studio; W. Herbert Dunton's home and studio had been a part of the Plaza upon the Loma, "as the small hill in the western part of town" was called; Ernest Blumenschein had converted a low, rambling adobe into a hacienda on the edge of the Loma; Walter Ufer's studio had been a Penitente chapel.[26]

Imhof, of course, had envisioned his own studio attached to his home, one he would build himself. He had money now, and he intended to create his own environment.

In this respect, he and Mabel Dodge Sterne had much in common. Mabel Dodge, the Grande Dame of New York City, had discovered Taos and the Indians about the same time as had Joseph Imhof.[27] The two would become neighbors and friends in their years in Taos, and each would build an adobe house that reflected the builder's character.

Mabel, however, moved to Taos in 1917, two years after the Taos Society of Artists formed. With her presence came added attention to the village, for members of her salon followed. The writers Carl Van Vechten and D. H. Lawrence visited, as did the psychoanalyst Carl Jung. Mabel invited Georgia O'Keeffe and Rebecca Strand, who became her houseguests in 1929. The visitors became news items that fed attention upon Taos. Then Mabel shed her husband and in 1923 married a Taos Indian, Antonio "Tony" Luhan. That alliance made more headline news in her hometown of Pittsburgh.

Taos so entranced Mabel that she is said to have written, "There is some strange charm about Taos, everyone . . . will agree. And there is no other place in America that stimulated and enchanted as many really significant Americans, as this small corner of the earth that has been called by the Indians 'the beating heart of the world.'"

For Joseph Imhof, the Indians represented "the beating heart of the world." Indeed, the Taos Indians, and everything about them—their costumes, their pueblo, and their sacred Taos Mountain—dominated not just the landscape of Imhof's life, but most of the lives of the artists living in Taos. Bert Phillips commented that all he had to do was "to hint of the meaning of a pose or show them my preliminary sketch to have them sense the idea of the picture."[28]

The Taos Indians, of course, had long since learned to accommodate intruders onto their lands. In the 1200s, the Taos Indians had settled at the lower slope of the Sangre de Cristo mountain range, and built four and five story apartments of adobe that appeared to be extensions of the land. They laid claim to Taos Mountain, a 12,282-foot peak that harbored Blue Lake from which they believed they had arisen, and which dominated their landscape and lives. Water from the mountain's sacred Blue Lake flowed in a stream from the mountain through the center of their pueblo. They farmed in relative peace until 1540 when the Spaniard, Captain Alvarado, led a detachment from Coronado's Expedition into their midst.[29]

From that moment, Taos Indians struggled against intruders who attempted to strip them of their land, their religion, and beliefs. When they rebelled, the Spaniards, and then the Americans slaughtered them.[30] Others came, of course, mountain men such as Kit Carson, and more Spanish priests such as Padre Antonio José Martinez whom Willa Cather alluded to in her novel, *Death Comes to the Archbishop*. Padre Martinez, who had been born in nearby Abiquiu into a well-to-do Martinez family, became one of the most powerful men in Taos. These latecomers, however, showed more respect for the Indians' autonomy. And the artists and writers respected the Taos Indians more than any others.[31]

The Indians paid a terrible price for accommodating all these people who wanted to share the Pueblos' environment and live in close proximity to their culture. Mabel Dodge Luhan observed in her book, *Winter in Taos*, "In those years before 1929, one could see the influence of American money in the Pueblo. Several Indians opened curio shops out there and neglected to cultivate their fields. They let the earth lie fallow, and they began to make cheap little drums, bows and arrows, small, uninspired pots, and even oil paintings of the Pueblo, Indian horses and men.

"There were so many tourists and they spent so much money, the Indians thought all the Americans in the States were coming here and that they were all rich!"[32]

The newly arrived Anglos—that wave of artists and writers who believed they had discovered then captured the soul and essence of Taos—would refer to the period between 1920 and 1940 as the "Golden Age of Taos."[33]

In the summer of 1929 when the Imhofs arrived, seven hundred Taos Indians lived in the Taos Pueblo. Among the Taos Indians whom Joe Imhof met that year was Gold Tooth John Mirabel. Sometime that summer or fall, Joe told Gold Tooth John Mirabel of the Imhofs' plans to build an adobe house in Taos and "that he would like to have an old beam from the mission destroyed by the U.S. troops in 1847."[34]

On July 26, that summer, Joe and Sallie purchased an irregular shaped parcel of land bounded on the north by the lands of the Taos Pueblo. The eastern sector of the land lay next to the *Acequia Madre del Pueblo*, and the southern portion butted up against the Brooks Subdivision.[35] On the western border was an alfalfa field which had been purchased in 1927 by Duane Van Vechten, an artist trained at the Art Institute of Chicago, in Europe and New York. However, she would not live on the land until she moved to Taos in 1929 and married Ed Lineberry two years later. After their marriage, they would turn the field into an eighteen-acre estate called El Rancho de la Mariposa de Taos. Duane was the niece of Carl Van Vechten, the journalist, photographer and novelist who had visited Mabel Dodge Luhan. Van Vechten would produce an extraordinary record of the great creative talent of his time. He counted among his friends Eugene O'Neill, George Gershwin, and Paul Robeson. In 1932, he began photographing celebrities and scenes of life in his era. In all, he left 15,000 photographs, most of them portraits. He would spend more and more time in Taos.[36]

Three days after the Imhofs' first land purchase, on July 29, they bought an additional parcel of land belonging to the Brooks Subdivision.[37] With this piece of land, they now owned two and a half acres that provided a magnificent view to the north of the Sangre de Cristo and sacred Taos Mountain.[38] The view of Taos Mountain constantly reminded them that within its folds rested the sacred waters of Blue Lake, "the source of all life for Taos . . . the repository for the souls of the departed Taos people."[39]

That Joseph Imhof clearly understood the religious significance of Taos Mountain and Blue Lake before he and Sallie arrived in Taos can be seen in his already formulated idea of the kind of adobe house he intended to build. After purchasing the property, he refined his plans before hiring a native

New Mexican and two helpers to select the pine trees to be felled, striped and dried for use in construction the next year.[40] It is also possible that the newly hired helpers set about making the sun-dried adobe bricks that needed to cure for almost a year before being used.

The ninety-two-foot-long by twenty-five-foot house needed adobe bricks that measured four-by-eight-by-sixteen inches and weighed one hundred pounds each. The Imhofs regarded the New Mexican they had hired a master craftsman and felt comfortable leaving him to supervise the work that needed to be completed that winter.[41]

As the Imhofs selected the materials for their new home and introduced themselves to the people in the community, they explored their surroundings. Less than a mile from the property they now owned lay a *Morada*, a small adobe chapel without windows that housed an altar and religious objects. The *Morada* served as the meeting place for the Penitentes who had descended from the Spaniards when they had occupied Northern New Mexico. During the occupation, the Penitentes had been a powerful political force. Their descendants continued to carry on the practices from the Flagellantes, people known to have lived in Europe during the Middle Ages.[42]

The self-punishing flagellations practiced by the Catholic, Hispanic members of the *Moradas* so horrified Archbishop Lamy when he arrived in 1899 that he banned the Penitente societies. That only drove them underground.[43] The Imhofs, years before when they had lived in Albuquerque, had first learned of the Penitente practices which still held a fascination for them.

During Lent, the Penitente brothers met in the *Morada* for prayers and instructions. On Friday nights, men in their first years of membership marched, naked to the waist, from the *Morada* whipping their backs with a fiber rope knotted with cactus spines. On Ash Wednesday, by drawing lots, a brother was selected to reenact the role of Christ, and on Good Friday the brother was fastened to the cross. If he died, the Penitentes secretly buried him.[44]

Moradas appeared on the canvases of Taos artists. In 1929, Joseph Imhof, using either his 4x5 camera with glass plates, or his tiny camera with bellows, photographed the *Morada* near his new property and the Penitente crosses at Truchas, a village about thirty-eight miles south of Taos. He entertained the thought of using the authentic building and crosses in one of his future paintings.[45]

After the Imhofs returned to New York to pack, they made the rounds to tell their friends good-bye and take a few nostalgic trips to the places they had lived. One such trip took them up the Hudson River to gaze upon the Spuyten Duyvil area where they hoped to catch a glimpse of the Connelly mansion where they had lived as newlyweds. Joe had painted the wisteria that covered the Connelly wall of balconies in 1898, and the Imhofs had made many hikes into the surrounding forested area. In 1930, they found instead a long line of ten-story apartment buildings and no evidence of trees and shrubs.[46]

Sallie, Imhof and unidentified woman on ship, ca. 1930.

All that spring, the Imhofs packed in order to ship their goods, including Joe's lithography press, the Rutherford flatbed hand press used by lithographers at Currier and Ives. This simple, cast-iron press patterned after English lithograph presses was used for printing lithographs directly from stone and metal plates.[47] In all probability, the Imhofs shipped the Rutherford on the same train that would take them to Raton, New Mexico. Once they arrived in Raton they, like other travelers, might have hired horse-drawn wagons that carried them and their goods into Don Fernando de Taos. While it is possible that the Imhofs took this route to reach Taos, since it is more direct, they could have taken the longer route to Lamy, then traveled back up to Santa Fe and eventually to Taos.

When the Imhofs arrived in Raton on Memorial Day, they became marooned once again by a heavy storm and impassable roads. When they finally arrived in Taos, they decided to take up residence at the Don Fernando Hotel, one of two hotels in Taos.[48] Gerson Gusdorf had completed the hotel in 1926, and liked to cater to the local artists, giving them special attention, and hosting an annual dinner for them that included after-dinner speeches. As a result, the Don Fernando Hotel became the gathering place for artists and their friends. Besides, the hotel was within easy walking distance for most who lived in Taos.[49]

As residents of the Don Fernando Hotel, the Imhofs could watch the famous, the talented, and well-educated come and go, and listen to their conversations and debates as they gathered. On a regular basis, Taos Indians danced in the hotel to entertain guests, and artists regularly hung their art for sale. Emil Bisttram arrived from Mexico where he had been studying under a Guggenheim Scholarship that same year. However, he had not yet opened his Heptegon Gallery, in the hotel's former barbershop, to become one of Taos's first art galleries.[50]

Joe and his helpers began work on the Imhofs' house immediately. Joe served as the sole architect and contractor. The New Mexican whom Joe had hired the previous year and his two helpers began laying the walls, after having cleared the land and dug deep trenches for each wall. Once the walls were laid, Joe hired Taos Indians to help mix the adobe plaster, and work on the vigas, the felled pine trees that served to brace the ceiling while, at the same time, they became exposed rafters that gave each room a decorative element. The Indians began carving the corbels, the heavy wood brackets used to brace each viga.[51]

"All this for a dollar and a half a day," Sallie remembered. "The regular wage was one dollar a day, and at this raise in pay they just flocked around. Their endurance seemed to be great. They would be up at daybreak attending to their home chores on the farm, and would arrive here at about seven, throw themselves on the ground and were asleep at once to arise at eight o'clock, start to work, and go merrily at it. They sang much of the day, brought their lunch, and we furnished coffee and a whole bologna daily, and they sat under the trees and sang again. At three we had lemonade and cookies with them, and every day was a social event for them."[52]

Imhof house in Taos, 1932.

The Taos Indians gave Joe his most treasured gift, a beam from their mission. During construction, Sallie said, " . . . the Indians with great ceremony brought the beam to him and it forms the arch beam in our living room. Its history is interesting. The forest service, from the tree rings, said the ponderosa pine was 200 years old when cut for the beam and was placed in the Mission in 1607. It was battered from the walls on February 3, 1847, [actually January 19, 1847] after the murder of Governor Bent. It is said that 100 [a more accurate figure is 175] were killed in the Mission and several in the hills beyond. It has always been a prized possession."[53]

Prized, yes, and a symbol of Joe's own rebellious nature. Governor Bent died horribly. When the Mexicans and Indians had banged on Bent's door that night, yelling at him, he had opened the door to speak with them, thinking he could calm them. They laughed and said "they did not intend to leave an American alive in New Mexico; and as he was governor, they would kill him first." They shot him with arrows, each arrow placed lightly in his eyes, his cheeks, his chest, just enough to torture him. When he fell back into the house, they followed and threw him to the floor and cut off his scalp.[54]

Imhof living room entry in Taos house displays beam from ruins of "old church"in Taos Pueblo.

He attempted to crawl through a hole that had been dug in the adobe wall by the women and children trying to escape. On the other side of the wall, the women pulled him through, but the Indians followed and killed him with guns. Then they nailed his scalp to the wall for all to see.[55]

In Santa Fe, Colonel Price gathered American troops, marched north, and pursued the rebels, finally cornering many of the warriors of Taos who had "collected in the pueblo church that stood at the northwest corner of the plaza. It was manned as a fort, with holes on the parapet and in the walls through which the defenders could shoot. The great terraced steps of the two pueblos were silent and empty, their ladders drawn up, their occupants waiting within like creatures in burrows listening for a favorable change of weather. In the fields on all sides the troops were drawn up, facing the clay wall that surrounded the town area. The howitzers were planted to effect a cross fire at a range of four hundred yards. Cannonading opened the battle, with flashes of fire, drafts of brown smoke, and black explosions over the snow. Dismounted soldiers charged in waves, the artillery moved up between salvos, and all converged toward the church. Its earthen walls were stout. 'An attempt was made to cut through the walls of the church . . . with axes,' reported a young artillery officer who commanded a six-pound howitzer in the battle, 'but they were so thick and the fire so deadly that it was found to be impracticable.' Still, the axes had thinned the three-foot thickness of the walls, and the young officer brought his howitzer up within sixty yards of the church and fired at the hacked part of the wall and 'soon made a breech large enough for five or six men to enter abreast. The roof of the church was then fired, and I ran the 6 Pdr. up within 30 feet of the breech, and poured grape shot into the church. Lighted shells were also thrown in, which bursted handsomely.' The attackers could see the interior. It was teeming with Indians, great numbers of whom fell dead and wounded. Rafters caught fire from the explosions. The noise was fearsome, chorded together with cannonades, the rattle of muskets, the shouts of the attackers, the cries of those hurt inside the church, and the roar and crack and tumble of burning timber. 'The order to storm the church was then given . . . and the storming party rushed it, so as we entered we found the smoke and dust so dense, that it was impossible to exist in it unless near the openings, and that the enemy had all retired except from the gallery, as we entered they fled, and were shot down by our troops from the neighboring walls.' Soon the roof fell in, and the blackened beams hung down, and the cold sunlight poured in from the bright blue sky."[56]

Joseph Imhof's attraction to one of those blackened beams that hung down from the church's roof, and the fact that he placed it in his home so that all who came would see it, may have been serving the same warning as that of the Indians who kept their partially destroyed mission. Perhaps the beam reflected Joe's statement about his own autonomy, that none should intrude upon it.

Among Anglos whom Joe met and immediately befriended was Walter A. Bailey, a thirty-five-year-old artist. Bailey had been reared in Kansas and had spent his boyhood drawing the Kansas landscape. He became art director of the *Kansas City Times*, the *Kansas City Star* morning edition, before moving to Taos to continue his scenic paintings.[57] In Taos, he also owned and operated the Taos Art Shop. In 1929, when Joseph Imhof walked into the Taos Art Shop, he and Walter began a friendship that would come to play an important part in the Imhofs' lives, enough so that Bailey would remark years later, "My wife and I were sorta adopted by the Imhofs while we were in Taos. The Imhofs wished I was their son."[58]

Bailey visited the Imhofs and the construction site regularly. Within the year, Imhof and his helpers had constructed one room and a porch where they planned to camp while they finished the house. The room had a large fireplace for warmth, and they felt comfortable living in the room.[59]

Within six months they had finished and roofed Joe's studio and two rooms on the upper floor where Joe intended to place his lithography press, and use the second room as a guest room. At this point, Sallie began to notice that Joe felt ill, a not unusual condition for a fifty-nine-year-old man who had changed locations, moved goods and furniture from three studios and one house, and worked compulsively at heavy labor for six months to build a new kind of home and studio.[60]

While making one of his regular visits to the Imhofs, Walter A. Bailey happened to find Joe lying face down in the dirt. Bailey picked up Joe and carried him into the house as Sallie rushed to bring Dr. Martin to examine her fallen husband. Dr. Martin diagnosed nervous exhaustion and recommended that the Imhofs take a vacation of rest for the winter on the West Coast.[61]

When Joe felt able to travel, he asked Walter Bailey to take responsibility for the continued construction of the adobe house. Bailey moved into the Imhof guest house. Then the Imhofs left by train for La Jolla where they possibly stayed with their friend, Joseph Keppler, Jr. The following Spring, in 1931, when the Imhofs returned, Joe showed his gratitude to Walter Bailey in two ways: by painting his portrait, one that depicted Bailey as right-handed when in fact Bailey was left-handed; and by giving Bailey a piece of Imhof land on which Bailey could build his own home.[62]

Bailey did build a house on the edge of the Imhof property. However, a dispute arose with the Taos Indians that Bailey's house encroached on Indian lands. The dispute continued for several years as Bailey's house was first torn down then rebuilt two or three times.[63]

Finally, said Phillips Kloss, the boundary dispute was settled in the

Imhofs' favor. By then, Walter Bailey had lived four years in Taos, and decided to move to Mexico City where he would maintain a studio in Coyoacán. Soon, he moved back to Kansas City, continued painting, and became an instructor of painting at Kansas City Art Institute. In 1940, he moved to Los Angeles to serve as staff artist, art columnist, and art editor for the *Los Angeles Herald-Examiner*.[64]

Gene Kloss and her husband, Phillips, a poet and writer, had first seen Taos in 1925, the year after Gene had received her baccalaureate degree, with honors in art, at the University of California in Berkeley.[65] In 1929, at the age of twenty-eight, Gene, with Phillips, had moved permanently to Taos. Gene Kloss' copper etchings, tonalities of aquatint, and drypoint began drawing attention and awards.[66] Within two years, this well-regarded artist, who was only five years younger than the Imhofs' daughter, and her husband would move into the Imhofs' guest house and become one of the Imhofs' most trusted and intimate friends.[67] Phillips Kloss would eventually publish ten volumes of poetry and musical compositions and be considered one of the true voices of the Southwest.

Sallie with guests in Taos yard. Pictured left to right: Sallie, unidentified, Dr. Martha Welpton's sister, Marie Trujillo, Phillips Kloss, Gene Kloss (partially hidden), Dr. Martha Welpton.

As the Imhofs finished their home in 1931, they worked at a more measured pace. Sallie would remark in her last years, "I say finished, but with adobe construction one never finishes. New ideas bring alterations, and it was in the fifties before we stopped changing doors and windows around."[68] In 1931, they spent more time becoming acquainted with those who would become their life-long friends. During this period, the Klosses saw them more frequently. They also met Lola Johnson, a teenager who lived on the other side of the Van Vechten property that separated the Imhofs from the Johnsons.[69]

The Imhofs may have first seen Lola, who would become Sallie's caretaker in her old age, riding her horse into the surrounding hills. In time they would learn that Lola, who had been born in 1918, had developed a debilitating disease as a child. The disease, possibly polio, affected her walk and caused one of her hands to wither. A Taos Indian, Joe "Sunhawk" Sandoval who was Geronimo's grandson, told Lola's parents that riding a horse would help the teenaged Lola. Sunhawk, who was also known as Geronimo of Taos and would become one of Joe Imhof's models, got a horse for Lola. As she rode into the hills, Lola said, she could see Geronimo watching her from a distance, taking care of her.[70]

The year of 1930 brought Helen and Frank Hall Kentnor who would become acquaintances of the Imhofs. Helen, who was twenty years younger than Sallie, would later serve as executrix of Sallie's will. By the time the Imhofs finished their home in 1931, Helen and Frank Kentnor had finished building El Chamiso Lodge in the sagebrush country south of Taos.[71]

Helen Kentnor had grown up in Wichita, Kansas and attended Simmons College in Boston, Massachusetts. She had been in Boston on Armistice Day in 1918 and, in the excitement, asked her parents' permission to join the Navy Secretarial Corp and become a Yeomanette. Of course they refused and she completed her business degree before returning to Wichita to work for the School Board.[72]

In 1927, she married Frank Hall Kentnor who had served in the Army where he had been trained in hotel management. Because he suffered from asthma, he and Helen decided to venture into the Taos Valley and build a twelve-room hotel on ten acres of land. They arrived in 1930, about the same time the Imhofs arrived. Frank's health improved immediately, and they began building their adobe hotel, using Taos Indians to lay adobe bricks, and their Spanish-American neighbors in Ranchos de Taos to become cooks and maids.[73]

They celebrated the opening with a Tin Can Dance, with the price of admission a bag of tin cans. A neighbor had carelessly dumped tin cans into an arroyo and the cans had washed onto the highway in front of the Inn after a heavy rain. The price endeared the Kentnors to the community. Shortly, the Kentnors changed the name of their hotel to the more easily recognizable name, Sagebrush Inn, which is the translation of El Chamiso.[74]

The Sagebrush Inn, with its picture window view of the Taos Valley and distant mountains, its Indian and Mexican architecture using adobe and viga (exposed raw beams) ceilings, Navajo rugs, and wood carvings and canvases of local artists, became an immediate success. Georgia O'Keeffe and the wife of Vice President John Nance Garner stayed at the Sagebrush Inn, as did the well-to-do from the East Coast who wanted to bask in the Southwestern flavor.[75] In time, Joseph Imhof's paintings would hang in the Sagebrush Inn.

One of the Imhofs' most well-known friends lived about a mile from them, on a twelve-acre piece of land where she built an elaborate adobe house. Mabel Ganson Evans Dodge Sterne Luhan regarded the Imhofs among her personal friends, and she would write in 1947 of Joseph Imhof's art in her book, *Taos and Its Artists*.[76]

Mabel had moved to Taos with her third husband, Maurice Sterne, a painter, who had come to New Mexico first in 1916, then written his wife suggesting that she come to "Save the Indians, their art—culture—reveal it to the world!"[77] Mabel had already made a name for herself in New York and in Europe. The Buffalo, New York heiress to a banking fortune had first married Karl Evans and, after his death, had taken their son to Europe. There she met Edwin Dodge, a Boston architect, whom she married. They had lived in Italy for ten years before Mabel divorced Dodge and returned to New York where she later married Maurice Sterne. It was during the time that the Sternes lived on Fifth Avenue that Mabel became so well-known for her salon of well-known writers, artists, and others who gathered in her home to discuss ideas and the politics of the times.

After Mabel moved permanently to Taos in 1917, her inspiration for purchasing the twelve acres on which she built her adobe home came from her nosey landlord. Their landlord had climbed upon their roof to eavesdrop one evening as the Sternes and houseguest, the artist Andrew Dasburg, discussed the war. The landlord had reported them to federal agents as German sympathizers. Not long after that the Sternes bought their own property.[79]

In the 1920s, Mabel divorced Sterne to marry Taos Pueblo Indian, Antonio "Tony" Luhan, the man to whom she would remain married for the remainder of her life. Mabel's home, during her marriage to Luhan, became the gathering place for her famous houseguests. She also presided over the social scene in Taos where she developed genuine friendships with the artists and became part of their lives.

She was a keen observer as well. She remarked in her book, *Taos and its Artists*, that the Imhofs had "built a beautiful house on the border of the Taos Reservation, facing the Indian fields that are seamed with the lovely wild-plum hedges; and from their windows they can watch all day the ever-changing aspects of the sacred mountain in front of them, rising above the Pueblo.

"In Imhof's large studio, there are a thousand evidences of his enduring relationship with the Indian people. Every variety of the objects they employ in their daily life is here, each so different from ours, in an aestheticism that is practical and imaginative. This room is a small museum of Indian lore and handicraft."[80]

The house was free of architectural adornment with its hand-made adobe bricks plastered with adobe mud. The walls had no true right angles and its rectangular, asymmetrical form cast irregular shadows on the land. The Imhofs' entire dwelling, it seemed, resembled a kind of personal museum of loved objects they had collected over the years. Imhof had divided the ninety-two-foot-long home into three basic sections seamlessly bound together. Their home, which ran east-west, had a center section comprised of a living and dining area, bedroom, kitchen and bath. While the Imhofs had built in the original style of an adobe house and had kept the number of windows to a minimum, a large picture window in their living room framed the sacred Taos Mountain. In the foreground, the Taos pueblo fields full of wild plums and sagebrush provided the only growth between their home and the Taos Mountain. In time, Joe would sculpt a rain god statue which would reside on the patio in the path of the picture window.[81]

The living room housed different paintings, among them an oil seascape of the Royal Fleet enroute to the East Indies. Various other paintings and lithographs of sailing ships, of the sea, and of seafaring people in New-foundland, Nova Scotia, Holland, and Brazil could be found throughout their home. Joe still loved the sea which he had come to know during his travels, and especially during his years growing up on Long Island Sound where he had spent long days watching seagulls and sailing ships. In 1930, while completing his home, he would finally copyright a lithography he had made in 1928, titled "Nieuw Amsterdam," regarded as one of his finest litho-graphs.[82]

In a letter describing the lithograph, Imhof wrote, "The lithograph is based on an old Dutch print made in 1653 which explains the date shown on the lithograph; the border is my own design and on an old Dutch frame. The beaver shown on the border represents the biggest trading in Nieuw Amsterdam, which was beaver pelts. Beaver always appeared on the early coat of arms of the colony . . . The lithograph is printed in a tint and black which appear on the proofs. The selling price is $50.00 each . . . ."[83]

In this lithograph of a many-masted ship in full sail, Imhof depicts in the foreground a canoe with two Indians, a boat of six men, and a row boat attached to the main ship. It is as if he had one lithograph with those ele-ments of life most important to him: the sea, ships, seamen, and Indians.

The Imhof home also strongly reflected Europe. In the dining/kitchen area hung a dated artist's proof of a Rembrandt self-portrait that had been in the Imhof family for generations; a collection of Delft plates, the leaded glass copy of Dürer's coat of arms, and wood-carved busts of a mermaid and merman that gave the area an eclectic feel. Sallie placed a William and Mary desk in the living room light since she used this desk for herself.[84]

The living room also housed two wood carvings said to be from Tibet, and that Joe noted had similarities with the *tablitas* worn on the heads of Pueblo women during corn dances. Among the other treasures gathered from around the world hung a photograph of Joe and their daughter, Elizabeth, after her graduation from high school in 1915.[85]

Joe's two-story studio occupied the western space. An adjacent room to the studio housed Joe's Currier and Ives Rutherford lithography press, the first press in Taos.[86] Clinton Adams, in his *Printmaking in New Mexico 1880-1990*, describes the lack of interest that the early Taos artists had in printmaking, particularly lithography. A few of these artists had served as lithographers' apprentices, and others associated lithography with the poorly-made nineteenth-century chromolithographs that had flooded the country. These factors caused the early artists, as well as critics, to dismiss the art of lithography.

"Nieuw Amsterdam, 1653," (lithograph, 30¼ X 36 in.),1930.

Imhof in his living room, Taos.

Etching enjoyed a better reputation because of the success of such nine-teenth-century artists as James McNeill Whistler and Peter Moran. In 1929, only a few of the artists in Taos had ever worked in printmaking, and few had an interest as keen as Gene Kloss and Andrew Dasburg. While Kloss primarily worked in copper etching, Dasburg, who had been invited to Taos as Mabel Luhan's guest, had made woodcuts. Dasburg, as a teacher, encouraged Kenneth Adams, in 1919 and 1920, and others to study in Taos.[87]

Adams' other teacher, B. J. O. Nordfeldt of Wichita, Kansas, encouraged Adams and others to work with lithography. Wichita, in fact, became one of the few places in the United States where artists could have their prints made. Most had to ship their work to New York, a less than desirable process since the artist then could not work directly with the printer to refine and make necessary changes. In 1926, Howard Cook received a commission to make woodcuts in Santa Fe for Willa Cather's serialized *Death Comes to the Archbishop*. The next year Cook met Barbara Latham, a young artist, in Taos. After they married, they returned to New York in search of an art gallery to exhibit their prints.[88]

Carl Zigrosser, the curator of Erhard Weyhe Gallery, immediately responded to Cook's work. Zigrosser took the train to Raton, then a bus to Taos in search of other artists' prints. Cook's success influenced other artists who worked in lithography to visit Taos. Because the area had no lithography press, though, most of the artists took their work back to New York to have it printed.[89]

Imhof's completed studio in 1931 spoke not only of what he intended to accomplish in lithography, but of his artistic interests. "Here one can see scrupulous studies of Indians in characteristic poses," Mabel Dodge Luhan wrote, "denoting in this painter an interest in research that is ethnological as well as artistic.

"Outside the large studio window, bundles of suet, dried meat, and last year's corn are fastened to the beams of the porch. There Imhof watches for hours the gathering of wild birds, and, quiet and invisible, is able to catch their free unhampered movement. He will spread out on the floor before you great sheets of drawing paper with studies of magpies in the very instant of changing movement, in that proximity that enables you to see what you never notice in their shy flight away from you, the exquisite blue-green fiery hues of the breast feathers.

"Acoma Pottery Maker," (lithograph, 13 X 17 in.).

"Water Carriers of Zuni Pueblo," (lithograph, 12 X 18 in.), ca. 1943.

263

"Pueblo Life," (lithograph, 20 X 13 in.).

"Acoma Firing Pottery," (lithograph, 13 X 17 in.).

"Lying in wait for the birds in his sly, unharmful way, Imhof has detected and snared upon canvas all the varieties of the hawk alone, in this valley. Plunging through the air, soaring, turning, diving, his large drawings of these fierce birds, upon a pale blue-gray paper, all breathtaking."[90]

"Magpies," (lithograph, 16½ X 12 in.).

Mabel Dodge Luhan's description of Imhof's unobtrusive and patient observations of birds could have been an accurate description of how he observed Indians and life within a pueblo. Imhof made known immediately his own sentiments about Indians to anyone who approached his home. Near a corn stalk Joe eventually painted on his front door he had scripted the words: "Corn the Indians gift to the white man."[91]

The painted words gave notice that Indians came first for Joseph Imhof, just as the charred beam served to signify his independence edged with a rebellious streak. Now that he had completed his home and studio, and served notice of his intentions, his next task lay in immersing himself into the world of the Pueblo Indians.

CHAPTER 14

DEATH REDEFINES FAMILY

At age sixty, Joseph Imhof had arrived at the place in life he had sought since he had received the box of watercolors on his fifth birthday from his godfather. He filled each day and evening painting, drawing and pulling lithographic prints, participating in art exhibitions, teaching, attending lectures given by fellow artists, making friends among the Indians.

As he and Sallie gradually established routines, their lives and personalities became more visible to the Taoseans. Many chose to like the Imhofs, while others found them strange. The behavior some found strange would soon become more exaggerated when the Imhofs suffered the greatest loss of their lives, the death of their daughter. For now, though, no one imagined such a tragedy awaited within two years.[1]

Each morning, Sallie and Joe walked into town to collect their mail, eat breakfast at the La Fonda Hotel, then walk home before Joe began work in his studio.[2] Sallie began to search for the work that would give her life meaning beyond serving as her husband's assistant and wife. In Taos she discovered an American Legion post in which she would become active, eventually moving up to a Service Officer in 1935. She would hold that position into her eighties.[3] She also learned that Dr. T. P. Martin needed assistance. She immediately volunteered and, by 1933, had become his secretary when the New Mexico State Welfare Department came into existence. Dr. Martin's work with Taos' social welfare agency became Sallie's work as well.[4]

During the first year the Imhofs lived in Taos, Joe finished a small room in the mezzanine above his studio where visiting Indians could stay. "We had many," Sallie said, "and during the fiesta many from other tribes. Many hours were spent evenings before the large fireplace where Joe learned to know the man and his character, and this he put on the canvas. He always said he could not paint a person until he knew his characteristics. The Indians said that no Taos artist except Joe could paint Indian eyes. His interpretation of hands was also beautifully done."[5]

Lola Johnson, the Imhofs' neighbor, described Joe's working relationship with Pueblo Indians similarly, saying, "Imhof used to have his models live in his home before he attempted to put them on canvas. He said he had to know the man before he could paint him. The Indians said that Imhof put a man's soul in his eyes. They said that the eyes reveal the inside of a man."[6]

Soon, Joe had numerous close friends among the Taos Indians. "He liked them better than Anglos," joked Kay Dicus, who would become a friend of the Imhofs when she and her artist husband, Richard, moved to Taos in 1945. Still later, in 1957, Kay would serve as secretary for the Harwood Foundation, an important Taos arts institution.[7]

"Indian Man With Squash Blossom Necklace," (lithograph, 17 X 14 in.).

"Santo Domingo Youth," (lithograph, 18⅞ X 12½ in.).

267

"Arapaho," (lithograph, 19 X 12 in.).

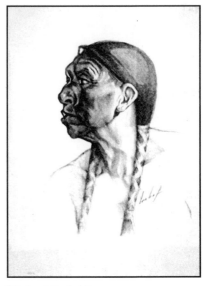

"Pedro Mirabel,"
(lithograph, 17 x 13 in.).

"It was hard to explain," Dicus said, when speaking of Joe Imhof's relationship with others in Taos. "Imhof was there, the art colony was over there, and the rest of the town over there. There seemed to be no connection. Joe was not anti-social, because he was outgoing, had a great sense of humor, and to individuals he was friendly. He [just] didn't take part in Taos life."[8]

Imhof had never been a joiner. Other than his membership in the St. Lucas Guild he had joined in Holland, he had not belonged to any organization. Nor did he participate in community activities except through his art. At that time in Taos, he was the only printer and, at that, working in lithography which other artists did not look upon with favor. He could usually be found in a nearby pueblo, or working in his studio wearing an apron and a green eyeshade. He differed from other artists in additional, critical ways. He did not number his prints; he rarely dated any of his work no matter what the medium; and he gave away his work to those he liked, and others who admired his work. This kind of behavior did not enhance the value of his or other artists' works. In fact, his actions tended to undercut the price of art. Finally, he hired an Indian to work as his lithography assistant. All of these behaviors added together did make the Imhofs seem strange to some in the community.

Sallie did participate in the community, yet some of her behavior did not endear her to others. Anneke Dicus Chittim said Sallie appeared to be "not a gentle person, feisty, and tight with money."[9] Sallie had learned to develop a mind of her own as manager of the Imhofs' finances that had ranged from near zero to "rich by all wildest dreams." The Imhofs had, after all, lived very full lives before they arrived in Taos, and Joe focused on exactly what he had to accomplish in the limited years remaining to him. Sallie intended to see that he fulfilled his goal.

In 1930, Joe volunteered to teach lithography and dynamic symmetry (the use of gridwork to balance a painting or lithograph) at the Taos Field School of Art.[10] Other Taos artists—Blumenschein, Berninghaus, Phillips, Dasburg, Ufer, Higgins, Lez Haas—also volunteered to teach courses in painting, sculpture, architecture and commercial art. The eight-week sessions took place during June and July, with classes held on Tuesdays, under the auspices of the University of New Mexico and at the Harwood Foundation. The School had started that year and already twenty to forty students had enrolled.[11]

Although Joe received neither payment nor recognition from the University of New Mexico for his instruction, he taught each summer from 1930 until the School disbanded during World War II. Then he resumed teaching until, as Sallie said, "the days of the bored G.I. who came to pass the time and not try to learn anything." This means Imhof probably quit teaching about 1946, when "after two summers," Sallie noted, "the class was discontinued." Sallie particularly remembered the years when Dorothea Fricke Whitcraft, a professor of art at the University of New Mexico, took her classes to study in Taos. As in Albuquerque years before, the Imhofs' home became a mecca for the students. The Imhofs were in their element. Sallie reported, "It was a party every Tuesday."[12]

Among teaching tools Imhof used were a grid system imposed on the sketch for a lithograph, and possibly the printed sheet titled, "Lithography," that Imhof had written. It read: "Lithography was invented by Senefelder in Bavaria in 1796. It is the art of putting designs on stone with a greasy material and of producing printed impressions therefrom.

Untitled lithograph
demonstrating Imhof's use of
grid marks, (19 X 14 in.).

"The process depends in the main, upon the antipathy between grease and water, which prevents a printing ink containing oil from adhering to parts of the stone not covered by design which have been dampened by water.

"The stone used is a compact, fine grained limestone of yellowish or grayish color. This is given a grain with carborundum or sand to suit the subject drawn.

"The greasy material used in making the design is called lithographic ink or lithographic crayon. The design may be drawn directly on the stone or may be transferred to the stone from paper on which the design has been drawn with greasy material.

"The completed design is etched by treatment with dilute acid and gum water, which renders the fatty matter more nearly insoluble and enables the blank portions of the stone to retain moisture. The stone is then, after washing, ready for the printing process. The above statement roughly describes the lithographic process."[13]

In all probability, the students who gathered at the Imhofs on Tuesdays used Joe's lithography press in their learning process. In the coming years, word would spread among the other artists that Imhof eventually refused to let others use his press.[14] The fallacy of this can be shown in Imhof's interactions with other artists, and possibly has something to do with the dissention in the Taos Society of Artists before it disbanded in 1927. It might also be one of the reasons why Imhof kept to himself as an artist and developed only a few close friendships with other artists. In fact, the very existence of the Harwood Foundation owed its life to the envy, petty jealousies, and exclusivity of the original Taos art colony members.

Burritt Elihu Harwood and Lucy Case Harwood had arrived in Taos in 1916. Burt had been born around 1855 in Charles City, Iowa where he had grown to manhood. While in his twenties, he had opened a photographic studio, then studied art at the Academy of Design in Chicago, the Art Students League in New York, and the *Académie Julian*. In 1889, he moved to Minneapolis where he painted portraits, and operated his own art school. In 1896, he married Lucy "Elizabeth" Case. The Harwoods moved back to France where Burt painted and his wife, who preferred to be called Elizabeth, ran a French Hospital during World War I.[15]

The year the Harwoods moved to Taos, Bert Phillips nominated Burt Harwood to membership in the Taos Society of Artists. The Society rejected Harwood, apparently because they did not believe his work to be good enough for membership. His rejection must have come as a terrible blow to such a man. When he died six years later, in 1922, his wife, Elizabeth, transformed their home on Ledoux Street into the Harwood Foundation, "To establish and maintain, in said town of Taos, New Mexico, a public library, a museum, and other educational agencies." The official Harwood stationary printed its activities: Art, History, Library. Thirteen years later, the Harwood became a part of the University of New Mexico by Elizabeth's "Deed of Conveyance." In 1929, the Harwood became the home to the University's Taos Field School of Art.[16]

In another display of discord, the Taos Society of Artists called a special meeting in 1919 "at which all members present voted to draft a letter requesting the deportation of fellow artist Henry Balink." The next year, Society members explored the possibility of posting a sign in the Taos Plaza that read, "the Taos Society of Artists does not approve of soliciting but would be glad to receive visitors and show their works upon request and after four p.m." Members then abandoned the idea.[17]

Two years later, in 1922, W. Herbert Dunton resigned his membership in the Society, stating, "he did not care to belong to a society in which sec'y [Ufer] referred to the president [Blumenschein] as a 'bald-headed S.B.'" By 1927, when the Society disbanded, it had accomplished its goals of creating a market for members' works of art. Over time, the burden of maintaining touring art exhibitions, publicity, and membership had become too time consuming for individual members.[18]

Still, negative remarks about other artists' works continued to find their way into the gossip circles and into print. Clinton Adams in his *Printmaking in New Mexico 1880-1990* observed that "Imhof, who prided himself on factual authenticity, nonetheless endows *Geronimo of Taos* with a dramatic haughtiness that perhaps reflects as much the temperament of the artist as that of the man portrayed."[19]

Phillips Kloss, a published writer and husband of the highly regarded Taos artist, Gene Kloss, who at one time lived in the Imhofs' guesthouse, remarked that the Taos Indian portrayed in "Geronimo," Joe "Sunhawk" Sandoval, was a medicine man and a Peyote cult Indian who had a Messiah complex. "Sunhawk was difficult, dangerous, and Imhof kept on guard around him," according to Kloss. Sunhawk, Kloss observed, also suffered from ptosis, a condition that caused his upper eyelids to droop.[20]

Imhof, who said he would never paint a portrait until he knew the person over a period of time, actually painted Sunhawk's reality: a medicine man who believed himself to be a kind of god. Imhof's painting depicts Sunhawk with his head erect and tilted slight back, his eyelids opened only into slits near the lower lids. The posture of Sunhawk's head and eyes could be interpreted as "dramatic haughtiness." But it is Sunhawk's temperament and drooping eyelids that Imhof painted, not Imhof's own attitude, as Adams suggests.[21]

As Imhof's and Sunhawk's friendship deepened, Imhof taught Sunhawk to paint and to assist Imhof run his lithography press. Imhof also gave Sunhawk art works. In the early 1980s when E. O. Floyd owned the Taos art gallery that sold Imhof's art, Sunhawk occasionally sold one of the Imhof works of art that Imhof had given Sunhawk when he needed money. E. O. Floyd said that on one occasion when he had gone to Sunhawk's house, Sunhawk had tried to sell him a copy of an Imhof he'd made. Floyd didn't want it, but saw an Imhof on a wall with about six nails in it. Floyd

"Geronimo,"
(lithograph, 15 X 10 in.).

said, "That's the one I want," and pointed to the wall.[22]

In Imhof's lifetime, Sunhawk shared his own art work with Imhof, and painted a circular 54-inch sandpainting next to the Imhofs' front door. Over the years, Sunhawk remained one of Imhof's favorite models, as well as a favorite for other artists, including Couse, Higgins, and Fechin. Sunhawk, with his fine bone structure and handsome features, had modeled since childhood for artists and understood their instructions for poses.[23]

"Joe's favorite . . . and long-time model," according to Sallie, was Taos Indian Cristino Mirabel.[24] In 1931, Imhof painted a 28-by-22-inch watercolor titled, "Cristino Mirabel (Hunta-Chuta) Head of 'Black Eyes'." The chest-high portrait depicts Mirabel as a man of serenity whose hooded eyes gaze into a distance of private thought, as he holds a ceremonial staff near his chest. A cloth draped just below his shoulders emphasizes his muscular body. The title gives his full name Cristino Mirabel, which was his Spanish nickname, followed by Hunta-Chuta, his Taos name. As head of "Black Eyes," a medicine society in Taos, Cristino Mirabel held influence within the Taos Pueblo society.[25] Cristino Mirabel served as chief of the Chiffonetti, sometimes referred to as the Black Eyes, a religious society in Taos. Their bodies are painted in stripes and spots and contrasting colors similar to the koshare of the Keres groups. They perform at the Feast of San Geronimo, the patron saint of Taos, in a two-day celebration that signals the close of the harvest season. Anglos sometimes call them "Clowns" because of their antics that cause others to laugh and feel entertained during the dance, but the Chiffonetti actually use their religious knowledge to call for physical well-being of their society.[26]

Knowing Cristino Mirabel and of his position in the Taos Pueblo, it seems only logical that Imhof would use him as the model for the painting titled, "The Cachique [sic]." Among the Pueblos, the term cacique, "designates the supreme village or town priest under the native government and ceremonial organization."[27]

As in his relationship to Sunhawk Sandoval, Imhof deepened his friendship with Cristino Mirabel throughout their lifetimes. "In the thirties Cristino Mirabal [sic] . . . needed money and offered the [company] robe [made of buffalo] for sale for fifty dollars, which Joe gladly paid him: the agreement was that whenever Cristino needed the robe he might borrow it for the ceremonial. Through all the years the agreement was kept."[28]

Joe lived the Indian saying, "Who comes as a friend is received as a friend," in his relationships with Pueblo Indians.[29] His acceptance by the Pueblos allowed him to become one of the first white men permitted to witness the sacred initiation rite of the Taos Pueblo. They took him into the underground kiva, their sacred ceremonial chamber, and practiced their religion that they kept secret from all other outsiders.

The Taos and other Pueblo Indians had cause to prohibit people other than members of their pueblo from viewing their religious ceremonies. After the Spanish retreated, the United States government in 1846 began a systematic program to destroy the Indian way of life, religion, and art.[30] The Americanization program meant ridding the Indians of what Congressmen and Indian Bureau officials regarded as "half-animal, sadistic, obscene." In the 1920s, one senator declared the Pueblo religious practices "un-American, . . . [and] inspired by Communist agents."[31]

"The American Bureau of Indian Affairs made a number of attempts to suppress native religion with a series of department regulations . . . This anti-Indian movement culminated in a set of regulations known as the Code of Religious Offenses which was used as late as the 1920s in an attempt to crush Pueblo religion.'" Not until 1934 did President Franklin D. Roosevelt's Commissioner of Indian Affairs, John Collier, bring the persecution to a halt.[32]

Early on, Indian art fared no better than Indian religion. Not until the early 1900s when artists living in Santa Fe and Taos colonies challenged the federal policy of "no Indian art" did government agents relax this policy.[33] Finally, officials reversed this policy in the 1930s during the same time period they reversed the religious persecution policy. However, it would take until 1970 before the Taos Indians reclaimed from the federal government Taos Mountain that harbored their sacred Blue Lake.[34]

For centuries, Taos Indians had made the two-day journey through Taos Mountain into Blue Lake to perform their most sacred ceremony at the site that cradled the souls of departed Taos people. Taos Indians, in their nature-oriented life, closely tie their emergence myth with Blue Lake. Although the Taos people have been "conditioned by centuries of teachings handed down by tribal elders to say nothing specific to anyone outside his own pueblo about the great religious concepts on which . . . life is based,.." Dr. Aurelio M. Espinosa and two or three other researchers obtained, before the 1930s, a fragment of the Taos Emergence myth.[35]

Dr. Espinosa's "informant told him that the people came up from the lake at Mount Blanca, near Monte Vista, Colorado. Having been created by our Father Sun, they came up in groups corresponding to the societies to be found today in Taos kivas, and scattered to the places to which Sun directed them, with instructions to meet at the Canyon of the Red Willows, Taos.

"First came the Feather People, who settled near Ranchos de Taos. Then came the Shell People, who went to a spot near the Colorado River. Then came the Water People, about whom an intriguing tale is told.

"They were first fish. They came over the mountain streams to the Santa Fe River. Then they swam up the Rio Grande and up the Taos River and to the Ranchos de Taos Creek until they arrived near the place where Fiadaina (Feather People) and Holdaina (Shell People) were living together. A Fiadaina girl went down to the river for water and saw the Water People in the water and ran to tell her people. When they came down they saw all the fish there standing up in the water. 'Those are some of our people,' said Fiadaina and Holdaina. They then got some bean plants and gave them to two girls. They told them to strike the fish with them. They struck them and they all became people.

275

"Groups arriving after the Water People were Big-Earring People, Knife People, Sun People, People of Feathers in Cold Weather (otherwise known as Old Axe People), Big Parrot Feather People, Lightning People and Day People. They all met finally at Taos."[36]

While the world of the Taos people began this way, it would end, Dr. Espinosa was told, "when they neglect their religious rites . . . ."[37] Not until 1906 did the Taos Indians face such a threat. That year, Theodore Roosevelt and Gifford Pinchot, without consulting the Taos Indians, gathered as much land as possible into the new National Forest system. Of that land, 130,000 acres belonged to the Taos people.[38] It had been granted them by the Spanish and confirmed by the Republic of Mexico. The United States, in the Treaty of Guadelupe [sic] Hidalgo with Mexico, pledged that Pueblo Indians . . . would be "maintained and protected in the free enjoyment of their liberty and property."[39]

When the Taos Indians realized that the United States government had confiscated their land for use in a national forest, they did not protest at first because they believed their sacred land would be protected from outside forces by becoming a part of Carson National Forest. Soon, however, loggers, campers, and hunters intruded and began destroying Taos prayer sticks.[40]

In 1926, after the Taos Indians spent years protesting and testifying before Congress, the Indians learned that the United States Indian Claims Commission confirmed the Indians' legitimacy to the land. When the government offered to pay for 50,000 acres of the land, since the other portion had already been taken by people who had settled on Taos land, which included the town of Taos, the Indians refused the money. They wanted clear title to the sacred Blue Lake. They even offered to give up all rights and titles to their land in and around Taos settled by outsiders.[41]

That year in 1926, John Collier, Sr., the longtime U.S. Commissioner of Indian Affairs who had actively tried to secure the return of the land surrounding Blue Lake to Indian control, attempted to ally fears raised by Congressmen. Since no white man had witnessed the sacred rites performed at Blue Lake, rumors circulated in Congress that the Indian ceremonies were not "true religious observances, but erotic orgies, which should be sternly forbidden."[42]

To combat the rumors, the Indians finally agreed to allow Collier and a companion, James W. Young, to accompany them to the lake and observe the ceremony. They set out with about three hundred Indians—men, women, and children—and many horses. However, halfway up the mountain, the Indians could not bring themselves to allow outsiders to witness their sacred ceremonies. They did allow the men to remain overnight at the first ceremonial ground.[43] There Collier experienced that same powerful transfer of forces that Joseph Imhof had experienced years earlier when he danced with the Cochiti Indians.

Collier described to the Senate and House Indian committees and in his book, *On the Gleaming Way*, what he experienced that night. "The fires lit the dance ground. Here were no colors, other than the fire's own color reflected from white and rusty robes. Here, with personal qualities shrouded, moved scores, hundreds of ghosts. They moved like masses of smoke, like wind made visible, like masses of cloud . . . . No casual motion, no gesture of one to another ever appeared; all was a mass rhythm which changed a hundred times during the night . . . .

"The song went out from fifty, sometimes a hundred singers. From ten o'clock until dawn there was never a full minute's interlude. Only once were the dancers still. That was when the mass singing ceased and one powerful voice for seven minutes sang alone . . . .

"That marvelous, ever-renewed, ever-increasing, ever-changing leap and rush of song was not only human song . . . . forces of the wild and of the universe had heard the call and taken the proffered dominion . . . . a strange release of energies took place . . . . the dynamic potentiality of ancient beliefs was realized, and . . . . there was expressed a rejoicing, passionate and yet coldly exalted."[44]

Collier saw this as the spirit of the Taos religion. "In this integration of human with mystical forces he could discern no asking, no adoration, no dread, but a simple sharing of Joy."[45]

In 1933, Congress passed legislation giving the Indians a fifty-year special use permit; then government agents violated the agreement by opening the area for recreation, even building on the land. In 1961, after another prolonged investigation, the Indian Claims Commission again ruled that the Taos people had been deprived of their land. When the Commission again offered to buy the land, the Indians refused. After a protracted effort by Congressmen and government agents to retain the land, Congress finally voted to return to Taos Pueblo their Blue Lake and the surrounding lands.

277

On December 15, 1970, President Richard Nixon signed the bill into law.[46]

Joseph Imhof, of course, would not live to see Blue Lake returned. In 1931, he was busy preparing for art exhibitions in Amarillo, Texas and Santa Fe. He worked as he always had, preparing to paint a canvas with oil, to draw on a lithographic stone, or create a watercolor. Using a pencil, he made a rough sketch of the art work's content. In numerous subsequent sketches, he refined the images that would appear on the final work. Finally, what had started as a sketch would appear in great and refined detail which he would use to draw upon the lithographic stone, or to paint.

At first, Imhof showed his lithographs and paintings only in group exhibitions. Sallie remembered, "He refused all honors. [He] never exhibited except the Fiesta Show in Santa Fe. He never liked his name in print."[47] Imhof may have never knowingly entered art competitions, but critics and art organizations did single out his work for praise and for an occasional award. Kay Dicus, one-time director of the Harwood Foundation, said Imhof simply did not care about awards. And, Joseph Imhof did show his work in more exhibitions than the Fiesta show.

In 1931, the Amarillo Art Association borrowed paintings from Taos artists for The Loan Exhibit of the Fine Arts Department of the Tri-State Fair in Amarillo. When the exhibit opened in September of that year, among the canvases were E. Martin Hennings's "Arroyo Foundation" and "Edge of the Sage," Herbert Dunton's "October Gold," and Joseph Imhof's two portraits: "Hunta Chuta" and "The Singers." *The Amarillo Daily News* reported, "Two Indians painted by Joseph Imhof of Taos have been chosen favorites by a large number of visitors."[48]

Regina Tatum Cooke, a well-known Taos art critic, then living in her hometown of Dalhart, Texas, commented that the exhibit "would have done justice to an art gallery anywhere."[49]

Two months later, The Museum of New Mexico's journal, *El Palacio*, reported, " . . . that the Fiesta Exhibition of this year surpassed any ever seen in Santa Fe . . . . W. Herbert Dunton's Singing Rain, and Imhoff's [sic] Taos Indian, along with Blanche Grant's Cochiti Bird, were among the most interesting Indian portraits . . . and Imhoff's [sic] Taos, dominated the water-color gallery." Among other Taos artists exhibiting at Fiesta were E. L. Blumenschein, E. Martin Hennings, Mary Greene Blumenschein, and Herbert Dunton.[50]

The Fiesta played an important part in the lives of New Mexico's artists. The Museum of New Mexico in Santa Fe had originated, housed and supervised the annual group art show to coincide with the Santa Fe Fiesta held in September to commemorate the seventeenth-century Spanish reconquest of Santa Fe. The Museum, which had been founded in 1909, had begun the shows in 1915 to call attention to Santa Fe artists. However, the Museum then broadened the show to include Southwestern artists, and its galleries became showcases for artists throughout the region. The Museum's journal, *El Palacio*, became the only publication to accurately report the world of artists and art in the state.

In the Fiesta artists' work could be seen the range in their interpretations of not only the state's, but Taos' landscape and its original inhabitants. Of the original founders of the Taos Society of Artists, which included Bert Phillips, Blumenschein, E. I. Couse, and Oscar E. Berninghaus, Pat Trenton, Curator of Art for the Denver Museum of Art wrote in *Picturesque Images from Taos and Santa Fe*, "Primarily illustrators, these first artists continued to paint their canvases in a decorative style with 'humanistic exuberance,' and romantic vision of the Indians as 'Noble Savages.'"[51]

By contrast, Trenton wrote, "Imhof has been frequently been called 'The Grand Old Man of the Pueblos' because of his dedicated study of all aspects of Indian life." Of Imhof's "Indian Camoufleurs," (see page 173) she wrote, "The artist's persistent interest in making a careful record of Indian rituals and ceremonies and his success in this endeavor is particularly apparent in this painting . . . . The dancers shown here are dressed to represent deer. The title suggests that the artist may have been impressed as much by the clever mimicry of the dancing as by the striking costumes." Of "Snake Dancer, Oraibi," Trenton said, "Although Imhof elected to portray only a single dancer, the implied movement of this strongly drafted figure suggests the entire chorus."[52]

Doris Ostrander Dawdy, in her *Artists of the American West A Biographical Dictionary*, repeated a frequent comment made by art critics when she wrote, "Imhoff's [sic] paintings of Indians are so anthropological that some critics have deprecated their importance as art. From his observations of Pueblo culture, he had become aware of the importance of corn in their lives and had used the medium of his art to explain its secular and ceremonial use . . . . [His] lithographs received better treatment from the critics."[53]

279

"Deer Dancers,"
(lithograph,
16½ X 12 in.).

It is this interpretation of the subject's internal life, the depiction of emotion that Pat Trenton alluded to in her comments, that Imhof worked toward: his effort to capture the subject's soul, the powerful relationship between Pueblo Indians and the universe as conveyed in a subject's or a ceremony's emotional release.

Frederick J. Dockstader, writing in *The American Indian Observed*, published in 1971, gives one of the best perspectives on the disadvantage that Indians and artists alike suffered when artists portrayed Indians in their own setting. Dockstader, who was Director of the Museum of the American Indian, Heye Foundation, New York City at that time, then commented on the effort that certain of the early Taos artists made to depict Indians in their environment.

"It is an unhappy fact that the history of the Native American has been largely written by his adversaries; it is equally true that the pictorial records of his culture have been primarily the product of non-Indians. As a result, the evaluation is not well balanced, and the portrayal of his life is one-sided."[54]

It was in the way in which white artists viewed the Indian that came the opinions and reactions of the country's larger population, "a case of white viewing through white eyes; the Indian had no interpreting role . . . . While there is little doubt that racism played a role, . . the non-Indian artist was an alien, in a new environment, with much to learn before he could hope to provide interpretation . . . . He was, after all, portraying a defeated people—an approach from which he could not detach himself. Likewise, his audience viewed the Indian from the point-of-view of victors. Add to this the presence of religious bias, economic position and social reaction, and the problems multiply.

"It is rare, for example that American Indian religious observances are presented naturally; either the native custom is regarded as something quaint and colorful, albeit heathen—or it is a savage, barbaric practice in which the violent or sanguinary aspects are sought out as foci of interest . . . . Peaceful everyday activities find little interest for these artists."[55]

Of the Taos School of artists that developed at the turn of the century, Dockstader singled out "Bert Phillips, . . a fine painter with a keen feeling for Indian life, Oscar Berninghaus and Ernest Blumenschein, [who] dominated the Taos area for many years. Joseph Imhof, best known as a lithograph artist, left a body of work in oil and outstanding portraiture in his watercolors.

"With these individuals, what there remained of The Old West disappeared, . . yet this is a part of The American Heritage—a vital thread of the fabric of a nation . . . [and] the cord is a strong bond holding together an astonishing range of individuals and cultures . . . ."[56]

It was this vital thread of the Indian heritage that Imhof sought to preserve for future generations. In 1931, not only did Imhof began exhibiting at recognized art shows, he and Sallie once again traveled to Cochiti and Santo Domingo Pueblos. At Cochiti, he learned that one of his old friends had died in the 1919 flu epidemic, but that his son, Juan José Suina, wished to continue his father's friendship. In time, Juan José Suina would become Imhof's faithful friend and advisor, particularly when Joe began his greatest work, the Corn Series.[57]

On one of the trips south of Taos, the Imhofs had themselves photographed in Peñasco, a community of less than five hundred Spanish descendants, located in a high valley in the Sangre de Cristo range near Las Truchas Peak (the trouts) and Jicarita Peak (small basket). Peñasco had few other buildings than the high school, and no historic remains, not even any churches or chapels of note. Yet it remained the largest town in the southernmost part of Taos County where other tiny villages dotted the valley.[58]

Sallie and Imhof near road to Peñasco, NM, 1931.

On these journeys farther south, the Imhofs carried dynamite to clear the roads of rock slides that blocked their car's path. They traveled through Embudo (funnel), a former Indian pueblo, then on to La Bajada where they negotiated the steep switchbacks. Cochiti and Santo Domingo Indians, in turn, made the journey to stay with the Imhofs on San Geronimo Day when held at the Taos Pueblo on September 30.[59] San Geronimo Day usually took place over a three-day period to celebrate a thanksgiving among the Taos

Indians. However, Pueblo and Plains Indians came from the surrounding area to help celebrate the day created in 1612 when the first church was built at the Taos Pueblo. At that time, the Spaniards selected San Geronimo as the Patron Saint of the Taos Indians.[60]

In this remarkably busy year of 1931, Imhof volunteered to print Helen Blumenschein's work on his Currier and Ives lithography press. Helen had joined her parents, Ernest and Mary Shepard Greene Blumenschein, in 1919, and had exhibited her art in Paris during 1930 and 1931. The results from Imhof's press, however, Helen found to be too pale for her liking. "He very kindly offered to print a lithograph for me," Helen said of the experience, "but it was so weak, I did not care for it and never had him do another." Clinton Adams commented that Helen "may well have encountered similar problems in the making of her nostalgic landscapes of the Taos valley" when she had her work printed by George C. Miller Lithographers in New York. Helen used bold and hard edges in her work, which differed greatly from Imhof's more softened images.[61]

By 1932, Emil Bisttram had returned to Taos where he, too, used Imhof's lithography press.[62] Bisttram's planned study in Italy on a Guggenheim Grant had been derailed by the threat of war in 1930. He then had secured permission to study with the Mexican muralist, Diego Rivera. He left his wife, Mayrion and her mother in Taos while he worked in Mexico.

Bisttram said of Rivera, then working on the famous National Palace murals in Mexico City, "Through an interpreter I found to my pleasant surprise that Rivera and I shared quite a few ideas in common, particularly Dynamic Symmetry, of which he approved if the artist would use it freely, as I had been doing for years." While Bisttram found his work rewarding, he had difficulty adjusting to the grinding poverty in Mexico City and its surroundings. Though his Guggenheim had been given for two years, Bisttram returned to the United States after the economic crash and joined his wife in Taos.[63]

In 1932, Bisttram opened Taos School of Art that offered courses in "Dynamic Symmetry, with its emphasis on the fundamental principles of composition, color theory, field and class work from models, problems in abstraction and non-objective painting." The school offered a dance department as well as instruction to students in ways the two creative forms embraced the same fundamental principles.[64]

The established artists did not embrace Bisttram or his ideas, according to his wife, Mayrion. One painter declared that "He [Bisttram] should be tarred and feathered and wheeled out of Taos for bringing in that crazy modern art."[65]

Imhof, long intrigued with dynamic symmetry, found Bisttram's work and ideas exciting. "Joe knew the science from New York associations," Sallie said, "but it was new here and he had for some time an evening class for the old established artists."[66] Other artists did finally express interest in Bisttram's work. "Eventually many, like Bert Phillips, who belonged to what was called the 'old hat' school, became friendly."[67]

E. I. Couse certainly used the principles of dynamic symmetry when he grided his photographs and compositional studies to transfer the figures to the canvases he painted.[68] Bisttram, who always capitalized the words dynamic symmetry when he wrote of the process, was able to demonstrate to his fellow artists that dynamic symmetry "was a method by which an artist used an amalgamation of linear constructs—lines drawn across the picture plane, aiding the creative hand and eye to perfectly balance and attune a composition to a precision of weight, mass and volume, thus allowing the artist to create order out of chaos."[69]

The Imhofs welcomed Emil Bisttram, who was only three years older than the Imhofs' daughter, Elizabeth. The older couple could empathize with the younger couple who, out of necessity, lived very frugally. Of the Bisttrams' early years, the late Lorraine Carr wrote in *The New Mexican*, "When the Bisttram's came to Taos they took up residence in a small studio built by the famous artist, E. I. Couse. A traditional Taos studio small but intimate with vigas, fireplace; even on the back portal; and a beautiful view of the Taos Mountains.

"Mayrion Bisttram has a flair for interior design. She painted the handmade studio bed, with book shelves at each end, a beautiful Chinese black lacquer.

"'Dear Me' said artists with less artistic ability. They were horrified. But his [Bisttram's] work of art blended with the Virgin Mary blue handwork and when piled high with lovely pillows made by Mayrion, it became a conversation piece.

"Very shortly all the artists were painting their studio bed black. Even Georgia O'Keeffe, a frequent visitor to Taos, succumbed to this daring color and used it in her Abiquiu studio."[70]

In speaking of Joe Imhof's, and possibly Bisttram's evening classes on dynamic symmetry, Sallie said, "We were not a large group and really it seems to me that there was no influx until after the Second World War. As usual, after a time, interest failed, but we had a large collection of Anderson of Rome photos of old masters and we would spend an occasional evening seeing just how near many of the paintings came to Dynamic Symmetry. It was surprising to find how very close they had followed one of the five routes."[71]

Into this milieu of fevered creative work and ideas appeared the Imhofs' daughter, Elizabeth, a thirty-five-year-old woman in 1933 who had been trained in nursing, according to Phillips who, with his wife, Gene, had known Sallie and Joe since the Imhofs had moved to Taos. No one remembered the exact year that Elizabeth arrived in Taos, but it was probably in 1932 or 1933. Phillips Kloss remembered, "Madeleine [sic] was blond, petite, rather arrogant, aloof. She had a married name which we've forgotten," he said. However, Gene Kloss remembered, "She was not married. She had a boyfriend, but [she] was not married."[72]

Elizabeth volunteered, Phillips Kloss said, "as a nurse for the local Taos dentist awhile, [and] apparently had a nurse's training."[73]

Except for the Klosses and Helen Kentnor, who owned the Sagebrush Inn, no one who knew the Imhofs remembered seeing Elizabeth in Taos. "I only saw their daughter once," Kentnor said, "at a distance, in a car with a local young man, and was told 'that is the Imhofs' daughter.' Shortly after that the town learned that the daughter had committed suicide in California. Sallie never ever mentioned her to me."[74]

Sallie and Joe apparently never mentioned what had happened to Elizabeth to anyone except the Klosses, but even they varied on the details of Elizabeth's life.

There seemed to be as many versions of her death as people who knew the Imhofs. Even in life, Elizabeth remained a shadowy figure. In the brief sketch Sallie wrote of Joe's life, she never mentioned Elizabeth's birth or full name. Apparently, Sallie made sure that the true nature of Elizabeth's death would never be known. The California Death Index does not list her name. Nor is there any record of her in San Diego where she is said to have died. New Mexico death certificates remain sealed except to next of kin. The Imhofs left no direct living relatives.[75]

We can only report, and then speculate on what happened. Harriet Ide Publicker, the daughter of the Imhofs' accountant, said, "I thought she committed suicide before going to Taos, in Brooklyn."[76]

Jackson Hensley, who purchased the Imhof house in Taos in 1967, said, "After a squabble with her parents over a pending marriage she went into the garage and asphyxiated herself."[77]

Walter Bailey, who had befriended the Imhofs in 1929 and then lived briefly in their new home in Taos, said, "She [Elizabeth] came to Taos the day I left in 1930. She came from New York [and] was living with the family for a few months. I was told she shot herself in the head."[78]

Michael Hensley, son of Jackson Hensley, said, "She [Elizabeth] committed suicide with carbon monoxide in the garage of the Taos home."[79]

Robert Erkins, who as a boy first met the Imhofs shortly after Elizabeth's death, remembered being told a different version of what had happened. Robert had been traveling with his parents, Albert and Charlotte Erkins, and sister, Charlene (Dady), on their many trips to the West from Ohio and Florida when the entire family first met the Imhofs. The Erkins then had become life-long friends of the Imhofs after the Erkins had, while on that stop in Taos, purchased Imhof's art. Their relationship was such that the Erkins knew Joe as "José," and each summer Robert and Charlene accompanied "José" on arrowhead searches and journeys into pueblos.[80]

According to Robert, "The daughter did commit suicide. She was with Sallie and Joe in Taos when she died. She was engaged to be married, found out she could not have children, and was despondent. She went out in the desert around Taos and disappeared. The Imhof dogs picked up the scent of her trail and found her. She had been despondent over a combination of romance and work."[81]

Charlene (Erkins) Dady confirmed Robert's story, as did Robert's mother, Charlotte Erkins, who added that the discovery of Elizabeth by the family dogs was why Sallie always liked dogs, because they had found the daughter. However, the Imhofs had always owned dogs.[82]

It appears that from the moment of Elizabeth's death on June 26, 1933, Sallie spent the remainder of her life burying their daughter from anyone's view.[83] Perhaps Gene and Phillips Kloss came the closest to knowing what happened.

Gene Kloss, only five years younger than Elizabeth, recalled that she and Phillips had gone to a gathering in a room behind Taos' drugstore to attend Emil Bisttram's lecture featuring notables such as Thornton Wilder. The Klosses had gotten there early and seen Joe Imhof sitting by himself and, since they knew him, they had sat beside him. Joe told them of the communication he had had from Sallie about their daughter. The Klosses, who had recently suffered the loss of Phillips' father, asked if they could do anything.

"Yes," Joe said, "you can help me close up the house."

After the lecture, the Klosses accompanied Joe to his house which they helped close, then took Joe to Albuquerque to the train. "Sarah Imhof rushed to San Diego and Joe followed," Phillips Kloss remembered, "leaving the sculptor, Gustave Hildebrand, and me to seal up, with adobe, the secret door to the attic an invaluable collection of dishes and Indian silver and turquoise handicraft there."

When the Imhofs returned, the Klosses drove to Albuquerque to pick them up from the train. When they all got in the car, Joe started to tell the story of his daughter's death when Sallie said, "Let me tell."

"She killed herself," Phillips Kloss said, "with potassium cyanide in San Diego, a copy of Rupert Brooke's poems still in her hand. She erroneously thought the hysterectomy she had under Dr. Welpton's supervision would de-feminize her."[84]

Carol Hale, who would assist Sallie in record keeping during her last years, said that Sallie and Martha Welpton had been life-long friends from the time that the Imhofs' daughter had been a child.[85] In 1933, according to historical records, Martha Welpton was a prominent physician in San Diego, and been the first woman physician in that city.[86]

In 1933, it was still possible to purchase poisons, such as arsenic and potassium cyanide, in drugstores and feedstores since people commonly used these poisons to kill rodents. Potassium cyanide is a lethal poison and kills instantly. Clearly, Elizabeth Imhof knew what she intended.

Rupert Brooke, a handsome and dashing Englishman, was a popular poet before and after his death in 1915 aboard a hospital ship on the Aegean Sea. He had died a soldier at age twenty-seven. He wrote of love, of having loved, and dying young. He titled two of his sonnets, "Oh! Death will find me, long before I tire," and "The Life Beyond." Two of his poems carried the title, "The Dead" and he named another, "The Funeral of Youth: Threnody."

287

He wrote of "The Great Lover," of "Dead Men's Love," and "The Vision of the Archangels."[87]

Had the unmarried Elizabeth become pregnant in Taos? In 1933, that event could have proven overwhelming to a middle-aged woman at a time when laws forbid abortion in the United States. However, such a procedure could be had just across the Mexican border near San Diego. Had Sallie accompanied Elizabeth to Dr. Welpton in San Diego to arrange matters in Mexico, only to have the procedure go awry and force Dr. Welpton to supervise Elizabeth's hysterectomy? Phillips Kloss also said that Sallie had been visiting Martha Welpton when Elizabeth drove out into the country and took poison.

Suicide, of course, represents the ultimate escape from this life. No one will ever know why Elizabeth felt so powerless, only that her self-esteem had reached its lowest. Whether fact or fantasy, Elizabeth believed she had no control over her life, and had never had since birth when her parents made her a part of their nomadic life. Elizabeth apparently did have one friend. Sallie left Mrs. Hester Bott Van Ness of Sacramento, California, and possibly of Towaco, New Jersey, one thousand dollars and two watches. Carol Hale identified the woman as possibly Elizabeth's friend.[88]

The only evidence that the Imhofs had had Elizabeth's body cremated can be found in an inventory that Sallie made in 1963 of their Taos home. Although Sallie never mentioned or wrote of her daughter, Sallie listed five photographs of Elizabeth in their home. In the living room could be found two photographs of "Joe with McGaha painting our daughter after graduation from high school—1915." In their bedroom, Sallie listed a photograph of "We three 1912," on the east wall; on the west wall, photographs of "our daughter in New York and in Albuquerque"; and finally, a photograph taken in La Jolla. This photograph had found a home in the Imhofs' bedroom, placed on the fireplace wall. Sallie noted, "1 photo La Jolla. Where our daughter's ashes were scattered."[89]

The Imhofs' lives would never be the same.

CHAPTER 15

FINALLY, A PATRON
WITH NEW ENTERPRISES

In the years intervening Joseph Imhof's first meeting with the Sioux traveling with William F. Cody, Imhof had rarely swerved from his goal of researching the Indian, meaning of corn to the Indian, and depicting the Indian in his natural state. The tragic death of his only child only intensified his efforts. Joe and Sallie had seen enough sorrow in their lives that each knew healing came through time, by surrounding themselves with those whom they loved, and by living a productive life. Still, Elizabeth's death changed their lives irrevocably.

Shortly after the Imhofs returned from La Jolla, California where they scattered Elizabeth's ashes, they invited Gene and Phillips Kloss to live in their guest house. Only a few years separated Gene Kloss' age from Elizabeth's age. This attraction to persons who approximated Elizabeth's age when she died, and to children from ages eight to twelve—the Erkins children, me and my brothers, Kay Dicus' daughter, Anneke—would become a pattern of the Imhofs for as long as they lived.

"We rented the [guest] house for a year in 1933," Phillips said, "[and] took Joe on sketching trips in our car, chauffeured Sal to relief work in town. Gene set up her Sturgis etching press there and Joe made the skids for it."[1]

The press weighed 1080 pounds, and "enabled me to do much larger plates than [had] the smaller presses I had owned previously," Gene said. " . . . It was geared, had a big wheel to turn, and an old-fashioned letter press built in below which gave it stability and an ideal place for dampening paper . . . ."[2]

"[It was] a congenial period," Phillips remembered. On Sundays, the

Klosses and Imhofs ate dinners together then talked into the afternoons, or climbed into the Klosses' car for a drive into the country.[3]

Sometime during this year, Imhof created, from sketches he had made while in La Jolla, California during 1933, a 21-by-15-inch lithograph of Father Junipero Serra. Using the title, "Fr. Junipero Serra," Imhof depicts the priest staring intensely, almost with hostility, at a cross he holds raised slightly above his left shoulder. Imhof did not date this lithograph of Father Junipero Serra, the eighteenth-century Spanish Franciscan missionary who directed the founding of nine Franciscan missions in California.[4]

"Fr. Junipero Serra,"
(lithograph, 25½ X 20 in.).

Is it possible that Imhof reflected his own state of mind in the lithograph? It is difficult not to speculate that Imhof still had not forgiven his father and the Catholic church for the sacrifices he had had to make to organized religion: the loss of his relationship with his father, and now the guilt suffered by the loss of his only child.

In 1935, after another visit in La Jolla, Imhof created a smaller 14¼-

by-11¼-inch lithograph titled, "Fr. Junipero Serra," that depicts the priest pressing a cross against his left shoulder. In this lithograph, the priest's face appears mellowed with kindness as he gazes into the distance as if contemplating a larger issue in life. The lithograph, like most of Imhof's work, does not carry a date, but is believed to have been created in 1935.[5]

"Fr. Junipero Serra," (lithograph, 21½ X 15¼ in.).

Sallie acknowledged, "Joe was deeply religious in his own mind although not a church goer."[6] Sallie might have made the same observation about herself. Helen Kentnor noted that although Sallie belonged to the Episcopal Church, "She did not participate in any church work regularly."[7]

Perhaps the Imhofs' close relationship with the Pueblo Indians influenced their religious understanding in ways that they chose not to discuss with anyone. "No Indian," D. H. Lawrence wrote of the Pueblo Indians' spiritual view of life, "saw himself as guided by an omnipotent being; rather he sought to merge himself with a life force that permeated all animate and inanimate objects. 'All is god,' in this 'vast old religion.'"[8]

Sallie expressed her beliefs in the way she lived, by helping others in her community. In 1933, when the New Mexico State Welfare office was first organized, Dr. Martin served as the Taos chairman. During this time Sallie, worked as Dr. Martin's secretary. As Phillips Kloss indicated, Sallie regularly pursued relief work.

Sallie, Taos.

Artists living in New Mexico could not have imagined themselves among the needy. However, in 1933 they began to feel the results of the 1929 financial disaster and subsequent Depression. It had taken three years for their art market to dry up. That year, fortunately, President Franklin D.

Roosevelt ushered in the first Public Works of Art Project (PWAP), a project established within the Treasury Department. The government situated the administrative headquarters in Santa Fe for Region Thirteen, which included Arizona and New Mexico. Artist Gustave Baumann received the appointment as area coordinator. It was his job to check on artists' progress, encourage and motivate them while, at the same time, supporting those who thought more about the quality of their work than their paycheck.[9]

Although this project originated to give financial support to needy artists, Baumann selected only competent artists. When the PWAP ended in 1934, the Federal Art Project of the Works Progress Administration (WPA/FAP) followed in 1934 to provide economic relief "regardless of the aesthetic result." Gene Kloss was among the few artists who met the criteria established for both programs. Baumann judged Kloss as the "project's one etcher most intent on giving value for money received."[10]

"Taos Sacred Mountain," a.k.a. "The Storm," lithograph, (16½ x 12½ in.).

In 1934, Imhof made prints, principally a lithograph titled "The Storm," also titled "Taos Sacred Mountain," for the WPA/FAP.[11] He also executed three murals, that depicted Pueblo dancers, in the University of New Mexico Student Union Building built by WPA funds.[12]

In addition, that year Imhof exhibited a lithograph in the galleries of the New Mexico Fine Arts Museum in conjunction with the Santa Fe Fiesta.[13] He also began making small lithographs of Pueblo Indians and Indian ceremonies that the Imhofs would use for their Christmas cards, thank you notes and as notes for special occasions. Imhof would follow this practice for the remainder of his life.[14]

The Christmas cards give more understanding of the way in which he worked. Few of the cards appear to be finished works of art. Several cards seem more like rough sketches on which Imhof has left ragged lines and unformed figures. He usually folded the completed card for the convenience of mailing. Imhof could be sloppy, Robert Erkins observed. "He was not a craftsman like [Henry F.] Farny," Erkins said, speaking of one of the most important nineteenth-century American painters whose paintings of Plains Indians reflected Farny's lifelong interest in Indians.[15]

"Many, Many Thanks...
The Imhofs," (lithograph,
11 X 8½ in.), 1948.

The smaller lithographs Imhof used for cards depict the wider range of subjects that interested him, and which he had already developed or would later develop into paintings and lithographs. Magpies quarrel in one lithograph, while two Pueblo women carrying water in ollas balanced on their heads appear in another lithograph. Another depicts deer dancers. Only one known card pictures the Imhofs, and it is so roughly drawn that they appear, as did their daughter in life, as shadowy figures. Imhof never executed a formal self-portrait, though he did make a few sketches and drawings of himself and Sallie. It was not within Imhof's nature to sit before a mirror and study his image. To do so would have meant introspection, and Imhof did not choose to focus his energies in such an enterprise.

Few critics mention Imhof's paintings of Plains Indians and works depicting life in the West. In these works, he used every medium—oil, casein, watercolor, ink, mixed media and lithographs. Perhaps so many other painters chose the same stereotypical subjects that Imhof's did not catch the interest of critics. In these works, Imhof depicts Sioux, Apache, Comanche and Arapaho Indians. He painted Plains Indians and cowboys racing across the plains; Plains Indians attacking a wagon train; Plains Indians in headdresses; cowboys in a corral roping horses; wild horses; a mining prospector with a donkey; hawks attacking magpies; a smiling Pueblo Indian with a wreath of leaves about his head. Since Imhof rarely dated any of his work, it is impossible to know when he created these varied works. However, many appear to be experiments, as if he were trying different ideas during the early 1930s when he began to use all of his time to create works of art.

The works he chose to exhibit at the Santa Fe Fiesta, however, seem to be some of the best of what he created, his lithographs of Pueblo Indian portraits. He exhibited at Santa Fe most of the years from 1931 until 1950.[16]

Several important events took place in the Imhofs' lives during 1935. They again traveled to La Jolla, California to visit their friends, the Kepplers, and then Dr. Martha Welpton, who still lived in San Diego.[17] It was during this stay in La Jolla that Imhof made sketches and notations for the second lithograph, "Fr. Junipero Serra," that depicts the subdued and more kindly appearing priest.

In Taos during 1935, the Imhofs met Marie and Arthur J. Merrill who, like other younger friends of the Imhofs, lived in the Imhofs' guest house.[18] Art Merrill, according to Carol Hale, appeared to be the stereotypical artist who wore a beret, lived in Taos during the summer and painted in Mexico during the winter. To the Imhofs, though, the Merrills became trusted friends. Although Joe was wary of his art being sanctioned by art dealers, the Merrills' gallery would represent Imhof's work for over fifty years.[19]

Marie Merrill said, "For a matter of a year and a half my husband, Arthur J. Merrill and myself lived in the guest house on their home property. During that time we were in and out of his several work studios several times a week and saw him painting or doing lithograph printing etc. We presented him in Merrill's Gallery over twenty years and with our association with him were very familiar with his type of art."[20]

When Arthur Merrill died in 1973, Marie sold Merrill's Gallery to Mrs. George (Lila) Deacon, who continued to carry Imhof's work. When Deacon sold Merrill's Gallery to E. O. Floyd in June of 1980, Floyd, too, carried Imhof's work until Floyd closed the gallery in 1986. At that time, Floyd sent the Imhof works, as willed, to the Heye Foundation in New York, thus ending a fifty-year association of Imhof with one gallery.[21]

The year that Joseph Imhof acquired a permanent art gallery happened to be the year that Dr. T. P. Martin died, leaving Sallie saddened and without her work in medicine. Not long after Dr. Martin's death, Sallie began to work with Dr. Gertrude Light, one of the few women medical doctors who had ever had a medical practice in New Mexico. Dr. Light probably had a professional association with Dr. Martin since he had helped organize the Talpa Water Users Association to handle their irrigation water and build reservoirs. Dr. Light lived in Talpa, a tiny settlement in a forested valley where three canyons—the Rio Chiquito, Little Rio Grande and Miranda Canyons—break out of the Sangre de Cristo mountains. Talpa had always been a part of Ranchos de Taos about four miles south of Taos.[22]

Dr. Light had received her medical degree in 1898 from Johns Hopkins University School of Medicine in one of the early classes of Baltimore's famed school. She had arrived in Ranchos de Taos in 1922 where she spent most of her medical career, which lasted into the 1940s.[23] Among her neighbors in Talpa had been Juan Pedro Cruz, a village weaver who had made his own loom and spinning wheel with which he supplied the Taos Indians most of their *serapes*, and the surrounding villagers with black, brown, and white checkered *jergas* (small rugs) with which they carpeted their dirt floors.[24]

Talpa also became the home to various artists, among them Andrew

Dasburg and Howard Cook. Talpa had one lodge that housed permanent guests by advance arrangement, and was frequented by Eastern artists who lived there during the summer. Medical doctors saw an entirely different side of life in Talpa's beautiful valley that artists painted. Living in the tiny sur-rounding communities were the poor who suffered with communicable dis-eases, ruptured appendixes, problem child births, and self-treatment for all variety of ailments and injuries.[25]

"Practice out in the countryside was largely a man's game, but a num-ber of women physicians chose to accept the special challenges inherent in practicing medicine away from the support systems of city medicine."[26] Dr. Light was only one of six women who practiced for more than four years in New Mexico during the 1920s and 1930s.[27] After Dr. Martin's death, Sallie Imhof began to drive Dr. Light, sometimes in the dead of winter, to treat patients throughout the countryside, assist Dr. Light with patients, and to keep the doctor's records.[28] Their association would last until Dr. Light be-came a patient herself in St. Joseph's sanitarium in Albuquerque.[29]

During this period in the late 1930s, Joseph Imhof began to develop a reputation for being impatient, even haughty to other artists. In *Printmaking in New Mexico, 1880-1990*, Clinton Adams writes, "Beginning in 1927 Alexandre Hogue spent three to seven months a year in Taos . . . where he became a close friend of the Blumenschein family. Hogue . . . stayed aloof from disputes among the Taoseño artists—a neutrality which bore fruit in 1936 and 1938 when Joseph Imhof (uncharacteristically) offered Hogue use of his lithograph press. Hogue describes Imhof as a 'loner' and 'difficult to know,' and believes that he (Hogue) may have been 'the only artist Imhof ever helped in Taos.'"[30]

Imhof had always been a loner from the time he left home at age fifteen. After his daughter's death, he became even more withdrawn from the people in the Taos community. He did help other artists in addition to Hogue, however. He offered his lithography press to Emil Bisttram who used it a number of times, as did his students at the Taos Field School of Art.[31] Prior to Hogue's use of Imhof's press, Helen Blumenschein used the press. And Van Deren Coke writes in his book, *Taos and Santa Fe: The Artist's Environ-ment, 1882-1942*, "As an artisan printer, Imhof gave freely of his time and knowledge of lithography to other members of the Taos art colony and to students."[32] Imhof gave generously to those with whom he felt *simpático*. The

July 16, 1936 *Taos Valley News* noted that "Mr. Joseph Imhof has generously given two lithographs to Miss Elflida Sprague to be raffled for the benefit of the Health Fund."[33]

Imhof had become, indeed, more impatient with those who impinged on his time and energy.[34] He was, in 1936, sixty-five years old and he hadn't even begun to formulate and rough sketch the Corn Series. That year must have brought financial worries, too, because the property that the Imhofs owned at 22 Willow Street in Brooklyn was cited for violation of the fire codes and reported as a fire hazard. Joseph Ide, the Imhofs' agent in New York, learned that the building, which the Imhofs had transformed into a duplex, had filled with smoke and gas after a fire had been started in the furnace. A Brooklyn building inspector determined that the flue was blocked, probably by bricks falling out of the walls between flues. The inspector ruled that the building was not fit for human habitation until the condition had been repaired.[35]

The Imhofs directed Joseph Ide to make the appropriate repairs.[36] Four years later they spent an additional five hundred dollars to alter and relocate a bathroom for the two family occupancy.[37] Finally, when the Imhofs' finances became even more tight and they knew they would never return to Brooklyn to live, they sold the building in 1944. But that was still eight years in the future and Joseph Imhof had not yet made peace with his daughter's death.

During this time, the Imhofs shared a close friendship with Helen and E. Martin Hennings, who lived traditional lives as artists, and Emil Bisttram.[38] Bisttram, like Imhof, had been treated as an outsider when he had arrived in Taos with his different views and experiences. Dorothy Brett had been one of the first artists to stand up for Bisttram, followed by Ernest Blumenschein, Kissel and finally Bert Phillips.[39] But Imhof had liked Bisttram from the very beginning. Part of their *simpático* stemmed from their mutual interest in and use of dynamic symmetry. Their similar philosophies, though, served to bind their friendship.

In 1938, Bisttram formed the Transcendental Painting Group that lasted for three years and, in those three years, caught the attention of the Soloman R. Guggenheim Museum, which exhibited seven of the members' paintings, and the Museum of Modern Art in New York, which exhibited ten members' work. Bisttram's philosophy matched that of Imhof's. According to Bisttram, "only that work from which the spiritual powers radiate, causing expression on the consciousness of the beholder, will enable man to better understand life and live more fully, more extensively and more intently or will have any reason and validity for existing."[40]

This transcendental philosophy reflected that which Joe and Sallie had come to accept from Dr. Adler, as well as the beliefs of the Pueblo Indians. Transcendental art held that "Harmony is the law of Life, of Nature and of her vibrations, and the two main fields in which Life works, to two main streams through which the Water of Life flows, Light and Sound. To apprehend and comprehend; to appreciate and analyze these two great forces, the two great faculties of man are used, sight and hearing. They go together. Remember that you cannot hear without seeing and that you cannot see without hearing.

" . . . You must understand the meaning of seeing. Seeing is not looking; seeing is opening the eyes. Most of us with eyes wide open see nothing, a few see much better with eyes closed. Seeing is understanding, comprehension. 'Oh, I see,' is said, when understanding is meant. Then you are right. Seeing and hearing are primarily and essentially mental, because it is necessary for the eye and the ear to have complete co-operation and the direct guidance of the higher mind in order to be able to do the work properly. In art, when I use the term 'developing of sight and hearing' I mean the perfecting of the higher mind, making a conscious mental effort to understand. You must make a willing attempt to use those functions more broadly. One of the secrets of the Law of Harmony is that real beauty lies under the surface."[41]

The Imhofs, while becoming more withdrawn, did not isolate themselves from their community and friends. A photograph taken in about 1936 or 1937 shows them standing before Tio Vivo (Uncle Lively), a hand-operated, hand-carved merry-go-round found in a barn in Peñasco. The Taos Lions Club bought the merry-go-round to use at community events, which included the celebrations at the September San Geronimo Fiesta. In the photograph, Joe wears an Iroquois Indian sash made of beaver hair, and Sallie wears a fiesta dress of her own design. While Joe smiles broadly and stands in a cocky stance, Sallie appears somber and stiff.[42]

The Imhofs must certainly have attended the dedication in May of 1937 of Taos' first community hospital, Holy Cross Hospital, because Dr. Gertrude Light was one of five physicians who used the twenty-bed facility.

The hospital had come into existence through the generosity of Mabel Dodge Luhan who had donated the home she had built for her son.[43]

Sallie and Joe Imhof in front of Tio Vivo, Taos, ca. 1936.

It was during this time in 1936 and 1937 that the Erkins family visited in Taos on one of their trips to Wyoming. Charlotte and Albert W. Erkins lived in Ohio where Albert was president of Mid West Glass and Manufacturing Company that had been organized in 1920 and did special automobile body design for General Motors cars. While in Taos, Charlotte and Albert had bought paintings by Sharp and Phillips, and their interest in art had motivated someone to suggest they see the Imhof art hanging in the Sagebrush Inn. When the Erkins family met the Imhofs, an immediate affinity developed. Mrs. Erkins bore a striking resemblance to the Imhof's daughter and, coincidentally, was about the same age as Elizabeth. So began a life-long friendship.[44]

In 1939, the Erkins began renting a home near the Taos Pueblo, and the two Erkins children, Robert and Charlene, began calling the Imhofs Uncle

Joe, or José, and Aunt Sallie. Over the years, the Imhofs took the Erkins camping and on painting trips. Joe taught Robert and Charlene to draw, took them to visit pueblos and dances, and on Indian arrowhead searches. Robert helped Imhof print lithographs, and Charlene would lie in quiet wait in Joe's studio as the two watched through the large living room window for magpies and other birds. The children gave rapt attention to Imhof's stories of Iron Tail, the Indian who had posed for the Buffalo nickel, and of Imhof's tales of Buffalo Bill.[45]

Imhof eventually painted a portrait of Charlene posed on a horse, dated the painting, and gave the oil to Charlene's father, Albert, as a birthday gift. Imhof, as he had for many of his paintings, hand-carved the frame. In 1941, Imhof gave the Erkins's daughter, Charlene, a lithograph of "Fr. Junipero Serra" and inscribed it, 1941.[46]

Imhof's habit and attitude about dating and cataloging his work is best described by Allen Willett, an art dealer in Carlsbad, California who first visited Taos in the summer of 1938. "I had the chance to meet a number of the old Taos artists, among them was Mr. Imhof," Willett said. "On one of my yearly visits to Taos I learned from Mr. Imhof that he was very disciplined in creating and pulling his stone lithographs. I seem to recall that he told me that he never knew how many of his prints would be in an edition because it all depended upon how crisp and sharp each print turned out. He printed as few as four or five or as many as fifty . . . I don't believe there is any record of the number of prints in each edition. I have sold many of his prints and have often been asked, 'How many prints in this edition?' As Mr. Imhof might say, 'Oh, I don't know. It all depends!'"[47]

On one of the Erkins' visits, Joseph Imhof showed the Erkins' family the hacienda and property at Abiquiu, which my aunt and uncle would eventually buy and name, Rancho de Abiquiu. Perhaps Imhof was trying to interest the Erkins in purchasing the property. Albert and Charlotte, however, found the property too rundown, too costly to renovate. The family preferred to rent property where they now spent entire summers camping, attending Pueblo dances.[48]

"One time," Robert said, "Joe used my back as a table for a sketch pad since no photographs were allowed [at a Pueblo ceremony]. All notes were by sketches and Imhof was accurate as to belt buckles and other articles." In his continued efforts to teach Robert to draw, "Imhof had a chair in his studio

301

that had lots of curves. He had me drawing that chair many, many times." Another time, Imhof inquired, "Bobby, did you ever shave a cat? To be an artist you need to shave a cat. Then you see the muscles and how the cat moves."[49]

The Erkins' children clearly admired the Imhofs. "I still have the sketch books," Robert said in the same conversation during the early 1990s, "for the aniline process Imhof made money on. It was big with bread companies. You could hardly buy a loaf of bread without a coloring book."

Robert then observed that "Imhof liked the brilliant background paintings of the day in Europe . . . all pink, blue or green sky and liked to concentrate on the face. Imhof had a broader scope than other Taos artists." Robert saw that Imhof liked to do "horrible things like extending arms, legs in a way the human body couldn't move."

Robert's observation can be seen in an Imhof painting, "Rebuilding the Mission," that appears in the booklet, *Representative Art and Artists of New Mexico*, published in 1940 by the School of American Research, Museum of New Mexico in Santa Fe. In the painting, the Pueblo Indians depicted haul enormous logs, their bodies bent in heavy labor as they rebuild a mission. A priest looks on, as if supervising, and all figures have elongated and curved bodies except the priest. The bent, elongated bodies of the Indians emphasize the slave-like life they lived under the erect-standing priest who holds a cross almost the height of his own body. The rebuilt mission looms toward the sky, dwarfing both the Indians and the priest. The painting is obviously another statement Imhof has chosen to make about the Catholic church (see page 170).

While the Erkins spent days and weeks in the home and studios of the Imhofs, Sallie reported, "We never showed the studio to tourists. All visitors were by appointment, and paintings were ordered or bought by our well-known friends here and abroad . . . . The years went on and on, we entertaining visitors from all lands who took many Indian paintings home and then would come letters from their friends asking for similar paintings, so many were bought sight unseen."[50]

By 1940, when *Representative Art and Artists of New Mexico* came off the press, the text noted that "many of the 146 artists listed are still at work," however the Golden Era of Taos had passed.[51] Economic growth had begun to invade Taos as did an ever-increasing number of tourists. At the same time, Taosans began to leave to join the military forces fighting World War II; and the Taos County Project came into existence to organize its citizens into groups to improve water wells, libraries, clinics and health services, adult literacy, education, livestock, water supplies, farming methods, mail service. The Taos Project was directed from the Harwood Foundation, and in all probability Sallie Imhof worked as a volunteer. It is known that Sallie began volunteer work for the local Selective Service Board.[52]

In 1941, Joseph Imhof exhibited in the Annual Exhibition of Painters and Sculptors of the Southwest held at the Art Gallery of the School of American Research and the Museum of New Mexico, Santa Fe in conjunction with Fiesta.[53] The next year, John Young-Hunter became a full-time resident of Taos. While the two men had quite different backgrounds and temperaments, they still enjoyed discussing their common interests: Buffalo Bill and dynamic symmetry which Young-Hunter also used while creating his works of art.[54]

Imhof and Sallie, Mesa, AZ, 1940.

At this time, Joseph Imhof began to concentrate more on the rough sketches for the Corn Series, and he and Sallie "attended most of the important dances, especially corn, and that meant work for both of us," Sallie reported. "Before we went I would receive my orders to pay special attention to some phase of the dance and report thereon. Joe's photographic mind would work at home where he would retire to his studio and draw notes of whatever he had put his mind to studying at that dance . . . . We certainly lived and thought Indian, but our lives were very happy and understanding. We took short trips to Arizona and California to see our friends and enjoyed what cultural events . . . Taos afforded."[55]

That year of 1942, my uncle, Winfield Morten, and my father, Robert (Hal) Howell Hopkins, Sr., had for two years been engaged in an enterprise to manufacture their "Victory Hut," a prefabricated housing unit that the United States armed forces purchased and used to house military personnel. The Victory Hut was the first innovation in military housing since the tent, and Morten's and Dad's six-acre plant in Dallas produced two hundred 16-by-16-foot Victory Huts per eight-hour shift to meet the demand for instant housing.[56]

While the Victory Hut represented only one of the several lucrative businesses Morten owned, the prefabricated housing became more well-known than any of his other enterprises. GIs the world over would soon either live in a Victory Hut, or see them on their bases. Within a year, the secret Los Alamos, New Mexico Manhattan Project that developed the Atomic Bomb would use the Victory Huts to house its personnel.[57]

My father spent vast amounts of time in Washington, D.C., fulfilling his responsibilities in an essential wartime industry during World War II. In those turbulent years, my father and mother took their three children, Robert, Morten, and me, to the Sangre de Cristo mountains in New Mexico. These journeys into the mountains helped revive Dad's spirits and afforded us children our first opportunity to learn from the pageant of men and women truly larger than life, people who equaled the magnificence of the surrounding landscape that spoke of the great drive to the West. After our introduction to the West, we knew we had more to see and learn of these experiences that refused to allow us to forget them.

In 1943, Winfield Morten, then thirty-nine years old, and his wife, Helen, my mother's sister, vacationed in New Mexico, partly as a respite from work and perhaps for Winfield to oversee their business. For Winfield, New Mexico felt almost like coming home, since he had visited there as a child. His mother, Blanche Morten Alexander, and his grandparents, Nellie and Edward Winfield Morten, who had reared the boy, had taken him to Pecos and Jémez Springs, which he remembered with enthusiasm.

Winfield Morten, like Joseph Imhof, had been rejected by his father. O. O. Alexander of Kansas City, Missouri, Winfield's father, had simply abandoned his wife, Blanche, and six-months-old son, Winfield. Blanche Alexander had taken her son and returned to her parents' home in Dallas, Texas.

Winfield's grandfather, E. W. Morten, who had originally come from the East, had amassed a fortune with his many enterprises in McKinney, Texas and in Dallas, where he lived.[58] E. W. reared Winfield in a surrounding of great wealth in the early 1900s, and eventually changed Winfield's last name from Alexander to Morten. Winfield lived in a world of extensive travel, cooks, chauffeurs, butlers, private schools. When E. W. died in 1929, he left Winfield a sizable estate of over twenty businesses, all of which had potential, but needed reorganizing. The condition of some of these businesses forced Winfield to develop his powers to adapt, overcome obstacles, and to use his inheritance as a tool to reach his goals. In the process, he became a man of vision. He was also a man of great integrity and generosity who trusted others would reciprocate that trust.[59]

Winfield lived in Dallas where he enjoyed living in social prominence, and it was here that he met Helen, his future wife who had moved to Dallas from Medora, Illinois.[60] Helen had style and verve, qualities that brought her a modeling career at Neiman-Marcus. This, plus her charm and beauty, attracted Winfield. It seemed only natural that Helen should share Winfield's love of New Mexico, and the Indian spirit and lore that had attracted him as a child.

When the Mortens arrived in Taos around 1943, friends introduced them to Joe and Sallie Imhof. At this first meeting with the Imhofs, Winfield purchased an Imhof painting, then commissioned Joe to create a lithograph for the Mortens' Christmas card. Winfield also remarked of his interest in buying property and Joe, of course, took the Mortens to the place that Joe would have liked to have bought had he had the money. For it was here that Joe liked to paint the spectacular multi-colored landscape: at Abiquiu near an old hacienda on the Chama River. The property had considerable acreage for sale. Winfield and Helen surveyed the old hacienda as Joe narrated its history. Like Joseph Imhof, Winfield Morten was a dreamer. The two men had other characteristics in common. Morten, like Imhof, was religious in his own way. Morten believed, like Imhof, that Indians had beliefs of worth that required study. Soon the Mortens envisioned the ranch in all its glory.

The area surrounding the village of Abiquiu had played host to at least ten prehistoric Pueblo sites before the ancient ones are said to have moved into the Chama valley and mesas around Abiquiu. In the century before the Spanish came in the 1500s, the ancient people migrated from the Abiquiu area toward the south to Santo Domingo Pueblo, westward to Acoma, Zuni, and Hopi villages.[61] Not until 1730 did people again settle in Abiquiu when the Spanish governor made a land grant to Bartolome Trujillo in 1734. Within the decade, twenty families joined Trujillo, as did Indians brought by the Spanish priest, Fray Carlos Delgado. A number of the people Father Delgado brought were descendants of the ancients who had lived there originally. In addition, "members of various tribes, as Pawnee, Wichita, Apache, Comanche, and Kiowa, who had been raised from childhood in Spanish households as 'servants' and were thoroughly Hispanicized, . ." moved to Abiquiu. These people were known as *genízaros*, people who had broken from their original culture. Over the next thirty years, repeated raids by Comanche, Navajo, and Ute dispersed the settlements until in 1770 the Spanish governor insisted that as a defense, the houses be built around the central plaza dominated by the church. In 1776, a population of 136 Spaniards and Indians lived in the town proper, and 254 persons lived in the area served by the mission.[62]

In 1943, six hundred lived in the village of Abiquiu built on a bluff some fifty miles north of Santa Fe.[63] The Chama River, which supplied water to Abiquiu, cut through the great sandstone cliffs and provided the color that attracted Joseph Imhof and Georgia O'Keeffe, who was by now spending her summers at nearby Ghost Ranch. In a letter to Arthur Dove in September 1942, O'Keeffe wrote, "I wish you could see what I see out the window—the earth pink and yellow cliffs to the north—the full pale moon about to go down in an early morning lavender sky behind a very long beautiful tree covered mesa to the west—pink and purple hills in front and the scrubby fine dull green cedars—and a feeling of much space."[64]

O'Keeffe would wait two more years before she would buy a house and three acres overlooking the Chama River and within view of the Rancho de

Abiquiu property owned by Helen and Winfield Morten.[65] For now, Abiquiu consisted of a run down, partially functional church, two bars, two Penitente *Moradas*, a post office, Martin Bode's Grocery Store next to the church, and Pilkington's Filling Station at the bottom of the bluff on Highway 84.

Winfield Morten began buying property in 1944 after he envisioned how the land and ill-repaired hacienda could be recreated to its original richness.[66] He was, in 1944, an ecologist before his time. But then Morten was ahead of his time in almost every endeavor he undertook. He and Helen bought ten thousand acres behind the hacienda in the Plaza Blanca Grant, and two other pieces of property which they planned to put under irrigation. These consisted of one thousand acres surrounding the hacienda and one thousand acres across the highway from the hacienda. Shortly after that, Winfield asked Imhof to work with him to restore the hacienda.

As Morten began his project in 1944, Robert Oppenheimer, the physicist responsible for the Manhattan Project, had already begun his work at the former Los Alamos Ranch School property, the site for the massive government development. At Oppenheimer's recommendation, the War Department on December 7, 1942, one year after Pearl Harbor, had taken over the Los Alamos Ranch and in 1943 moved the boys who attended the private school to the Sagebrush Inn in Taos for a year. Oppenheimer had known of the Los Alamos property since he had spent his summers at a home he owned at Pecos, a small community twenty-five miles east of Santa Fe. The Victory Huts that sprang up overnight in Los Alamos changed the remote forested mountain region into a mining camp appearance where workmen had scraped the land bare before the unadorned brown box-like buildings sprang up overnight.[67]

Within ten years, the population in Los Alamos would spill over into a sagebrush-covered mesa ten miles southeast, and produce another new town, White Rock. No one was thinking about another new town in 1943, however, for no one in the surrounding towns and villages knew about the secret project brewing in their hills and forests.

By the time the Los Alamos Manhattan Project neared completion in 1944, Morten and Imhof were restoring the hacienda. Joe dug around the area to find the best adobe material, and found it across Highway 84 on Morten property. Imhof then supervised the hacienda restoration while my father managed the ranch restoration project.

307

The rebuilding continued during the summer months, so my father brought my mother and us three children—myself, and brothers Robert and Morten—to live in Santa Fe. When workmen finished the two ranch manager houses, a bunk house, and a cook shack at Rancho de Abiquiu, the Mortens and Hopkinses moved into the two managers' houses.

Although neither the Mortens nor Hopkinses had any knowledge of the Imhofs' finances, it became clear within a few years that the Imhofs' meager financial situation had influenced Joe's decision to work under Winfield's commissions. Joe carved the front door to the ranch house and the mantel piece over the living room fireplace. The carving read: "La Casa del Valle Feliz," The House of the Happy Valley. For the ranch house patio, Imhof sculpted a "Rain God" statue identical to the one at his Taos home. He made wood carvings on the doors that led to bedrooms for two Hopkins' children. For Robert, a racing horse; for me, a deer.

Imhof then painted murals over three door openings at the ranch house. The living room mural depicted Oñate and his soldiers entering the valley. The mural over the dining room showed Indians winnowing corn. A third mural painted over the trophy room door portrayed Winfield, Helen, and some of my family. The inscription: "Enjoy Life While You Are Living, You Will Be A Long Time Dead."[68]

In 1945, with the Mortens' home near completion, Joe began to select furnishings from his Taos house to furnish Rancho de Abiquiu. He chose his favorite color, blue, and incorporated his Delft plates into the decor, as well as antique chests, a pair of mermaid and merman pults that had at one time braced the mantel of a European's fireplace, and a medieval metal plate dated 1590.

Winfield Morten had met a dreamer with whom he could communicate, and with whose ideas on art, decor, architecture, nature, Indian spirit and lore he agreed. It's possible that the wealth that surrounded Winfield as he grew to maturity tended to isolate him, and contributed to his inability to communicate his ideas to others. My father served that function for Winfield's business relationships. Winfield and Joe, however, spoke the same language and needed no interpreter. Winfield not only purchased Imhof's art, he purchased the many treasures that Imhof had collected since his early twenties.

Rancho de Abiquiu itself became a treasure, attracting the editors of *Life Magazine* who would eventually send the photographer, W. Eugene Smith, to capture the unique hacienda and its owners. While the World War II events preempted Rancho de Abiquiu's story on *Life Magazine's* pages, the photographs remain in the magazine's archives.[69]

Helen and Winfield began to invite their friends and neighbors to dinner parties. They placed guests at the hand-made table that seated fourteen. At any dinner party, guests might include Fathers Placido Martinez and Francis Nava of the St. Thomas Catholic Church in Abiquiu, the Mortens' new friend, Georgia O'Keeffe, the Imhofs, the well-regarded Dallas merchant Stanley Marcus, and Clara and Leo F. Corrigan of Dallas who had amassed a fortune in real estate, actor Joseph Cotten, and dress designer Agnes James, who had created a line of clothing similar to clothes worn during Fiesta time, and who came often to Abiquiu to find her colors.[70]

Helen and Winfield Morten in living room of their Rancho de Abiquiu home, Abiquiu, NM, February 25, 1947.

309

Of course, the Hopkins family of five attended many dinners. At dinners when most of the guests consisted of family and close friends, Joe Imhof would bring several of his many hats. After dinner, he would instigate games, wearing the hats. Sometimes we would all play charades, and even Sallie seemed to enjoy these.

At gatherings that both O'Keeffe and Imhof attended, they rarely, if ever, discussed their art. Their philosophies on art so diverged that each had little to discuss, which is not to say they did not treat each other with respect and interest. O'Keeffe did visit the Imhofs in their home.[71]

The Morten dinners held special pleasure for the Catholic Fathers because Winfield contributed handsomely to the rebuilding of Abiquiu's Catholic church. At one point, Winfield had brought four Victory Huts to Abiquiu and placed them beside the newly completed church for parishioners to use as a community hall. The sight so appalled O'Keeffe that she described to Winfield how awful his huts looked. Winfield agreed to stucco the buildings so that they blended with Abiquiu's adobe church and buildings.[72]

Imhof in one of his many hats.

Within a short time, Georgia O'Keeffe, Aunt Helen and Uncle Winfield became good neighbors and good friends. I can remember visiting Georgia's home in Abiquiu, and eyeing the plywood dining table placed in the corner with bancos, the seats built into the walls of adobe homes. On another visit, I studied what I decided must be a blue egg in a painting I found hanging on one of her walls. Years later I discovered that I had been looking at a pelvis bone through which I could see the blue of the sky, though I have often wondered if I actually was looking at an unfinished painting. Not long after that, Georgia called my Aunt Helen and asked if she had anyone at Rancho de Abiquiu who could come to her house and crate a painting. Aunt Helen sent my brother, Morten, and his friend, Kenny Mathis, who crated Georgia's painting.

When Georgia O'Keeffe visited my aunt and uncle, she especially enjoyed visiting with the men present, though she made keen observations about Rancho de Abiquiu and others present. Once she told my mother, Aunt Helen and me, as she observed the three of us dressed in blue jeans, that Mother and Aunt Helen looked better in their jeans than I did. Nancy, she said, was too thin. She was, of course, correct.

A Dallas family who visited as guests of the Mortens, LaRue and Hans Glitsch, who had built a fortune in the manufacturing of parts for the oil industry, and their young daughter, Carol, would receive the gift of Joe's time and knowledge when Carol became an artist herself one day. "My first teacher was Jose Imhof," Carol recalled, "an old man when I first met him. He told me where to begin and how . . . . He thought my pastel of a Teddy Bear was very nice, but it would be okay to draw things that move too. And to show them moving as well. He knew this wasn't easy, but the time to start is now not later, no matter when now is . . . . He told me not to listen to what anyone said, but just listen to their tone of voice—that would tell me all I needed to know.

"He was very patient with me and asked questions about why I did this and that, this way or that way. Then he listened intently to my answer. Very strong medicine for a very young girl. He said something later when I was moaning about my draftsmanship and how really hard liquid color was for me to handle. He said don't worry—keep working—somewhere around middle age it would all come together. I think then he said, 'everything does.'

"We spoke of drawing methods . . . [and] if I was lucky, I would be

311

thrown into interesting art classes. But to remember you can quit a class and not quit working—all of the work he'd gotten done was outside one, but they were important."[73]

Imhof painting in Taos Pueblo.

Sallie Imhof, 1945.

As Joe's own work on the Morten projects progressed, Sallie Imhof made it obvious to Winfield and Helen Morten that she (Sallie) was not happy with Joe's arrangements with Winfield. It took too much time away from Joe's painting and research for his Corn Series.[74] She realized, she said, that the financial arrangement was necessary, but she didn't have to like it. In 1945, Joe had reached seventy-five years of age and he still had not started painting the Corn Series.

Joe, however, still wanted to bring us Hopkins children into his daily activities. When I first met him as a ten-year-old, he remarked that I reminded him of his daughter. From that moment, he took me and my brothers on adventures to the Puye Cliff dwelling on Santa Clara Pueblo lands to the south and west of Abiquiu, and to many Pueblo dances and ceremonies. Puye Mesa is a crescent-shaped cliff more than a mile in length and honey-combed with two levels of caves that housed the ancient cliff dwellers. On the top of Puye Mesa we explored the ruins of the Great Community House, which originally had twelve hundred rooms for daily living, and provided us the possibility of artifacts.[75]

As Joe and I walked the land, he taught me how to listen to the wind steal the dust and envision whispered stories of the Indians who had lived upon the land. The only arrowhead we ever found came when we walked upon this land and one day Joe exclaimed, "Look what I've found!" In his hand glistened an arrowhead, which he then gave to me. Only years later did I learn that he had brought the arrowhead from home, then slipped it out of his pocket into his hand before he had reached to the ground to scoop up some dirt with the arrowhead.

Joe took me with him into a kiva during ceremonies, and he took my brother, Robert as well, although Robert hadn't known that it would be necessary for him to stand while there. When they attended the Santo Domingo Corn Dance, Joe dressed in Indian costume and danced with the Santo Domingo.[76] Morten, the youngest, rode horseback with Joe in late evenings to the white cliff Palisades that O'Keeffe painted so often. There, at sunset, Morten sat and watched Joe paint for the several hours until darkness enveloped them.[77]

We children listened, entranced, by Joe's stories of the Penitentes, of the Penitente ring he had which was an exact replica of the official ring used by the Major Domo Penitente to cut across the left shoulder of the initiate.

313

Its initials "JS" meant Jesus Salvatorum, he told us. After Joe's death, I learned that Sallie had given the ring to the University of New Mexico Maxwell Museum of Anthropology.[78]

The land around Abiquiu was rich in ways only Imhof could imagine. Imhof told us children of stories about ancient creatures that had lived near Ghost Ranch as long as 175,000,000 years ago. Paleontologists did discover excellent phytosaur remains, as well as bone fragments of complete skeletons of coelophysis, the earliest of the lizard-like dinosaurs.[79] With Imhof, my brothers and I existed in an idyllic world, our days rich with adventure and promise. I suspect that Joseph Imhof experienced a similar sensation about those days surrounded by children who loved him, and having found a patron who not only would finance his every endeavor, but dreamed his dreams with him. Imhof's relationship with Morten must have been what Imhof had hoped to receive from his own father.

Other friends of the Mortens, however, had interests other than lost peoples and dinosaurs. Retired Major General Charles H. Corlett, who had served under Generals Bradley and Eisenhower, and his wife, Pauline, who then lived in Española, New Mexico, often attended the Mortens' dinner parties where the conversations always turned to the secret business at Los Alamos.[80]

Did the Mortens feel afraid, the General wanted to know, when they lived only nineteen air miles from the secret something in Los Alamos that used Morten's housing units.

"We're safe," Winfield replied, when, in reality, they lived only a few miles from the atomic bomb project.

On August 6, 1945, with the frightful event of the atomic bomb explosion on Hiroshima, we learned about the Manhattan Project in Los Alamos and their first test bomb on July 16, 1945 in New Mexico area known as *Jornada del Muerto* (Journey of Death). As scientists came into Santa Fe's La Fonda Cantina to celebrate that August day in 1945, my parents, Hal and Pauline Hopkins, who had been sitting in the Cantina, only then learned how their family huts had been used in Los Alamos.

In May on VE Day in 1945, Frank Kentnor had died in a hospital room in Albuquerque.[81] When Helen Kentnor reopened the Sagebrush Inn as a lodge and it once again became the gathering place for artists and people who lived in the surrounding area, life in Taos seemed to return to normal.[82]

If the Imhofs had any thoughts about the atomic bomb, we never heard them spoken. Nor could we have guessed their thoughts by their behavior. Life simply moved on. In July of 1945, Joseph Imhof received the First award in Pastel and Print for his print, "The Sage Philosopher," at the ninth annual art festival held at Western State College, Gunnison, Colorado. E. Martin Hennings received an honorable mention for an oil.[83]

The next year, 1946, Arthur J. and Mrs. Merrill moved into the Sagebrush Inn from where Arthur conducted a gallery for Taos artists.[84] That same year, Kathleen (Kay) and Richard Dicus moved to Taos and settled in Cañon a few miles east of Taos on Highway 64 where they opened a guest ranch. They had first, however, looked at property in Abiquiu and rejected it. Georgia O'Keeffe would buy the property.[85]

And this was the year that Winfield Morten had begun to plant alfalfa to enrich the soil, and to raise cattle and sheep on the land around Abiquiu. Almost immediately, a great mystery arose. In one alfalfa field, the irrigated water simply disappeared. It was Imhof, with his knowledge of ethnology and archaeology, who deemed it worthy of research. It took three years before they discovered that caves, where ancient people had lived, lay beneath Winfield's land. Winfield's irrigation water had found the caves long before the archaeologists.[86]

In March of 1946, *El Palacio* reminded its readers that Portales, a community of five thousand and seat of Eastern New Mexico College, played an outstanding role in the development of fine arts in New Mexico. Not only did the county art society sponsor the Museum of New Mexico Exhibitions in Portales, but the College boasted of a permanent collection of paintings which included the works of Joseph Imhof.[87]

Sallie Imhof finally became the center of attention in July of 1946 when she received the Selective Service Medal and Certificate authorized by the Congress of the United States, and signed by President Harry S Truman, at a ceremony at the New Mexico State Capitol in Santa Fe. Sallie's award was given "in acknowledgment and appreciation for those who rendered more than two years of faithful service, without compensation, to the administration of the Selective Training and Service Act of 1940."[88]

El Palacio commented in its September issue that a Joseph Imhof drawing of an Indian, hung in the 1946 Santa Fe Fiesta exhibit at the Art Museum, had employed a harsh technique and yet was curiously successful. The next month, an *El Palacio* feature capsuled the Taos art colony, its artists

315

who included Imhof, and noted that the Taos Field School of Art by the University of New Mexico had become active again, stating that, "One afternoon a week Joseph Imhof instructed in the art of lithography." According to Sallie, this and the next year would the last that Joe taught lithography at the Field School of Art.[89]

For printmakers in New Mexico, an important event transpired in 1947: in February the Fine Arts Museum in Santa Fe organized a group exhibition devoted solely to prints. Clinton Adams stated, "This exhibition, which reflected, and undoubtedly encouraged, increased printmaking activity, became the first in a series of twelve annual exhibitions . . . . As might be expected, these annual exhibitions included prints by many of the artists who had established themselves as New Mexico's leading printmakers in the years before the war: Adams, Baumann, Cook, Imhof, Kloss, Latham, Shuster, and Sloan."[90]

In April, the Santa Fe *New Mexican* newspaper reported, "Joe and Sal Imhof to La Jolla for two weeks, just to relax and feed the gulls." While there, Imhof painted the sea again, executing a small watercolor, an 11½-by-16-inch work that portrayed a rather placid scene of green knolls, and sand washed by the sea. Joe signed and dated the work, 1947.[91]

Imhof at party after Dallas Museum of Fine Arts Show, 1948. Pictured left to right: Hans Glitsch, Helen Morten, Robert H. Hopkins, Jr., Robert H.(Hal) Hopkins, Sr., Imhof, La Rue Glitsch, Winfield Morten, Pauline Hopkins.

In September, Imhof's work once again appeared in Santa Fe, this time at the annual Painters and Sculptors of the Southwest exhibition during Fiesta. Then during December, the Museum held a second Print Exhibition, declaring that New Mexico's printmakers had never been "fully appreciated." *El Palacio* reported that among the works of art were, "The fine portraits of Indians by Joseph Imhof (lithography)."[92]

The next year, 1948, Joseph Imhof stayed as busy as the previous year, producing lithographs and paintings. In Dallas during February, the Dallas Museum of Fine Arts held the First Southwest Print Show sponsored by the Dallas Print Society. Joseph Imhof's "Jacarillo Apache," a lithograph, hung in the exhibition which ran from February 2 through 29. Various festivities accompanied the show.[93] My parents, Hal and Pauline Hopkins, hosted a dinner party for the Imhofs at Dallas' Century Room, Hotel Adolphus. Sallie was noticeably absent. During the exhibition, Joe gave my brother, Robert, the lithograph, "Taos Sacred Mountain." To my mother, he gave a copy of Mabel Dodge Luhan's book, *Taos and Its Artists.* He inserted a bookmark at the page where Mabel Dodge Luhan commented on Imhof. "Page 22," Imhof inscribed on the bookmark, "–and of such tripe history is made."[94]

In March, the same exhibition opened in Santa Fe from March 6 until March 25. During September, Imhof traveled once again to Santa Fe to participate in the annual Exhibition of Painters and Sculptors associated with Fiesta.[95] That year one of the Imhofs' friends, James F. "Buck" Burshears, who had served as the Fish and Game Warden at the Taos Fish Hatchery at Questa, would become associated with the Boy Scouts of America Koshare Indians in La Junta, Colorado. "Buck" Burshears would soon introduce the Koshare Indian Scouts to the Imhofs in ways neither Joe nor Sallie could imagine.[96]

By 1949, so many tourists had discovered Taos that the village trustees decided to install parking meters throughout the town. Television invaded as well. The Imhofs purchased a television set and that brought to Sallie one of her favorite forms of entertainment: boxing. She shared the excitement of the fights with the Dicuses' daughter, Anneke, since Anneke's parents did not own a set. Anneke had reached the age of about ten and become another surrogate child to the Imhofs, calling them Aunt Sallie and Uncle Joe, as had other children. She and Sallie, in their own idyllic world, spent many of their days sitting on the sofa, watching television.[97]

While watching television one day, Anneke said, "A bat landed on the sofa beside me. When I screamed, Sallie ran to the kitchen and got a pan to catch the bat which she took outside. She probably never washed the pan after she captured the bat." Then Anneke observed. "Sallie wasn't too good of a housekeeper. In their kitchen a Hoya plant, which gave off a bad odor, covered the wall and ceiling. I took a cutting," she confessed, "of this same plant and it now grows in my bedroom on the wall and ceiling."[98]

Most mornings Sallie called Anneke's mother, Kay, and gave a detailed account, accompanied by right hook, left blow, of the boxing or wrestling match she had watched on television the night before. Sometimes Anneke overheard the sharp remarks the two woman exchanged with each other, since both spoke with such frankness to the other.[99]

In 1950, Joseph Imhof exhibited again, this time with only nine other artists from Taos, in the New Mexico Museum of Art during Fiesta.[100] Sallie, who had spent most of her life anxiously watching over Joe's work, goals, finances and health now became so concerned with Joe's age and health that she questioned their family physician, Dr. Hausner, if he thought Joe should undertake the task of painting the Corn Series, his life's project that he hadn't even begun to paint. "His answer was that Joe had dreamed of this for fifty years, and the joy of doing it at last would sustain him," Sallie said.[101]

The world had entered the nuclear age, but Sallie Imhof spoke only of unfinished business: Joe's Corn Series. Still, life held a few unanticipated events. Winfield Morten had another project that intrigued Joe, and the Koshare Indian Museum had just opened and wanted Joe's work.

CHAPTER 16

THE CORN SERIES ENDS
THE PARTNERSHIP

Joseph Imhof had been making sketches of the Pueblo Indians since 1907 when the Imhofs had first come to Albuquerque. In 1908, as he had danced with the Cochiti Indians in their ritualized Corn Dance, he had had his vision of painting the Corn Series. He had then spent the remainder of his life researching and visualizing how he would depict the meaning of corn to the Indians.[1]

He wanted his paintings to convey more than just the detailed daily care of corn, and the reverence the Indian had for this plant that had sustained them spiritually and physically since the beginning of their existence on earth, as told through their own stories. Imhof wanted to get at the deep seated, harmonious rhythm of the universe that permeated the Indians' life every moment of every day.

"He kept methodically working on the Corn Series," Sallie said, referring to the years since Imhof had had his vision in 1908. "He was that sort of man. When he made up his mind to do something he did it. He might not do it then, but eventually he did it. No doubt about it. He kept his mind straight on what he was doing."[2] And Sallie knew he expected her to help him to stay focused.

Now in 1950, at the age of seventy-nine, Imhof's sketching intensified as he determined that he needed sixty paintings to record this story of corn and the Indian. "He announced it would take him four years to paint those 60 paintings," Sallie said.[3] She knew of the urgency that his Corn Series called to him, and yet she watched with alarm as other projects pulled at him, grabbed at his interests. With all the power of the pecking hen boss, as Helen

Imhof's photograph for preliminary study of painting, "Procession, Pueblo of Picuris," (oil, 4 X 5 ft.). See page 188.

Imhof's sketch for preliminary study of painting, "Procession, Pueblo of Picuris," (oil, 4 X 5 ft.). See page 188.

Kentnor once described Sallie's managerial capabilities, Sallie cast herself into all of the events that impinged on Joe, determined that nothing should distract her husband from the goal he had set for himself since 1908.[4]

She welcomed her first obstacle, the Koshare Indian Museum's interest in and acquisition of Imhof's art. In 1950, Joseph Imhof gave the Koshare Indian Museum the lithograph, "Geronimo Gojathlay."[5] The Museum's interest in Imhof's work brought with it James F. "Buck" Burshears' subsequent request to bring Koshare Boy Scouts to visit Joe in his studio. This particular group of scouts attracted the Imhofs' interests just as had General McAlpin's scouts years before in New York.[6]

"Geronimo Gojathlay, 1834–1909,"
(lithograph, 17 X 11½ in.).

The Koshares had originated in 1933 when a group of boys in La Junta, Colorado had begun to meet to study Indian lore. Over the years, thousands of seventh grade boys who had achieved the best school grades and scout records became Koshares. Now the boys who joined Koshares came not only from La Junta but from the surrounding towns as well. As the organization evolved, the scouts learned more about Indians than just lore.

They began to build Indian costumes, use beadwork, learn Indian crafts and Indian dances. In summer and winter at their compound they performed their repertoire of over one hundred dances from various tribes. They now had, among other elements, a kiva and the Koshare Indian Museum.[7]

The second obstacle Sallie had to face involved one of Winfield Morten's dream projects. By 1950, retired Major General Corlett had become vice president of Morten's housing company, renamed New Mexico Housing Company, with the headquarters in Santa Fe.[8] Corlett had grown up in Monte Vista, Colorado and had a working knowledge of Colorado's silver mines. In 1950, he told Winfield that he (Corlett) had mining interests in Silverton, a small town of 1,375 people nestled in Southern Colorado's San Juan Mountains. Corlett invited Winfield to join him on a trip to Silverton to inspect the mining interests.[9]

While in Silverton to inspect Corlett's silver mines, Winfield instead became entranced with the surroundings and envisioned the area as a vacation paradise. Silverton, he realized, could become the vacation destination of travelers who embarked on the narrow gauge train at Durango and rode it through the mountains to Silverton. On a second visit in 1951, Winfield took an interest in the sixty-eight-year-old Grand Hotel that had been owned and operated by Edna Frecker since 1944.[10]

Silverton and the Grand Hotel had just the kind of romance attached to it that had always attracted Winfield. Of all the many mining camps built along the headwaters of the Rio de las Animas (River of Lost Souls) in the 1870s, only Silverton remained. The Ute Indians, who had ruled these rugged mountains, had repelled intruders for many years, and used the mountains as a fortress from which they raided other Indians and settlers. And the mountains themselves were hostile to even one acre of agriculture. Still, prospectors knew that the inhospitable mountains had veins peppered with gold and silver. So many men died trying to invade the mountains to mine for riches that in 1868 the United States negotiated a treaty with the Ute, then further reduced the Ute holdings in 1873 when the Ute ceded the San Juan Mountain area to the United States. By the next year, two thousand men had descended upon Silverton.[11]

The San Juan Mountains did not give up its treasures without a heavy price. All goods had to be packed over the mountains on the backs of men and mules. Snows in winter and even the summer prevented passage into or out of Silverton for months at a time. In 1882, the Denver and Rio Grande Railway opened a narrow gauge railroad between Silverton and Durango. By 1884, Otto Mears, the "pathfinder of the San Juans," completed a toll road from Silverton to Red Mountain mines and would go on to build four hundred miles of toll roads and his own railroad to transport ore from mines to smelters.[12]

Into this mix of daring and riches came W. S. Thomson of London to look after his interests in the Martha Rose Smelter in Silverton. He recognized the opportunity in building a fine hotel. For sixty thousand dollars, he built the Grand Hotel, a three-story building with a solid stone masonry foundation, graceful French plate-glass windows at street level, round-top windows on the second floor, and a mansard roof.[13] The lushness within could be seen immediately in the entrance door knob that bore the state seal of Colorado. The lobby woodwork had been painted chocolate and cream, and the walls enhanced with paintings. A dining room that seated one hundred had been outfitted with expensive carpeting and marble-topped sideboards. Thomson spared "no pains or expense . . . to make this house equal in comfort and convenience to the best hotels in the East." When the hotel opened in 1883, Silverton's millionaires chose it as their hotel, and it became known as "the home of the silver kings."[14]

Lillian Russell performed there when she visited with her escort, "Diamond Jim" Brady. Other celebrities gave the Grand a kind of luster. Prohibition brought an end to the hotel's income and, in 1920, Henry Frecker bought it at a tax auction. Upon his death, his daughter, Edna, began operating it in 1944.[15]

Winfield, the visionary, saw it in all its glory. With Corlett's encouragement, Winfield bought the hotel in 1951 for twenty thousand dollars and made Corlett president of the hotel company. He then embarked on a $350,000 remodeling program to refurbish the entire structure within a year.[16] He immediately spoke with Joseph Imhof, asking him to assist in determining the decor and art that would hang throughout the hotel.

That year in 1951, Imhof had been actively painting the Corn Series. His friend, Henry Sauerwein, who liked to help Joe, had been driving him to different Pueblo ceremonies. The excursions enabled Joe to gather finite details of fact. As Sallie said, "Joe would travel with four to five cameras."[17]

Sauerwein, a friend of Kay and Richard Dicus, had visited the Dicuses in Taos during 1945, then returned permanently in 1951. His doctorate in modern languages did not hold great promise for employment in Taos, so someone told him that the Bookmobile needed a driver. Sauerwein learned to drive and took charge of Taos' Bookmobile. In his friendship with the Imhofs, he volunteered to drive Joe to pueblos to sketch. As they drove, they talked. At Cochiti, the Indians sprinkled Joe and Henry with corn pollen to make them invisible. As invisible beings, they then participated in the Indian dances.[18]

In 1951, Sauerwein helped the Imhofs celebrate Joe's eightieth birthday, and photographed the couple posed with a beautifully carved banco Richard Dicus had created. In the photograph, Sallie wears a dark-colored fiesta-style dress that highlights her Indian squash blossom necklace.[19] As she sits on the banco, she leans her head slightly into Joe standing behind the banco, his hands spread on either side of Sallie on the top of the bench. The photograph, which conveys the love and comfort the Imhofs felt for each other, would become the photograph the local newspaper published when announcing all the important events in the Imhofs' future.

During 1951, Imhof kept busy with other art projects in addition to his work on the Corn Series. He carved the St. Francis for the Sagebrush Inn fireplace after Helen Kentnor sold the Inn that year to Mrs. Amy Kling, who wanted the saint represented in the Inn. St. Francis was the patron saint of Ranchos de Taos.[20]

Then when Winfield described his newly purchased hotel to Joseph Imhof, Joe immediately visualized Winfield's dream of a luxury hotel set in a vacationer's paradise. Joe agreed to work on restoring and decorating the historic hotel. Sallie Imhof balked at Joe's new assignment. My father, Hal Hopkins, went further and made his feelings known. He told my mother, "Winfield's going to run out of money one of these days bailing himself out of his dreams."

To placate Sallie, and to help the Imhofs with their financial situation, Winfield promised to send the Imhofs a monthly check until Joe finished the Corn Series. Winfield further promised that upon completion of the Series, he would acquire joint ownership of the Corn Series with the Imhofs. Upon Joe's death, Winfield would place the Series in the appropriate museum. Sallie grudgingly agreed.[21]

Winfield renamed the Grand Hotel, Grand Imperial Hotel, combining the two names the hotel had carried since its birth in 1883. He commissioned Imhof to execute a painting of Chief Ouray, regarded as the most outstanding leader of the Ute Indian chiefs.[22] Chief Ouray had been a great friend to Kit Carson and had, in 1868, traveled to Washington to sign a treaty between the United States and Ute.

"Chief Ouray," (media and size unknown). Imhof and Helen Morten, opening of Grand Imperial Hotel, Silverton, CO, 1952.

Imhof and Morten, in undertaking their dream project, remodeled the entire hotel. For Morten, this meant adding private baths to each room, a gift shop, a ballroom, a fireplace in the lounge now known as the Chief Ouray lounge, a new kitchen to suit the French chef Winfield hired to prepare continental meals, huge skylights on the third floor that formed a dome over the lounge below and added natural light, telephones, and a museum. Morten placed expensive Navajo rugs on the polished floor of the lobby and Chief Ouray lounge.[23]

Imhof contributed his larger-than-life-size painting of Lillian Russell, and a drawing of Otto Mears. Art works hung on walls in the lounge, dining room, gift shop, museum, office, lobby, and private dining room. Imhof also hung the oil, "Indian Deer Dancers." He placed in the hotel the model of Henry Hudson's ship, *Half Moon*, that he had carved years earlier for the city of New York and used as a model for his lithograph, "Nieuw Amsterdam." He added rare and beautiful antiques from mining and by-gone Western days.[24]

Imhof's model ship, "Half-Moon," in his studio.

When the hotel opened in 1952, Imhof left evidence that he obviously had been having a good time in Silverton. He scripted this message on the wall of the restaurant which he frequented and was owned by Helen Waite: "The proprietor of this restaurant is Helen Waite. If you wish credit for your meal, go to Helen Waite [hell and wait] for it." Phillips Kloss remarked that Joe's inspired message reflected his sense of humor.[25]

When Morten and Imhof finished their dream project, the Grand Imperial was everything its name implied. The wire services and local Colorado newspapers covered the opening in July of 1952. A photograph of Joseph Imhof standing beside me appeared in the *Denver Post* along with many other photographs covering the hotel's opening on July 2, 1952. Laura Gilpin, the famous photographer who recorded the lives of the Navajo, made photographs of the hotel, some of which were used for postcards.[26]

Imhof and Nancy Hopkins Reily at opening of Grand Imperial Hotel, Silverton, CO, 1952.

MUSEUM—Miss Nancy Hopkins of Dallas, Tx., looks over an item that will be included in a museum which will be part of the Grand Imperial. Joe Imhof (above) of Taos, NM., noted western authority, is in charge of organizing the museum. Miss Hopkins wears a blouse from the Gay Nineties era.

Major motion picture stars, James Cagney and John Derek, had themselves photographed lounging on the staircase under the Lillian Russell painting. Later, more motion picture stars came to stay for weeks in Silverton when making the westerns "Maverick Queen," "Great Day in the Morning," "Run for Cover," "Ticket to Tomahawk," and "Night Passage."[27]

327

Lounge of Grand Imperial Hotel, Silverton, CO, featuring Imhof paintings, 1952.

My father's prophesy proved all too true, however. After all the money Morten had poured into the hotel, and the elegance with which he furnished the Grand Imperial that brought news coverage, Morten lost the hotel to the mortgage company within ten years.[28] Not only had he spent too much money rebuilding and furnishing the hotel, he had the misfortune of hiring an inadequate management, and paid a tax rate regarded as too high. In addition, Silverton's population of 1,400 did not approve of the Grand Imperial's new decor, or the French chef who prepared continental meals. They had preferred eating in the hotel's old cafe. Neither did the locals like Morten's idea of decorating the hotel's interior by mixing miners with Indians and cowboys. The locals preferred the original decor that reeked of the old mining days.

Allen Nossaman, Archive Director of the San Juan County Historical Society in Silverton, agreed that Morten was a man ahead of his time, saying, "Morten was indeed a man who foresaw the increasing tourist interest in Silverton and southwestern Colorado, and both the narrow gauge railroad and the Grand Imperial Hotel have been key elements in what has been steady but slow growth in that respect since the 1950s. It is unfortunate he was not able to find more reward in his vision, but he did save the hotel building from a questionable fate during a depressing period in Silverton's history, and we are in his debt for that."[29]

Sallie would be in Morten's debt as well, but she never mentioned his name in any of her recordings. In fact, in August 1954, Sallie told Fred Mazzulla, a well-regarded amateur historian, photographer, and lawyer of Denver, Colorado, and his associate, Jack P. Riddle, who had come to make a twelve-minute, 16 mm. motion picture documenting Imhof working at his lithography press, "I wouldn't want Silverton mentioned in it [the documentary]. It's [the Corn Series] not going to be in Silverton. That's a thing of the past, that idea."[30] Her adamant statement referred to their question about Morten's discussion of placing the Corn Series in Silverton, Colorado.

The year of 1952 brought events that pleased Sallie more. The Koshare Indian Museum acquired Imhof's painting, "Singers of the Plain," a 30-by-22-inch oil of three Indians in profile (see page 179).[31] Joe also sold the Museum five prints for twenty-five dollars. Joe wrote Burshears on May 12, 1952, " . . . one was for Burshears as a gift for your new house—an old world custom, for luck in the new home—therefore I shall give you credit on your next purchase or send you a check to cancel the sale. The price of lithographs was and is $25.00."[32]

Sallie reported, "By this time the Koshare Boy Scouts were coming to Taos several times a year from La Junta, Colorado, and they always came to the studio . . . and sometimes there were sixty of them. They would sit cross-legged on the studio floor and Joe would talk to them on many subjects—Indian of course—because although having an Indian name and doing beautiful Indian dances, they had little time to study Indian lore."[33]

Earlier in the year when Sallie and Joe had celebrated their fifty-fifth wedding anniversary, they had hosted a dinner party for their friends at the Sagebrush Inn, inviting only those friends in Taos.[34] Even then one or more of the guests believed the rumor and erroneous stories that circulated about a

329

wealthy Texan who planned to build a kiva to house Imhof's Corn Series.[35]

Over the next three years, Joe concentrated painting the Corn Series which, when seen together, tell the daily, social and religious significance of corn to the Pueblo Indian lifestyle. In painting the story of corn, "He meant them [the paintings] to be for instruction, education," Sallie said, "but [he] painted carefully as if for sale."[36]

She knew only too well that the Series signified the statement he planned to leave for others. "His art was a totally different type than most artists," Sallie observed. "They have the idea of painting a picture, but then once the picture is painted, that ends the episode. Joe's is a continuous story. The Corn Series has been on his mind since we came out here."[37] Perhaps without his knowing, though, the Corn Series became a metaphor for his own, and all life on the planet.

In paintings, which range in size from 1½-by-2 feet to eight-by-twelve feet, Imhof used all the materials and skills he had developed over a lifetime: gouache on board, crayon, oil, oil on linen pasted on Upson Board, oil on muslin pasted on Upson Board, line pencil over gouache, casein, watercolor. For each painting's content, he religiously drew upon his hundreds of photographs, sketches, articles of clothing, ceremonial objects and tools that he had collected since 1907 (see pages 179-192).[38]

Imhof obviously felt compelled to leave an accurate historical record. "This is all based," he wrote, "on observations & sketches & photographs before 1910. These pictures are absolutely correct. The story of corn as lived by the Indians of the Rio Grande and other Pueblos. Corn was the everyday staple of food, so naturally it pervaded all the day's work and thought. From the rising sun to night, corn was in the thoughts & activities. In these pictures we will follow 'corn from the cradle to the grave.' Mostly from the ceremonial standpoint & entirely from the pictorial view so that all may understand what these ceremonies look like & what they mean.

"This is a picture story, first & last, & the explanations will concern directly the pictures. Sufficient text will be added to hook up a complete story. A Guide book at 50 cents is your admission," he wrote.

"These are story pictures and no artistic liberties have been taken with them," he again emphasized.[39]

Imhof then sketched his idea of how the paintings should be exhibited. He placed as his centerpiece his 8-by-12-foot painting of the Santo

Domingo Corn Dance (see page 192). The surrounding paintings, which have no particular order, seem to speak as a metaphor of events in Joe's life as much as they speak of events in all peoples' lives. It is as if Imhof wanted people to understand that if you live long enough you will experience all these things, all these emotions. His point seems to be that people must accept life's events in harmony with nature.

The paintings recorded not just Taos Pueblo Indians' relationship to corn, they recorded the peoples in all the Rio Grande Pueblos Joseph Imhof had studied, including Acoma, Isleta, Santo Domingo, Cochiti, Taos, Picuris, and San Felipe. In them can be seen the colors that Imhof so loved in the European paintings: blues, pinks, beige, purple, yellows, red, lavender, orange, violet.[40]

While it is not known in what order Imhof painted the sixty works, he clearly depicts the physical aspects of corn: Pueblo Indians digging irrigation ditches, plowing, planting, harvesting, preparing to dry corn, grinding it, and baking bread. In paintings that show the use of corn in the Pueblo Peoples' life cycle, Imhof portrays the newborn infant being symbolically sprinkled with corn pollen, the governor presiding while seated with a corn tassel in his hand, a just deceased being sprinkled with pollen at burial, and other ceremonial and ritual events.[41]

As Imhof painted the ritual events in Pueblo Indians' lives, he and Sallie became participants in their own ritual events. On February 3, 1954, Sallie and Joe celebrated their fifty-seventh anniversary by inviting friends to a cocktail party in their home.[42] And, in August of that year, Fred Mazzulla and his film crew assembled in the Imhofs' home to film and record Joe's lithography work. The repartee between the Imhofs, heard in one of the Mazzulla tapes, gives a telling insight into their relationship.[43]

After they had finished filming a segment, Joe said to Fred Mazzulla, "I'm gonna get the missus." He paused, then said, "She'll say, . ." he paused again before commenting, "she likes to check, tell you all about what she saw and what we didn't do right." Then he chuckled.

As Sallie entered the room, Joe said, referring to the filming equipment, "Look at all this mess they have to have."

"A mess," Sallie noted, "this isn't a mess."

"Don't trip, Mother," Joe cautioned, "over all this."

"Would you like some whiskey?" she asked.

"Not just now," he said. "We're all gonna have some."

"No," she insisted, "I don't mean them. I meant you just right now."

"No, dear, no," he said.

"Are you tired?" she questioned.

"Not a bit," Joe said.

"Wouldn't you like to have something to snap you up?" she persisted.

"Don't worry about me," he chuckled.

"I'm not worried about you, but," she paused, "thought you deserved one by now."

After they finished another taping session, Joe and Sallie discussed what Joe should wear during another filming segment.

"You look more handsomer in a smock," she observed.

"But then I'll have to take off my shirt," he groused.[44]

Sallie's concerns about Joe's well being had a basis in fact. A few months after they finished the film, Jack Riddle's letter, dated in January 1955 and addressed to Sal and Joe noted: "We are most happy to hear that Joe is getting back on his feet. It'll probably mean he'll be hard at work again."[45] Doctors had discovered cancer in Joe and, while he worked more slowly, he continued painting the Corn Series. In mid-April, he finished the paintings.[46]

On April 15, my wedding day, he and Sallie selected and shipped to me and my husband, Don, a 24-by-20¼-inch oil of a prominent lone tree, surrounded by smaller trees, standing on a hill set against a typically colored Imhof mountain and sky. In the lower left, Joe had written, J. Imhof (see page 167). The gift remains a significant last act of kindness by Joe to one woman among many who substituted for his beloved daughter, Elizabeth.

On June 13, Sallie noticed that Joe seemed "unusually happy." He had, after all these years, discovered himself, and completed his work. He had apprenticed himself to the Indians, and learned what they had always known: that he was a being in a greater universe swayed and shaped over time by learning to live in harmony with nature, and by rhythmic pulses.

CHAPTER 17

SALLIE COMPLETES THEIR WORK

When Joseph Imhof went to bed that night, two months after he had completed the Corn Series, he slipped into a coma and died at ten o'clock the next evening, on June 14, 1955.[1] So ended a useful life. He had completed what he had set as his life's goal: the accurate record of a people, of all people.

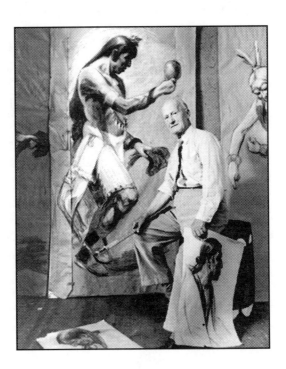

Imhof in his Taos
studio, ca. 1954.

Obituaries appeared in Taos, and other New Mexican newspapers, as well as papers in San Francisco and Denver. Sallie requested friends not send flowers to her or Joe, but to contribute to the Taos County Heart Association.[2]

A telegram to Sallie from the Koshare Indian Boy Scouts read: "We have just been advised tonight that great man has joined his forefathers. May the peace of the 'Great Spirit' rest with you who remain behind. We are mourning with you in this loss of one whom we regard as the greatest of the great among artists and men, Aunt Sally. We want you to know that Uncle Joe will be long remembered and sadly missed by hundreds of boys who have had the privilege of knowing him. We want to extend you our deepest sympathy and sincere affection in this time of trial and want you to know that you also have a place in all Koshare hearts right along side of Joe. You are both part of our large family."[3]

Joe's funeral services were held at eight o'clock in the morning at the Garcia Funeral chapel where Dr. A. F. Wassen conducted a short service that consisted of reading the Twenty-third Psalm and the Lord's Prayer. Sallie then had Joe's body taken to Fairview Park Cemetery in Albuquerque where it was cremated.[4]

Joe then came to rest with the departed souls of Indians. Sallie recorded, "On the 24th at dawn a plane flew over unannounced, but I wakened early and was out with his beloved dogs. The plane encircled the house, then flew west then again around the house and flew south, then came again and flew east, and then, just as the sun reached the tip of the sacred mountain it flew to Blue Lake, to Sacred Canyon and then over the Pueblo, and the ashes having been scattered in all three locations, it flew away. Later the Governor of the Pueblo sent me a message to say 'Now he is always with us and we are glad.'"[5]

On July 10, an article by Jack P. Riddle and Fred Mazzulla titled, "The Master Lithographer of Taos," appeared in the *Empire Magazine* of the *Denver Post*.[6] It was a fitting tribute to a man who had begun his life's work as an apprentice lithographer at age fifteen.[7]

Joseph Adam Imhof left his entire estate to his wife, Sallie, who served as his executrix. Helen Kentnor, who worked as a legal secretary for Beutler and Brandenburg, Attorneys-at-Law in Taos after having re-taught herself shorthand, acted as Notary Public.[8]

Within three days after Joe's death, Sallie asked Kay Dicus if her daughter, Anneke, would want Joe's Rutherford lithography press for the Verde Valle School that Anneke attended in Sedona, Arizona. Kay immediately set about working with Sallie. She telephoned the head of Verde Valle's art department who accepted the press, then she secured a trailer while Sallie persuaded several Indians to uproot the heavy press, and carry it downstairs for its journey to Sedona.[9]

"The only thing Sallie wanted," Kay said, "was a little plaque saying it was given in memory of Joseph A. Imhof and was a Currier and Ives press. No one ever did the plaque. Sallie also gave the school all his forty-five lithography stones and twelve lithographs. The art teacher at Verde Valle was not interested in print making, so the press was sold to the Art Barn, then sold to Northern Arizona University where it is being used by students every day. This is what Sallie wanted . . . for it to be used."[10]

After Sallie settled the Currier and Ives press into its new home, she contacted their friend, Frederick J. Dockstader, then Assistant Director of the Museum of the American Indian, Heye Foundation, New York City. At Sallie's invitation, Dockstader came to Taos to appraise Joe's vast collection of objet d'art, Indian relics, and work. He placed Joe's lithographs at Merrill's Gallery to sell for the Heye. Dockstader worked with Kay Dicus, who had become secretary for the Harwood Foundation in 1957, to place one of each lithograph with the Harwood.[11]

To Fred and Juanita Parrett, who lived in the gardner's house on the Van Vechten property next to the Imhofs, Sallie gave Joe's work table.[12] Joe had made frames on the work table he had equipped with a mitre box, grind stone, T-square and triangle. Over the next five years, Sallie sifted through and recorded the content of six studio rooms. While working at the task Joe had left her to complete, she continued to pursue other projects that interested her. Helen Kentnor recalled, "She was a hard worker for the church [Episcopal]. She helped with the building project [in 1960], though I don't know about her financial support for the project.

"We were friends. She was a boss. That's probably why we got along. She and my mother were like chickens pecking. I went along with people while my mother and she were both bosses with different ideas. She had good ideas."[13]

In executing her idea of placing the Corn Series, Sallie signed a Deed of Trust on August 10, 1960, conveying to the Helen and Winfield Morten Foundation a gift of certain paintings, photographs, archaeological and ethnological materials, books and miscellaneous items of personal property, and transparencies of the Corn Series from the collection of Joe Imhof, to be used by the Foundation as it deemed to be in its best interest. Helen Kentnor notarized the document. Sallie hoped the collection would be held together and known as "The Joseph A. Imhof Collection," adequately maintained, and displayed from time to time in suitable surroundings.[14]

It would be retired General Charles Corlett who would negotiate the arrangement between Sallie and the Mortens, and then place Imhof's collection at the Maxwell Museum of Anthropology at University of New Mexico in Albuquerque. His actions can be seen in a letter he wrote on January 20, 1965, to make sure University officials recognized the Mortens at the opening exhibition of the Corn Series. Corlett addressed the letter to Dr. Frank C. Hibben, Director, Maxwell Museum of Anthropology, University of New Mexico, Albuquerque.

"After Joe died, Winfield and Sallie persuaded me that I should find a proper home for Joe's remarkable series of paintings, the 'Story of Corn.' It was rather an unwelcome task for an old soldier, but I told them I would do the best I could.

"As I understand it, Winfield and Helen Morten financed Joe for several years while he was working on the Corn Series which, when completed was to be owned jointly by the Imhofs and the Mortens.

"In searching for the proper place for the Series, I think it could have been sold for a very considerable sum of money to one of the Corn Products Companies, but neither the Mortens or Sallie Imhof wanted this. They wanted it to stay in the South West at a place where it would be viewed by many people.

"Before I approached the University of New Mexico, I tried the Museums at Santa Fe and the Desert Museums at Ghost Ranch and Tucson in which Arthur Pack was interested. Neither of these Agencies could properly handle the Series.

"Fortunately, Tom Popejoy [President, University of New Mexico] and I were at a party in Santa Fe together. I got Tom in a corner and told him about the 'Corn Story.' He was immediately interested, and sent Doctor Hill [Chairman, Department of Anthropology, Maxwell Museum] to my house in Española and I took him to Taos and introduced him to Sallie. These two made the preliminary agreement to give the Collection to the University. Everybody appeared to be happy with the arrangement, and I think they still are."[15]

Sallie wrote General Corlett on April 19, 1961: "This is to let you know that today I signed over to the Morten Foundation the entire Indian collection of Joseph A. Imhof.

"Howard Brandenburg was preparing the papers for Morten to sign transferring it to the University of New Mexico.

"Now it would seem that all I have to do is await the coming of ethnologists, packers, etc.

"Again, dear General Corlett, I want to express my thanks for all you have done in this matter; I realize fully that it has been your interest and sacrifices of valuable time to bring all this to pass.

"While I am happy to have Joe's dream realized, happy to have it go to Albuquerque where the dream began, still I feel as if a veritable part of me goes with it. I feel also that God has kept me here to see it through."[16]

On April 21, 1961, the Helen and Winfield Morten Foundation made a Deed of Gift of Joe's collection to the University of New Mexico. In a letter to Dr. W. W. Hill, Winfield wrote: "Mrs. Imhof is very satisfied to know that the University will become the owners of this work of art and the Indian relics they have spent a life time in collection so they might be of historical and educational value for generations to come in their new home."[17]

During May, Joe's collection filled a large moving van and two station wagons, which transported the artifacts as varied as headdresses, baskets, and cradle boards to hunting tools, to the Maxwell Museum. The *Albuquerque Journal* reported on July 6, 1961: "The Joseph Imhof collection of Pueblo Indian ceremonial materials valued at $100,000 had been presented to the Museum of Anthropology at the University of New Mexico." The newspaper account "termed the collection a 'major gift,' the largest contribution made to the Museum in recent years . . . through the Winfield Morten Foundation."[18]

Sallie continued living in the adobe home she and Joe had built, though the house had begun to deteriorate through the lack of maintenance. Sallie filled part of her days taking long walks with the Imhofs' large dog, Sage, holding her aging body erect with a walking stick taller than herself.

Often she sat on the bench outside her kitchen door on the south side of the house. Above her and nailed to the wall, as if acting as guards, was a wood carving of two heads, one a Spanish Conquistador, and the other a Classic Roman profile.[19]

She did not lack for people who cared about and for her.[20] Each Easter, a group of Koshare Boy Scouts came to visit and bring her the Easter lily they had formerly given to Joe.[21] Mrs. Clarence (Lola) Johnson, who had been a long-time friend of the Imhofs and a special nurse who had cared for Phillips Kloss' mother, checked on Sallie each day, brought her meals, and chauffeured her about town. A Pueblo woman cleaned her house and managed any work the yard needed, and the people who rented the guest house helped as well. Carol Johnson Hale, Lola's daughter who was in college, soon began to keep Sallie's accounting notes in a spiral notebook. Carol remarked, "Sallie was always generous in paying me for my bookkeeping."[22]

On Tuesday, April 9, 1963, the Department of Anthropology of the University of New Mexico held the formal opening for the Maxwell Museum of Anthropology. As part of the celebration, the Museum had mounted a major exhibition of Indian artifacts. Curators devoted two cases to the Imhof collection; one case of figurines from the Taos Kiva, and another case of relics from the Cochiti Pueblo.[23]

Sallie, now ninety-one years old, lay in Taos' Holy Cross Hospital, felled partly by hemorrhages in her eyes.[24] Still, Sallie enjoyed the exhibition from a distance, pleased that her efforts and Joe's labor had borne fruit. Regardless of hospitalization, Sallie continued her work. On April 27, 1963, Sallie wrote Dr. Hill: "This is to inform you that the Imhof Story [*I is for Imhof - Indian Idolater*] is typed . . . . It covers time from his birth to June 23, 1955 [sic] when the plane took his ashes over the pueblo. I have tried to keep it simple and unpretencious [sic] as he was and I hope you will be satisfied with it . . . . I have Dr. Coke's book [*Taos & Santa Fe: The Artist's Environment 1882-1942*], which has been read to me in bits here and there. The book reviews and reviewers seem eo [to] agree that little environment seems to reach the reader. Sorry he had not been here long enough to understand the painting life of the old men."[25]

Van Deren Coke, a historian and artist, had written of Imhof, "Always fascinated with the Indians, Imhof was more of an anthropologist than artist. Rather than publish his findings, he elected to use naturalistic paintings to recount his major theme—the importance of corn in the secular and religious life of the Pueblo peoples. These pictures have considerable value as verification of ceremonies he observed and studied. As works of art, they are modest in value, due to the artist's concentration on distinct renderings of facts to serve didactic purposes. It was as a printmaker that Imhof showed his European art training and skill as a draftsman . . . these were artistically respectable and served as historic notations due to their authentic and particularized treatment."[26]

That year, Van Deren Coke became director of the University Art Museum in Albuquerque. In an inaugural exhibition, Coke included works of New Mexico's major printmakers. The exhibition included only seven prints. Among them were Imhof's work.[27] Curiously, Van Deren Coke in his observation about Imhof's work had come closer than any other in discovering what Joe had set out to accomplish. Still, Coke didn't have it quite right either. The answer lay there waiting to be discovered in the epiphany Joe had experienced in 1908 at Cochiti.

On Sunday, February 7, 1965, the University of New Mexico Maxwell Museum of Anthropology presented the first time exhibit of Joseph A. Imhof's Corn Series. Curators determined that the exhibition would run until August 4, the date Santo Domingo Pueblo Indians performed their major Corn Dance.[28]

Retired General Corlett made sure that Winfield and Helen Morten received the deserved recognition in having placed the Series. In his January 20, 1965 letter, in which he established his relationship to the University's president, General Corlett noted to Dr. Hibben, Director of the Maxwell Museum, "The purpose of this letter is to suggest that in addition to Sallie Imhof, that Winfield and Helen Morten be included as Honored Guests at the 'Reception and Exhibition of the Corn Series' on February 7th [1965] at the University. I feel sure it would make them very happy."[29]

Helen and Winfield Morten did not attend the opening that Sunday. In the weeks before the opening, Helen had asked Winfield, "Honey, don't you want to go to the opening?"

Winfield did not hesitate in his answer. "No, Hon, this is Sallie's day."[30]

General and Mrs. Corlett attended in the Mortens' place.

Sallie dressed in a navy blue ensemble accented with a gardenia corsage when she attended the afternoon reception in the building a scant few blocks from the Imhofs' Albuquerque home in 1910. Sallie arrived with Kay and Richard Dicus, Lola and Clarence Johnson, Susan Johnson and Carol and Bruce Hale. Sallie gave her greetings to Dr. Tom Popejoy, the University president, Dr. Frank Hibben, and J. J. Brody, the exhibition's curator.[31]

Brody installed the show in the center of the Museum's main hall, and used thirty paintings from the Series, interspersing the paintings with ethnological material, such as a digging stick, Joe had collected throughout his career. Although lack of funds had prevented the University from producing a catalogue for the exhibition, Brody's arrangement led the viewer through Imhof's story of the Indians' relationship with corn.[32]

While Sallie did have her day, as Winfield knew, she could not rest for now. Two days later, Lola Johnson wrote this letter for her to Dr. Hibben: "Thank you and Mr. Brody and the whole crew at the Museum of Anthropology for the wonderful job you did on the *Corn Series*. Words cannot express my feelings. Now that the Corn Series is well in hand, my thoughts turn to stone lithography. I am so happy that the University has started again a class on Stone Lithog. There is so much I would like to discuss with you if only you had time to come to Taos and bring with you the new teacher Garo Antreasian, printer & painter. My ideas are not fully formed but briefly I would like you and Garo Antreasian to select a few of Joe Imhof's best lithographs from my collection to keep in the Stone Lithography Dept. for students' reference.

"Do you know that on several very hot August mornings in the press room Joe did a film titled how to make a Stone Lithograph. This was filmed by Fred Mazzulla the prominent photographer & lawyer of Denver, Colo. It is in his possession. I have 5 stills in my possession which I can show you of the Currier and Ives press, work shop & Joe at work. You asked about Joe's work from 19[??] to 1929. If you have time to listen I could sketch a fascinating tale. When you come please come in the near future because time sort of presses on one. We're around home in Taos at 10 o'clock. Mrs. Imhof stood the trip & all like a trooper. We had a wonderful day it will be remembered for years to come. And we want to say Thanks for a job well done. Do come & see us—soon—it's later than we think. Kind of stormy out today. Just sitting & looking out our beautyful [sic] ol [sic] Taos Mountains."

The letter was signed, Sallie Imhof & Mrs. Johnson.[33]

Garo Antreasian had joined the University of New Mexico Lithography Workshop faculty in 1963 to prepare fellows for the Tamarind Lithography Workshop, Inc. in Los Angeles. Tamarind would then complete the students' training designed to create master lithographic printers. Antreasian had taught since 1948, first at John Herron School of Art in Indianapolis, then at Tamarind before coming to New Mexico. In addition to his work preparing fellows, Antreasian conducted regular courses for art students during the academic year, and, in the summer, conducted an artist-teacher fellowship program.[34]

In 1965, Sallie did give the University of New Mexico College of Fine Arts eleven of Joe's lithographs, and Antreasian incorporated the Imhof works into his instruction program. Antreasian stressed the importance of Imhof's lithographs. They served as example of how lithography creates a "more direct and spontaneous" medium than other graphic arts. "It requires no chiseling, carving or engraving. As the artist just draws on the stone, he finds greater freedom in the use of one or more colors, ease in the use of materials and wide opportunity for imaginative creativity."[35]

The next year, in February 1966, the University of New Mexico Art Galley in Albuquerque opened an exhibition that featured Mrs. Joseph A. Imhof's collection, which included Joe's Oriental prints. The show also included drawings by Andrew Dasburg, and the collection of William H. and Rebecca Salsbury James.[36]

The same year, Buck Burshears purchased ten Imhof oil and watercolor paintings for the Koshare Indian Museum.[37] On Sunday, May 29, 1966, the Koshare Museum opened an exhibition of thirty Imhof paintings. By then, except for the Maxwell Museum, the Koshare had the largest collection of Imhof paintings in the country. The exhibition drew people from seven states.[38]

Lola Johnson attended for Sallie who lay in the Taos Hospital. The *La Junta Tribune* reported on June 1, 1966, "The widow of Joseph Imhof, whose friendship for the Koshares made possible the acquisition of the paintings, was not present. She is in the hospital quietly predicting her own death during the month of June. Present, however, for the exhibition was Mrs. Imhof's companion and nurse during recent years, Mrs. Clarence (Lola) Johnson . . . . Mrs. Johnson says that Mrs. Imhof said that her husband had died in June, that a child had died in June. That was why she said that she, too, would die in June."

The loyalty the Imhofs engendered in others can be seen in the newspaper's quote from Lola Johnson. " . . . That Imhof is the finest of the documentary painters of Indians is an unquestioned fact to Mrs. Johnson. Moreover, she thinks he is likely the last of the great ones. First, because the new Taos art colony is lacking in the firm discipline that the old-timers had. 'They think if they go bare-footed and let their beards grow, it makes them an artist,' she said. 'It is too hard for them to paint portraits which show character.

"'Too, there are no longer models from which to paint. The old Indians are gone. The new generation just doesn't have it. They are pressing to put electricity into the pueblo. So even if the new artists wanted to paint real Indians they wouldn't have any to paint.'"[39]

Lola Johnson returned to complete her work with Sallie. Among the duties she performed was writing a letter to Mabel V. Pease, Commander, The National Yeomen F, First Enlisted Women, United States Navy, requesting permission for Sallie to be buried in her Naval uniform of dress blues.[40] And, finally, in one of her last gestures, Sallie directed Lola, to "give Ora a picture." Mrs. Ora Belle Chase, a nurse who cared for Sallie in the hospital, received "Superstition Mt."[41]

Sallie died, just as she had predicted, on June 26, 1966, in the Taos Holy Cross Hospital, the hospital founded by her neighbor, Mabel Dodge Luhan. Two days later friends held a simple funeral service for her near the Taos Pueblo. Her Navy hat lay atop her casket. After services, she was cremated at Fairview Crematorium in Albuquerque.[42]

The Note Book, published by the National Yeomen F, reported, "Sarah Russell Imhoff [sic] . . . was 94 when she died in Taos, New Mexico. She walked in all the local parades there until a few years ago in full uniform. She was so proud of her service and her uniform and left detailed Last Wishes, which were, that she be laid out in her white uniform and her blue uniform, hats and badges all be cremated with her and the ashes scattered over the Taos Sacred Mountain and over the Imhoff [sic] home place which bordered on Pueblo land. Her two big loves of her life were her Navy Service and the Indians of Taos community."[43]

In her will, with Helen Kentnor named Executrix, Sallie completed her partnership with Joe. She left an estate valued at $112,588.69. She returned to their proper place all the objects she and Joe had collected over a lifetime. She paid her debts and gave gifts of cash, paintings, and personal objects to the Imhof friends, Museum of the American Indian, Heye Foundation, Harwood Foundation, College of Fine Arts of the University of New Mexico, and the Museum of New Mexico, Santa Fe.[44] She returned all that had been given. She had managed well.

EPILOGUE
PEOPLE AND EVENTS SURROUNDING
THE IMHOFS AFTER THEIR DEATHS

John Young-Hunter died August 9, 1955, shortly after finishing his memoirs, *Reviewing the Years*.

Joseph Keppler, Jr. died on July 4, 1956. He left his collection of Indian artifacts to the Southwest Museum in Los Angeles and the Museum of the American Indian in New York, Heye Foundation. Keppler's wife left the *Puck* material to the New York Historical Society Museum in New York.

E. Martin Hennings died in 1956.

Pauline Hopkins, my mother, in 1955 enrolled at Southern Methodist University in Dallas, Texas for courses in interior design after my father, Hal Hopkins, died in 1954. From 1955 until 1957, she managed the Grand Imperial Hotel Gift Shop, Silverton, Colorado. She then married Archie Castleberry and, within a few years, purchased property in Southern Colorado in an effort to create for her children and grandchildren the experience and understanding of the West that she and her family had received from Helen and Winfield Morten at Abiquiu.

Mary Greene Blumenschein died in 1958, to be followed by her husband two years later.

Winfield and Helen Morten lost their Rancho de Abiquiu in May 1957 when New York Life Insurance foreclosed on Rancho de Abiquiu. Winfield could not pay the interest on the loan. Morten had, as my father predicted, lost the majority of his wealth bailing out his dreams. On April 14, 1960, Georgia O'Keeffe wrote Helen and Winfield, "I miss you very much and think of you often. Your light gone from the house across the valley makes me very sad. Every night I look for it. I have had visitors off and on but it isn't like knowing you are across the river. I will keep looking for your light." The Grand Imperial Hotel in Silverton was sold the same year on a

345

mortgage foreclosure. Alva A. Simpson, a New Mexico rancher, acquired the ranch property at Abiquiu in 1969. He sold seven thousand acres to a group that built the Dar al-Islam (Place of Peace or Surrender) mosque and school on a bluff near Abiquiu overlooking the Chama River. In the early 1990s, the Rancho de Abiquiu hacienda and acreage was purchased privately. In mid-1990, the brick home adjoining the Rancho de Abiquiu property was listed in the National Register of Historic Places.

In 1963, Sallie entrusted Fred Mazzulla with the lithograph, "Nieuw Amsterdam 1653," to be given to her hometown's Philadelphia Art Museum. In her letter to Mazzulla, she remarked that her ancestors, the Russells, had come over in 1683 with William Penn. The current museum has no record of the lithograph.

Mabel Dodge Luhan died in 1962.

Martha Welpton, M.D., died on August 13, 1967 in San Diego, California.

In 1967, the artist Jackson Hensley, a native of Portales, New Mexico who had been living in Connecticut, purchased the Imhof adobe home in Taos. The Hensleys lived there for twenty years before selling the house to Linda and Robert Attiyeh of Los Angeles.

Winfield Morten died of cancer at age sixty-four in 1968 while living in Dallas, Texas. On August 10, Georgia O'Keeffe wrote to Helen Morten, "Last evening in the midst of hard rain and thunder and lightning, Emilia phoned in and told me about Winfield. It is sad I had for days been thinking about the two of you and intending to write but just did not get to it I regret to say. I would have liked to speak to him. As I sit here, early this morning with every thing outside very wet so the sun even has a hard time trying to come up, and I think of Winfield. It is as if he will always be with us even if he had gone through the door into the great unknown. My deepest sympathies to you." Helen Morten died in 1984. Although the Mortens lived in reduced circumstances, they had lived their dreams and, like the Imhofs, had left something of value for others. Pope Pius XII had awarded Winfield a citation in 1956 for his work in revitalizing the Catholic Church in Abiquiu; and the Grand Imperial Hotel, after having had several ownerships before the current owners, is the focal point for the daily train excursions for tourists riding the narrow gauge from Durango to Silverton.

Under Garo Antreasian's leadership, the University of New Mexico

Lithography Workshop became so successful that, in 1970, the Tamarind Institute in Los Angeles moved to Albuquerque and merged with the University of New Mexico College of Fine Arts with Antreasian as director.

Mrs. Elizabeth Murphy, Joseph Imhof's sister, died in 1960 at the age of eighty-seven.

Cristino Mirabel, one of Imhof's favorite models, died on June 21, 1961.

Retired Major General Charles H. Corlett died on October 14, 1971.

Theodore T. Murphy, Joseph Imhof's nephew, retired from the Brooklyn Union Gas Company, moved to Florida, and died in 1983 at seventy-eight years old.

Georgia O'Keeffe died on March 6, 1986 while living with Juan Hamilton and his family in Santa Fe.

Joe "Sunhawk" Sandoval died December 19, 1987 at age eighty-five.

Helen Blumenschein died in 1989.

Helen Kentnor died in May 1995, just four days short of one hundred years.

Henry Sauerwein remained a devoted friend to Sallie after Joe's death, even as his responsibilities increased with his appointment as director of the Wurlitzer Foundation in Taos that administers grants and housing to artists in the community.

Gene and Phillips Kloss continued to live in Taos until their deaths, respectively 1996 and 1995.

The Erkinses all became collectors of Imhof works of art. Mrs. Erkins died in Arizona. Charlene Erkins Dady moved to Oregon, while Robert settled in Idaho.

The Harwood Foundation remained an invaluable library, museum, and gathering place for people throughout New Mexico, artists, and writers. Sallie's nine thousand dollar gift enabled the Harwood to build an addition to the library in 1972. The addition became known as the Imhof Reading Room.

On October 30, 1994, the George Gustav Heye Center of the Smithsonian Institution, National Museum of the American Indian opened at the newly renovated Alexander Hamilton United States Custom House. The New York museum, the first of three being created around the Heye artifacts by the Smithsonian Institution, controls the collection. "This is about cultural reclamation," said W. Richard West, Jr., an Oklahoma Cheyenne and director of the museum . . . . "it is a return of ownership to Indian people."

The new museum represents the acknowledged value of this land's native people. Joseph Imhof spent his life recording the story of the Pueblo people so that all people might learn the history of all mankind.

DOCUMENTATION ABBREVIATIONS
IN NOTES

ACM*   Amon G. Carter Museum, Ft. Worth, TX, Fred
                  Mazzulla Collection, Imhof File.
ACM-JAI***   Amon G. Carter Museum, Ft. Worth, TX, Fred
                  Mazzulla Collection, Imhof File, Oral History Tape,
                  Sallie and Joseph Imhof with Jo and Fred Mazzulla,
                  John Riddle, Jack Miles in the Imhof home, Taos, NM,
                  Aug. 28, 1954, 1:30 p.m.
ACM-SRI***   Amon G. Carter Museum, Ft. Worth, TX, Fred
                  Mazzulla Collection, Imhof File, Oral History Tape
                  with Sallie Imhof and Jack Riddle, 1955.
BR*   Brooklyn City Records, Census and City Directory.
CIIVG**   Craig, McClain, *Currier and Ives, An Illustrated Value
                  Guide* (Radnor, PA:Wallace-Homestead Book Co, 1987).
DP-EM**   Fred Mazzulla, Jack P. Riddle, "The Master Lithographer
                  of Taos," *Denver Post Empire Magazine*, July 10 (1955):8,9.
IIFI***   Sarah Russell Imhof, *I Is For Imhof - Indian Idolator* (sic),
                  unpublished manuscript, 1963. There are copies at ACM,
                  NMAI-SI(1), and KCMF.
KCMF*   Kit Carson Memorial Foundation, Inc., La Morada de
                  Don Fernando de Taos, Taos, NM, Imhof files.
MNM-HL*   Museum of New Mexico, Santa Fe, NM, History Library.
NA**   David Hurst Thomas, Jay Miller, Richard White, Peter
                  Nabokov, Phillip J. Deloria, *The Native American, An
                  Illustrated History* (Atlanta, GA: Turner Publishing Co.,
                  1993).

NHR***   Nancy Hopkins Reily, author, interviews and correspon-
           dence.
NJR*   New Jersey Deed Records, Morris County, Township of
           Montville.
NMAI-SI(1)* National Museum of the American Indian - Smithsonian
           Institute, Heye Foundation, NY, NY, Box V-L, Folder 2.
NMAI-SI(2)* National Museum of the American Indian - Smithsonian
           Institute, Heye Foundation, NY, NY, Box OC 204B,
           Folder 1.
NMAI-SI(3)* National Museum of the American Indian Smithsonian
           Institute, Heye Foundation, NY, NY, Box FD 25, Folder 7.
NMR-B*   New Mexico Records, Bernalillo County.
NMR-T*   New Mexico Records, Taos County.
NYCR*   New York City Records, Census and City Directory.
PNM**   Clinton Adams, *Printmaking in New Mexico, 1880-
           1990* (Albuquerque, NM:University of New Mexico
           Press, 1991).
SADC***   Susan Anneke Dicus Chittim, Santa Fe, NM,
           interviews and correspondence.
SAM**   Peggy and Harold Samuels, *Samuels' Encyclopedia of
           Artists of the American West* (Secaucus, NJ: Castle, a
           Division of Book Sales, 1985).
TAIA**   Mabel Dodge Luhan, *Taos and Its Artists* (NY:Duell,
           Sloan and Pearce, 1947).
TPH**   John Sherman, *Taos, A Pictorial History* (Santa Fe, NM:
           William Gannon, 1990).
TSA**   Robert R. White, *The Taos Society of Artists*
           (Albuquerque, NM:University of New Mexico Press,
           1983).
TSF**   Van Deren Coke, *Taos and Santa Fe, The Artist's
           Environment, 1882-1942* (Albuquerque, NM:University
           of New Mexico Press, 1963).
UNM-GA**   Winifred S. Ritter, "Golden Alumna," *University of New
           Mexico Alumnus* 37(Oct. 1965):14.
UNM-HF*   University of New Mexico, Albuquerque, NM,
           Harwood Foundation, Taos, NM, Imhof File.

UNM-HF-KD*** University of New Mexico, Albuquerque, Harwood
      Foundation, Taos, NM, Kay Dicus Oral History Tape
      on Joseph Imhof, Interviewed by David Witt and Kit
      Egri, Taos, August 6, 1981.

UNM-MMA* University of New Mexico, Albuquerque, NM,
      Maxwell Museum of Anthropology, Imhof File.

WIT**   Mabel Dodge Luhan, *Winter in Taos* (Denver,
      CO:Sage Books, Inc., 1935).

 * Archives, Collections and Records
 ** Published Sources
*** Unpublished Sources

NOTES

CHAPTER 2: BEGINNING IN BROOKLYN

1. IIFI, p.1.

2. Ibid.

3. CIIVG, p.3.

4. BR, Kings Co. Deeds 1865-1880 did not list John Imhof at 492 Atlantic Ave. as grantor or grantee.

5. BR, Kings Co. Liber 641, pp. 112-115, John Imhof purchased 408 Atlantic Ave. (between Bond and Nevins Streets) on Aug. 29, 1864 for $4,000.00. BR, Kings Co. Liber 987, pp. 44-47, John Imhof sold 408 Atlantic Ave. on Mar. 20, 1871.

6. BR, 1855 Census showed that John was born in Germany, was an alien, and had been in the United States two years.

NMAI-SI(1), There is a page out of a magazine with a photograph captioned, "Big Gun Drill at the Old Imhoff Battery (now demolished), the Castle, Cape Town, circa 1860." Sallie did not explain the photograph but it obviously had some significance to Joe Imhof's family.

NMAI-SI(3), Sallie filled out the biographical form and wrote, regarding Joe's mother, "Magdalena Reidel, not sure of spelling, she died before I met Joe." As a postscript on the form, Sallie stated, "On second thought I believe his mother's maiden name was Rippell."

7. BR, 1860 Census.

8. BR, 1880 Census.

9. David McCullough, *The Great Bridge* (NY:Simon and Schuster, 1972) pp. 103-8.

10. *Encyclopedia Britannica*, 1969, s.v. "Long Island."

11. David Ment, *The Shaping of a City, A Brief History of Brooklyn*, Prepared by Brooklyn Rediscovery (Brooklyn Educational and Cultural Alliance) in cooperation with the Board of Education (NY:City of New York, 1979) pp. 6-8.

12. Ibid., p. 6.

13. David M. Ellis, James A. Frost, Harold C. Syrett, Harry Carman, A *History of New York State* (Ithaca, NY:Cornell University Press, 1957) pp. 9-10.

14. William N. Fenton, *Parker on the Iroquois* (Syracuse, NY:Syracuse University Press, 1968) pp. 13-14.

15. Ment, *Shaping of a City*, p. 6.

16. Ibid., pp. 12-14.

17. Ralph Foster Weld, *Brooklyn in America* (NY:Columbia Press, 1950) p. 18.

18. Ibid., pp. 86-87.

19. Ibid., p. 88.

20. Ibid., pp. 98-99.

21. Ibid., pp. 88-91.

22. Ibid., pp. 92-93. McCullough, *Great Bridge*, pp. 39-62.

23. In *Germans to America, 1852-1855*, John Imhof (age 24) with Joseph (15) and Ottilie (male 17) sailed on the SS *Goethe*, Bremen to Baltimore, arriving Oct. 24, 1853. This was Joseph Imhof's father if I assume John's birth date was correct as stated in the Brooklyn 1875 and 1892 Censuses.

Magdalena Elizabeth Imhof, Joe's mother, was not listed on the SS *Goethe* passenger list. No marriage certificate was found for John and Magdalena Imhof in New York or Brooklyn. I assume because Magdalena lists her birth place as Wertenbergh, Germany on the Census records that she came from Germany about the same time as John.

Although I did not research any documents on the spelling of Imhof, I believe that the original spelling, Imhoff, was shortened to Imhof. Both Imhoff and Imhof were found on early census and directory records. Joseph A. Imhof always used the Imhof spelling.

24. KCMF, "List of Antiques in Imhof House, Feb. 1963."

25. BR, City Directory, 1856, John Imhof is listed: boots and shoes, 429 Atlantic, home same. BR, Kings Co., There was no listing for John Imhof at 429 Atlantic Ave. as grantor or grantee.

26. McCullough, *Great Bridge*, pp. 24, 103-107.

27. Ibid., pp. 29, 43, 46-50, 68, 153.

28. Ibid., p. 112.

29. Ibid., pp. 21, 28-31, 83. *Encyclopedia Britannica*, 1969, s.v. "Railway." Keith L. Bryant, Jr., *History of the Atchison; Topeka, and Santa Fe Railway* (Lincoln, NE:University of Nebraska Press, 1974) p. 1.

30. McCullough, *Great Bridge*, pp. 25-26, 187, 564.

31. IIFI, p. 1.

32. BR, 1880 Census. BR, Liber 1139, pp. 382-5 lists John Imhof buying 493 Atlantic Ave. (between Nevins and Third Streets) for $8,300.00 on Jan. 3, 1874.

33. BR, 1875 Census lists John Imhof as a naturalized citizen.

34. McCullough, *Great Bridge*, p. 565.

35. IIFI, p.1.

36. Ibid.

37. ACM-SRI.

38. *Encyclopedia Britannica*, 1969, s.v. "Art Education, United States."

39. L. A. Cremin, *The Transformation of the School* (NY: Alfred A. Knopf, 1968) p. 20.

40. William W. Brickman, *Educational Systems in the United States* (NY: The Center for Applied Research in Education, Inc., 1964) pp.20-21.

41. IIFI, p.1.

42. Ibid.

43. McCullough, *Great Bridge*, pp. 538-541.

44. Ibid., pp. 530-533.

45. Ibid.

46. BR, 1880 Census.

47. IIFI, p. 1.

48. UNM-HF-KD.

CHAPTER 3: ON HIS OWN

1. IIFI, p.1.

2. In the UNM-MMA Imhof File is a letter dated Mar. 1, 1966, from an Imhof relative, Theodore T. Murphy, 389 Locust Ave., Uniondale, NY. This offered my only clue to any of Joe's relatives. In 1980 I began researching Uniondale records for Mr. Murphy. Murphy was listed in the Nassau County Directory, 1967-70, but was not listed in the Directories from 1970 to 1972. Finally, I located, through the county tax records, Murphy's neighbors on Locust Ave. One, Mrs. Pat Hettrick, told me that she knew Murphy and his sister, Frankie. Hettrick said that Theodore and Frankie moved to Beverly Hills, Florida around 1978. Frankie died shortly after they arrived in Florida. A *St. Petersburg Times* Obituary, Mar. 21, p. 7B, revealed Murphy's death in 1983. Wills were located for Theodore T. Murphy, St. Petersburg, FL, Pinellos Co., Estate Copy, 83-2913-ES and Frances (Frankie) C. Murphy, Citrus Co., FL. The wills listed several people, including Veronica and Wilford Herron of Sarasota, Florida. I attempted to contact all the names but located only the Herrons. When I talked with Veronica Herron on the telephone on Jan. 19, 1994 and identified myself, and explained my interest, she replied, "Yes, I knew Mr. Murphy and knew of Mr. Imhof. I am sitting here looking at two Imhofs." Mrs. Herron described the paintings, the earliest Imhof works I have found. Mrs. Herron helped with the two Murphy wills and indicated that the Theodore T. Murphy will mentioned two family priests.

3. IIFI, p. 1.

4. Ibid, pp. 1-2.

5. DP-EM. ACM-JAI.

6. CIIVG, p. 14.

7. IIFI, pp. 1-2. DP-EM. CIIVG, p. 13.

8. Harry T. Peters, *Currier and Ives, Printmakers to the American People* (NY:Doubleday, Doran and Co., 1942) p. 4. Colin Simkin, Ed., *Currier and Ives America* (NY:Crown Publishers, 1952) p. 1.

9. Peters, *Currier and Ives, Printmakers*, p. 12.

10. Ibid.

11. CIIVG, p. 120.

12. Simkin, *Currier and Ives' America*, p. 1. Peters, *Currier and Ives, Printmakers*, p. 7.

13. Peters, *Currier and Ives, Printmakers*, p. 7.

14. CIIVG, pp. 10, 11. Peters, *Currier and Ives, Printmakers*, p. 5.

15. *Collier's Encyclopedia*, 1989, s.v. "Currier and Ives."

16. Peters, *Currier and Ives, Printmakers*, p. 2.

17. Simkin, *Currier and Ives' America*, p. 4.

18. *Collier's Encyclopedia*, 1989, s.v. "Currier and Ives."

19. Peters, *Currier and Ives, Printmakers*, p. 11.

20. Simkin, *Currier and Ives' America*, p. 7.

21. DP-EM.

22. DP-EM, Imhof states that he usually pulled twelve prints from a lithography stone. I assume that because Currier and Ives pulled twelve prints per stone that this is where Imhof began his practice. Peters, *Currier and Ives, Printmakers*, p. 14.

23. ACM-JAI.

24. DP-EM.

25. ACM-JAI. DP-EM.

26. "Artest," *E. S. Lawrence Gallery Newsletter*, Taos, NM, Winter, 1986-87, p. 3, states that Imhof brought the first lithography press to Taos. TSF, pp. 84-85; UNM-HF-KD, Joe's lithography press was used by Currier and Ives. The markings on the Rutherford Press are on the yoke of the press by a top screw: Rutherford Press, Rutherford Machinery Co., (division-General Printing Ink Corp. New York) serial number HPZ, model number 9924. When Northern Arizona University bought the press there were 45 stones with it, but no prints.

27. PNM, p. 44. Garo Antreasian, *The Tamarind Book of Lithography*, (Los Angeles, CA:Tamarind Lithography Workshop, Los Angeles, 1971) pp. 13-15.

28. This is the painting owned by Veronica and Wilford Herron, Sarasota, Florida as described to me on the telephone Jan. 19, 1994.

29. Ibid.

30. Mary Ann DiNapoli, my research assistant in Brooklyn, telephoned the Brooklyn Union Gas Co. The Urban Affairs Department stated that the Brooklyn Gas Light Co. merged with others in 1895 to form Brooklyn Union Gas Co.

31. ACM-JAI, When asked, "What does the A stand for?" Imhof replied, "They argue about it, so we just leave it A. Officially that's correct."

32. ACM-JAI.

33. IIFI, p. 2.

34. Ibid.

35. Ibid.

36. Ibid.

37. Howard Hibbard, *The Metropolitan Museum of Art* (NY:Harrison House, 1980) pp. 7-27.

38. Mary Beal, Edwin Bowes, Waldemar Januszcak, *Techniques of the Great Masters* (Secaucus, NJ:Chartwell Book, 1985) p. 60.

39. Horst de la Croix, Richard G. Tansey, eds., *Gardner's Art Through the Ages* (NY:Harcourt Brace Jovanovich, Inc., 1980) pp. 774-775.

40. Dore Ashton, Denise Hare, *Rosa Bonheur, A Life and A Legend* (NY:Viking Press, 1981) pp. 144-157.

41. Hibbard, *Metropolitan*, pp. 318, 332.

42. NMAI-SI(3), Last Will and Testament of Sarah Russell Imhof, Dec. 22, 1964, Section II, Section j. KCMF, "List of Antiques in Imhof House, Feb. 1963," p. 3, "Said by the curator [of the Rijkmuseum] to be the most successful copy of the Baron he had ever seen."

43. Hibbard, *Metropolitan*, p. 345. Beal, *Techniques*, p. 64.

44. Beal, *Techniques*, p. 22.

45. Ibid., p. 56.

46. Ibid., p. 86.

CHAPTER 4: BUFFALO BILL AND THE SIOUX

1. *Encyclopedia Britannica*, 1969, s.v. "Art, Societies of." *Academic American Encyclopedia*, 1994, s.v. "Academies of Art."

2. *Encyclopedia Britannica*, 1969, s.v. "Art, Societies of."

3. Ibid.

4. *Academic American Encyclopedia*, 1994, s.v. "Guilds."

5. *Encyclopedia Britannica*, 1969, s.v. "Art, Societies of." *Academic American Encyclopedia*, 1994, s.v. "Academies of Art."

6. *Academic American Encyclopedia*, 1994, s.v. "Academies of Art." *The New Encyclopedia Britannica*, 1991, s.v. "Arts, Practice and Profession of the."

7. *Encyclopedia Britannica*, 1969, s.v. "Fine Arts."

8. *Academic American Encyclopedia*, 1994, s.v. "Academies of Art."

9. Charles C. Eldredge, Julie Schimmel, William H. Truettner, *Art in New Mexico, 1900-1945, Paths to Taos and Santa Fe* (NY:Abbeville Press Publishers, 1986) pp. 44-47.

10. *The New Encyclopedia Britannica*, 1991, s.v. "Arts, Practice and Profession of."

11. Croix, Tansey, *Gardner's Art*, pp. 775-776.

12. *Encyclopedia Britannica*, 1991, s.v. "Art, Societies of."

13. Croix, Tansey, *Gardner's Art*, pp. 655-656.

14. Ibid., pp. 660-662.

15. ACM, "Red Star Line Cabin Passenger List," SS *Noordland* from New York to Antwerp, Apr. 1, 1891. IIFI, p. 2, Sallie states in her biography: " . . . sailed on the Red Star Line Steamer Noordland, April, 1890." ACM, the actual cabin passenger list is dated April 1, 1891, from New York to Antwerp. It has a handwritten notation on it, "April, 1891, first trip, Cody aboard, returned NY, Oct., 93."

16. Annette Stott, *American Painters Who Worked in the Netherlands, 1880-1914*, Ph.D. diss. Vol. 1 of 2 (1986), Boston University Mugar Memorial Library, Boston, MA, p. 55.

17. *Encyclopedia Britannica*, 1969, s.v. "Antwerp, History."

18. *Baedeker's Netherlands, Belgium and Luxembourg from A to Z*, (Englewood Cliffs, NJ:Prentice Hall, Inc.) pp. 82-91.

19. IIFI, p. 2.

20. ACM.

21. BR, Liber 2035, pp. 459-460, on April 1, 1891 John Imhof bought 227 Wyckoff St. for $3,800.00.

22. ACM, "Red Star Line Cabin Passenger List," SS *Noordland*. "Passengers on the Ocean," *New York Times*, Apr. 1 (1891)8.

23. Amon Carter Museum catalogue, *The Wild West or, A History of the Wild West Shows, Being an Account of the Prestigious, Peregrinatory Pageants, Pretentiously Presented Before the Citizens of the Republic, Crowned Heads of Europe and Multitudes of Awe-Struck Men, Women and Children Around the Globe, Which Created a Wonderfully Imaginative and Unrealistic Image of the American West* (1970) p. 44.

24. Joseph J. Arpad and Kenneth R. Lincoln, *Buffalo Bill's Wild West* (Palmer Lake, CO:Filter Press, 1971) p. 1. *Encyclopedia Britannica*, 1969, s.v. "Cody, William Frederick."

25. Paul Fees, Curator, Buffalo Bill Museum, Cody Wyoming, letter to NHR, Apr. 21, 1987.

26. Arpad and Lincoln, *Buffalo Bill's West*, p. 14.

27. Ibid., p. 10. Nellie Snyder Yost, *Buffalo Bill, His Family, Friends, Fame, Failures and Fortunes* (Chicago:Sage Books, The Swallow Press, Inc., 1979) pp. 189, 198.

28. John Burke, *Buffalo Bill, The Noblest Whiteskin* (NY:G. P. Putnam's Sons, 1973) p. 216. Richard J. Walsh, *The Making of Buffalo Bill, A Study in Heroics* (Indianapolis, IN:The Bobbs-Merrill Co., 1928) p. 294.

29. Yost, *Buffalo Bill, Family*, p. 221.

30. Burke, *Buffalo Bill, The Noblest*, p. 190.

31. Eleanor Tufts, *Our Hidden Heritage, Five Centuries of Women Artists* (NY:Viking Press, 1981) p. 150.

32. Burke, *Buffalo Bill, The Noblest*, p. 190.

33. Ashton and Hare, *Rosa Bonheur*, p. 155.

34. Yost, *Buffalo Bill, Family*, p. 224.

35. "Col. Cody Gets His Indians," *New York Times* Mar. 7(1891)4.

36. ACM-JAI. Paul Fees, letter to NHR, Feb. 9, 1987.

37. ACM, *The Wild West, History*, p. iii.

38. Isabelle S. Sayers, *Annie Oakley and Buffalo Bill's Wild West* (NY:Dover Publications, Inc., 1981) p. 16. From the Buffalo Bill Museum, an 1885 Wild West show program, "Mr. Nate Salsbury, Director," a biographical sketch, sent to NHR Apr. 21, 1987.

39. Yost, *Buffalo Bill, Family*, p. 230.

40. ACM-SRI. IIFI, p. 3.

41. ACM, "Red Star Line Cabin Passenger List," SS *Noordland*.

42. Paul Fees letter to NHR, June 2, 1994.

43. ACM-JAI.

44. ACM-JAI. IIFI, p. 3.

45. Yost, *Buffalo Bill, Family*, pp. 230, 231.

46. Arpad and Lincoln, *Buffalo Bill's West*, p. 10. Burke, *Buffalo Bill, The Noblest*, p. 214.

47. Arpad and Lincoln, *Buffalo Bill's West*, pp. 9, 10.

48. Col. W. F. Cody, *An Autobiography of Buffalo Bill (Col. W. F. Cody)* (NY:Winchester Press, 1969) pp. 320, 321.

49. TAIA, p. 21.

50. IIFI, p. 3.

51. "John Young-Hunter Dies at 80," *The New Mexican* Aug. 9(1955).

52. IIFI, p. 3.

53. John Young-Hunter, *Reviewing the Years*, (NY:Crown Publishers, 1963) pp. 72-74.

54. SAM, p. 64.

55. Arpad and Lincoln, *Buffalo Bill's West*, p. 18.

56. *Academic American Encyclopedia*, 1994, s.v. "Wister, Owen."

57. Arpad and Lincoln, *Buffalo Bill's West*, p. 18.

58. Ibid., pp. 18, 19.

59. IIFI, p. 3.

60. MNM Library, Santa Fe, Imhof file, Sarah Russell Imhof, "Joseph A. Imhof," unpublished biographical sketch.

61. Robert P. Welsh, *Piet Mondrian's Early Career, The "Naturalistic" Periods* (NY:Garland Publishing Inc., 1977) p. 14.

62. Michel Seuphor, *Piet Mondrian, Life and Work*, (NY:Harry N. Abrams, Inc., 1956) p. 399. I did not locate any definitive information on the St. Lucas Guild. I located facts in bits and pieces to assemble some idea of the Guild. I established that Piet Mondrian was a member of the Guild, then used this information as a guide; Mondrian's art does not resemble Imhof's art.

63. Hans L. C. Jaffe, *Piet Mondrian* (NY:Harry N. Abrams, Inc., 1970) Jacket cover text.

64. IIFI, p. 3.

65. Ibid., pp. 3-4.

66. Ibid., p. 4.

67. Evelyn Graham, *Albert, King of Belgians* (NY:Dodd, Mead and Co., 1929) pp. 45-49. *Encyclopedia Britannica*, 1969, s.v. "Albert I."

68. IIFI, p. 4.

69. *The Encyclopedia of World Art*, 1966, s.v. "Human Figure."

70. IIFI, p. 4.

71. UNM-MMA, Sallie Imhof letter to Dr. W. W. Hill, Oct. 29, 1961, University of New Mexico, Dept. of Anthropology, Albuquerque, NM.

72. *Encyclopedia Britannica*, 1969, s.v. "Daguerre, Louis Jacques Mande," and "Camera Lucida and Camera Obscura."

73. Naomi Rosenblum, *A World History of Photography* (NY:Abbeville Press, 1984) pp. 239-242.

74. Ibid., pp. 240-241.

75. Michel Auer, *Encyclopedia International of Photographers, 1839 to Present*, Camera Obscura, CH-1248 Hermance, Switzerland.

76. Beaumont Newhall, *The History of Photography from 1839 to Present* (Boston, MA:Little Brown and Co., 1982) pp. 69-70.

77. For years, I kept in a closet a large wooden box filled with prints. I knew the prints had come from my aunt and uncle, Helen and Winfield Morten, and that the prints had belonged to Imhof. Miraculously, I kept them, and, as I wrote the Imhof biography, I realized the box contained the Anderson of Rome and "Gallery of Masterpieces" prints.

78. IIFI, p. 4.

79. SAM, p. 436.

CHAPTER 5: A NEW FAMILY

1. I did not locate a death certificate for Joe's mother. For the following reasons I concluded that Joe's mother had died by the time he returned to the United States in Oct. 1893: NMAI-SI(3), In a biographical form that Sallie Imhof filled out in the 1960s for the NMAI-SI(3), Sallie states that Joe's mother died before she met Joe. In IIFI, p. 4, Sallie states that shortly after Joe returned from Europe in Oct. 1893, she met Joe; Joe's father, John, lived from 1874-1891 at 493 Atlantic Ave., Brooklyn. On the same day (Apr. 1, 1891) that Joe sailed for Europe, John bought a house at 227 Wyckoff. On July 18, 1906, when John sold the house, he is listed as a widower; IIFI, p. 2, Sallie states that while Joe was in Europe he arranged for his mother to send him a monthly check; BR, 1892 Census, John and Magdalena Imhof are listed. The census was taken on Feb. 16, 1892. Thus I concluded that Joe's mother died between Feb. 16, 1892 and mid-Oct. 1893.

2. IIFI, pp. 2, 3, 5.

3. IIFI, p. 4. BR, Liber 2035, pp. 459-460, states that John Imhof bought 227 Wyckoff on Apr. 1, 1891.

4. IIFI, p. 4.

5. IIFI, p. 5. Dorothy Harmsen, *American Western Art* (Denver CO: Harmsen Publishing Co., 1977) p. 106.

6. IIFI, pp. 5-6.

7. NYCR, 1896-97 New York City Directory.

8. IIFI, pp. 4-5.

9. Ibid. Stanley Appelbaum, *Nineteenth Century Stage in Advertising Woodcuts* (NY:Dover Publications, 1977) p. 142.

10. Appelbaum, *Nineteenth Century*, p. 26.

11. General Services Administration, Military Personnel Records, St. Louis, MO, #173-90-35 provided an accurate physical description of Sallie. IIFI, p. 4.

12. IIFI, p. 5.

13. Ibid.

14. Ibid.

15. NMAI-SI (3).

16. Ibid.

17. NMAI-SI (3). KCMF, Sallie made notations that when she was born that her parents lived at 909 Walnut St., Philadelphia, PA. Further notations state that her father died in 1893. In notes given to me by Carol Ann Johnson Hale (the daughter of Lola Johnson, Sallie's companion in her latter years) of Wichita Falls, TX is a sheet listing Laurel Hills Cemetery, Philadelphia, PA. Research conducted at this cemetary causes me to believe Sallie's parents may have been interred there. MNM-HL, "Jolly Rancher," listed Sallie as Sarah Russell Stuart. Stuart may have been her mother's maiden name.

18. 1880 Pennsylvania Census, Philadelphia Co., City of Philadelphia, Microfilm, T-769, Roll 124, Vol. 64, ED 139.

19. NMAI-SI (3).

20. IIFI, p. 5.

21. Ibid.

22. Ibid.

23. *Encyclopedia Britannica*, 1969, s.v. "Long Island."

24. NA, pp. 224-234.

25. IIFI, p. 5.

26. Ibid., p. 6.

27. Susan Wagner, *Cigarette Country, Tobacco in American History of Politics* (NY:Praeger Publishers, 1971) pp. 32-47.

28. Ibid., pp. 32-39.

29. Ibid., pp. 37-38.

30. Richard B. Tennant, *The American Cigarette Industry, A Study in Economic*

Analysis and Public Policy (New Haven, CT: Yale University Press, 1950) pp. 23-24, 42.

31. IIFI. p. 6. Ray Dellenbaugh, Sunnyvale, CA owns one set of fifty cards, in the Indians series, which includes the Imhof Indian cards. He purchased the set from a collection, "American Indian Chiefs" by Allen and Ginter of Richmond, VA, Lithographer Eddy and Clauss, NY. On the back is marked, "Allen and Ginter." Dellenbaugh stated that in addition to this set, he owns fifty more cards in the series, and that three or four Imhof cards contain printing errors.

Mr. Chuck Hynes, Minnetonka, MN has a collection of over 7,000 cigarette packages. Hynes wrote me a letter describing his own research. "I have one of the Indian head series of Allen & Ginter cards, titled Man & Chief. It is the second from the left in the photo from *Life Magazine*. The reverse side of the card shows that there were 50 individual cards in the series and gives the title of each. The card was lithographed by Lindner, Eddy, and Clauss of New York. The identity line clearly says, 'Allen & Ginter . . . Richmond, Virginia.' In my opinion, the Indian Head Series did NOT come packed with the brand Sweet Caporal. That name was owned by the Kinney Tobacco Co., of New York, not Allen & Ginter. At the time these cards were printed, these two companies were competitors. Allen & Ginter went into business in 1875. They produced several brands, the first of which was 'RICHMOND STRAIGHT CUT No. 1.' Other brands were BON-TON, NAPOLEONS, THE PET, and OPERA PUFFS. I believe that the Indian series of cards may have been packed in any one of ALL of these brands, INITIALLY! Allen & Ginter was acquired by 'Buck' Duke and became a part of the American Tobacco Co., just prior to 1900. When the anti-trust suit was won by the Federal Government, American Tobacco was forced to divest itself of some of the companies it had acquired. The assets and brand names of Allen & Ginter were turned over to Liggett & Myer of St. Louis, Missouri. At about the time that Duke bought out Allen & Ginter, he also bought Kinney Tobacco Co. Following each acquisition, the words, 'Manufactured by American Tobacco Co., Successor' appears on the package. Those words would be printed on the cards as well. Since the card DOES NOT have these words, I feel certain that it was produced prior to Duke's acquisition of Allen & Ginter . . . . These same cards [Indian Chiefs] may have been used in Sweet Caporal at a later date, but the original issues probably were packed with some of the earlier Allen & Ginter Brands (Dubec, Bon-Ton, and Napoleons are my best estimate). Later issues of the card may possibly have been packed in SWEET CAPORAL."

"Early Advertising," *Life* 28(1952):39-43. *Life* 28(1952) Photo caption: "Cigaret-makers helped blaze another advertising trail; they were among the first to discover selling value of a device that now seems second nature—a pretty girl."

32. ACM-JAI.

33. Ian M. Thompson, "Historic Silverton Hotel Purchased," *The Durango-Cortez Herald* Feb. 1972.

Allen Nossaman of the San Juan Historical Society, Silverton, CO, in a May 4, 1994 letter to me stated, " . . . a bar-stool variety storyteller told that the 'Lillian

Russell' painting was done by a man (whose name he did not know) who had been commissioned to paint several great actresses of the period; this is supposedly one of those seven which are in different places around the West."

34. SAM, pp. ix, 434.

35. Ibid., p. 86.

36. Ibid., pp. 52-53.

37. Ibid., pp. ix, 454-455, 460-461.

38. Ibid., pp. ix, 45-46.

39. Ibid., pp. ix, 102.

40. Ibid., pp. ix, 333-334.

41. Ibid., pp. ix, 184, 355-356.

42. Ibid., p. 249.

43. Ibid., p. ix.

44. *Encyclopedia Britannica*, 1969, s.v. "Oklahoma."

45. Richard Brookhiser, "Deerslayer Helped Define Us All," *Time* Nov. 9(1992)92. *Encyclopedia Britannica*, 1969, s.v. "Cooper, James Fenimore."

46. *Encyclopedia Britannica*, 1969, s.v. "Bandelier, Adolph Francis Alphonse." Warren A. Beck, *New Mexico, A History of Four Centuries* (Norman, OK:University of Oklahoma Press, 1974) pp. 318-319.

47. Beck, *New Mexico, A History*, pp. 318-319.

48. UNM-MMA, Letter to Captain Jack Riddle from Joseph Imhof, Mar. 3, 1955.

49. TSA, pp. 1-2. Robert R. White, *Artists of Territorial New Mexico, 1846-1912* (Albuquerque, NM:University of New Mexico Press) p. 158. White states that the first artist to live in Taos was Clementine A. Brown who was a Presbyterian missionary teacher sent to Taos from Utah about 1883. Her duties in the mission school included teaching art.

50. SAM, p. ix.

51. Ibid., pp. 219-220.

52. Ibid., pp. 235-236.

53. Jack Cowart and Juan Hamilton, *Georgia O'Keeffe, Art and Letters*, (Boston, MA:Little, Brown and Co., 1987) pp. 291-294.

54. IIFI, p. 6.

55. Ibid., p. 5.

56. *Encyclopedia Britannica*, 1969, s.v. "Museums and Galleries," "Art Education." Sherman E. Lee, ed., *On Understanding Art Museums* (Englewood Cliffs, NJ:Prentice-Hall, Inc., 1975) pp. 163-166.

57. BR, City Directory, 1891-1892; BR, Liber 36, pp. 43-44, John Imhof sold 227 Wyckoff on Oct. 4, 1905.

58. BR, Liber 27-440, Blk. 179, Section 1, Lot 44, listed as a widower (July 18, 1906).

59. ACM-SRI.

60. IIFI, p. 8. KCMF, "New York Tree," Sallie Imhof.

61. Ibid.

62. Ibid.

63. *Encyclopedia Britannica*, 1969, s.v. "Bennett, James Gordon."

64. James D. McCabe, *Lights and Shadows of New York Life; or the Sights and Sensations of the Great City* (NY:Farrar, Strauss and Giroux, 1970) p. 703.

65. IIFI, p. 8. KCMF, "New York Tree," Sallie Imhof.

66. KCMF, "New York Tree."

67. Ibid.

68. IIFI, p. 6.

69. IIFI, p. 6; In the biography that Sallie wrote in 1963, their daughter is never mentioned by name. The daughter is listed as Madeleine Elizabeth Imhof on Sallie's U.S. Navy Records. NMAI-SI(3), On a biographical form Sallie filled out, she spelled her child's name: Magdalen Elizabeth. In deciding which name to refer to their daughter, I decided upon Elizabeth because in an obituary on Sallie their daughter is listed as Elizabeth.

70. *Encyclopedia Britannica*, 1969, s.v. "Spanish-American War."

71. IIFI, p. 6.

72. Ibid.

73. Antreasian, *Tamarind*, p. 76.

74. Ibid., p. 75.

75. "Joseph A. Imhof, of New York, New York, Assignor to H. A. Thomas and Wylie Lithographing Co., A Corporation of New Jersey, Pictorial Device," Patent No. 687155 dated Nov. 19, 1901, United States Patent Office, Washington, D.C.

76. "Joseph A. Imhof, of New York, New York, Assignor to American Lithographic Co., A Corporation of New York, A Pictorial Device," Patent No. 698838, dated Apr. 29, 1902, United States Patent Office, Washington, D.C.

77. IIFI, p. 6.

78. Ibid.

79. Ibid., pp. 6-7.

80. Ibid., Sallie referred to the train as the Dolly Varden.

81. *Encyclopedia Britannica*, 1969, s.v. "Dewey, George."

82. IIFI, p. 7.

83. NA, pp. 98, 161.

84. Ibid., p. 238.

85. Ibid., pp. 268-269.

86. Ibid., p. 98.

87. SADC, NHR, Interview Sept. 16, 1993. My research on Kay Dicus indicated she had a daughter, Susan. After searching ten years for Susan, I learned she called herself, Anneke. I located her on Sept. 1, 1993, and she told me that there were so many Susans in Verde Valle School, Sedona, Arizona in the 1960s that she decided to go by Anneke.

88. IIFI, p. 6.

CHAPTER 6: THE BIRTH OF STYLE AND SUBJECT

1. IIFI, p. 7.
2. Ibid.
3. Stott, *American Painters*, pp.55-57.
4. *Baedeker's Netherlands*, pp. 79-81. Nina Nelson, *The Netherlands* (Longdon:B.T. Batsford Ltd., 1967) p. 50.
5. IIFI, p. 7.
6. Stott, *American Painters*, p. 179.
7. Ibid., pp. 179-180.
8. IIFI, p. 7. Stott, *American Painters*, p. 181; p. 195, "The common practice in Laren was to hire one or more local cottages, thereby reserving the sole right to paint those interiors and to use the inhabitants as models for a specified period."
9. IIFI, pp. 7, 12. Stott, *American Painters*, p. 182: "He [Henry Ward Ranger] . . . enjoyed lively art discussions with the Dutchmen and other artists who gathered evenings at the Vergulde Postwagon."
10. IIFI, pp. 7, 12.
11. Nelson, *Netherlands*, pp. 136-137.
12. I purchased the European scene from Woodrow Wilson of W. Wilson Fine Arts, Santa Fe, NM on Sept. 17, 1993. Wilson said he bought it many, many years ago and had it in his home. He said that it was an early Imhof of a European scene.
13. I visited the Brandywine Galleries, Ltd. in Albuquerque during 1989. Louise Abrums, the owner, told me of two unsigned Imhof oil paintings. They had been in her gallery from an estate. Abrums gave me enough information that I located the parties involved in the estate of Marjorie Williams of Corrales, NM. I telephoned her grandson, Leon Loughridge of Littleton, CO to discover that Williams had purchased some of the furnishings of my family's Rancho de Abiquiu. The two paintings were eventually sold to Jim Raughton, Denver, CO. When Raughton sent me a photograph of one of the paintings, "Outside Munich, 1900," I realized it was the same as the black and white photograph in the MNM, Photo Archives. Raughton described "Outside Munich, 1900," as "One of the earliest Imhofs. Imhof celebrates the tranquility of open space outside Munich, Germany. This is a relatively late summer scene, painted in 1900. While the palette is similar to Imhof's work in New Mexico the scene is lush with a landscape full of trees. Impressionist style includes solid brush strokes up to and including half inch." The second painting is unsigned, measures 12-by-9-inches, has a tree in the foreground, a far horizon and no house.
14. IIFI, p. 7.
15. Ibid., pp. 7-8.
16. Ibid., p. 8.
17. *Encyclopedia Britannica*, 1968, s.v. "New York."

18. Ibid., "Iroquois."

19. Ment, *Shaping of a City*, p. 9.

20. *Encyclopedia Britannica*, 1969, s.v. "New York."

21. Fenton, *Parker*, p. 16.

22. *Encyclopedia Britannica*, 1969, s.v. "New York."

23. Ibid., "Iroquois."

24. Ibid., "New York."

25. Ibid., "Delaware Indians."

26. Ellis, *A History of New York*, p. 10.

27. Ibid., NA, p. 97.

28. NA, p. 156.

29. Ibid.

30. Ibid.

31. *Encyclopedia Britannica*, 1969, s.v. "Huron."

32. Ibid.

33. Ibid.

34. Ibid.

35. Roger C. Owen, ed., *The North American Indians, A Source Book* (NY:Macmillan Co., 1967) p. 566. *Encyclopedia Britannica*, 1969, s.v. "Iroquois."

36. IIFI, p. 8.

37. Ibid., pp. 8-9.

38. Ibid., p. 9.

39. Ibid.

40. Ibid.

41. Ibid.

42. Ibid.

43. ACM, "Holland-America Line, Passenger List, 'Postsdam' Saturday, November 19, 1902." Listed were: Mr. J. Imhof, Mrs. J. Imhof, Miss M. Imhof. Sallie wrote on the passenger list: "Our second trip. Returned 1904."

44. IIFI, p. 9.

45. Ibid.

46. Ibid., p. 9. *Baedeker's Netherlands*, pp. 85-86.

47. IIFI, p. 9.

48. Ibid., pp. 9-10.

49. Ibid., p. 10.

50. Ibid.

51. Ibid.

52. Ibid.

53. I called the Wisconsin Historical Society, Racine, Wisconsin. They supplied the obituaries for Clifford Snyder in the following newspapers: *Racine Journal* 3 Jan. 1928; *Walworth County Independent* 26 Jan. 1928; *Elkhorn Independent* 5 Jan. 1928.

54. IIFI, p. 10.

55. Ibid.

56. Ibid., Stott, *American Painter*, p. 334: "Veere attracted more attention from American painters than any other town in Zeeland. George Wharton Edwards (1859-1950) devoted an entire chapter of his book *Holland of Today* to Veere, apart from the chapter on Zeeland. He described it as 'the deadest town in all Zeeland,' and for those who sought the picturesque and old-fashioned, Veere's deadness became an asset. It offered a ruined fortification, an ornate old town hall, and a massive cathedral for painters of the town . . . [who] were drawn to Veere by the little children who still wore the entire traditional costume after children in other towns in Holland had abandoned such clothes."

57. IIFI, p. 11.

58. Ibid., p. 12.

59. Ibid., p. 11.

60. Ibid.

61. Ibid., pp. 11-12.

62. Ibid., p. 12.

63. Ibid.

64. Walsh, *The Making of Buffalo Bill*, p. 294. Burke, *Buffalo Bill, The Noblest*, p. 216.

65. IIFI, p. 12.

66. Ibid.

67. Ibid.

68. Ibid.

69. *World Book*, 1969, s.v. "Lorelei."

70. IIFI, p. 12.

71. Ibid., pp. 12-13.

72. Ibid., p. 13.

73. Ibid.

74. Ibid.

75. Ibid.

76. Ibid., pp. 13-14.

77. Susan Poole, *Frommer's Belgium, Holland and Luxembourg*, (Englewood Cliffs, NJ:Prentice-Hall, Inc., 1990-1991) p. 125.

78. IIFI, p. 14.

79. Fedja Anzelewsky, *Dürer, His Art and Life*. Translated by Heide Grieve (NY:Alpine Fine Art Books, 1980) p. 136. "In a letter of 26 August 1509, Dürer told Jakob Heller that he had finally delivered the carefully packed altar panels to Hans Imhoff who would be responsible for their transport to Frankfurt." Peter Strieder, *Albert Dürer, Paintings, Prints and Drawings*, NY:Abaris Books, 1981) p. 19: "An inventory notation dated 1573-74 of the collection of Willibald Imhoff of Nuremberg speaks of two portraits, also painted on vellum, as being likewise the work of Dürer."

p. 147: "Portrait of the Emperor Maximilian I, Tempera on Canvas; 32 3/4" x 33 1/ 2". Formerly in Willibald Imhoff's collection." p. 60: "The inventory of the collection built up by Willibald Imhof, an upper-class citizen of Nuremberg, lists portraits of his Strasbourg master and his wife as Dürer's work." p. 81: "At first the accounts for the money collected in Nuremberg and in Venice were kept by the Paumgartners in Nuremberg; from 1491 to 1515 the trading firm of Konrad Imhoff and Sons was in charge of the fund."

Ludwig Grote, *Dürer* (Skira, 1965) p. 110: "The North German, Italian, and Portugese merchant houses had branch offices in Antwerp; the Nuremberg families with agents there included the Tuchers, Imhofs and Hirschvogels."

H. Knackfus, *Dürer* (Bielefeld Leipzige, Germany, 1911) p. 135: " . . . portrait, which has been supposed to represent Hans Imhof the elder of Nuremberg, hangs in the Prado Gallery at Madrid in a place of honour among the most select master-pieces of various nations and centuries, together with Dürer's own portrait of 1498." p. 143. "He produced a relief, cast in silver, with a graceful female figure, for a casket which was presented to a young lady of the Imhof family, and is in the possession of that family at Nuremberg to the present day."

80. Max Steck, *Dürer and His World* (NY:A Studio Book, The Viking Press, 1957) p. 85. Grote, *Dürer*, p. 110. IIFI, p. 14. BR, 1890 Census, I researched Joseph Imhof's genealogy to his father, John Joseph Imhof. From this point to Hans Imhof I did not research. From Sallie's biography we know that Joseph A. Imhof was of the same lineage as Hans Imhof. Robert R. White told me of Steven Ozmont's book, *Magdalena and Balthasar, An Intimate Portrait of Life in 16th Century Europe Revealed in the Letters of a Nuremberg Husband and Wife* (New Haven, CT:Yale University Press, 1989), which contains the Imhof name. The letters dated 1582-1598 reveal the Imhof names of Andreas, Sebastian, Katherina, Wilhelm, Jorg, Marina and Jakob. They are of interest because they were average people of the times.

When the University of New Mexico Maxwell Museum of Anthropology opened the Corn Series Exhibition, Feb. 7, 1965, among the guests was Mrs. Robert Imhof of Brewster, KS. In 1992 correspondence with Mrs. Robert Imhof, she stated, "I didn't know Joseph Imhof personally—I did know his wife and enjoyed her company very much." In a telephone conversation on Sept. 13, 1992, Mrs. Robert Imhof (now of Colby, KS) said, "Sallie and I tried to establish the relationship but got stuck in the German language. Sallie wanted me to call her Aunt Sallie as she wanted relatives. I attended the exhibition with a special invitation and enjoyed it very much." Mrs. Robert Imhof suggested I read William Dell Davidson's *Family Connection*, housed in Cherokee County Kansas Genealogical-Historical Society, Inc., Library, Columbus, KS, which traces some of the Imhof line. There were many Imhofs named but I could find no connection.

81. Poole, *Frommer's Belgium*, pp. 371-372.

82. Ibid.

83. IIFI, p. 14.

84. Poole, *Frommer's Belgium*, p. 371.

85. Harold Osburn, ed., *Oxford Companion to Art* (Oxford: Clarendon Press, 1970) pp. 337, 340.

86. Ibid.

87. Ibid.

88. Ibid.

89. Steck, *Dürer and His World*, p. 85.

90. Ibid., p. 112.

91. IIFI, p. 14. Research in 1994 indicates this painting is not in the Gardiner Collection of the Boston Museum.

92. Knackfus, *Dürer and His World*, p. 135.

93. NMR-T, District Court Probate No. 126, Book W, p. 481, Last Will and Testament of Sarah Russell Imhof. KCMF, "List of Antiques in Imhof House, Feb. 1963."

94. IIFI, p. 14.

95. Poole, *Frommer's Belgium*, p. 331.

96. IIFI, p. 14.

97. Ibid.

98. Ibid.

CHAPTER 7: JOINING PHILOSOPHY WITH ART

1. IIFI, p. 15.

2. Ibid.

3. Tennant, *The American Cigarette*, p. 57.

4. Ibid., pp. 35, 133.

5. Wagner, *Cigarette Country*, pp. 40-44. Tennant, *The American Cigarette*, p. 134.

6. Wagner, *Cigarette Country*, pp. 32-40.

7. Tennant, *The American Cigarette*, p. 39.

8. Ibid., p. 21.

9. Ibid., p. 35.

10. Nannie M. Tilley, *Bright-Tobacco, 1860-1929* (NY:Arno Press, 1948) pp. 583-584.

11. Tennant, *The American Cigarette*, pp. 50-51.

12. IIFI, p. 15.

13. Tilley, *Bright-Tobacco*, p. 585.

14. IIFI, p. 15. My research on the mechanism that Joe invented did not reveal a definite invention under Joe's name. Of the people who knew Joe, and who I interviewed, all suggested that the invention was some type of mechanism to open a cigarette package. Sallie, in her biography, stated that the invention was the mecha-

nism and that it was patented. In a letter to NHR from Walter A. Bailey, Los Angeles, CA, Mar. 1987, Bailey stated, "I don't think he invented the package. It was the 'pull string' that opened the package, I heard."

Chuck Hynes, Minnetonka, MN, an authority on cigarette packages wrote: "It was not until moisture barrier materials were developed that a mechanism was needed to open a cigarette package. Cigarettes were packaged in various configurations of boxes in the early days. The only seal on the boxes was the Federal Tax stamp. It was placed over one of the joints of the box in such a position that it had to be broken to open the package and get at the cigarettes. It was actually illegal to open a package without tearing the tax stamp. This was done to prevent re-use of the stamp. (The post office went to cancellation stamps since postage stamps could be soaked off and re-used.)

"In the late 1800s the 'Bonsack' machine was perfected by J. B. (Buck) Duke. Prior to then cigarettes were hand-rolled and production was a slow process. From the time of manufacture to the time of consumption the tobacco retained enough moisture to burn properly. Stale cigarettes (dried out tobacco) burn very rapidly and very hot.

"Once the Bonsack machine was perfected, it became possible to produce millions of cigarettes per week. This led to the broader distribution of ready-made cigarettes to rural areas. Up to then most farmers 'rolled their own' from tobacco sold in tins. The 'tin can' prevented evaporation and kept the tobacco fresh.

"As more and more cigarettes were manufactured and as distribution reached into the countryside, often the cigarettes were stale on a shopkeepers shelf before they were sold. This created a need for a wrapping material that had moisture barrier properties. Inner package liners made of paper and metal foil were developed. Prior to World War II LEAD foil was actually used. While this improved the shelf life, it did not totally solve the problem.

"A product called 'Glassine' was developed, and not too long afterward came 'Cellophane.' By sub-wrapping with foil-lined inner wrappers and OVER-WRAPPING with cellophane or Glassine, AND SEALING the over-wrap, shelf life was extended to about six months.

"Now, you could no longer use your fingernail to open the top of a cigarette pack. It was at this point that TEAR TAPE was invented. It was a tough strip of tape with a loose end that you could pull to 'un-zip' the cellophane wrapper. The same process is used today, except the tape is now made of nylon and the over-wrap is made of polyprophylene.

"If Imhoff [sic] invented anything, it had to be TEAR TAPE or the combination of tear-tape with the inner-liner. The first real innovation in opening a pack of cigarettes came from BROWN & WILLIAMSON. They introduced a *vertical* tear-tape on Viceroy cigarettes and then had an arrangement on KOOL'S that they called the 'POP-TOP' package. When you pulled the tear-tape, it opened the outer wrapper and when it came to its end it was fastened to the inner wrapper. By giving the tape a final tug, the inner wrapper popped open."

15. IIFI, p. 15.

16. Ibid.

17. Richard Samuel West, *Satire on Stone, The Political Cartoons of Joseph Keppler* (Chicago:University of Illinois Press, 1988) pp. 3, 19, 124.

18. IIFI, p. 15.

19. West, *Satire*, p. 430.

20. Ibid., pp. 3-4, 7.

21. Ibid., pp. 7-8.

22. Ibid., pp. 8-9.

23. Ibid., pp. 9, 12.

24. Ibid., p. 19.

25. Ibid., pp. 19, 72.

26. Ibid., pp. 72-73.

27. Ibid., pp. 73, 124.

28. Ibid., p. 287.

29. Ibid.

30. Ibid., pp. 351-352.

31. Ibid., pp. 352, 297.

32. Ibid., p. 397.

33. Ibid.

34. Edwin Emery, *The Press and America, An Interpretative History of Journalism* (Englewood Cliffs, NJ:Prentice-Hall, Inc., 1962) p. 506. Frank Luther Mott, *American Journalism* (NY:Macmillan Co., 1962) pp. 374-376.

35. Emery, *The Press*, pp. 347-348.

36. Ibid., p. 349.

37. Ibid., p. 377.

38. Ibid., p. 507.

39. Ibid., pp. 421-422.

40. Ibid., pp. 422-423, 572.

41. Ibid., pp. 422-423.

42. Ibid., p. 451.

43. Ibid., pp. 478-479.

44. IIFI, p. 15. My research on the Sloane newspaper syndicate was not successful. Sallie recorded, "Then came the Sloane newspaper syndicate and a silent arrangement in which Joe shared a portion of the profits." The only mention of Sloane is the device he created for J.V. Sloane of American Lithographic. I was unable to determine if these were the same.

45. *World Book*, 1969, s.v. "Pulitzer, Joseph."

46. IIFI, p. 15.

47. Ibid.

48. Ibid., p. 16.

49. NJR, Deed Book I, 18, pp. 411-412, Feb. 21, 1905, James E. Bott and Joseph A. Imhof.

50. IIFI, p. 16.

51. IIFI, p. 16. Horace L. Friess, *Felix Adler and Ethical Culture, Memories and Studies* (NY:Columbia University Press, 1981) pp. 33-34.

52. Friess, *Felix Adler*, pp. 16-20.

53. Ibid., pp. 20-21.

54. Ibid., pp. 21, 27.

55. Ibid., p. 32.

56. *Concise Columbia Encyclopedia*, 1983, s.v. "Kant, Immanuel."

57. Friess, *Felix Adler*, pp. 33, 38.

58. Ibid., p. 8.

59. Ibid., p. 64.

60. Ibid.

61. Ibid.

62. Ibid., p. 6.

63. Ibid., p. 49.

64. Ibid., pp. 8, 162.

65. IIFI, p. 16. Lillie G. McKinney, *History of the Albuquerque Indian School* Master's thesis, University of New Mexico, 1969, pp. 38, 46-50: From 1903 to 1908 there were several superintendents at the Albuquerque Indian School. J. K. Allen was from 1903 until May 27, 1906. B. Custer resigned Feb. 17, 1908. R. Perry began as superintendent Feb. 18, 1908. So it is difficult to determine with which superintendent Joe corresponded. Ward Alan Minge, *Acoma Pueblo in the Sky* (Albuquerque, NM:University of New Mexico Press, 1991) p. 76.

66. Howard Bryan, "Off the Beaten Path," *Albuquerque Tribune* June 22(1953).

67. Friess, *Felix Adler*, pp. 163, 175.

68. Ibid., pp. 209, 211-212, 222.

69. Ibid., pp. 212, 222, 229.

70. Arno Gruen, *The Betrayal of the Self, The Fear of Autonomy in Men and Women* (NY:Grove Press, 1986) p. 30.

71. Gruen, *The Betrayal*, pp. 1, 4, 30-32.

72. Friess, *Felix Adler*, pp. 229, 231, 253.

73. IIFI, p. 16.

74. Friess, *Felix Adler*, p. 233.

75. Lisa Couturier, "Speaking in Silence," *New Woman* Mar. (1992):60.

76. Ibid., p. 61.

77. Ibid.

78. IIFI, p. 16.

79. Ibid.

80. Ibid.

81. Ibid.

82. Ibid., pp. 16-17.

CHAPTER 8: ALBUQUERQUE BOUND

1. IIFI, p. 17. Dorothy Harmsen in *American Western Art*, p. 106, states that the Imhofs came to New Mexico in 1905 and built their studio in 1906. However, my research in City Directories does not establish the Imhofs in New Mexico in 1905 or 1906.

2. IIFI, p. 17.

3. Ibid.

4. Ibid.

5. Ibid.

6. Minge, *Acoma*, pp. 74-75.

7. Ibid., pp. 75-76.

8. Ibid., p. 72.

9. Ibid., p. 80.

10. Ibid., pp. 76-80.

11. Keith L. Bryant, Jr., *History of the Atchison, Topeka and Santa Fe Railway* (Lincoln, NE:University of Nebraska Press, 1982) p. 3. Lesley Poling-Kempes, *The Harvey Girls, Women Who Opened the West* (NY:Paragon House, 1991) pp. 2, 5.

12. Bryant, *History*, p. 3. Poling-Kempes, *Harvey*, p. xvii.

13. Bryant, *History*, pp. 1-3. Poling-Kempes, *Harvey*, p. 13.

14. Poling-Kempes, *Harvey*, p. 30.

15. Ibid., pp. 30-31.

16. Ibid., p. 31.

17. Ibid., pp. 33-34.

18. Ibid., p. 34.

19. Ibid., pp. 34-35.

20. Ibid., pp. 35-36.

21. Ibid., p. 35.

22. Ibid., pp. 36-37.

23. Ibid., pp. 37, 41.

24. Ibid., p. 42.

25. Ibid., p. 43.

26. Ibid., pp. 55-56.

27. Ibid., pp. 37, 41.

28. Bryant, *History*, p. 113.

29. Ibid.

30. Ibid., p. 121.

31. Bryant, *History*, p. 119. Poling-Kempes, *Harvey*, pp. 68, 157-158.

32. Poling-Kempes, *Harvey*, p. 157.

33. Ibid., p. 156.

34. Sandra D'Emilio, Suzan Campbell, *Visions and Visionaries, The Art and Artists of the Santa Fe Railway* (Salt Lake City, UT:Peregrine Smith Books, 1991) pp. 8-9.

35. Ibid., pp. 10, 17.

36. Ibid., p. 17. Ellen J. Landis, ed. *Eanger Irving Couse, Imagemaker for America* (Albuquerque, NM:Albuquerque Museum, 1991) pp. 240-241. Couse established his first permanent summer residence in Taos in 1906. In 1907 Jerry Mirabel of Taos Pueblo posed for Couse. Mirabel would eventually become a model for Imhof. In 1914 the Santa Fe Railway used the Couse painting, *Wal-si-el, Good Medicine*, on its calendar.

37. D'Emilio and Campbell, *Visionaries*, pp. 24-26.

38. Ibid., p. 21.

39. NHR telephone conversation with Mrs. Barbara Brenner, Taos, Oct. 15, 1994. Oscar Berninghaus created a menu cover for the Santa Fe Railway in 1915. Brenner conferred with her mother, Dorothy B. Brandenburg, as to whether Berninghaus created any menus for the Santa Fe Railway in 1907. Barbara replied to me, "Mother can't say if he did any menus but possibly, so say probably." So it is probable that Imhof saw work by Berninghaus. TSA, p. 104, " . . . Couse paintings were used on Santa Fe Railway calendars every year from 1923 to 1938."

40. D'Emilio and Campbell, *Visionaries*, p. 27.

41. Ibid.

42. Ibid.

43. IIFI, p. 17.

44. Ibid.

45. Poling-Kempes, *Harvey*, pp. 154, 233.

46. Ibid., p. 154.

47. IIFI, p. 18.

48. Ibid., p. 17.

49. Ibid.

50. Poling-Kempes, *Harvey*, p. 157.

51. IIFI, pp. 17-18.

CHAPTER 9: LIFE IN ALBUQUERQUE

1. Erna Fergusson, *Albuquerque* (Albuquerque, NM:Armitage, 1947) p. 37. The Alvarado Hotel was closed in 1969 and later demolished.

2. IIFI, p. 18.

3. "North End of Sandia Mountains, Albuquerque" is not dated but it is believed to have been painted during 1907-1912 when Imhof was living in Albuquerque.

4. IIFI, p. 19.

5. Robert L. Casey, *Journey to the High Southwest, A Traveler's Guide* (Old Saybrook, CT:The Globe Pequot Press, 1993) p. 275.

6. Ibid., p. 275.

7. Ibid.
8. Ibid., pp. 275-276.
9. Ibid., p. 276.
10. Ibid., pp. 276-277.
11. Ibid., p. 277.
12. Ibid.
13. Ibid., pp. 277-278.
14. Ibid., p. 278.
15. Ibid.
16. Ibid., pp. 278-279.
17. Ibid., p. 279.
18. Ibid., p. 280.
19. Ibid.
20. Ibid., pp. 280-281.
21. Ibid., p. 281.
22. Ibid.
23. Ibid., p. 282.
24. Ibid., pp. 282-283.
25. Ibid., p. 283.
26. Ibid.
27. Ibid., p. 284.
28. Ibid., p. 286.
29. Ibid., pp. 286-287.
30. Ibid., p. 287.
31. Ibid.
32. Ibid.
33. Ibid.
34. IIFI, p. 18.

35. Ibid. Donald A. Gill, *Stories Behind the Street Names of Albuquerque, Santa Fe and Taos* (Chicago:Bonus Books, Inc., 1994) p. 74: "Gold was named by Colonel Walter G. Marmon, after a mineral, apparently an indication of the hope that Albuquerque would be a major shipping point for the mining industry after the railroad arrived in 1880. He chose Coal, Gold, Copper, Lead, Silver." p. 37: "When the railroad came in 1880, New Albuquerque was created by lot sales of New Mexico Town Co. developed by the Santa Fe Railway and Franz Hunning, William Hazeldine and Elias Stover. Colonel Walter Marmon, a civil engineer, laid out townsite and plat names."

36. IIFI, p. 18.

37. Dorothy Hughes, *Pueblo on the Mesa* (Albuquerque, NM:University of New Mexico Press, 1989) p. 17.

38. Frank D. Reeve, *History of the University of New Mexico*, Ph.D. diss. (1928) p. 1.

39. Reeve, *History of UNM*, pp. 1-2.

40. Ibid., p. 2.

41. Ibid.

42. Hughes, *Pueblo*, pp. 19-20.

43. Reeve, *History of UNM*, p. 3.

44. Hughes, *Pueblo*, pp. 17-33. "The Pueblo University and University Campus, Location and Environment," Bulletin of UNM, Sept. 1908. *The Mirage* (UNM Students)4 (1909).

45. Hughes, *Pueblo*, p. 21. Reeve, *History of UNM*, p. 36.

46. Reeve, *History of UNM*, p. 36.

47. Hughes, *Pueblo*, pp. 23, 25.

48. Ibid., p. 25.

49. Ibid., pp. 25, 27.

50. "The Pueblo University," 1908.

51. Hughes, *Pueblo*, pp. 27, 29.

52. Ibid., p. 29.

53. Ibid., pp. 29, 33.

54. Ibid., p. 38.

55. UNM-GA.

56. Ibid.

57. Reeve, *History of UNM*, p. 50.

58. Hughes, *Pueblo*, p. 41. UNM-MMA, Letter to Dr. W. W. Hill, Director, Dept. Archaeology, UNM, Albuquerque, NM, from Sallie Imhof, Feb. 16, 1962.

59. UNM-GA.

60. NHR telephone conversation with Robert Joki, Portland, OR, 1989. Joki owns this painting. For years he has tried to identify the man in the portrait but is unable to do so.

61. Croix, Tansey, *Gardner's Art*, p. 666.

CHAPTER 10: DISCOVERING THE PUEBLOS

1. IIFI, p. 19. ACM, glass plate negative, "Imhof in Covered Wagon," an undated photograph depicts Imhof seated in a covered wagon pulled by mules.

2. IIFI, p. 19.

3. Ibid., p. 20.

4. Joe S. Sando, *Pueblo Nations, Eight Centuries of Pueblo Indian History* (Santa Fe, NM:Clear Light Publishers, 1992) p. 181.

5. Ibid., pp. 183-184.

6. Ibid., p. 181.

7. Ibid.

8. Ibid., pp. 181-183.

9. IIFI, p. 20. Sando, *Pueblo Nations,* p. 181.

10. Sando, *Pueblo Nations,* p. 184.

11. Ibid., p. 21.

12. Ibid., pp. 1, 26-28.

13. Paul Weatherwax, *Indian Corn in Old America* (NY:Macmillan Co., 1954) p. 48.

14. *Native Americans: Behind the Legends, Beyond the Myths* Atlanta, GA:Turner Broadcasting Co., 1994.

15. Ibid.

16. Ibid. Sando, *Pueblo Nations,* p. 22.

17. Sando, *Pueblo Nations,* p. 190.

18. Ibid., p. 22.

19. Ibid., p. 28.

20. Ibid., p. 8.

21. Joseph P. Hedrick, Jr., "Blessed by Tradition," (Santa Fe, NM: unpublished manuscript, 1990) pp. 6-7.

22. Ibid., p. 7.

23. Ibid., p. 8.

24. Ibid., p. 9.

25. Sando, *Pueblo Nations,* pp. 8-9.

26. Edgar L. Hewett and Wayne L. Mauzy, *Landmarks of New Mexico* (Albuquerque, NM:University of New Mexico Press, 1953) p. 84.

27. Sando, *Pueblo Nations,* p. 24.

28. Hedrick, "Blessed Tradition," p. 16.

29. Sando, *Pueblo Nations,* p. 24. Hedrick, "Blessed Tradition," p. 16.

30. Herbert J. Spinden, "Indian Dances of the Southwest," *American Museum Journal* 15(1915):103-115.

31. Sando, *Pueblo Nations,* p. 32.

32. UNM-MMA, Inventory of Imhof Collection, May 2, 1961.

33. IIFI, p. 20. Letter to NHR from Bob Dauner, Albuquerque Museum, Albuquerque, Dec. 2, 1987, stated that Sallie's spelling of Maria Chi que que in the biography she wrote is correctly spelled Chewiwie.

34. IIFI, p. 19.

35. UNM-HF-KD.

36. Casey, *Journey Southwest,* p. 270.

37. IIFI, pp. 19-20.

38. Ibid., p. 2.

39. Minge, *Acoma,* p. 1.

40. "Pueblo of Acoma, Acoma, Sky City," Acoma Tourist Visitor Center, Acoma, NM, 1995.

41. Ibid.

42. Minge, *Acoma,* pp. 4-5, 36-37.

43. Lucille Enix and I traveled to places Imhof had been in New Mexico, including the pueblos of Isleta, Santo Domingo, Cochiti, and Acoma. At Acoma, we walked the land, climbing from the mesa top to the valley floor via the well-worn footpath, using handholds that the ancients as well as Imhof had used. As I viewed the dramatic surroundings, it became obvious to me why Imhof felt so inspired with such country and the Indian way of life. The experience provided another reason why I have dedicated so many years of research into Imhof's life.

44. Minge, *Acoma*, p. 4.

45. Ibid., p. 21.

46. Ibid., p. 4.

47. Ibid., pp. 64-66.

48. Ibid., p. 166.

49. Sharyn Rohlfsen Udall, *Santa Fe Art Colony, 1900-1942* (Santa Fe, NM:Gerald Peters Gallery, 1987) pp. 24-25.

50. Minge, *Acoma*, p. xiii.

51. Ibid.

52. Sando, *Pueblo*, p. 34.

53. Ibid., p. 40.

54. Ibid., p. 33.

55. Ibid.

56. Hedrick, "Blessed Tradition," p. 27.

57. Sando, *Pueblo*, p. 43.

58. Weatherwax, *Indian Corn*, p. 238.

59. Ibid., pp. 113-120.

60. Ibid., p. 223.

61. UNM-MMA, Inventory of Imhof Collection, May 2, 1961.

CHAPTER 11: A HOME AT LAST

1. IIFI, p. 18.

2. NMR-B: Deed Book 48, p. 5, May 4, 1910, Mrs. Martha L. Thielmann to Joseph A. Imhof, an undivided one-third interest in two strips of land in Township 10, north of Range 3 east, containing 10.3 acres. State of New Mexico, Bernalillo County; Deed Book 48, p. 6, May 20, 1910, Joseph A. Imhof to Ada M. Netherwood, quit claim deed to an undivided interest in land in Township 10, north of Range 3 east, containing 10.3 acres.

3. IIFI, p. 18. NMR-B: June 18, 1912, Microfish, Bk 6, Grantee 1910-1917, pp. 180-209, p. 207: Warranty Deed, Ila M. Stewart to Joseph A. Imhof, lots 6, 7, 8, Block One of University Heights (plat filed in July, 1906), Bk 50, p. 255.

4. IIFI, p. 18.

5. The first street south of Railroad Ave. (now Central Ave.) was Silver St. The

second street south of Central Ave. was Coal St. which was changed to Lead St. The third street south of Central Ave. is now Coal St.

6. IIFI, p. 18.

7. Kenneth C. Balcomb, *A Boy's Albuquerque, 1898-1912* (Albuquerque, NM:University of New Mexico Press, 1980) pp. 60-61.

8. IIFI, p. 18. A photograph from NMAI-SI, "Home of J. A. Imhof, Albuquerque, NM, photo by J. A. Imhof, 1912," negative number 19312.

9. IIFI, pp. 18-19.

10. Ibid.

11. IIFI, p. 19.

12. Ibid.

13. Reeve, *History of UNM*, p. 49. UNM-GA. IIFI, p. 21.

14. Reeve, *History of UNM*, p. 49.

15. KCMF, *Albuquerque Journal* July 6, 1961.

16. UNM-HF-KD.

17. E. A. Burbank, *Burbank Among the Indians* (Caldwell, ID: The Caxton Printer, Ltd., 1944) p. 17.

18. *New Mexico, A Guide to the Colorful State*, compiled by Workers of the Writer's Program of the Works Projects Administration in the State of New Mexico. American Guide Series Sponsored by the Coronado Cuarto Centennial Commission and the UNM (NY: Hastings House, 1940) p. 243.

19. Arnold Vigil, "Backtracks, Time Travels Through New Mexico," *New Mexico Magazine* (1994)60-61. *New Mexico Guide*, p. 243.

20. Hewett and Mauzy, *Landmarks*, p. 72.

21. Frank Waters, *Masked Gods . . . Navaho and Pueblo Ceremonialism* (Albuquerque, NM:University of New Mexico Press, 1950) pp. 263-264.

22. Waters, *Masked Gods*, p. 264.

23. Ibid., pp. 264-266.

24. IIFI, p. 19. UNM-HF-KD. ACM-SRI.

25. Eldredge, Schimmel, Truettner, *Art in New Mexico*, p. 93.

26. This painting has inscribed at the bottom right: To Kitty and Marion Sulzberger. The inscription is in the same color of paint and the same writing style as signed by the artist in the lower left.

27. When I reviewed Joe's photography file at the MMA I reviewed over 1130 prints of the surrounding pueblos.

28. UNM-HF-KD. KCMF, *Albuquerque Journal* July 6, 1961.

29. Charles H. Lange, *Cochiti, A New Mexico Pueblo, Past and Present* (Albuquerque, NM:University of New Mexico Press, 1990) p. 4.

30. Ibid., pp. 57-60.

31. Ibid., pp. 4, 7, 426.

32. Ibid., p. 24.

33. Ibid., p. 49.

34. Ibid., pp. xviii, 51-53.

35. Ibid., p. 53.

36. Ibid., pp. 51, 54.

37. Ibid., pp. 54, 228.

38. Ibid., pp. 78, 124-140.

39. Ibid., pp. 175-179.

40. Ibid., p. 315.

41. Vincent Scully, *Pueblo:Mountain, Village, Dance* (NY:The Viking Press, 1975) pp. 185-186.

42. Ibid.

43. Lange, *Cochiti*, p. 315.

44. Ibid.

45. UNM-HF-KD.

46. Lange, *Cochiti*, p. 232.

47. Ibid.

48. Ira Moskowitz, *American Indian Ceremonial Dances* (NY:Bounty Books, 1972) p. 127.

49. Friess, *Adler*, p. 3.

50. UNM-HF-KD.

51. Craig Martin, "All in a Day, Tent Rocks," *New Mexico Magazine* Sept.(1994)22.

52. IIFI, p. 20.

53. Ibid.

54. Ibid.

55. David A. Remley, *Erna Fergusson* (Austin,TX:Steck-Vaughn Co., 1969) pp. 9-10.

56. Remley, *Erna Fergusson*, pp. 10-11. Poling-Kempes, *Harvey*, pp. 42, 150-151.

57. *The Mirage* vii(1911):27.

58. UNM-GA, "She [Sallie] remembers Charles Lembke and 'Beans' Gladding taking part." Microfilm, Zimmerman Library, UNM, *UNM Weekly*, Jan. 9, 1909 - May 8, 1917. "Rose O'Plymouth Town Proves Most Enjoyable," *UNM Weekly* XIII(1911)1. "The scenery for the play was painted for the occasion by a friend of the University, who also superintended the settings." The play was held May 30, 1911 at the Elks Opera House.

59. IIFI, p. 21.

60. UNM-GA. IIFI, p. 20. Legend has it that Imhof taught the first lithography class at UNM, however there are no UNM records of this class. I assume when Sallie writes in her biography that the students of the University came to the Imhof studio, that Joe taught lithography for no fee. Reeve, *History of UNM*, pp. 47, 52.

61. IIFI, p. 20.

62. Ibid.

63. A biographical publication obtained from the Albuquerque Library.

64. IIFI, pp. 20-21.

65. Hughes, *Pueblo*, p. 122.

66. NHR interview with SADC Sept. 16, 1993.

67. *Mirage* vii(1911)27. UNM-MMA, Letter from Sallie Imhof to Dr. W. W. Hill, Dir. Dept. of Anthropology, UNM, dated Feb. 16, 1962.

68. NMR-B:Deed Records, Microfish, Bk 6, Grantee 1910-1917, pp. 180-209, Ila M. Stewart to Joseph A. Imhof, Lots 6, 7, 8 of Block One of University Heights, Bk 50, p. 255 or 258, for $1,250.00.

69. NMR-B:Mortgage Deed Records, 9MD, p. 2, Microfish Bk 6 (H-L) Grantor 1910-1917, p. 218: dated Sept. 10, 1912, Joseph A. Imhof to First Savings Bank and Trust Co., Albuquerque, promissory note for $500.00, payable two years after date, 8% interest, Lots 6, 7, 8, Block One, University Heights.

70. NMR-B, Microfish, Bk 6, Grantee 1910-1917, p. 107, Joseph A. Imhof Grantee, First Savings Bank and Trust Co., Grantor, Aug. 20, 1913, release, Filed 3 MTG 58, Instrument dated Aug. 13, 1913, lots 6, 7, 8, Block 1, University Heights. There was no record of this for a copy to be made. It was only listed in the Index.

NMR-B, Microfish, Grantor, 1910-1917, (H-L), Bk 50, p. 462. P. 218, Received Aug. 20, 1913, Joseph A. Imhof and wife, Sara Russell Imhof of the Township of Montville, NJ, Co. of Morris, State of NJ, Warranty Deed to Katherine I. Bakes, wife of Frederick C. Bakes of Albuquerque, Date of Instrument: Aug. 13, 1913, for consideration of $900.00, lots 6, 7, 8, Block 1, University Heights and all houses, buildings, trees, waters, profits and privileges.

71. IIFI, p. 21.

72. Ibid.

73. IIFI, p. 21. *The National Cyclopedia of American Biography* (NY:James T. White and Co., 1920)17:348.

74. *National Cyclopedia*, p. 348.

75. IIFI, p. 21. Sallie's quote, "It was amusing to be greeted with joy to civilization after those years of roughing it in the Southwest," was not included in the final version of the biography she wrote. I found this quote in some rough notes of the biography in material sent to me by Carol Johnson Hale, Nov. 1993.

CHAPTER 12: NEW YORK AND FINANCIAL SECURITY

1. IIFI, p. 21.

2. NJR, Township of Montville, Recorded Deed Bk I 18, p. 411-412, James E. Bott of New Jersey sold to Joseph A. Imhof, 2-21-1905.

3. IIFI, p. 21.

4. United States Patent Office, Washington, D.C., Joseph A. Imhof of New York, New York, Assignor to Kaufman & Strauss Co. of New York, a corporation of New York, Patent No. 1,094,995, "Display-Stand," filed Nov. 17, 1913.

5. United States Patent Office, Washington, D.C., Joseph A. Imhof of New York, New York, Assignor to Kaufman & Strauss Co., of New York, a corporation of New York, Patent No. 1,157,542, "Display Stand," filed Dec. 23, 1914.

6. IIFI, p. 21. NYCR, 1915 Census.

7. Milton W. Brown, *American Painting From the Armory Show to the Depression* (Princeton, NJ:Princeton University Press, 1955) pp. 182-183. *Encyclopedia Britannica*, 1969, s.v. "New York City, Greenwich Village."

8. Brown, *American Painting*, p. 4.

9. Ibid., p. 6.

10. Ibid.

11. Ibid., p. 9.

12. Ibid., pp. 6, 9-10.

13. Ibid., pp. 12, 40.

14. Ibid., pp. 12-13.

15. Ibid., p. 37.

16. Ibid., pp. 38, 48.

17. Ibid., pp. 47-49.

18. Ibid., pp. 47, 50.

19. Ibid., pp. 7-8.

20. Ibid., pp. 7-8, 10.

21. Ibid., p. 6.

22. Ibid., p. 160.

23. Ibid.

24. Ibid., p. 161.

25. SAM, p. 203.

26. Jay Hambidge, *Dynamic Symmetry - The Greek Vase* (New Haven, CT:Yale University Press, 1920) p. 7.

27. SAM, p. 203.

28. Brown, *American Painting*, p. 164.

29. SAM, p. 203.

30. Walt Wiggins, *The Transcendental Art of Emil Bisttram* (Ruidoso Downs, NM:Pintores Press, 1988) p. 16.

31. Brown, *American Painting*, p. 12.

32. IIFI, p. 28.

33. Ibid., p. 22.

34. Robert W. Peterson, *Boy Scouts, An American Adventure* (American Heritage, 1984) pp. 17, 20.

35. Ibid., pp. 20, 23.

36. Ibid., pp. 23, 52.

37. IIFI, p. 22.

38. *New York Times* 4 Feb., 1915; 9 Feb., 1915; 13 Apr., 1917.

39. IIFI, p. 22.

40. ACM-SRI.

41. IIFI, p. 22.

42. "Indian Chief Opens Tercentenary Fair," *New York Times* 8 Nov. 1914.

43. Ibid.

44. "Rodman Wanamaker," biographical sheet distributed by a photography gallery in Santa Fe, NM.

45. Ibid.

46. John Young-Hunter, *Reviewing the Years* (NY:Crown Publishers, 1963) p. 76.

47. IIFI, p. 22.

48. Edgar I. Stewart, *Custer's Luck* (Norman, OK:University of Oklahoma Press, 1955) p. 409. "Indian Chief," NYT 1914.

49. IIFI, pp. 22-23.

50. UNM-MMA, Letter to Dr. W. W. Hill, Dept. of Anthropology, UNM, Albuquerque, NM, from Sallie Imhof, dated Jan. 8, 1962.

51. IIFI, p. 24. William Young, Editor, A *Dictionary of American Artists, Sculptors and Engravers, From the Beginnings Through the Turn of the Twentieth Century* (Cambridge, MA:William Young and Co., 1968) p. 334.

52. IIFI, p. 24.

53. Ibid. ACM, negative (fragment of an 8x10) #43 of Theodore Roosevelt, standing in office. ACM, negative #44, 8x10 negative of Theodore Roosevelt standing in military uniform beside tent. For years I had a print of negative #44 in the Imhof memorabilia but did not know from where it came.

54. UNM-MMA, Letter to Dr. W. W. Hill, Dept. of Anthropology, UNM, Albuquerque, NM, from Sallie Imhof, dated July 15, 1961.

55. IIFI, p. 24. Anne Morand, Curator of Art Collections, Gilcrease Museum, Tulsa, OK letter, Dec. 2, 1992 to NHR: "I have no record of a life cast by Imhof being given to the collection. If this occurred before 1955, the gift could have been part of the Foundation or family collections that were not transferred to the Institute that year (and) unfortunately, few records of those collections exist. If the cast was given between 1955 and 1962 when record keeping was scanty, I have no way of tracing it. As of 1963, the Institute collections did not include the cast."

56. UNM-MMA, Letter to Dr. W. W. Hill, Dept. of Anthropology, UNM, Albuquerque, NM, from Sallie Imhof, dated July 15, 1961.

57. IIFI, p. 23.

58. KCMF, "List of Antiques in Imhof House, Feb. 1963," Item No. 57, photograph of daughter when she graduated from high school in 1915. NYCR 1915 Census.

59. IIFI, pp. 24-25.

60. Joseph Bruchac, "The Heye Center Opens in Manhattan With Three Exhibitions of Native Arts," *Smithsonian* 25(1994):40. Brad Darrach, "A House of the Spirits, Trove of Native Americana Harbors a Vital Legacy," *Life Magazine* (1994):120.

61. NMR-T, District Court, Final Order, Judgment & Decree, Will of Sarah Russell Imhof, District Court, Recorded Book W, p. 481, Probate No. 126, filed Feb.

11, 1969. KCMF, The letterhead on the official Navy stationery reads, "The National Yeomen F, First Enlisted Women, U.S. Navy." United States Department of Military Personnel Records, St. Louis, MO, Enrollment Records, Sarah Russell Imhof Serial No. 7635, No. 1739035. IIFI, p. 6.

62. IIFI, pp. 6, 23. KCMF. United States Department of Military Personnel Records, St. Louis, MO, Enrollment Records, Sarah Russell Imhof Serial No. 7635, No. 1739035.

63. Ibid. for USN Records only.

64. IIFI, p. 23.

65. Ibid. NHR telephone interview with Robert Erkins, Feb. 13, 1992: Erkins said that Joe was sitting in a barber's chair when he thought of his idea for invisible paintings. He shared the profits from his invention with his barber and attorney.

66. United States Patent Office, Washington, D.C., Joseph A. Imhof of New York, New York, Assignor to Invisible Color Print Corporation of New York, a corporation of New York, "Method of Producing Color Prints," Patent No. 1,384,663, filed May 23, 1921, patented July 12, 1921.

67. IIFI, pp. 23-24.

68. Imhof filed three patents in 1922: (1)United States Patent Office, Joseph A. Imhof of New York, and John Charters of Astoria, New York, Assignors to Invisible Color Print Corporation of New York, New York, a corporation of New York, Patent No. 1,447,723, filed October 31, 1922, patented March 6, 1923, Print and Process of Making Same." (2)United States Patent Office, Washington, D.C., Joseph A. Imhof of New York, New York, Assignor to Invisible Color Print Corporation of New York, New York, a corporation of New York, Patent No. 1,507,358, filed April 7, 1922, patented September 2, 1924, "Art of Printing." (3)United States Patent Office, Washington, D.C., Joseph A. Imhof of New York and John Charters of Astoria, New York, Assignors to Invisible Color Print Corporation of New York, New York, a corporation of New York, Patent No. 1,528,925, filed October 31, 1922, patented March 10, 1925, "Process of Making Prints."

69. IIFI, p. 23.

70. Ibid., pp. 23-24.

71. Ibid. p. 23. NJR, Morris Co., Township of Montville, Deed Bk S-27, pp. 462-465, Joseph and Sallie Imhof, 6 1/4 acres, May 10, 1922.

72. IIFI, p. 24. BR, Kings County, Borough of Brooklyn, Deed Bk, #86503, pp. 380-382, July 12, 1923, Basil O'Connor and Elvira M. O'Connor to Joseph A. Imhof, 22 Willow St., Section One, Block 214. McCullough, *Great Bridge*, p. 549.

73. Goldstone and Dalrymple, *History Preserved*, p. 419.

74. Ibid., p. 417.

75. BR, Kings County, Borough of Brooklyn, Deed Bk, #86503, pp. 380-382, July 12, 1923, Basil O'Connor and Elvira M. O'Connor to Joseph A. Imhof, 22 Willow St., Section One, Block 214.

76. Ibid., p. 421. A photograph of 22 Willow St. in the Brooklyn Heights

Historical District is in text of Goldstone and Dalyrymple, *History Preserved*, p. 423.

77. IIFI, p. 24.

78. Richard Goldstein, *Superstars and Screwballs, 100 Years of Brooklyn Baseball* (NY:Dutton, 1991) p. 140.

79. IIFI, p. 24.

80. Goldstein, *Superstars*, p. 141.

81. IIFI, p. 23.

82. Ibid., p. 25.

83. Karen S. Young, Millicent Rogers Museum, Taos, stated that the dolls were made by Sallie Imhof, and decorated by the Indians in the 1920s. There was a second set of dolls in Gallup, NM, possibly with the trader, Jay Evertts.

84. IIFI, p. 25.

85. NHR telephone conversation with Walter A. Bailey, Los Angeles, CA, Feb. 10, 1987. Bailey indicated that he knew many stories about Imhof but was reluctant to tell them to me on the telephone. He had included them in his memoirs and asked if I would write his biography.

86. Telephone conversation with Harriet Ide Publicker, Beverly Hills, CA, May 3, 1995.

87. Ibid. Obituary for Joseph Ide, *New York Times* 9 Dec. 1965. David B. Ide, Ft. Lauderdale, FL letter to NHR, Sept. 18, 1995: "I knew Mr. Imhof I guess all my life until he died, but my knowledge of him was not very strong. I do remember my father telling me that he and Mr. Imhof were teachers in the New York City school system and had become quite good friends. It seems to me the story goes that at some time (I don't have the vaguest idea when) Mr. Imhof was to move to the south west and that his financial affairs would be handled by my father. There was some sort of an oral agreement that there would be a reimbursement at the time of Mr. (and Mrs.) Imhof's death."

88. IIFI, p. 25.

89. KCMF, Sallie included in the *Morada* file her handwritten notes about the testimonial dinner given in her honor and a letter from the National Commander.

90. Ibid.

91. IIFI, p. 25.

CHAPTER 13: HOME IN TAOS

1. IIFI, p. 25. MNM-HL, Taos File, *Taos Valley News* ca. 1929.

2. TPH, p. 14. "Historic Taos," information contained in a city of Taos hand-out sheet dated June 29, 1987.

3. UNM-MMA, Letter to Dr. W. W. Hill, Dept. of Archaeology, UNM, Albu-querque, from Sallie Imhof, Jan. 6, 1963.

4. The Imhofs owned their Brooklyn home at 22 Willow St. until 1944 when

they sold it. It is speculation that Elizabeth lived at 22 Willow St. during the time the Imhofs were moving and getting settled in Taos. Walter Bailey letters to NHR, Feb. 19, 1987 and March 12, 1987 stated that Elizabeth came from New York to Taos the day he left in 1930. Bailey helped with building of the Imhof house, so I assume it was late 1930. Phillips Kloss letter to NHR, March 8, 1988 stated that Elizabeth stayed a few months doing volunteer work for a Taos dentist because she had a nurse's training.

5. TSF, p. 10.

6. TPH, p. 26.

7. TPH, p. 28. "The Taos Art Colony," *El Palacio* 53(1946):318. In the Albuquerque Museum are three paintings of early Albuquerque: #85.4.1 "Plaza of Albuquerque," Joseph Eaton (1815-1896), watercolor on paper; #85.30.12 "Albuquerque, San dei Mountains, June 25, 1869," Vincent Colyer (1825-1888), watercolor on paper; #76.115/1 "Old Town, Albuquerque, 1885," Leon Trousset, oil on canvas.

8. SAM, p. 377. TPH, pp. 27-28.

9. TPH, pp. 27-28.

10. SAM, p. 436.

11. Ibid.

12. SAM, p. 51. "The Taos Art Colony," *El Palacio* 53 (1946):318.

13. "Taos Art," *El Palacio* p. 318.

14. TSA, p. 104.

15. Ibid., pp. 1-2. TPH, p. 113.

16. TSA, pp. 2-3. TSF, pp. 13-15.

17. "Taos Art," *El Palacio* p. 318.

18. TSF, pp. 18-22.

19. TSA, pp. 2-3. SAM, pp. 51, 147.

20. Virginia Couse Leavitt, "Yesterday and Today in Taos County and Northern New Mexico," *Taos and the American Art Colony Movement: The Search for an American School of Art*, Taos County Historical Society (Taos, NM,:Winter, 1987) p. 4.

21. Ibid., pp. 3, 5.

22. Ibid., p. 3.

23. Ibid.

24. TSA, pp. 17-21, 23. Gordon E. Sanders, *Oscar E. Berninghaus, Taos, New Mexico, Master Painter of American Indians and the Frontier West* (Taos, NM:Taos Heritage Publishing Co., 1985) p. 24: "Until July 1915, The Society was informal and usually referred to as the Taos Art Colony. However, it is evident there was a verbal agreement among the painters, and that some organizing had previously been done by Bert Phillips. The 'St. Louis Republic' ran a full-page cover story in its art section dated August 11, 1913 that featured reproductions of works by a number of the original six artists. The article also stated that Oscar Berninghaus had joined the Taos Art Colony. All of the paintings used in the pictorial section were dated 1912, lending credibility to the 1912 agreement theory."

25. TSA, pp. 12, 14, 15, 28.

26. Cooke, "Taos Artists." MNM-HL, Taos File.

27. TAIA, inside jacket copy. Mabel Dodge Luhan was well aware of the art being created in the U.S. and Europe. In her opinion, "Perhaps the most unusual art colony in the world is the closely knit community of Taos . . . . During the past thirty years, has come some of the most interesting and important art in America; an art whose style is as varied as the personalities of its creators, producing alike the studio portraits of John Young-Hunter and the surrealism of Thomas Benrimo, the Indian scholarship of Joseph Imhof, and the abstractions of Emil Bisttram."

28. Laura Bickerstaff, *Pioneer Artists of Taos*, (Denver, CO:Sage Books, 1955) p. 75.

29. TPH, pp. 5, 9. John Nichols, *If Mountains Die, A New Mexico Memoir* (NY:Random House, 1979) p. 8.

30. TPH, pp. 9-16.

31. Ibid., pp. 23-27.

32. WIT, p. 35.

33. TPH, p. 67.

34. IIFI, pp. 26-27.

35. NMR-T, Warranty Deed Record, Bk A-30, p. 194, Susan B. Brooks to Joseph A. Imhof and Sarah Russell Imhof, July 26, 1929. NMR-T, General Index Direct, A-Z, 1930 to 1941, p. 75, Jan. 21, 1932, Grantor, J. A. Imhof, Grantee, S. R. Imhof, Quit Claim D, recorded in Book A-32, p. 502.

36. *Life Magazine* (1995):29. Cooke, "Taos Artists," MNM-HL, Taos File. After Duane Van Vechten Lineberry died, Ed Lineberry remarried. Ed and Novella Lineberry turned part of their property into the Van Vechten-Lineberry Taos Art Museum featuring Van Vechten along with a fine representation of many Taos artists, including their former neighbor, Joseph Imhof.

37. NMR-T, Warranty Deed Bk A-30, p. 195, Susan B. Brooks to Joseph A. Imhof and Sarah Russell Imhof, July 29, 1929.

38. IIFI, p. 26.

39. Marcia Keegan, *The Taos Pueblo and Its Sacred Blue Lake* (Santa Fe, NM:Clear Light Publishers, 1991) p. 47.

40. IIFI, p. 25.

41. Ibid., p. 26.

42. Francis I. Fugate, Roberta B. Fugate, *Roadside History of New Mexico* (Missoula, MT:Mountain Press Publishing Co., 1989) "Penitentes," pp. 257-258.

43. Ibid.

44. Ibid.

45. ACM-SRI.

46. KCMF, "New York Tree."

47. Garo Antreasian, *The Tamarind Book of Lithography* (Los Angeles, CA:Tamarind Lithography Workshop, 1971) p. 343.

48. IIFI, p. 25.

49. TPH, pp. 50, 89.

50. Ibid., pp. 67, 78, 85.

51. IIFI, p. 26.

52. Ibid.

53. Ibid., p. 27.

54. Paul Horgan, *Great River, The Rio Grande in North American History* (NY:Rinehart & Co., 1954) p. 765.

55. Ibid.

56. Ibid., pp. 767-768.

57. Brochure on Walter A. Bailey, published by Art Made Famous, Ltd., Santa Barbara, CA.

58. NHR telephone interview with Walter A. Bailey, Feb. 10, 1987. Mr. Bailey indicated that he had written his memoirs which included mention of Imhof. His memoirs are in the possession of Mrs. James Bailey, Fair Oaks, CA.

59. IIFI, p. 26.

60. Ibid.

61. NHR telephone interview with Doris Bailey Wakeland, Silver City, NM, Dec. 4, 1994. Letter to NHR from Doris Bailey Wakeland, Silver City, NM, Dec. 30, 1986.

62. Letter to NHR from Doris Bailey Wakeland, Silver City, NM, Dec. 30, 1986: "We visited him [Bailey] in June, at which time, I suggested the idea of offering the portrait for exhibit. I thought it was a good piece of work, in addition to the interesting point that it is the only painting of a non Indian, according to Mrs. Imhof. I had called upon her in the mid fifties, introducing myself as Walter Bailey's daughter. She was unaware that he had had a child, since his sojourn in Taos was subsequent to his divorce from my mother. When I attempted to convince her that I was indeed related, witness my possession of a photo of a portrait of my father by Imhof, she denied it saying that 'Imhof only painted Indians.' Needless to say, the visit was not prolonged.

"My dad, who has clear recollections of his earlier life, tells of the days when he lived in a guest house on the Imhof property. At one time, Imhof gave him a piece of land on which to build his own house. It turned out that the property line was inaccurate, and part of the house was on government land. It was then torn down.

"Walter also had a small portrait painted by Leon Gaspard who was a good friend. I was lucky enough to find Gaspard at home on the same trip to Taos mentioned above. He was most gracious and allowed us to see his private gallery of his paintings."

63. NMR-T, No deed to Bailey for any property was recorded in the County Clerk's office. NHR telephone conversation with Walter A. Bailey, Feb. 10, 1987: Bailey said that Imhof sent him a watercolor seascape from La Jolla.

64. Letter to NHR from Phillips Kloss, Jan. 1988. Walter A. Bailey brochure.

65. "Gene Kloss, Print Retrospective," The Harwood Foundation Museum of the University of New Mexico, July 29-Sept. 24, 1994, p. 5.

66. PNM, p. 38. SAM, p. 269.

67. Letter to NHR from Phillips Kloss, Jan. 1988.

68. IIFI, p. 26.

69. In Jan. 1990, Tom Noeding of Governor Bent Gallery, Taos, told me that Lola Johnson had a daughter. After several years of research I located Lola's daughter, Carol Johnson Hale of Wichita Falls, TX. Carol Hale became my primary source on Lola Johnson, Sallie's friend, and, in her last years, her companion and nurse. NHR telephone interview Carol J. Hale, Nov. 8, 1993, Jan. 8, 1995. In Nov. 1993 Carol J. Hale mailed me her files on Imhof; I photocopied them and returned them to her.

70. NHR telephone conversation with Carol J. Hale, Wichita Falls, TX, Jan. 8, 1995.

71. When I telephoned the St. James' Episcopal Church, Taos, in Jan. 1995, to inquire of Sallie's membership, Claire Brandenburg answered the telephone. She identified herself as the daughter of Helen Kentnor, one of the participants in the Imhof story.

72. Claire W. Brandenburg, "Portrait: A Woman of Courage," unpublished paper, pp. 1-2.

73. Ibid., p. 2.

74. Ibid., pp. 2-3.

75. Ibid., p. 3.

76. TAIA, p. 165. In the biographical listing: "JOSEPH A. IMHOF, No information obtainable."

77. TPH, p. 42.

78. WIT, jacket cover.

79. TPH, p. 42.

80. TAIA, pp. 22-23.

81. NHR conversation with Michael Hensley, Taos, Jan. 21, 1995. Hensley stated that Geronimo drew the twelve-foot snake on the wooden board above the front gate. At the time, vines covered the gate.

82. KCMF, "List of Antiques in Imhof House, Feb. 1963." Also in the house were two paintings by Imhof which were copies of Old Masters in the Rijksmuseum, Amsterdam: "Baron Von Hasselear" and "Mimi." UNM-MMA, Letter to Fred Mazzulla, Denver, CO from Sallie, July 24, 1963: "The background is from an old print of Nieuw Amsterdam which Joe owned. It was made by a Dutchman who visited there and returned to Amsterdam where the print was made. It represents the shore line of what was later called the Battery. The ship is Dutch of the same model as Heinrich Hudson's 'The Half Moon' the original model was and is in the Rijksmuseum in Amsterdam where Joe measured and sketched it. The following year 1654 the first 23 Jewish emigrants arrived saved from pirates by a French ship of war which brought them in. The Jews of New York had a great celebration in 1954 and

the fantastic story of their wanderings appeared in the New York papers."

83. UNM-MMA, Letter to Capt. Jack P. Riddle, Denver, CO, from Joe Imhof, Nov. 3, 195? (illegible date). UNM-MMA, Letter to Dr. W. W. Hill, Dept. of Anthropology, UNM, Albuquerque, from Sarah Russell Imhof, Jan. 8, 1962: "Would you be at all interested in the lithograph of Nieuw Amsterdam 1653? The background was made from a print of that date made by a visiting Dutchman who returned to Holland and made the print there. Joe once owned it but being Joe he probably gave it to some friend." KCMF, "List of Antiques in Imhof House, Feb. 1963": On the east wall of the bedroom hung art by Imhof: a watercolor, "Halifax, Nova Scotia," watercolor "La Jolla, 1921," and a painting on wood "Room in Brewer's Guild, Antwerp, 1891," sketch of Sarah Russell Imhof made in 1902, Guenwald near Munich on a picnic, painting of Quebec with Hotel Frontenac in distance, painting St. John's, Newfoundland showing ships unloading salt—the codfish industry and light on hill, painting of La Jolla, 1947.

84. KCMF, "List of Antiques in Imhof House, Feb. 1963."

85. Ibid.

86. PNM, p. 78. There is little reference to the types of paper Imhof used. NMAI-SI, There were a few notations on the lithographs and sketches such as Gabriano, Strathmore artist paper, Marquet stock, Weave Text Strathmore. UNM-MMA, Letter to Sallie from W. W. Hill, Mar. 22, 1963: "The reason for its selection was not only because of the excellence of the lithography but because it was placed on a bluish-gray paper which lent substantially to its effectiveness. Being no art critic I was glad to discover that the artists agree with me since I have always been enthusiastic about it."

On the back of two prints I own from the Imhof Collection was a cardboard piece cut from a shipping box. The printed matter on the cardboard read: Label:SAXO . . . , Paper Produ . . . , 240 West 18th St., Type Right with Sphinx Paper. In handwriting: 100 sh 22 x 34 64# P L Buff; 200 sh 251/? X 30½ 220# Blu Sa . . . ; 1000 sh 25 1/? X 30½ 280# Blue Sa . . . . These are the only clues I found to the paper Imhof used.

87. PNM, pp. 26-27.

88. Ibid., pp. 27, 32-33, 35.

89. Ibid., pp. 35-36.

90. TAIA, pp. 22, 33.

91. KCMF, photograph dated 1965.

CHAPTER 14: DEATH REDEFINES FAMILY

1. UNM-HF-KD. NMAI-SI(3), Biographical form filled out by Sallie.

2. UNM-HF-KD.

3. "Fifty-Five Years Ago," newspaper clipping (1952), UNM-HF, Imhof Research File.

4. Letter to NHR from Helen Kentnor, Taos, NM, Jan. 1988.

5. IIFI, p. 27.

6. KCMF, *La Junta Tribune* June 1, 1966.

7. UNM-HF-KD.

8. UNM-HF-KD. Helen Blumenschein letter to NHR, Nov. 15, 1987, "They [Imhofs] were both very pleasant but did not socialize with the art group."

9. NHR interview with SADC Sept. 16, 1993.

10. IIFI, p. 27.

11. *The Harwood Foundation of the University of New Mexico, Taos, 1923-93, A Brief History and Collection Listing Published on the Seventieth Anniversary of the Foundation*, Produced by the staff of the Harwood Foundation (Wichita, KS.:Printing, Inc., 1993) p. 14. David Witt, "A Brief History of the Harwood," an unpublished paper (Taos, NM:Harwood Foundation, 1993) pp. 1-9.

12. IIFI, pp. 27-28. UNM-GA.

13. Carol J. Hale package of Imhof material to NHR, Nov. 1993. I came across this information sheet many times during my research in art galleries, and through owners of Imhof art. I assume the sheet was written for a hand-out. ACM-JAI: Sallie: "I hope the beer bottle doesn't appear in the picture." Joe: "A good lithographer will put beer on the stone." Sallie: "Mabel Dodge Luhan in her book [*Taos and Its Artists*], the beer bottle is in the picture." Joe also commented that he used butter as his grease.

14. UNM-HF-KD.

15. *Harwood Foundation*, Harwood Foundation, pp. 7-9.

16. Ibid., pp. 9, 11, 13-14. UNM-HF-KD. By 1930 when the Imhofs arrived in Taos the Harwood was well on its way to becoming what Elizabeth Harwood envisioned. The Harwood became a favorite of the Imhofs although Kay Dicus states that she is not sure the Imhofs ever knew Elizabeth Harwood.

17. TSA, p. 9.

18. Ibid., pp. 10, 12.

19. PNM, p. 18.

20. NHR telephone conversation with Phillips Kloss, Mar. 7, 1988. Letter to NHR from Phillips Kloss, Jan. 1988.

21. NHR conversation with Rena Rosequist, Taos, Jan. 20, 1995. Rosequist stated that Sunhawk modeled as a child. Imhof taught Sunhawk to paint and Sunhawk painted a few works but stopped. When Imhof asked him why he stopped, Sunhawk said, "Can't eat paintings."

22. NHR telephone conversation with E. O. Floyd, Taos, Sept. 29, 1993.

23. "Joe 'Sunhawk' Sandoval Dies," *Taos News*, Dec. 23, 1987. NHR conversation with Martha Reed, Taos, Oct. 28, 1995. Reed stated that shortly after Joe Imhof died, Sallie prepared to burn some of Imhof's work. Sunhawk asked if he could have some of the art to be burned. Sallie gave Sunhawk the art. Sunhawk gave Martha Reed two of the pieces of art.

24. UNM-MMA, Letter to Dr. W. W. Hill, Dept. of Anthropology, UNM, Albuquerque, from Sallie Imhof, Aug. 2, 1961. Sawnie Morris, "Eva Mirabal, Taos Pueblo Artist," *Taos Magazine* VI(1989):32: "When Mirabal was a child, her father, Pedro Mirabal, frequently posed for artists Maurice Stern [sic] and Joseph Imhoff [sic]."

There are conflicting spellings for Mirabel/Mirabal. Some listings are: Koshare Indian Museum, Catalogue No. PA314, Jerry Mirabel; Koshare Indian Museum, Catalogue No. PA324, Cristino Mirabel; Roswell Art Museum and Art Center, Cristino Mirabel; Oklahoma City Art Museum, 1964.021, Pedro Mirabel; *Taos Magazine* July(1989):32, uses Eva Mirabal; NHR telephone conversation with the grandson of Imhof model, Pedro, Jonathan Warmday, Taos, Feb. 29, 1996 said that Mirabal is the correct spelling; UNM-MMA, Letter to Dr. W. W. Hill, Dept. of Anthropology, UNM, Albuquerque, from Sallie Imhof Aug. 2, 1961, Cristino Mirabal; Millicent Rogers Museum of Northern New Mexico notes from Oscar Berninghaus exhibit, July 1994 on a cartoon that Berninghaus drew, "Taos Plaza, 14 x 30, mixed media, 1931, cartoon with Dorothy Brett, M.D. Luhan and Jerry Mirabel." The notation on the side reads: Jerry Mirabel the Indian who met and entertained all tourists (when sober and even more than when he was not).

25. *Kennedy Quarterly* XIV(1975):101, 124. Imhof is also mentioned in *Kennedy Quarterly* XIV(1975); X(1970).

26. John J. Bodine, *Taos Pueblo, A Walk Through Time* (Santa Fe, NM: Lightning Tree, Jene Lyon Publisher, 1977) pp. 45-46. UNM-MMA, Letter to Dr. W. W. Hill, Dept. of Anthropology, UNM, Albuquerque, from Sallie Imhof, Aug. 2, 1961.

27. UNM-MMA, Imhof Collection Inventory, May 2, 1961, #61.3.47. Joe S. Sando, *The Pueblo Indians* (San Francisco, CA:The Indian Historian Press, American Indian Educational Publications, 1976) p. 240. UNM-MMA, Letter to Dr. W. W. Hill, Department of Anthropology, UNM, Albuquerque, from Sallie, Aug. 2, 1961: "I do not know whether statistics interest you but Cristino Mirabal chief of the Chiffonetti and Joe's long time model—he modeled for the Cacique painting died July 21st found dead in bed heart failure."

28. UNM-MMA, Letter to Dr. W. W. Hill, Dept. Archaeology, UNM, Albuquerque, from Sallie Imhof, Sept. 16, 1962.

29. TAIA, p. 43.

30. A. M. Gibson, *The Santa Fe and Taos Colonies, Age of the Muses, 1900-1942* (Norman,OK:University of Oklahoma Press, 1988) pp. 148-149.

31. John U. Terrell, *Pueblos, Gods and Spaniards* (NY:Dial Press, 1973) pp. xx-xxi.

32. Ibid.

33. Jeanne O. Snodgrass, "Indian Art Today," *Western Review* 2(1965):29-30.

34. Keegan, *Taos Pueblo*, pp. 49-52.

35. Claire Morrill, *A Taos Mosaic, Portrait of a New Mexico Village* (Albuquerque, NM:University of New Mexico Press, 1973) p. 58.

36. Ibid., pp. 59-60.

37. Ibid., p. 60.

38. John T. Whatley, "The Taos Saga of Blue Lake," *The Indian Review* 2(1969):24.

39. Philip Reno, *Taos Pueblo* (Denver, CO:Sage Books, 1963) p. 21.

40. Keegan, *Taos Pueblo*, p. 49.

41. Ibid., pp. 49-50.

42. Morrill, *Taos Mosaic*, pp. 60-61.

43. Ibid., p. 61.

44. Ibid., pp. 61-62.

45. Ibid., p. 62.

46. Keegan, *Taos Pueblo*, pp. 50-52.

47. NMAI-SI(3), Biographical Form.

48. "Panhandle Patrons Look to New Mexico for Art," *Southwest Art Magazine* Apr.(1993):85.

49. *Amarillo News* Sept. 27, 1931.

50. MNM-HL, *El Palacio* 31(1931):303-6; *El Palacio* recorded years from 1929-1976 that Imhof exhibited at Santa Fe: 1931 watercolor "Taos"; 1934 drawings and lithographs; 1935 listed; 1936 watercolor Indian; 1937 listed; 1941 listed; 1946 Indian; 1947 March PrintMakers exhibition, a Santa Fe first time exhibition, September listing, December PrintMakers exhibition; 1948 listing; 1950 Prints and Drawing exhibition.

51. Pat Trenton, *Picturesque Images from Taos and Santa Fe*, An Exhibition sponsored by the First National Bank of Denver and the Denver Art Museum, Jan. 12-Mar. 17, 1974, p. 5.

52. Ibid., p. 131.

53. Doris Ostrander Dawdy, *Artists of the American West, A Biographical Dictionary* (Chicago:Sage Books, Swallow Press, Inc. 1974) p. 123.

54. Frederick J. Dockstader, *The American Indian Observed* (NY: M. Knoedler and Co., Inc., 1971) p. 7.

55. Ibid., p. 8.

56. Ibid., p. 11.

57. IIFI, p. 27.

58. KCMF, photograph of Imhofs captioned, "Old trees near old road to Penasco, 1931, Mr. and Mrs. Imhof." MNM-HL, Taos file, 5-21-1936, Blanche Grant, "S-700, Cities, Towns and Villages, Peñasco."

59. UNM-HF-KD.

60. MNM-HL, Taos File, *The New Mexican* Sept. 25, 1936.

61. SAM, pp. 51-52. PNM, pp. 63-64. Letter to NHR from Helen Blumenschein, Nov. 1987.

62. IIFI, p. 28. UNM-HF-KD.

63. Wiggins, *Transcendental Art*, p. 19.

64. E. A. Davis, ed. *The Historical Encyclopedia of New Mexico* (Albuquerque,

NM:New Mexico Historical Association, 1945) pp. 83-84. IIFI, p. 28. Gibson, *Taos & Santa Fe*, p. 66.

65. Wiggins, *Transcendental Art*, p. 20.

66. IIFI, p. 28.

67. Wiggins, *Transcendental Art*, p. 20.

68. Landis, ed. *Eanger Irving Couse*, p. 21.

69. Wiggins, *Transcendental Art*, p. 16.

70. Ibid., p. 21.

71. IIFI, p. 28. UNM-MMA, Imhof File, Letter to Dr. W. W. Hill, Dept. of Anthropology, UNM, Albuquerque, from Sallie Imhof, Oct. 29, 1961.

72. Letter to NHR from Phillips Kloss, Mar. 8, 1988; NHR telephone conversation with Gene Kloss, Jan. 9, 1995.

73. Phillips Kloss letter to NHR, Mar. 1988.

74. Helen Kentnor letter to NHR, Feb. 1988.

75. In over fifty years association with the Imhof name and over fifteen years of research, I discovered scant information on the Imhofs' daughter. Of the people I interviewed, few knew the Imhofs had a daughter. If they knew of the daughter they knew almost nothing about her. I documented only three references to the daughter by name. NMAI-SI(3), After Joe died Sallie filled out a biographical form for the NMAI, Heye Foundation listing children: "1 daughter, Nov. 19, 1898, Huguenot, Long Island, NY. Magdalen Elizabeth died June 26, 1933, San Diego, Cal, about to begin a late medical education, very talented and like me always wanted to be a surgeon." U.S. Navy Records: Sallie lists child as Madeleine Elizabeth Imhof. *Denver Post*, June 28, 1966; Sallie's obituary lists the daughter as Elizabeth Imhof. MNM-HL, "Imhof Rites Set Monday at Taos," *The New Mexican*, June 26, 1966. I was unable to document that Magdalena Elizabeth Imhof married. She did not appear on the marriage records in NMR-T, Marriages No. 7 Book 1928-32, Marriages No. 8 Book, 1932-35, Marriages No. 9 Book, 1935-37; San Diego Co., CA. Marriages, 1912-1936.

76. NHR telephone conversation with Harriett Ide Publicker, Beverly Hills, CA, May 3, 1995.

77. *Jackson M. Hensley - An American School Painter*, a biographical sheet. Hensley, a native of Portales, NM and a painter, lived in CT. As Hensley's success escalated, he chose to forego all the awards which he thought might detract from his concentration and creativity. He moved back to New Mexico and purchased the Imhof home, which was in disrepair. He remodeled the home and added a sizable horse farm. NHR conversation with Jackson Hensley, Taos, Nov. 6, 1987.

78. Letter to NHR from Walter A. Bailey, Los Angeles, CA, Feb. 1987.

79. NHR conversation with Michael Hensley, Sept. 28, 1993.

80. NHR telephone conversation with Robert Erkins Feb. 13, 1993. NHR telephone conversation with Charlene Dady, Wilsonville, OR, Feb. 29, 1996.

81. NHR telephone conversation with Robert Erkins June 17, 1994.

82. NHR telephone conversation with Charlene Dady, Sept. 29, 1994.

83. NMAI-SI(3), Biographical form filled out by Sallie stated Magdelena Elizabeth (no last name given) died June 26, 1933, San Diego. Carol J. Hale material, Nov. 1993, a notation in Lola Johnson's handwriting that the Imhofs' one child died June 12, 1933. I question if the date was an error; perhaps she died on June 12 and the ashes were scattered on June 26. ACM, I was never able to identify a young girl photographed standing in front of what appears to be the corner of the Imhofs' Taos house. However, I feel certain this is the Imhofs' daughter.

84. NHR telephone conversations with Gene Kloss, Jan. 9, Feb. 22, 1995. Letter to NHR from Phillips Kloss, Mar. 1988.

85. NHR telephone conversation with Carol J. Hale Jan. 8, 1995.

86. San Diego Historical Society, Oral History Collection, interview with Dr. Rieta Campbell Hough, Feb. 19, 1977, by Billie Jean Meade, pp. 1, 4-5.

87. Frank N. Magill, ed. *Critical Survey of Poetry, English Language Series*, Authors, A-Chat, No. 1 (Englewood Cliffs, NJ:Salem Press, 1982) pp. 302-308. George E. Woodberry, ed. *Collected Poems of Rupert Brooke* (NY:Dodd, Mead & Co., 1915) pp. 15-17.

88. NHR telephone conversation with Carol J. Hale, Aug. 8, 1993. Carol indicated that she thought Hester Bott Van Ness was a childhood friend of Elizabeth Imhof. NJR, County of Morris, Township of Montville, Deed Book I 18, pp. 411, 412, Feb. 21, 1905. James E. Bott and Emma, his wife, sold Joseph A. Imhof of New York 6¼ acres. In the deed it mentions the land next to this 6¼ acres belonged to James E. Bott. When I talked to a librarian in Montville, she indicated that the name Bott and Van Ness were common names in Morris County. NMAI-SI(3), Last Will and Testament of Sarah Russell Imhof leaves Mrs. Hester Bott Van Ness, 2608 "O" Street, Sacramento, CA or Towaco, New Jersey, "the sum of $1,000.00 and my two watches." KCMF, There is a letter dated Jan. 5, 1966 to "Mother Imhof and Lola" from a Hester. Hester mentions Oscar, New Jersey relative, and that they received a copy of Sallie's biography. Research in the Sacramento, CA City Directory established that Mrs. Oscar Van Ness was listed as living in Sacramento from 1966 to 1973. I conclude that Elizabeth Imhof probably knew Hester Bott Van Ness in New Jersey. Hester married Mr. Van Ness and moved to Sacramento. Elizabeth and Hester remained friends through the years.

89. KCMF, "List of Antiques in Imhof House, Feb. 1963."

CHAPTER 15: FINALLY, A PATRON WITH NEW ENTERPRISES

1. Letter to NHR from Phillips Kloss Jan. 1988.

2. PNM, pp. 38-40.

3. Letter to NHR from Phillips Kloss Jan. 1988. NHR telephone conversation with Gene Kloss Jan. 9, 1995.

4. Imhof did not date his art as a general rule. The only clues to when he created these two lithographs of Father Junipero Serra: UNM Art Museum has two, dated 1933, of the same pose with the priest holding the cross above his left shoulder and a book in his hand. KCMF, The lithograph "Fr. Junipero Serra" with the cross on the priest's left chest appeared in a La Jolla newspaper photograph in "Art Comment" by Hazel Boyer Braun dated in 1935. NHR telephone conversation with Charlene Dady Sept. 29, 1994, Dady stated that the "Fr. Serra" lithograph was inscribed by Imhof to her in 1941. NMAI-SI, Acc. 159. We know that the "Fr. Serra" with the cross above his left shoulder was done in 1933. "Fr. Serra" with the cross over his left chest was done before 1935 or in 1935. We speculated that due to the essence of the two lithographs that the "Fr. Serra" with the cross above his left chest was done at the time of Imhofs' daughter's death, and the "Fr. Serra" in 1935 was done after his daughter's death.

5. Ibid.

6. ACM-SRI.

7. Letter to NHR from Helen Kentnor Mar. 1988.

8. Eldredge, Schimmel, Truettner, *Art in New Mexico*, p.69.

9. Kathryn A. Flynn, Editor, *Treasures on New Mexico Trails, Discover New Deal Art and Architecture* (Santa Fe, NM:Sunstone Press) pp. 125-128. PNM, pp. 37-38.

10. PNM, p. 38.

11. Ibid., p. 144. Flynn, *Treasures*, p. 28. This same lithograph Imhof titled, "Taos Sacred Mountain."

12. Flynn, *Treasures*, p. 22: "Albuquerque, WPA Art in WPA Buildings, A., Anthropology Annex. The Anthropology Building was formerly the Old Student Union Building built by WPA funds. The Annex portion houses three Joseph Imhof murals depicting pueblo dancers." In the summer of 1970 I went to the UNM campus to see the Imhof art. I was directed to a large auditorium with stair-step seating. I remember seeing on the far wall large black and white paintings of Indian dancers. I remember being disappointed that they were in black and white. In 1996 when Marian Rodee toured me though the UNM campus to see the Imhof art, I asked about the murals referred to in the Flynn book that stated the Imhof murals were part of the WPA project. Rodee did not know of any art resembling the Imhof murals. She showed me the auditorium that could possibly have housed the murals. None were there and she did not know of any being there previously. I am uncertain whether my memory failed, Flynn's book listed the murals by Imhof in error, or if the murals had actually been there and something happened to them.

13. MNM-HL, *El Palacio* 37(1934).

14. My research lists the earliest known dated Christmas card as 1934-35.

15. NHR telephone conversation with Robert Erkins Feb. 13, 1993.

16. See Chapter 14, Endnote No. 50.

17. IIFI, pp. 28-29.

18. E. O. Floyd gave me a photocopy of his files on Imhof from the time Floyd

had his art gallery, the former Merrill's Gallery. The file contained a letter on Merrill's Gallery stationery marked Lila Deacon, Director, addressed To Whom It May Concern, from Marie Merrill, May 20, 1978.

19. NHR telephone conversation with Carol J. Hale Jan. 8, 1995.

20. E. O. Floyd, Imhof file, Marie Merrill letter dated May 20, 1978.

21. E. O. Floyd, Imhof file, letter to Roland Force, NMAI-SI, from E. O. Floyd, Apr. 23, 1981. NHR telephone conversation with Marie Merrill Oct. 18, 1993.

22. Letter to NHR from Helen Kentnor Mar. 1988. James A. Burns, "S-700 Cities, Towns and Villages, Talpa," May 23, 1936, MNM-HL. "Tempo," *Taos News,* June 6, 1996. After Dr. T. P. Martin died, his widow, Helen, opened the Hotel Martin (Taos Inn) on June 7, 1936. Among those assisting at the opening reception was Mrs. Joseph Imhof.

23. Jake W. Spidle, *Doctors of Medicine in New Mexico* (Albuquerque, NM:University of New Mexico Press, 1986) pp. 46, 203.

24. Writer's Program, NM, *New Mexico, A Guide to a Colorful State* (NY:Hastings House, 1940) p. 376.

25. MNM-HL, Taos File, 5-23-1936, Burns, "S-700 Cities," pp. 1-2.

26. Spidle, *Doctors of Medicine,* p. 184.

27. Ibid.

28. Letter from Phillips Kloss to NHR, Mar. 1988.

29. MNM-HL, Taos File, Ruth Fish, *The New Mexican,* May 13, 1946.

30. PNM, p. 44. NHR conversation with Ted Egri, Taos, Nov. 1987: "Imhof did lithography for others in Taos because he had the only press, but got mad and withdrew."

31. UNM-HF-KD.

32. TSF, p. 85.

33. MNM-HL, *Taos Valley News* July 16, 1936.

34. UNM-HF-KD.

35. BR, Dept. of Buildings of the Borough of Brooklyn, Violation Report 607/36 Jan. 1936 Tax Block 214, Lot 17, Census Tract 1.

36. Ibid.

37. BR, Dept. of Housing and Buildings, Brooklyn, Application No. 1206, March 28, 1940, Block 214, Lot 17, Section 1, Volume 6.

38. UNM-HF-KD. Notes to NHR from Carol J. Hale Jan. 8, 1995.

39. Wiggins, *Transcendental Art,* p. 20.

40. Ibid., p. 29.

41. Ibid., pp. 87-88.

42. From a photograph provided by Charlene Dady Oct. 25, 1994. NHR telephone conversation with Carol J. Hale Jan. 8, 1995.

43. MNM-HL, *The New Mexican* May 4, 1937.

44. NHR telephone conversation with Robert Erkins Feb. 13, 1993.

45. Ibid. Letter from Charlene Dady, Oct. 25, 1994.

46. NHR telephone conversations with Charlene Dady Sept. 29, Nov. 1, 1994. Imhof painted the portrait of Charlene Dady for her twelfth birthday as a present to her father, A. W. Erkins. This portrait among many other portraits disclaims Sallie's remark that Joe only painted Indians.

47. Letter to NHR from Allen Willett, Carlsbad, CA Sept. 25, 1991. ACM-JAI, Imhof states that he made twelve prints. DP-EM, Imhof states that he made twelve prints.

48. NHR telephone conversation with Charlene Dady Sept. 29, 1994.

49. NHR telephone conversation with Robert Erkins Feb. 13, 1993.

50. IIFI, pp. 27-28.

51. *School of American Research, Representative, Art and Artists of New Mexico* (Santa Fe, NM:1940) p. ii. Gibson, *Santa Fe and Taos Colonies*, p. 267.

52. MNM-HL, Taos file, "Taos County Folk Celebrate Cultural Project Success." Dr. J. T. Reid, *It Happened in Taos* (Albuquerque, NM:University of New Mexico Press, 1946) pp. 1-3, 16-17.

53. MNM-HL, *El Palacio* 48(1941):194.

54. UNM-HF-KD. MNM Library, "Jolly Rancher," "Sugar and Spice," News Straight from the Jolly Rancher (Wheatridge, CO:Sept.-Oct., 1971) p. 2.

55. IIFI, pp. 28-29.

56. "A Prefabricated House in Forty Minutes," *Click Magazine, The National Picture Monthly*, 6(1943):8. One house could be manufactured in 7 minutes, erected in 40 minutes. The first shipment of Victory Huts went to Pearl Harbor shortly after Dec. 7, 1941.

57. "Los Alamos, Beginning of an Era," Los Alamos Historical Society, Los Alamos, 1993. Although they are not identified by name, these are the units supplied by the Texas Pre-fabricated Housing Co. as shown on pages 11, 14, 23, 37, 56. The "Victory Hut" name was eventually changed to "Dallas Hut."

58. In another of those coincidences that has marked my writing of Imhof's life, E. W. Morten is buried on Long Island, NY. However, his wife, Blanche, is buried in Grove Hill Cemetery, Dallas, TX only several blocks from the residence of my co-author, Lucille Enix. Each time I drove by the Morten cemetery plot at Grove Hill on my way to Lucille's I was amazed at the paths E. W. Morten, Winfield Morten and Imhof were taking me.

59. "Civic Leader Rites Slated for Monday," *Dallas Times Herald*, Aug. 11, 1968. Morten was a graduate of Terrill Prep School in Dallas. He attended a business school at age 17 in Dallas, just a few years before his grandfather died in 1929. He was a sports enthusiast, sponsored the Pan American Polo Tournament in Dallas in 1935 and was active in the Dallas Polo Club. He also donated the sanctuary at the Church of Incarnation, Dallas.

60. Helen, my aunt who eventually became Morten's wife, had first married in Medora, IL, at age 16, the son of a wealthy farmer. They moved to Dallas. Helen's brother, who had tuberculosis, had by then moved to Dallas for his health. Helen

and her first husband divorced. Then Helen married a prominent Dallas Judge. They divorced. When she met Winfield, she said, "I've been looking for Winfield all my life."

61. Gilberto Benito Cordova, *Abiquiu and Don Cacahaute: A Folk History of a New Mexican Village* (Los Cerrillos, NM:San Marcus Press, 1973) pp. 15-19.

62. "New Mexico Historic Sites," A Survey Prepared by the Staff of the Museum of New Mexico, State Planning Office (Santa Fe, NM 1967) pp. 22-23.

63. *Sixteenth Census of the United States, 1940, Population Characteristics of Population,* Part 4, Minnesota to New Mexico, U.S. Government Printing Office, Washington, D.C., Vol. II, p. 1007.

64. Cowart and Hamilton, *Georgia O'Keeffe, Arts and Letters,* pp. 233, 293.

65. Ibid., p. 293.

66. NMR, Rio Arriba County, Index to Real Property, Indirect, Jan. 1, 1937-1949, #60785, 1-5-44, Book 25A, p. 582, Warranty Deed, Winfield Morten, grantee, under Juan Jose Lovato Grant. Morten began buying his property about this time. He did not buy all his land at one time, but in pieces.

67. *Los Alamos, Beginning of an Era, 1943-5* (Los Alamos, NM:Los Alamos Historical Society, 1993) pp. 9-10. Winfield Morten and Hal Hopkins with their Texas Housing Co. would later provide all the prefabricated housing for the Los Alamos community known as White Rock.

68. The Rancho de Abiquiu dining room wall containing the mural was demolished in a recent renovation. However, the remaining murals in the trophy room and living room are still on the walls but have been covered with paint.

69. These photographs were made Feb. 25, 1947. The negatives are housed at Life Archives, Time and Life Building, Rockefeller Center, Rm 2858, NY 10020, Set #22973. Pauline H. Castleberry recalled that the day the photographers arrived to photograph Rancho de Abiquiu they were fascinated with a dining room table arrangement that she had made of tumbleweeds. "Texas Hospitality, Charm Found at Morten Ranch in New Mexico," *Daily Times Herald* Nov. 30, 1950, "The story of their Shangri-La is as picturesque and colorful as an Indian legend. The land on which their adobe house is erected belonged to a Spanish family for 100 years. The Mortens are the first Anglos to own the land. Before the Dallasites purchased the expanse of land the soil had not been touched for 50 years. Their work has been to plant grass and irrigate. The Mortens' love for the land challenged them to develop the acres. They avidly discuss the irrigation process which turned poor land into excellent soil. They own 1,000 acres 'under the ditch' and 10,000 acres of ranging land. Mrs. Morten admits that she wasn't interest in soil conservation until she met Mr. Morten. She tells that he even discussed it on their first date. 'In fact,' she chuckled, 'I don't think he would have married me if I hadn't shown some enthusiasm for irrigation, soil conservation and ranching." NHR telephone conversation with E. Morten Hopkins Sept. 8, 1995. Hopkins stated that the big irrigation ditch from the Chama River to the ranch was engineered by Winfield Morten. It was quite

a conversation item at the time because to the eye the water appeared to flow upstream.

70. Often my family visited with Joe and Sallie in their Taos home. Aunt Helen, Mother and I dressed in our Agnes James fiesta dresses worn with our silver and turquoise concho belts and squash blossom necklaces. Sallie and Joe's house was full of artifacts. The house always had a ladder on the outside. Lunch was always refreshing, especially in the summer when the watermelon dessert was cooled in the stream running by the house. Gene Cavallo, "Agnes James at 81. A Living New Mexican Treasure Remembers Frontier Womanhood," *The New Mexican* June 23(1981):1-3. Lorraine Carr, "It Happened in Old Santa Fe," *The New Mexican* Aug. 13(1956):10. Agnes James, born in Rockwall, TX in 1900, married Jimmy James, a traveling patent medicine salesman. They traveled the "Southwest in a fringed surrey selling his wares. Jimmy suddenly died leaving Agnes and her young son, Bill. She attend SMU, did social work in Albuquerque. Having talent as a dressmaker she opened several women's clothes stores in New Mexico. She made adaptations of native Spanish and Indian costumes. She went to mother earth for her colors, the most popular is Abiquiu Clay which she got from the reddish hills near Abiquiu. She hand-dyed all her fabric in a big pot in her kitchen. Her clothes became a success in her stores Pins and Needles and Town and Country located in Santa Fe at the corner of Lincoln and Marcy. New York showed an interest and her first big show was at the Biltmore Hotel. Saks Fifth Avenue was her biggest buyer." Cordova, *Abiquiu*, p. 80. Father William Bickhaus was priest at Abiquiu from Aug. 1932 to Nov. 1946. He may have been a guest in the Mortens' home.

71. NHR telephone conversation with Harriet Ide Publicker May 3, 1995.

72. As a result of Morten's donating his Dallas Huts to the St. Thomas Church in Abiquiu, he was cited by Pope Pius XII, Mar. 4, 1949. Napoleon "Paul" Garcia, Sr., Abiquiu, in Jan. 1993, related, "The church was never closed at the time we were 2 Mission of the El Rito (San Juan Nepomocino Parish) under Father Bichouse [sic]. It is true in 1944 Mr. Morten brought in two of his prefab houses and we got 2 permanent priests and 4 nuns (sister). The people build a permanent school and convent in late 1942 and early fifties. The El Rito Parish was split then which was a big parish. And the Mother part of the parish was being headed from Cuba, New Mexico. The New Church was finished in 1939 under the direction of the El Rito Parish. The Old Church was built in the 1800s."

73. Theodore D. Kurrus, "Indescribable Carol Glitsch Burnett," *Southwest Art Magazine* Sept.(1979):66. Letter to NHR from Carol G. Burnett, Sept. 9, 1979. Biographical information supplied by Burnett's daughter, Mrs. Charles (Galen Burnett) Haynes, Midland, TX Oct. 18, 1994: "Carol Glitsch was born in Dallas, Texas 1936. Studied color theory and pastels at age 8 with Ethel Brodnax. At 11 years of age studied a short time with Jose Imhof of Taos, New Mexico, one of our foremost New Mexico and European artists. She studied commercial art with the Art Institute in Connecticut, and had a small advertising agency in 1960-63. Won a scholarship to

Texas University Fine Arts Department, but elected to go to SMU where she studied under DeForrest Judd and Stella LaMonde. Studied one summer with Leszgk Muzscynski of the Royal Academy, London. Studied creative photography with Elliott Eliasofan, photographer and painter—Director of New York Museum of Modern Art, 1965. The artist works in and around the realist manner without becoming obsessive in detail—the quality of light being of paramount interest, swinging between the use of color and lack of it. Working in acrylic on canvas and wood, the artist ranges in subject matter from rodeos to museums and from still life to carnivals. She has had previous shows in Dallas, 1974, 2719 Gallery; 1976, Fairmount Gallery; 1978, Roughton Gallery. Also showing in Jamison Galleries, Santa Fe, NM."

74. ACM-SRI.

75. Hewett and Mauzy, *Landmarks New Mexico,* pp. 18-20.

76. NHR conversation with Robert H. Hopkins, Jr.

77. NHR conversation with E. Morten Hopkins Sept. 5, 1988.

78. UNM-MMA, Letter to Dr. W. W. Hill, Dept. of Anthropology, UNM, Albuquerque, from Sallie Imhof Aug. 2, 1961.

79. Arthur N. Pack, *We Called It Ghost Ranch* (Abiquiu, NM:Ghost Ranch Conference Center, 1965) pp. 92-93.

80. Major General Charles H. Corlett, *Cowboy Pete, The Autobiography of Major General Charles H. Corlett* (Santa Fe, NM:Sleeping Fox Enterprises, 1974) pp. 77, 106.

81. Brandenburg, *Portrait of Courage,* p. 3.

82. TPH, p. 104.

83. MNM-HL, *El Palacio* 52(1945):168.

84. MNM-HL, Taos File, *Santa Fe New Mexican* May 16, 1946.

85. NHR telephone interview with SADC Sept 1, 1993. Kay Dicus was born in England, lived in New York and Baltimore where she met Richard Dicus. In Baltimore Kay was secretary in the Engineering Dept. at Johns Hopkins University where she was a friend of Henry Sauerwein. Kay and Richard married and visited her sister in Albuquerque in 1941. They liked New Mexico, but WWII began; Richard joined the Navy and had reached the rank of Commander when the war ended. They moved to Taos, settling in Cañon where their daughter, Anneke, recalled that they hosted many important guests, one being Millicent Rogers with her child, nanny, chauffeur and dogs. Richard designed several Taos houses, owned "Workshop," making Spanish American furniture in a shop on Guadalupe Plaza.

86. NHR telephone conversation with E. Morten Hopkins Sept. 5, 1988. NHR telephone conversation with E. Morten Hopkins Sept. 13, 1993: Morten thinks the dig took place near Dood Newsome's house (which is directly across the northern most entrance to the ranch, off the highway north of Abiquiu). Dood lived in an adobe house about 300 yards off the highway. It was in an alfalfa field that Morten mowed in flat fields close to the Chama River. Winfield Morten said the water for irrigating was being lost in the ditch. Imhof brought people from Albuquerque to

excavate. They found caves where people had lived. Water ran through the earth and disappeared. There may have been two excavations going on at the same time. NHR correspondence with Napoleon "Paul" Garcia, Sr., Abiquiu, NM, Jan. 25, 1995. Mr. Garcia stated: "It was never a proven fact. They also claimed to have lost some heavy equipment where it got stuck."

87. MNM-HL, *El Palacio* 53(1946):63.

88. KCMF, Letter to Sarah Russell Imhof from Rufus Sedillo, State Director Selective Service, Santa Fe, July 8, 1946.

89. MNM-HL, *El Palacio* 53(1946):235, 322.

90. PNM, p. 57.

91. Dixie Lee Yaple, "Taos Briefs," *Santa Fe New Mexican* Apr. 25, 1947, MNM-HL. NHR interview with Helen Morten Oct. 23, 1979: Helen stated that in 1947 Imhof painted the La Jolla watercolor that she owned. NHR telephone conversation with Walter A. Bailey Feb. 10, 1987. Bailey said that he had a La Jolla watercolor seascape that Imhof sent him from La Jolla. Bailey said that he would sell his.

92. MNM-HL, *El Palacio* 54(1947):188, 277.

93. MNM-HL, *El Palacio* 55(1948):121. "First Southwestern Print Exhibition at the Dallas Museum of Fine Arts, February 1 to February 29, 1948," sponsored by the Dallas Print Society, Dallas Museum of Fine Arts Library.

94. When my parents moved into their new home ca. 1947 in Dallas, Imhof gave them a painting of his favorite tree. This is the same favorite tree as seen in the painting on loan from Mel Weimer, Colorado Springs, CO to the Van Vechten-Lineberry Taos Art Museum.

95. MNM-HL, *El Palacio* 55(1948):121.

96. NHR telephone conversation with Carol J. Hale Jan. 8, 1995.

97. NHR interview with SADC Sept. 16, 1993. "Taos Village Is to Get Park Meters," *The New Mexican* May 19, 1949, MNM-HL.

98. NHR interview with SADC Sept. 16, 1993. Letter to NHR from M. Jon Kolomitz, La Junta, CO July 14, 1992: "I recall visiting Mr. Imhof at his studio in Taos on one or two occasions. His home was a magnificent adobe structure filled with his works, props, artifacts, dust and dogs!"

99. NHR telephone interview with SADC Sept. 1, 1993.

100. MNM-HL, *El Palacio* 57(1950):382.

101. IIFI, p. 29.

CHAPTER 16: THE CORN SERIES ENDS THE PARTNERSHIP

1. ACM-SRI.

2. Ibid.

3. IIFI, p. 29.

4. Letter to NHR from Claire W. Brandenburg Jan. 19, 1995.

5. Koshare Indian Museum, La Junta, CO, Inventory, Catalogue No. PA 389, Accession date Dec. 31, 1950, Reference No. 87.10.341.

6. IIFI, p. 28. Koshare Indian Museum, Imhof file, Letters to Joe from J. F. Burshears, Mar. 17, 1951; Apr. 7, 1952; Jan. 18, 1954.

7. *Koshare Dancers*, Koshare Indian Museum, La Junta, CO souvenir booklet.

8. Corlett, *Cowboy Pete*, p. 110. Corlett was a West Point graduate. In another coincidence, Corlett's wife, Pauline, was from Groveton, TX where my husband, Don Reily, was born. The New Mexico Housing Co. stationary indicated the company had two offices, although I'm not sure when each office opened. One was located at 108 W. Palace, the other at 207 W. Water St. Each office was just a few blocks from the building at the corner of Sheridan and W. Palace that served as the check-in point for the Manhattan Project. Corlett, after his active duty in the U.S. Army, retired to his ranch at Española, NM. He held several political offices before becoming vice president of New Mexico Housing Co.

9. "The Grand Imperial Hotel Has Grand Opening This Weekend," *Silverton Standard and the Miner* Grand Imperial Hotel Edition, July 18, 1952, p. 1.

10. Ibid.

11. Jack Benham, *Silverton and Neighboring Ghost Towns* (Ouray, CO:Bear Creek Publishing Co., 1981) p. 7.

12. Ibid., pp. 7, 16, 36. Lucius Beebe, Charles Clegg, *Narrow Gauge in the Rockies* (Berkeley, CA:Howell-North, 1958) pp. 94-95.

13. Sandra Dallas, *No More Than Five In a Bed, Colorado Hotels in the Old Days* (Norman, OK:University of Oklahoma Press, 1967) pp. 87-89. *Silverton Standard* July 18, 1952. Ian Thompson, "Historic Silverton Hotel Purchased," *Durango-Cortez Herald* XXI(1972):1, 8.

14. Dallas, *No More*, pp. 87-88.

15. Ibid., pp. 88-89. "Imperial Hotel in Same Family for Thirty Years," *Silverton Standard* July 18, 1952.

16. "The Grand Imperial Hotel Has Grand Opening," *Silverton Standard*. Thompson, "Historic Silverton."

17. UNM-HF-KD. ACM-SRI, Sallie stated that Imhof used some of these cameras two weeks before he died.

18. NHR telephone conversation with Henry Sauerwein, Taos, Oct. 14, 1994. MNM-HL, Taos file, *Taos News, The Foundations*, Sept. 11, 1969. Mrs. Helene Wurlitzer set up the Wurlitzer Foundation of New Mexico that made grants, provided residences and financial aid to all types of artists.

19. ACM, newspaper clipping dated June 23, 1955. NHR interview with SADC Sept. 16, 1993.

20. Letter to NHR from Helen Kentnor Nov. 1987. NMR-T, Record of Mortgages, Deed Book J-19, pp. 243-244, Nov. 23, 1951, Helen Kentnor and J. P. Brandenburg, Taos, to Amy Kling of Rochester, NY.

21. UNM-MMA, Major General Charles H. Corlett letter to Dr. Frank C.

Hibben, Albuquerque, NM, Jan. 20, 1965. NHR interview with Helen Morten, Dallas, TX, Oct. 23, 1979.

22. Dallas, *No More*, p. 89. *Durango-Cortez Herald*, p. 1.

23. "The Grand Imperial Has Grand Opening This Weekend," *Silverton Standard*.

24. Letter to NHR from Allen Nossaman, Archive Director, San Juan County Historical Society, Silverton, CO, Nov. 22, 1993: "The ship model is no longer in the hotel or in Silverton. The last owner of the hotel, Ken Marlin, had renovated an old schooner into a restaurant and sold it just before coming to Silverton about ten years ago. He was from Newport Beach and had a good deal of experience with sailing and model building. He was attracted to the model in the hotel, and was soon telling people he built it. I knew he hadn't but I wasn't sure where it had come from . . . only that it was in the hotel when I moved to Silverton in 1963. He ended up taking the model with him when he sold the hotel to the current owners in 1992." ACM, Sallie Imhof obituary, *Denver Post* June 28, 1966.

25. Letter to NHR from Phillips Kloss Mar. 1988.

26. "Old Splendor Lives Anew, Famed Silverton Hotel Reborn," *Denver Post* July 2, 1952, ACM.

27. Lucius Beebe, "All Aboard For the Old West!" *Houston Post This Week Magazine* May 25, 1958, pp. 14-18.

28. Dallas, *No More in Bed*, p. 90.

29. Allen Nossaman letter to NHR Nov. 22, 1993: "The only relationship between Imhof and Silverton that I am aware of was that Dallas real estate man Winfield Morten, in his 'restoration' of the Grand Imperial Hotel here during the early 1950s, hung a number of Joseph Imhof's paintings of Indian subjects in the refurbished lounge area of the hotel. Imhof's work was very impressive, but Morten's ideas of restoration for an old Victorian hotel were inappropriate. Instead of playing on the 1880s and 1890s decor and the mining heritage of this community, he scrapped or sold antiques and imposed a cowboys and Indians theme on the interior. The Imhof paintings were one of the more respectable aspects of this effort, and Morten's work did leave the hotel better off as far as plumbing, wiring and heating were concerned, but the overall effort was unsuccessful, and Morten ended up losing the hotel for fuel and utility bills."

30. "Stone Age Still Exists in New Mexico," *Western Printer and Lithographer* June 1955, p. 58, ACM. ACM-SRI.

31. NHR telephone conversation with Del Orr, Koshare Indian Museum, Feb. 29, 1996. "Singers of the Plains," Catalogue PA-310. Koshare Indian Museum, Imhof file, J. F. Burshears letter to Joseph A. Imhof, May 1, 1952, states that the Koshare Museum got an earlier Imhof painting, "The Chanters," a couple of years before.

32. Koshare Indian Museum, J. F. Burshears letter to Joseph A. Imhof, May 12, 1952.

33. IIFI, p. 28. NHR telephone conversation with Del Orr, Koshare Museum,

Feb. 29, 1996. "I came to the Imhof house as a boy with the Koshares. I remember the house had a Rembrandt on the wall."

34. MNM-HL, *El Crepusculo* Feb. 7, 1952. Guests were: Kay and Richard Dicus and their daughter Susan; Helen and E. Martin Hennings; Mrs. and Mrs. C. D. Weimer, a businessman; Weimer's daughter and son-in-law, Corrine and Paul Albright; Mrs. Amy Kling of the Sagebrush Inn fame; Henry Sauerwein; and Laura Young. The guests honored Sallie and Joe by giving them a love bird and Sallie a corsage of orchids. Susan Dicus read a poem written especially for the event.

35. UNM-HF-KD.

36. ACM-SRI.

37. Ibid.

38. KCMF. Regina Cooke, "UNM Given Imhof Indian Paintings and Rare Items," *Taos Artists.*

39. UNM-MMA, Inventory of Imhof Collection, May 2, 1961, No. 61.3.809.

40. NHR telephone conversation with Robert Erkins, Feb. 13, 1993. Erkins said that Imhof admired certain colors from European paintings.

41. KCMF, "Pageant of Corn Exhibit Planned at Anthro Museum."

42. MNM-HL, *El Crepusculo,* Feb. 11, 1954: Guests included Mrs. and Mrs. E. Martin Hennings, Mr. and Mrs. C. D. Weimer, Mr. and Mrs. Paul Albright, Mrs. Minnie Sauerwein, Henry Sauerwein, Susan Dicus and Victor White (an Austrian who taught in Dallas and authored books on Austria). Letter to NHR from Melvin W. Weimer, Colorado Springs, CO, Aug. 28, 1989: "Mr. Imhof was a good friend of my family also and perhaps you may have known some of them, Alex and Bertha Gusdorf or their daughters, Elsie Weimer who was my grandmother, and her sister, Corinne Wyle Albright."

43. UNM-MMA, Letter to Imhof from Jack Riddle, Denver, CO, Nov. 17, 1954. Frances Melrose, "How Fred Mazzulla Collected the West," *Rocky Mountain News* Aug. 25, 1975, ACM: Mazzulla was an attorney, photographer and collector of Western Americana. He was constantly on the lookout for first-hand stories and collectible items from old timers. He sold his collection to ACM in 1975. ACM, Letter addressed to Jim: "Here is the tape on Joe Imhoff [sic]. This is how it all came about. Joe and Sallie Imhoff [sic] invited us down to make a film and a tape. Jim Miles, Jack Riddle and Pat Evans borrowed some 16 mm S.O.F. equipment from one of the colleges and made a film. It is owned by Miles and Riddle. I took along a tape recorder and a couple of Leica cameras. Jo [Mazzulla] and I made a series of Kodachromes using flash. The tape ends rather abruptly as we started down stairs. We usually name all persons present at the end of the tape. This time we were too slow. Present were Joe and Sallie Imhof, Fred M., Jo M., Jack Riddle, Jim Miles, Pat Evans and the Imhof dogs." MNM-HL, or ACM, Jim Forrest, Santa Fe, Director of MNM in 1965, was given a duplicate of the tape.

44. ACM-JAI.

45. UNM-MMA, Letter to Sallie Imhof from Jack P. Riddle, Jan. 20, 1955.

Letter from Joseph Imhof to Jack P. Riddle, Mar. 3, 1955: "About the tape recordings - I have been too ill and am still not well enough to give them any thought; I hope ere long to get my strength back and to be able to concentrate on that big job; at the present time I can do nothing about it."

46. IIFI, p. 29.

CHAPTER 17: SALLIE COMPLETES THEIR WORK

1. IIFI, p. 29. ACM, Obituary with photograph, June 23, 1955. Imhof's survivors included his beloved sister, Elizabeth Imhof Murphy, several nieces and nephews (among them Theodore T. Murphy and Frances C. Murphy). NMAI-SI, There are two of the same lithograph; "Juan-Taos," Acc. No. 190, marked "Last stone," notation on back of lithograph: Juan de Jesus Martinez, last litho made by Imhof. NHR telephone conversation with Robert Erkins, Feb. 13, 1993: "I have one lithograph written by Sallie, 'last one.'"

2. ACM-SRI. ACM, Obituary, June 23, 1955.

3. NMAI-SI(1), "Taos Art," newspaper clipping, June 23, 1955.

4. IIFI, p. 29. ACM, Obituary with photograph June 23, 1955.

5. IIFI, p. 29.

6. DP-EM.

7. NHR conversation Sept. 8, 1995 with my brother, E. Morten Hopkins. In July 1955, just as Imhof was approaching his last days, Winfield Morten became terribly sick with his stomach ulcer. Subsequently, my brother, a 17-year-old, ran Rancho de Abiquiu with Helen Morten. The ranch had 75 people on the payroll, and ran 24-hour shifts cutting and baling the alfalfa crop.

8. NMR-T, District Court, Will dated Oct. 29, 1954, filed June 21, 1957 as completed, Probate No. 7. If Sallie predeceased Joe, then Joe mentioned in his will: Elizabeth Imhof Murphy, his Columbia Baking Co. and American Locomotive Stock; Winfield Morten, Overland Oil Stock and the entire contents of his studio; Helen Morten, his personal property and Sallie's personal property; Frances Murphy, $1,000.00; Theodore Murphy, $1,000.00; Annie M. Thomas, $1,000.00; Susan Anneke Dicus, $1,000.00; Pamela Ferret, $1,000.00; Henry Sauerwein, $2,000.00; Juan Jose Suina, $500.00; Joseph H. Ide, $40,000.00 to cover any charges for any and all services that he may have rendered during his lifetime.

9. UNM-HF-KD.

10. Ibid.

11. Ibid.

12. UNM-MMA, Letter to Mrs. Joseph A. Imhof from J. J. Brody June 2, 1965: "I heard something about the work bench you mentioned, and remember informing them again to see if they might be able to use it." UNM-MMA, Letter to UNM from Mrs. Fred (Juanita Lola) Parrett Apr. 23, 1965: "Some years ago when

Mr. Imhof died his widow gave us his workbench. We are moving and would like to give it to the University since you have a permanent collection of his work. It has a miter box, grind stone, tee square and triangle. If you are interested in coming after it please let us know and we will either personally give it to you, or if we have moved by then, will leave it next door at Ila McFee [sic] Turners White Horse Studio to be picked up. We live directly opposite the Post Office in Taos." My research to locate Imhof's work bench proved futile. However, in talking with Mrs. Bruce (Victoria) Parrett (daughter-in-law of Mrs. Fred Parrett) she told me that she had Imhof's easel. Mrs. Freddine Parrett Heisey, Chilicothe, MO letter to NHR Apr. 1995: Fred Parrett was an electrical contractor who lived in the gardener's house on the Van Vechten-Lineberry property. He checked the house and grounds when Ed and Duane Lineberry were away.

13. Letter to NHR from Claire W. Brandenburg Jan. 19, 1995.

14. UNM-MMA, Deed of Trust signed by Sarah Russell Imhof Aug. 10, 1960.

15. UNM-MMA, Letter to Dr. Frank C. Hibben, Albuquerque, from Major General Charles H. Corlett, Española, Jan 20, 1965.

16. UNM-MMA, Letter to Major General Charles H. Corlett from Sallie Imhof Apr. 19, 1961.

17. UNM-MMA, Deed of Gift, Helen and Winfield Morten Foundation, Dallas, TX, Apr. 21, 1961. "UNM Gets Famed Art Treasures," *Denver Post* July 17, 1961, KCMF. "Imhof Indian Paintings are Presented to UNM," *Albuquerque Journal* July 6, 1961, KCMF: gifts are given through the Helen and Winfield Morten Foundation. UNM-MMA, Sarah Russell Imhof letter to Dr. W. W. Hill, Dept. of Ethnology, UNM, June 14, 1961: "Mr. Morten sent me the architect's plan for the so-called aged housing and enclosed your letter to him in answer to his inquiry. I note you thank him for many kindnesses. I hope he has been kind but I wonder what he has done for the UNM except the gift of Joe's gift of the corn series. I am curious!" UNM-MMA, Letter to Dr. W. W. Hill, Dir. Dept. Ethnology, from Winfield Morten, Apr. 26, 1961.

18. KCMF, *Albuquerque Journal* July 6, 1961. On Oct. 25, 1994, Charlene Dady sent NHR a copy of the letter that Sallie sent to Erkins family on May 7, 1961: "Now at long last the University of New Mexico at Albuquerque has accepted as a memorial gift all Joe's corn series paintings and his entire ethnological collection and his books, etc. for a permanent home in Albuquerque. They are overwhelmed with the scope of his 50 years of research and thankful to be the recipients. One of those huge Beakin's trucks came on Tuesday at 8 am and the packers, ten of them worked until 4 pm when the truck was filled to capacity. We had to take out the big studio window and just as Joe had always said there was 2 feet to spare so the big paintings went out OK. Now there are six empty rooms but the paintings I have for sale which I have kept in the spare room I am going to hang in the big studio, and after a fashion show them but the UNM warns me to hold them at a much higher price than I have been doing as soon as the exhibition is in place there will be a large

demand for Joe's work. It is really queer—first the Ghost Ranch museum was interested through the Pack Foundation. Then Santa Fe, then the Taylor Museum in Colorado Springs and the Heye Foundation in New York but none had the facilities to house so much Indian and the UNM had the money to build. This is the plan— now the ethnology dept. has a new building and the pottery, stone implements and all things ethnological will be temporarily shown there; the Dept. Fine Arts has just completed a large wing to the new large building and there some of the paintings will be hung in a corridor temporarily—next year they will build a large building with a huge auditorium and there the entire collection will be permanently hung and housed and the valuable books on the Pueblo Indian mostly long out of print will be kept in what they call locked reference shelves, and while I last I shall be advisor as to what Joe would want and they are so anxious to carry out his wishes so far as possible. I feel that a great weight is lifted from my shoulders and in the very town where within view of the University Joe lived and began his interest in the Corn Dance and all the rest of it."

19. NHR telephone conversation with Carol J. Hale Jan. 8, 1995. Carol stated that Sallie gave Lola Johnson the wood carving of two heads, one a Spanish Conquistador and the other a Classic Roman profile.

20. Letter from Mrs. Freddine Parrett Heisey May 1995: "We had an arrangement with Mrs. Imhof, she would call every morning so we would know she was all right." The Parretts lived on the Van Vechten property next door to the Imhofs.

21. IIFI, p. 28.

22. NHR telephone conversation with Carol J. Hale Aug. 8, 1993. KCMF, "List of Antiques in Imhof House, Feb. 1963." Some items included: "Seascape of Royal Fleet in Route to East Indies" by Friet Schoof; Delft plates bearing the hallmarks of seventeenth century makers; seventeenth century steins; Flemish chests; beidermeier clock; Ming dynasty vase; mezzotint by Sir Henry Raeburn, Scottish painter; two wood carvings from Tibet with *tablitas* on their heads similar to ones used in Native American corn dances; etching by John LaFarge of Tibetan dancer; Anderson photograph of "Victory of Samothrace"; eighteenth century French wig table; Gothic chest; old Imhof family table. KCMF, Two spiral accounting notebooks kept by Sallie. In them were names and addresses, some printed in large handwriting. The "Account Book for 1965" contained her income and expense accounts, her bank account information for a Philadelphia bank and a New York bank. In addition, she listed those who were helping her in 1965, some of whom included Lola Johnson, Anna Sandoval, Roserita Sandoval, Frank Mascoranas, Ralph Steebe, Sophie, Joe, Don Garcia, Dorothy Morten and David Chacon.

23. UNM-MMA, Letter to Mrs. Joseph A. Imhof from Dr. W. W. Hill, Dept. of Anthropology, UNM, Apr. 29, 1963.

24. ACM, Letter from Sallie to Fred Mazzulla, July 24, 1963, regarding the biography: "Alas I cannot read much of it even with strong magnifiers since that unfortunate eye hemmorrhage. I must now ask you to overlook typing errors; al-

though I can type after a fashion I cannot read what I have typed . . . but at 91, I must remember that time marches on." NMAI-SI, Box V-K, No. 4A, Letter to Mrs. Imhof from Vera Keppler, July 3, 1963: "I was very deeply distressed to know of your eye condition . . . It is fortunate indeed that your distant vision is not affected too much and that you have such courage in facing your handicap." ACM, On this copy of the biography, Sallie had penciled in "tired eyes."

25. UNM-MMA, Letter to Dr. W. W. Hill from Sallie Apr. 27, 1963. KCMF, *La Junta Tribune* June 1, 1966: "In fact, Mrs. Johnson pressed Mrs. Imhof to put in writing the story of her husband's life—something which he never had the time to do for himself. And then eventually to dictate the story of her own life, a tape recording that was only recently completed." Letter to NHR from Carol J. Hale, Nov. 1993 had a large empty envelope addressed to the Sisters of Loretto, Santa Fe. On the edge of the envelope was a handwritten note: "For Lola Johnson, Thanks for the letter. I'm praying for 'her' and for you, SMA. Lola, dear I sent these up to you as soon as I received your letter. Sr. B (from here) spent the long week-end in Taos—called your house a dozen times. Was on her way to the hospital to see if she could catch . . . . She brought the tapes and this back to me. My Love, to Mrs. Im and yourself, Sr. Marie Anthony." I concluded that Sallie must have made a tape of her life. Carol Hale stated that she thought a Catholic nun interviewed Sallie much later than 1955. I did not conclude anything about the existence of the tapes except there were some. Carol Hale said that Frederick Dockstader convinced Sallie to give him the tapes and other material. Carol Hale stated that Dockstader said that on his way back to New York his luggage was lost. If Sallie made a tape of her life, I did not find it. KCMF, Several pages of handwritten notes by Sallie that formed the rough draft for a biographical sheet on Imhof. The sheet was typed, printed and used as handouts about Imhof.

26. TSF, pp. 84-85.

27. PNM, p. 73.

28. KCMF. NHR telephone conversation with Robert Erkins Feb. 13, 1993: Erkins stated that he saw a Diorama with pueblo in background, and a foreground with figures 1 1/2 times actual life size in the exhibit at the UNM after Joe died and before Sallie died. This was at the time Sallie gave paintings to UNM. There was no place to house the Diorama, and Erkins did not know what happened to it.

29. UNM-MMA, Letter to Dr. Frank C. Hibben from Major General Charles H. Corlett Jan. 20, 1965.

30. NHR interview with Helen Morten Oct. 23, 1979. NHR interview with Pauline H. Castleberry May 25, 1984: "After 1957, on one of Archie and my trips to Colorado, we stopped by to visit Sallie in the hospital. Sallie mistook me for Helen. She gave me a pastel of one of Joe's favorite formations just north of Española. I considered it a parting gesture to Helen." As the years progressed, we kept up our friendship with Sallie. When my children, Mark Hopkins Reily and Donna Carolyn Reily, were born, Sallie sent them each a tiny pair of leather Indian moccasins.

409

31. KCMF, Seven hundred and fifty invitations were issued. Refreshments were served by wives of the Anthropology Dept., including Mrs. W. W. Hill, Mrs. Frank Hibben, Mrs. John Campbell, Mrs. Harry Basehart, Mrs. Karl Schwerin, Mrs. Stanley Newman and Mrs. J. J. Brody. Hostesses included graduate and undergraduate students associated with the dept. Sallie, age 93, greeted guests: from Taos, Mr. and Mrs. Richard Dicus, Mr. and Mrs. Allen Dicus, Mr. and Mrs. Thomas Tarleton, Mr. and Mrs. Don Blair, Miss Helen Blumenschein, Eugene Williams, Miss Louise Dicus, Mr. and Mrs. [Lola] Clarence Johnson, Mr. and Mrs. Ralph Streebe, Mrs. Robert Imhof of Brewster, KS, who had visited Sallie while working of the Imhof genealogy. From Española, Gen. and Mrs. Charles Corlett, Mrs. Agnes James. From Santa Fe, Dr. and Mrs. Albert Egenhofer and Kay, Mr. and Mrs. George Russell Wilson, Dr. Bertha Dutton, Miss Rose Evans. From Las Vegas, Mrs. and Mrs. Bruce D. Hale. From Albuquerque, Mr. and Mrs. Kenneth Adams, Mr. and Mrs. Murel Prinkey, Mr. and Mrs. Rolland Feight, Mr. and Mrs. Charles Fox, Mrs. Fred Muller, Mrs. Raymond O. Ryan, Mrs. Rainey Woolsey, Mrs. Ann Marshall, Mrs. Dorothea Whitcraft, Mrs. Margaret Ferrett and Mrs. Rainey Wollsey. From Buhl, Idaho, Robert Erkins. UNM *Alumnus Magazine* 37(1965): Sallie wrote, "I . . . was deeply impressed by the work that was put into the arrangement . . . . I have a deep affection for the University and it is satisfying to have a part in things that go on there." ACM-SRI, Sallie would also comment, "Joe would have changed many things in hanging the show, had many ideas in arranging the show." KCMF, *Albuquerque Journal* Aug. 15, 1965, states the exhibition was extended through late Sept. KCMF, newspaper article, "Corn Series in Anthropology Museum, Imhof Work Exhibited at UNM."

32. KCMF, "'Corn Series' in Anthropology Museum, Imhof Work Exhibited at UNM."

33. UNM-MMA, Letter to Dr. Frank C. Hibben from Sallie Imhof Feb. 9, 1965. UNM-MMA, Letter to "Dearest Friends," written by Lola Johnson for Sallie Feb. 10, 1965, Taos: "Thanks so very very much for such a wonderful day. Words cannot express my feelings as to what a wonderful job you've done on the Corn Series—I hope you will understand how happy you have made me—you put in much work and feeling into the display I can just say thanks. I know you'll understand. It was such a wonderful day. We are still reliving it over and over—Had a grand trip home arrived at 10 bid all my kids good-bye and rested. We are having snow today and looks like we will have it all night. Will be looking forward to a visit around Easter when you go to Colo. Springs. We were going to stop in Santa Fe and dance but nothing looked exciting after such a pleasant day with all of you, Sallie." Mrs. Johnson added in the same letter, "The trip didn't tire Mrs. Imhof very much. Had a good dinner before we left Albuquerque and she was still young strong when we got home—What a lady—We wrote to Dr. Hibben too—Haven't written to Mr. Hill—Will write him 'if' he helps you re-hang the pictures. Hope he helps you. Lola Johnson."

34. KCMF.

35. KCMF, "Lithography Offered to U. Students."

36. KCMF. UNM-GA, Sallie interviewed by Winifred S. Ritter and Bob Lalicker. She was classified as perhaps the oldest living alumna. At the interview Sallie gave the Alum Association a poem by President Gray which he autographed for her on Mar. 4, 1912. NHR research revealed that Sallie's comments contained several erroneous bits of information.

37. KCMF, *La Junta Tribune* June 1, 1966. Koshare Indian Museum, Letter from Otto T. Noeding, Bent Gallery, Taos to J. F. Burshears, Koshare Indian Museum Nov. 25, 1966: the letter states that the Koshares are interested in buying five lithographs (Plains Indians, Sandoval Taos, Mirabel-Taos, Santo Domingo Youth-Antonio Tonerio, Apache-Geronimo) and one watercolor, PH Woohlon, meaning Medicine Deer of the Taos Pueblo - Juan de Jesus Archuleta. Currently, the Koshare Indian Museum collection contains many paintings Imhof had presented to them. This may make the Koshare Indian Museum the most representational collection of Imhof art since Imhof retained these works of art for himself. The current inventory of Koshare Indian Museum lists more than ten Imhofs bought in 1966.

38. KCMF, *La Junta Tribune* June 1, 1966.

39. Ibid.

40. KCMF, Letters to Lola Johnson from the National Yeomen F Commander Mabel V. Pease July 6, 19, 1966.

41. NHR telephone conversation with Ora Chase, Taos, Nov. 5, 1989.

42. Obituary, *Denver Post* June 28, 1966, Denver Public Library. KCMF, *La Junta Tribune* June 1, 1966. UNM-HF-KD. MNM-HL, Taos file, Obituary, *The New Mexican* June 26, 1966.

43. Letter to NHR from Carol J. Hale Nov. 1993. *Notebook, Published in the Interest of National Yeoman F* XXXV(1966)3. Telephone conversation with Carol J. Hale Nov. 8, 1993. Carol stated that she had a box full of Sallie's medals and patches from Sallie's navy days.

44. NMAI-SI(3), Last Will and Testament of Sarah Russell Imhof Dec 22, 1954. NMR-T, District Court, Book W, Jan. 48-Nov. 68, Probate Docket 1, Probate No. 126, p. 481. Last Will and Testament of Sarah Russell Imhof filed June 29, 1966. Kathleen Dicus, Taos, $1,000.00; Dr. Martha Elizabeth Howe, Taos, $1,000.00; Mrs. Hester Bott Van Ness, Sacramento, CA or Towaco, NJ, $1,000.00 and two watches; Mrs. Judith White, Del Rey Beach, FL, topaz jewelry; Charlotte Erkins, Old Trail Ranch, Wilson, WY, diamond engagement ring; Joseph H. Ide, Beverly Hills, CA, $30,000.00 and one small painting; NMAI-SI, any prints and paintings selected by Frederick Dockstader; Dr. Frederick J. Dockstader and wife, Alice, one painting of his choice; Harwood Foundation, Taos, one painting selected by Dockstader and $1,000.00 for books at Harwood Library; Robert A. Erkins, Buhl, ID, two copies of two portraits by Franz Hals entitled "Baron Hessalaer" and "Mimi"; Lola Johnson, Taos, $1,000.00 (In letter from Carol Hale to NHR Nov. 1993, an additional amount of $8,803.90 was given to Lola Johnson); College of Fine Arts, UNM, two old lead transparencies pertaining to Albert Dürer; Museum of New Mexico, Santa Fe, an-

tique furniture in home except antique corbels, hardware, and beams built into the home. (The MNM waived their right to these items, Probate No. 126, Mar. 1, 1967); NMR-T, District Court, Probate No. 126, Last Will and Testament of Sarah Russell Imhof, filed June 29, 1966. UNM-HF-KD, In Sallie's will there was no mention of her bequest to Harwood for a library room. But Dicus knew Sallie wanted the money to go to the library addition. Mabel Dodge Luhan had donated her books as the nucleus of the library. Often Sallie had remembered people's birthdays with a book for the library. So Dicus and Toni Tarleton, the Harwood chief librarian, worked for two years for the money to go to the library addition. UNM-HF, Board Minutes: In January, 1965 the Board recognized the need for space. In October, 1967 the Harwood Foundation received $7,000.00 from the Sarah Russell Imhof Estate. UNM-HF-KD, Hattie-Louise Browning donated the furniture for the library addition. Browning was a friend of Dicus and is the woman in the portrait by John Young-Hunter which hung in the Imhof Reading Room at one time. The three-fourths posed portrait with Browning's hands in her lap was made at the request of Browning's mother, Blanche Fallon Hall. Browning wanted the portrait cut down, so Dick Dicus cut it down. Dick framed the hands in a small frame and sent it to Browning with the note, "Pale Hands, I love."

CREDITS:
BLACK AND WHITE ILLUSTRATIONS

OPPOSITE TITLE PAGE
Joseph Imhof in his Taos home, 1945. Photograph reprinted by permission of National Museum of the American Indian, Smithsonian Institute.

CHAPTER 1
Page 26: "Enjoy Life While You Are Living, You Will Be A Long Time Dead." Photograph courtesy of Nancy and Don Reily.

Page 30: Imhof's studio sign at Taos home, ca. 1955. Photograph reprinted by permission of Amon G. Carter Musuem, Ft. Worth, TX.

CHAPTER 2
Page 41: Site of the Ridley Mansion at the corner of Beekman and William Streets, New York City, undated. Photograph reprinted by permission of Amon G. Carter Museum, Ft. Worth, TX.

CHAPTER 3
Page 48: Imhof demonstrates how to make a lithograph, 1954. Photograph reprinted by permission of Museum of New Mexico, (Neg. No. 20071).

CHAPTER 4
Page 68: Imhof's sketch of a hand. Photograph reprinted by permission of University of New Mexico, Albuquerque, Maxwell Museum of Anthropology (No. 61.3.801).

Page 69: Anderson of Rome photograph of Jacopo Tintoretto's "Miracle of St. Mark," demonstrating dynamic symmetry and quality of reproduction, date unknown. Photograph courtesy of Nancy and Don Reily.

CHAPTER 5
Page 75-6: Imhof's cigarette cards as featured in *Life*, 1950. Photograph courtesy of

414

CHAPTER 12

CHAPTER 13

CHAPTER 14

CHAPTER 15

Page 310: Imhof in one of his many hats. Photograph reprinted by permission of National Museum of the American Indian, Smithsonian Institute.

Page 312: Imhof painting in Taos Pueblo. Photograph reprinted by permission of Museum of New Mexico, Photo Archives, (Neg. No. 20067).

Page 312: Sallie Imhof, 1945. Photograph reprinted by permission of National Museum of the American Indian, Smithsonian Institute.

Page 316: Imhof at party after Dallas Museum of Fine Arts Show, 1948. Photograph courtesy of Nancy and Don Reily.

CHAPTER 16

Page 320: Imhof's photograph for preliminary study of painting, "Procession, Pueblo of Picuris." Photograph reprinted by permission of University of New Mexico, Albuquerque, Maxwell Museum of Anthropology, (No. 61.13.875A).

Page 320: Imhof's sketch for preliminary study of painting, "Procession, Pueblo of Picuris." Photograph reprinted by permission of University of New Mexico, Albuquerque, Maxwell Museum of Anthropology, (No. 61.3.801).

Page 321: "Geronimo Gojathlay, 1834-1909," lithograph. Photograph courtesy of Nancy and Don Reily.

Page 325: "Chief Ouray." Imhof and Helen Morten, opening of Grand Imperial Hotel, Silverton, CO, 1952. Photograph courtesy of Nancy and Don Reily.

Page 326: Imhof's model ship, "Half-Moon," in his studio. Photograph reprinted by permission of Amon G. Carter Museum, Ft. Worth, TX.

Page 327: Imhof and Nancy Hopkins Reily at opening of Grand Imperial Hotel, Silverton, CO, 1952. Photograph reprinted by permission of Amon G. Carter Museum, Ft. Worth, TX and *Denver Post*.

Page 328: Lounge of Grand Imperial Hotel featuring Imhof paintings, 1952. Photograph reprinted by permission of Roach Photos, Inc., Denver, CO.

Page 333: Imhof in his Taos studio, ca. 1954. Photograph reprinted by permission of Museum of New Mexico, Photo Archives, (No. 20068).

CREDITS: COLOR ILLUSTRATIONS

Jacket Cover: "Santo Domingo Corn Dance," (Nancy and Don Reily. Photograph Courtesy of Gerald Peters Gallery, Santa Fe, NM).

Page 177: "Santana Sandoval," (Koshare Indian Museum).
Page 178: "The Governor of the Pueblo," (Koshare Indian Museum).
Page 178: "The Singers of the Plains," (Koshare Indian Museum).
Page 179: "The Governor of Taos," (University of New Mexico, Maxwell Museum. Photograph by Damian Andrus).
Page 180: "Winnowing Corn," (University of New Mexico, Maxwell Museum. Photograph by Damian Andrus).
Page 181: "Cleaning the Ditch," (University of New Mexico, Maxwell Museum. Photograph by Damian Andrus).
Page 182: "Braiding Corn, Acoma," (University of New Mexico, Maxwell Museum. Photograph by Damian Andrus).
Page 183: "Husking Colored Corn," (University of New Mexico, Maxwell Museum. Photograph by Damian Andrus).
Page 184: "Grinding Corn, Acoma," (University of New Mexico, Maxwell Museum. Photograph by Damian Andrus).
Page 184: "Making Wafer Bread," (University of New Mexico, Maxwell Museum. Photograph by Damian Andrus).
Page 185: "Baking Cornbread," (University of New Mexico, Maxwell Museum. Photograph by Damian Andrus).
Page 186: "Burial Ceremony, Taos Pueblo," (University of New Mexico, Maxwell Museum. Photograph by Damian Andrus).
Page 187: "Koshares at Kiva," (University of New Mexico. Photograph by Damian Andrus).
Page 188: "Ceremonial Smokers," (University of New Mexico, Maxwell Museum. Photograph by Damian Andrus).
Page 188: "Procession, Pueblo of Picuris," (University of New Mexico, Maxwell Museum. Photograph by Damian Andrus).
Page 189: "Winter People Resting, Pueblo of Santo Domingo," (University of New Mexico, Maxwell Museum. Photograph by Damian Andrus).
Page 190: "Apache Visitors to Corn Dance," (University of New Mexico, Maxwell Museum. Photograph by Damian Andrus).
Page 191: "Votive Offering During Corn Dance, Santo Domingo," (University of New Mexico, Maxwell Museum. Photograph by Damian Andrus).
Page 191: "Prayer After Dance, San Felipe," (University of New Mexico, Maxwell Museum. Photograph by Damian Andrus).
Page 192: "Corn Dance," (University of New Mexico. Photograph by Damian Andrus).

INDEX

[NOTE: Page numbers in *bold italics* refer to illustrations.]